Striking a Light
The Bryant and May Matchwomen and their Place in History

Louise Raw

BLOOMSBURY ACADEMIC

LONDON · NEW YORK · OXFORD · NEW DELHI · SYDNEY

BLOOMSBURY ACADEMIC
Bloomsbury Publishing Plc
50 Bedford Square, London, WC1B 3DP, UK
1385 Broadway, New York, NY 10018, USA

BLOOMSBURY, BLOOMSBURY ACADEMIC and the Diana logo are
trademarks of Bloomsbury Publishing Plc

First published in Great Britain 2009
Revised paperback edition published 2011
Reprinted 2011, 2012
Reprinted by Bloomsbury Academic 2013, 2015, 2016 (three times), 2018, 2019

A catalogue record for this book is available from the British Library.

A catalog record for this book is available from the Library of Congress.

ISBN: HB: 978-1-8472-5147-3
PB: 978-1-4411-1426-6

Typeset by Pindar NZ, Auckland, New Zealand
Printed and bound in Great Britain

To find out more about our authors and books visit
www.bloomsbury.com and sign up for our newsletters.

STRIKING A LIGHT

Contents

Illustrations

Map

For Phil and Sam,
and in memory of the Bryant and May matchwomen.

Acknowledgements

Thank you to everyone who helped and advised me during the writing of this book. I am particularly indebted to the descendants of the matchwomen Eliza Martin, Mary Driscoll and Martha Robertson. Their grandchildren – respectively Jim Best and his wife Mary; Joan Harris; and Ted Lewis and his wife Bett – did them proud in bring these remarkable women, and their long-vanished East End, into sharp focus. I hope I have done justice to their stories.

Without tutors like Nigel Morter and the late Pat Hayes, my research would probably never have begun: Professors Mary Davis and Steve Jeffreys at London Metropolitan University helped it to continue.

Love and thanks to Phil and Sam.

Thanks also to my adoptive mother Jennifer, and her mother Joyce, the women who first showed me that 'the past' mattered, and provided empirical lessons in female strength in adversity. Much loved, always missed.

Foreword

Louise Raw's book examines how the working class women who planned, thought and organised the 1888 strike at Bryant and May's East London factory have been eclipsed in subsequent accounts. The names of Mary Driscoll, Eliza Martin and Sarah Chapman have faded from historical memory, although the 'match girls' strike in which they played a leading part has lived on to become symbolic of women's trade union organising. Louise Raw notes how the very term 'match girls' contributes to the sentimentalized portrayal of meek and vulnerable victims; many of the dockers who also went on strike in the late 1880s were young too but would never be referred to as 'boys'.

Louise Raw has painstakingly examined the original written sources, showing how the socialist Annie Besant publicized and supported the strikers' cause but did not act as their leader. Indeed, the employers, Bryant and May, understood this at the time by secretly keeping tabs on a group of five women they had identified as the instigators and perpetuators of rebellion; among them were Mary Driscoll and Eliza Martin.

By piecing together material from their grandchildren, Louise Raw has enabled us to learn more than simply their names. She has discovered how the resourceful Mary Driscoll was only 14 when the strike occurred in 1888, but was already aware of her Irish heritage and a staunch supporter of the Republican cause. Hopes had been raised of Home Rule a few years before the strike, only to be dashed and the bitterness lingered on. Mary Driscoll was already aware of politics when she became involved.

Striking a Light reveals the tenacity of memories within working class communities which counter the dominant versions of events. Eliza Martin's grandson, Jim Best, informed Louise Raw confidently, 'Eliza told Dad that she and her friends started the strike and we were proud of that'.

By making use of oral sources from descendents Louise Raw has also been able to fill in what happened subsequently to the women who went on strike in 1888. All too often working class women flash momentarily into view in exceptional moments such as strikes or demonstrations, only to vanish once again into oblivion. Mary Driscoll married a docker and after his death ran a shop. Independent and resourceful to the last, she passed on her sense of dignity and democratic entitlement to her grand children: 'Always hold your head up. Remember you're as good as anyone'.

Not only did the women communicate their memories of resistance to their own families, the strike left an institutional legacy in the Match Women's Union. This survived for fifteen years and former striker Sarah Chapman would go on to represent it at the Trades Union Congress. Even after the independent union dissolved, the habits of organizing persisted. By 1912 the Bryant and May match workers were to be found in the National Union of Gas Workers and General Labourers. In 1923 the local Labour MP John Scurr attributed the continuing unionization of the factory to the 1888 strike. Scurr himself was a left winger, sympathetic to women's rights; and he had been active in the United Irish League – East London radical traditions died hard.

Louise Raw's book is to be welcomed for meticulously unpicking the construction of the 'match girls' supposed naivety and helplessness. *Striking a Light* restores the women's activism, and it indicates how they were affected by a wider consciousness of their rights which drew on the political movements around them. In enabling us to see how this was by no means a momentary awareness, she brings into view the context in which the strike took place. Workplace, community and family traditions combined to constitute an entwining sense of collective power.

She has been able to draw on an accumulative heritage of work on women's labour history which has sought out ways of complementing the lack of written source material by gathering information from a variety of places and gaining personal evidence through family memories. Feminist historians also have been particularly aware of the relevance of personal networks in enabling women to take public action and Louise Raw demonstrates the strong bonds of personal solidarity displayed by the young women before they took part in the strike.

Striking a Light is a fascinating, in depth account of a particular strike which acted as a catalyst for wide scale militancy. Though the strike itself is well known, Louise Raw has covered new ground which enable her to present it in a new light. Her findings leave us with a tantalising question: What of the other women who participated in strikes all over Britain during the late 1880s and early 1890s?

More generally, Louise Raw's work provides a valuable contribution to our understanding of class, gender, ethnicity and historical agency. Largely hidden from view by the dominant versions of history, working class women's restricted entry points have been skewed. Despite a great wealth of feminist inspired women's history showing the extent of collective action and continuous conscious rebellion on the part of working women in many lands, we still hear of them as victims, moved by transient emotions into the visible arena.

Striking a Light is at once an inspiring reminder of the matchwomen's resolution and courage, and of how many other stories remain still to be told.

Professor Sheila Rowbotham, 2010

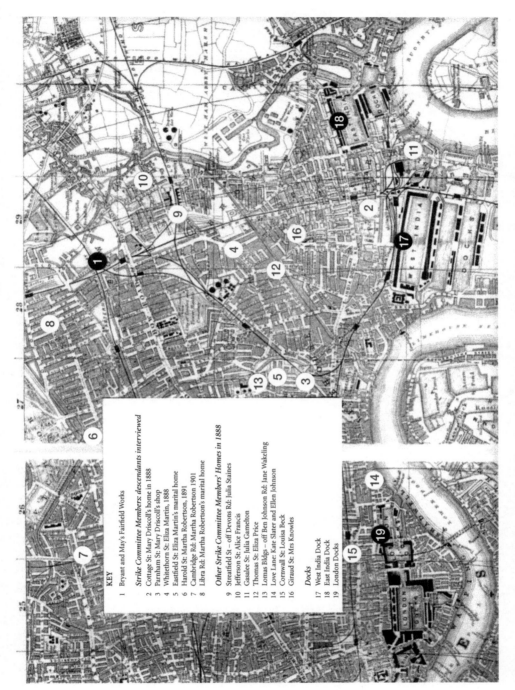

KEY

1   Bryant and May's Fairfield Works

Strike Committee Members: descendants interviewed

2   Cottage St: Mary Driscoll's home in 1888
3   Parnham St: Mary Driscoll's shop
4   Whitethorn St: Eliza Martin, 1888
5   Eastfield St: Eliza Martin's marital home
6   Harold St: Martha Robertson, 1891
7   Cambridge Rd: Martha Robertson 1901
8   Libra Rd: Martha Robertson's marital home

Other Strike Committee Members' Homes in 1888

9   Streatfield St – off Devons Rd: Julia Staines
10   Jefferson St: Alice Francis
11   Gaslee St: Julia Gamelton
12   Thomas St: Eliza Price
13   Lomas Bldgs – off Ben Johnson Rd: Jane Wakeling
14   Love Lane: Kate Slater and Ellen Johnson
15   Cornwall St: Louisa Beck
16   Giraud St: Mrs Knowles

Docks

17   West India Dock
18   East India Dock
19   London Docks

Mapping the Strike Committee: the women's homes and workplaces in the East End

Introduction, Methodology and Review of Literature

INTRODUCTION

In the summer of 1888, fourteen hundred workers, mostly young women and girls, walked out of Bryant and May's match factory in Bow, East London – and, effectively, into the history books.

When it came to popular appeal, the strike had it all: an almost fairy-tale-like struggle between rich, powerful factory owners, and desperately poor workers with all the photogenic waif-likeness of Hans Christian Andersen's martyred 'Little Match Girl', a staple of the Victorian nursery.

Before the strike the matchworkers were regarded as part of the 'lowest strata of society':[1] during it they met with MPs, and were the subject of editorials in *The Times*. After it, they formed the largest union of women workers in the country.[2] They earned the dubious accolade of being threatened by the serial killer 'Jack the Ripper', or someone claiming to be him, and they attracted the more wholesome attentions of celebrity socialists George Bernard Shaw, William Morris, Eleanor Marx – and, most significantly, Annie Besant: a Fabian journalist and, according to all previous sources, the leader of the strike.

No wonder that the matchworkers captured the public imagination then, and have not relinquished their hold on it yet: plays and musicals were being written about them into the 1960s (to the chagrin of Bryant and May, then still making matches in Britain, and also still trying to live down the national scandal caused by the strike), which continue to be performed today.

Sheila Rowbotham famously observed that the lives and experiences of most working-class women have been 'hidden from history'.[3] If British labour history can provide an exception to prove this rule, then the matchwomen must be it: in fact, their strike has been written about so often that it has become almost a cliché of the genre. When Sarah Boston was writing about women workers and trade unions in 1987, she found that most people she told about her work responded, 'Oh . . . the matchgirls' strike and all that?'; this was not just the most familiar, but often the *only* example of female industrial action which even those with a good knowledge of labour history knew anything about.[4] This was not just the case in Britain: in 2007, Danielle Thornton also found that everyone assumed her thesis on Victorian female factory workers must be about 'the matchgirls,' even though she was in Australia, and subject was actually Melbourne seamstresses.[5]

For many labour historians, this is precisely the problem. As E. H. Carr reminds us, history is not just a neutral record of the past: historians effectively decide which events deserve to be picked out of the great morass of human experience, then polished and elevated to the status of 'historical fact'.[6] The matchwomen, to many, made it into the history books more by luck than merit. They were in the right historical place at the right time; just before a wave of strikes swept the nation, from the East End to Aberdeen and Dublin. The Great Dock Strike of 1889 was one of the most celebrated of these disputes. 'New Unionism' led to the unionization of tens of thousands of unskilled and semi-skilled workers, eventually sowing the seeds of the Independent Labour Party (ILP). It is generally regarded as the starting point of the modern labour movement.

The matchwomen's action took place just over a year beforehand, and in the same part of London: Bryant and May's Fairfield Road factory was (and the shell of it still is) less than two miles from the dock where the '89 strike began. Even today, with much new development in between, it takes less than 40 minutes to walk from one to the other. Both groups of workers were exploited, badly paid and largely at the bottom of the Victorian labour hierarchy. The docks and the match factory were the largest employers of, respectively, male and female 'casual' labour in the East End.

However, the matchwomen's strike is still generally dismissed as happening too soon, and among workers 'too different' – in ways which are never specified – from the dockers for their strike to have influenced the men, let alone to be judged the true beginning of New Unionism.[7]

The dock strike spread so fast that within a week 'half of East London was out',[8] and it would eventually involve hundreds of thousands of workers. Compared to this, a short, relatively small stoppage at a match factory, supposedly orchestrated entirely by middle-class outsiders, does not have the ingredients of a serious 'fact' of labour history.

The matchwomen's strike is in some ways a victim of its own success. The story as it stands is easy to dismiss as all style and no substance – and I've encountered irritation in some learned quarters that such a 'trivial' event still interests people. One eminent historian I spoke to felt, quite vehemently, that the matchwomen had ridden into the pages of history on the coattails of the dockers, and only remained there for reasons of political correctness.

Still, historians seem as unable to resist the allure of the matchwomen's story as the public, and so the conventional version continues to be repeated; but it has never been judged worthy of having an entire book devoted to it, until now.

On the subject of Annie Besant, and the leaders of the dock strike, history is voluble: all have numerous biographies devoted to them, and have published their own memoirs – several times, in Besant's case. It is true that it's hard to resist the adjective 'colourful' in summarizing Besant's life, a sweeping *fin de siècle* search for meaning encompassing devout Christianity and marriage to a clergyman, scandalous divorce, atheism, a trial for obscene libel, and relationships with famous – and sometimes notorious – men like the atheist MP Charles Bradlaugh, and George Bernard Shaw. Besant ended her life as the *de facto* leader of a new religion and a venerated figure in India, where her body was cremated on a funeral pyre.

Though any matchwoman would have been hard-pressed to compete with all that, there is no reason why their lives shouldn't have been considered equally noteworthy. However, the record is completely silent on the women who walked out of Bryant and May's gates on that July day. There is a strike fund register, compiled by Shaw and others, which gives more than 700 of their names, but beyond that we know nothing – not what they thought of the strike, nor whether they survived it by many years to marry and raise children, or succumbed to what they themselves called 'phossy jaw', the grisly and potentially fatal disease of matchmaking. They remain silent, nameless faces regarding us solemnly from a black-and-white photograph, frozen forever in one moment in time.

If their strike had indeed been as marginal as many suggest, then this might not matter unduly. There are, after all, innumerable lives, particularly of women and working people in general, waiting to be rescued from historical obscurity. However, I have discovered that there are serious and previously undiscovered flaws in the conventional story of the strike which, once exposed, revolutionize the traditional view of the strike and its main players.

With famous exceptions – the David Starkeys and Simon Schamas – it is generally frowned upon for historians to bring themselves into their work, and rightly so for the most part. The researcher's own experiences must always inform their work to a degree, however – and at times they are indispensable to it. The Italian oral historian Alessandro Portelli has written beautifully about the relationship between researcher and 'informant'. Portelli discovered in the course of his early work, with Italian communists, that attempting to separate his own life and beliefs from his work in pursuit of a mythical academic neutrality was not only impossible, but counter productive. Only when his interviewees knew more about him, and he stopped being just 'that man from the university', did they begin to trust him enough to allow the meaningful work to begin.[9] Without my own experiences, both in and outside the workplace, my research would never have begun.

I had learned from experience the 'us-against-them' solidarity that working at the less attractive end of the labour hierarchy can foster. I'd worked, and gone on strike, with women from East End families, and could imagine vividly how *they* would have responded to being told to give up their wages, and probably their jobs, to walk out purely because a middle-class outsider said so. Though this was almost a hundred years after the matchwomen, it was still my own working past which initially sparked my curiosity: how had one woman, apparently acting alone and never having actually set foot inside a match factory let alone worked in one, brought 1,400 virtual strangers out on strike?

Most people who knew Besant seemed to have found her a compelling orator, and an attractive and charismatic personality, with some exceptions – Mrs Pankhurst was not an admirer, Beatrice Webb frankly couldn't stand her and George Bernard Shaw, though initially beguiled, called her humourless. Even so, the matchwomen were among the poorest of workers, living hand-to-mouth, completely dependent for survival on their earnings. Even the most minor rebellion against the factory rules could lead to instant dismissal. To have succeeded in bringing them out for her own ends, Besant would have needed organizational genius. As most histories have accepted Besant as the strike's prime mover, this should make it a rare, if not singular, event in British labour history – a true example of worker action being provoked purely by a politically motivated outsider. Not just trade unionists, but employers and the wider establishment, would obviously have vested interests in knowing how Besant achieved this feat: I therefore expected to find numerous and detailed examinations of Besant's tactics. I was genuinely surprised to discover that the classic texts not only failed to provide answers about this, but did not even ask the questions.

Without personal experience of strikes from the workers' perspective, I would probably never have questioned the orthodox history of the matchwomen. My first stroke of luck, then, was that I came at the story from a trade union, rather than a traditional academic, background. I began my research as part of a project for the Transport and General Workers' Union, and I will always be grateful to them for the education in Labour history that they gave me. London Metropolitan University allowed me to continue researching the strike to master's degree and then doctoral level – taking a chance on a student who had left school before her 16th birthday and had no first degree. Throughout the years I found more and more conclusive proof that Besant did not lead, and actually couldn't have led, the strike. I also discovered that Bryant and May, whilst only too happy to go along with the Besant-led version of events in public, privately identified five women who they believed were the real leaders of the strike.

I wanted to go further than this, however: to somehow get closer to the matchwomen's own perspective on events. There were no known autobiographical accounts, and the participants are long dead, which presented me with what academics call a 'methodological problem'. I decided that the only logical thing I could do was try to trace surviving relatives of the five 'ringleaders'. This was an unusual approach to take and I was warned, quite sensibly, that this would probably result in a time-consuming and expensive wild goose chase. It certainly did absorb a good deal of time and money, but after several fascinating and frustrating years in pursuit of the 'real' matchwomen through the pages of history and East End memory, I was finally able to meet and talk to men and women who had known the women, including the grandchildren of two of the women who, I now believe, were the true leaders of the strike.

This book is for them. I hope it will go some way towards giving the matchwomen back the voice and the power that history has so far denied them. I would like it to serve both as a rewriting of the very beginnings of modern British labour history, and as a tribute to the women whose courage and determination made possible the 'tremendous harvest' of New Unionism.[10] Their actions gave hope and inspiration to hundreds of thousands of desperately exploited workers and they should, I believe, now be acknowledged as the mothers of modern trade unionism.

SEARCHING FOR THE MATCHWOMEN: SOURCES AND RESOURCES

I started my research by looking for and studying every previous account of the strike I could find. In some pieces of historical research this would be reasonably straightforward: the researcher would probably begin with a shrewd idea of where to look for evidence, and a relatively clear path to follow in tracking the development of knowledge on their chosen subject.

However, the matchwomen's case is a curious one. Knowledge about the strike can't be said to have developed in any meaningful way since it ended, leaving the women in a historical dead end, locked in an old-fashioned story of Great Individuals helping The Poor. It's remarkable how attractive the idea of helpless girls rescued by Mrs Besant has proved, in the teeth of both the evidence and new schools of historical thought. In some cases, in fact, Victorian commentators were somewhat more enlightened in their view of the matchwomen's own role than later writers have been.

Rather ironically, Bryant and May proved extremely helpful to my research. Their company archives became publicly available in the 1980s, and box after box of ephemera as well as serious documentation bears witness to the firm's decades of continued, almost obsessive, interest in all matters pertaining to the strike and to its own public image, spanning the years from original copies of Besant's paper, the *Link*, to playbills of musicals about the matchwomen from the 1960s. Amongst this, I made two major discoveries concerning Besant's beliefs about strike action and the employers' views about the strike's real leaders.

Accordingly, a little more lateral thinking was necessary. Because there are no previous books which concentrate solely on the strike, the search for 'secondary' accounts (written after the fact by historians or writers who were not witnesses) involved surveying a wealth of general histories of the period: histories of trade unions, of London and the East End, of industrialization, of women and work in the Victorian era and so on. In hopes of finding something new which might not have made it to publication I also contacted historians of the period such as Anna Davin, Jerry White and Paul Thompson, and met with the director of Raphael Samuel's archives (Samuel was Professor of History at the University of East London and involved in the groundbreaking History Workshop movement, and collected an immense amount of data). Between the hardback and paperback editions I've continued to research and revise and have been grateful for the advice of Terry McCarthy, former director of the People's History Museum in Limehouse and author of *The Great Dock Strike 1889*.

Because the strike was such a *cause célèbre* in its day, there was a wealth of media coverage. I surveyed national and local papers, journals and periodicals from June 1888 to the end of the dock strike in 1889. The collections in the

British library's newspaper division at Colindale, London, are unrivalled, but I also found the East London local history library, in the Bancroft Library in Mile End, invaluable. It provides a comprehensive selection of the many local newspapers published in the area at the time, and has the added advantages of having not only census records but librarians with an excellent knowledge of the area, under the same roof.

Beyond this, I had to find and visit, or at least contact, each archive, museum, library and collection which might contain some previously unseen primary evidence. I wrote to archivists in India, Canada and the USA, and wrote features for both Irish and English national newspapers about my search.

I also looked at the letters and diaries, both published and in their original form, of key figures like William Morris and George Bernard Shaw and Sidney and Beatrice Webb.

I never did discover one single 'Holy Grail' – an elusive letter or matchwoman's diary from 1888, casually sitting in a box of papers. Even in my extended years of research, I may have missed it; or it may simply not exist.

My search for descendants began as an attempt to mitigate the unfortunate necessity of conducting an investigation without testimony from its most vital witnesses. The grandchildren I interviewed contributed to a series of breakthroughs which combined to completely transform the story of the matchwomen.

There follows a more detailed account of my research and review of previous literature on the matchwomen.

PRIMARY SOURCES

Media accounts were, of course, no more neutral in 1888 than they are today. They have to be approached with some caution, and consideration of the dominant ideas of the society which produced them; and this is especially pertinent in the matchwomen's case. The 'woman question' was being hotly debated in the 1880s, and the relatively new figure of the 'factory girl' was causing controversy and alarm in some quarters: the kind of working-class female militancy embodied by the strikers was therefore bound to be unpalatable to some. These factors, combined with class prejudices, inevitably colour accounts of the strike, sometimes translating into perceptions of the women as helpless and powerless and, as strikers, the pawns of socialist agitators.

It is not unexpected that the right-wing press should have found this a more acceptable version of events, and that Bryant and May should have encouraged it. However, sections of the 'left-wing' press of the period also showed a surprising willingness to identify the strikers with the victimized 'little matchgirl' stereotype of popular contemporary fiction. It is impossible to know how far this was a tactical attempt to gain sympathy for their cause, rather than an accurate reflection of the writers' own perceptions. However, the declared beliefs of several leading socialists of the time on women show that they were by no means immune to the influence of 'bourgeois' domestic ideology, which held that a woman's place was at home.

Furthermore, socialist organizations like the Fabian Society and the Social Democratic Federation (SDF) had little interest in trade unions as vehicles for class struggle: nor did they believe that workers outside the union movement could, or should, successfully take on their employers.

Overall then, we must remember that contemporary media accounts of the strike are largely, as Chris Willis puts it, 'filtered through the middle-class consciousness' of journalists and commentators, and do not necessarily represent the truth of the women's actions.[11] As to the women's own views of the strike, little attempt was made to record them. They were almost always seen and written about (as the Victorian working-class poor often were) as an undistinguishable 'mass', and one which had in any case been manipulated by outside forces.

Accordingly, within four days of the strike, *The Times* had attributed it to 'interference from outside', by unnamed individuals who had 'carefully prepared' the ground by writing 'inflammatory articles' with gross exaggerations of working conditions, and who had promised the workers financial help if a strike took place.[12]

Although I've found that the matchwomen had traditions of militancy of which their employers must have been aware, Bryant and May management eagerly encouraged the 'reds under the beds' scenario, no doubt grateful for the opportunity to focus attention away from their own poor record as employers. Besant was a convenient scapegoat who allowed them to appear the wronged party, and to attack the strike without seeming to directly attack their workers. Accordingly William Bryant claimed, at the 1888 company annual general meeting, that relations with the workforce had always been good until socialist interference had 'upset (their) minds'.[13] This is patently untrue: there had been at least three strikes in the preceding seven years, and Bryant and May had a list of the five women they felt to be the most likely 'trouble-makers'.

Once the battle lines were drawn, the different 'sides' in the dispute, not unexpectedly, presented versions of events which portrayed them in the best possible light, and/or favoured their political beliefs. This must apply equally to the accounts of Annie Besant, the main witness to the strike whose writings almost all secondary sources use as their basis.

Annie Besant was the middle-class journalist and Fabian socialist whose name would forever after be linked with the matchwomen, and who is often almost universally accepted as having led the strike. She had reported on conditions at Bryant and May for the *Link*, which she produced along with fellow Fabian Herbert Burrows. The well-known article 'White slavery in London', published in the *Link* on 23 June 1888, forms the basis of the assumption that the strike was her doing: but never at any time in the course of the brief (less than two full columns long) piece does she ever suggest the women should strike. In the concluding lines, she exhorted readers to try a far less radical solution: '. . . let us . . . avoid being "partakers in their sins" by abstaining from using their commodities'.

Besant, then, had a straightforward boycott in mind. It might be thought that she was tactically concealing her true aims here: proposing one course of action while secretly planning a strike. It is, after all, Besant and this piece which *The Times* had in mind when making its thinly veiled and condemnatory reference to the writer of 'inflammatory articles'.

However, I found that Besant had actually written in the same copy of the *Link*, on the page after the 'White slavery' article, of the sheer impossibility of organizing a union or leading a strike with 'the girls of Bryant and May, mentioned in another column'.[14] They would simply be dismissed, she argues, and easily replaced from the London 'residuum' of unemployed workers.

Although Besant's words appear to clearly challenge her own myth as strike leader, they can only be used as pieces in the jigsaw puzzle of evidence which must be assembled in the absence of a full account in the strikers' own words.

Reports of the matchwomen's own words are rare but do exist, albeit quoted by others. Besant quotes a note from them, apparently verbatim, at one point during the strike. The journalist covering the strike for the *Star* spoke briefly to the women, and the comments that he reports appear authentic, allowing for the previous provisos about media reports. Only one oral account also exists in the British Library sound archive in which a working-class eyewitness, being interviewed on another topic, gives us a very brief but vivid flash of the women on strike.

These, and in particular the last, have been scrutinized in order to extract as much meaning from them as possible. The tape features East Ender Samuel Webber, a boy at the time of the strike, talking about street and popular songs of the period. At one point Webber breaks into a snatch of song apparently sung by the matchwomen as they marched through the East End collecting strike funds. I've researched the words sung in detail, and found a fascinating trail leading from a Welsh method of working-class justice associated with political revolt and especially with women – to a Civil War marching song.[15]

The note from the matchwomen quoted by Besant, unsigned and hand-delivered, also reveals a great deal about her relationship with them – that the women were not regularly meeting with her; were not known to her by name (it is formal in style as well as unsigned); that they had at least a passing interest in politics, as they ask when the next socialist meeting is likely to be held; and that they were reacting as they saw fit to management intimidation, uninfluenced by Besant or any third party.[16]

FACTS AND FICTIONS: SECONDARY SOURCES

Looking at both primary and secondary sources on the strike, I was struck by the extent to which many of the commentators and labour historians who deal with it all – and there are those who don't think it important enough to mention – tend to downplay its importance, and to make mistakes about even the most basic details of the dispute.

Surprising too is the minimal use which generally seems to have been made of the quite extensive primary evidence on the strike, which probably explains the differing versions given of the most basic facts about it. There is a general consensus in favour of Besant's 'leadership', but on all the other elementary points – dates, numbers on strike and so on – accounts differ so widely, and apparently carelessly, that it seems doubtful that much primary research has been done at all.

Even those who were in a good position to provide first-hand evidence treat the facts of the dispute rather casually. Sidney and Beatrice Webb were founding Fabians and chroniclers of the union movement, and close associates of Besant at the time of the strike. Despite being so close to the action they say that Besant's piece 'White slavery in London', which they imply began the strike, was published in 'July 1888', when it actually appeared in June. They are oddly precise, though wrong, about the number of strikers too: '672'. In fact the *East London Advertiser* put the number of strikers variously at 1,500 and 1,100; *The Times* and *Star* at 1,300; and Besant at 1,400.[17] The Webbs give no source for their figure. The strike fund register, which records only those strikers who received payments from the fund, records 712 names, which is at least in the right area, but the Webbs' precise but erroneous figure is still puzzling: all the more so given that Sidney Webb's lifelong friend, George Bernard Shaw, was present when the register was compiled, and even personally recorded some of its entries. It's also possible that Beatrice Webb's personal animosity towards Besant, strongly expressed in her journals, may have muddied the waters, perhaps making Webb unlikely to approach Besant to verify details or, maybe, to want give her too much credit for a fairly large strike.

Pelling's *A History of British Trade Unionism* is one of many sources to index its account of the strike under 'Besant, A.' rather than 'matchwomen' or 'Bryant and May'. Pelling deals with it in seven lines as a preface to three pages on the dock strike, and is the source with the lowest number of strikers, writing that 'a few dozen' women struck successfully '. . . with the help of Mrs Besant and other socialists'.[18] Pelling gives no source for his figures, and I have not been able to find any primary or secondary source giving low enough numbers to have misled him.

Soldon[19] agrees that 'Mrs Besant deserves the lion's share of the credit' for the dispute, and says that the women 'went on strike after hearing Annie Besant speak',[20] giving no source for this incorrect assertion. He gives the rest of the credit not to the strikers, but to Clementina Black of the Women's Protective and Provident League (WPPL).[21]

Morton and Tate[22] state that 700 women came out on strike, and that 'Mrs Besant and another socialist, Herbert Burrows . . . organised them' after 'Mrs Besant published a startling exposure of their conditions in the *Link* in July'[23] (again, rather than June). Morton and Tate give no source for their figure, but it's probably based on the number on the strike fund register.

Paul Thompson, as well as placing Besant and Burrows at the head of the strike, also strongly refutes any suggestion that the matchwomen were part of New Unionism:

> The strike of matchgirls in July 1888 organised by socialist Annie Besant ... [was] relatively isolated and consequently given exaggerated publicity. The real start of the New Unionism in London was not until the gasworkers' agitation of 1889.[24]

Thompson provides no evidence to back up his assertion.

Harrison's *Late Victorian Britain* is unusual in not referring directly to Annie Besant, but devotes no more than half a sentence to the matchwomen. The entry on New Unionism begins with the dock strike, listing its achievements before working backwards to the matchwomen whose strike 'had shown that it might be possible to organize even the poorest and most exploited groups of workers'.[25] This choice of words is interesting: it makes the women themselves passive, a group which has surprisingly proved capable of being organized despite their lowly status, rather than demonstrating a capacity for self-organization. The dockers' victory, on the other hand, is theirs: it is 'the Great Dock Strike', and not the organization of the dockers or the actions of their leaders, which 'wrested from the employers "the dockers' tanner"'.[26]

Hobsbawm's *The Age of Empire*, covering the period 1875 to 1914, makes no mention at all of the matchwomen's strike, but has three references to Annie Besant. The first highlights her role as one of '. . . the handful of emancipated British women in the revival of the labour movement after 1888: of Annie Besant and Eleanor Marx . . .'.[27] While at least attributing some importance to the efforts of women, this perfectly illustrates the way in which the matchwomen's achievements are 'hidden' by class. Over a thousand women are by no means a 'handful', but despite Hobsbawm's excellent working-class history credentials, he mentions only middle-class 'great individuals'.

In his *Labour's Turning Point 1800–1900*, a collection of contemporary documents, Hobsbawm allows that the strike broke out 'unexpectedly', but

> after Mrs Annie Besant, Socialist and later theosophist and leader of the Indian National Congress, had exposed conditions in the factory in her paper, The *Link* [May 1888]. Largely with the help of the Socialists, the strike was won. With it began the movement of 1889–92.[28]

Again the date for the *Link* article is wrong. Hobsbawm next includes an interesting extract from 'Toilers in London', quoting one of the matchwomen as saying the strike '. . . just went like tinder, one girl began, and the rest said "yes", so out we all went'.[29]

However he does not point out that if 'one girl began' the strike, logically Besant could not have 'begun' it. A great deal of detail is given about Besant, but none about the women: who they were, where they lived, even how old they were.

The impression given here is that Besant and 'the Socialists' led or organized the strike. Though Hobsbawm does conclude that the strike 'began the movement of 1889–92', this is slightly contradictory. If the movement really began with the strike, then clearly its dates should be *1888*–92.

Hobsbawm also refers on the next page to the union formed at the Beckton works – more than six months after the matchwomen had formed theirs – as 'the first of the new unions of unskilled workers'.[30]

Hobsbawm's total entry on the matchwomen takes up half a page, while the Beckton Gasworks organization is given two pages, and the dock strike seven. The reader is left with the impression that the matchwomen were somewhat peripheral to New Unionism.

Other historians write that even the rather sketchy attention given to the matchwomen by their colleagues has been more than their strike warranted. Paul Thompson strongly refutes any suggestion that the matchwomen were part of New Unionism:

> The strike of matchgirls in July 1888 organised by socialists Annie Besant ... [was] relatively isolated and consequently given exaggerated publicity. The real start of the New Unionism in London was not until the gasworkers' agitation of 1889.[31]

Barbara Harrison agrees:

> It could be argued ... that claims made for the strike owed more to the publicity it received from its socialist/feminist supporter Annie Besant than to its actual uniqueness; especially as there were other examples of strike action ... occurring spontaneously at this time.[32]

In 2004 Alastair Reid's general labour history devoted three pages to the dock strike but only eleven lines to the matchwomen's, and in a separate section on 'Women and Organisation'[33] Reid calls the strike an 'apparent breakthrough', but then stresses that 'when the matchgirls themselves were faced with determined employer opposition their organization simply collapsed'.[34] In fact the union survived the turbulent years after the peak of New Unionism, though many did not: Besant said that it was still strong and active in 1893.[35] It survived as an independent union for fifteen years, before an unsuccessful strike defeated it. Even so, the matchwomen did not give up on trade unionism: by 1912, most Bryant and May workers were members of the National Union of Gas Workers and General Labourers.[36] In 1923, Labour MP John Scurr said of the factory that 'Every person there is a trade unionist',[37] and attributed this to the victory of '88.

DELUSIONS OF GENDER? WOMEN AND HISTORY

Two significant works on women and British labour history do offer a fresh perspective on events. Though both Sarah Boston and Mary Davis consider the strike in general histories and so do not look at it in great detail, Boston comments on Besant's negative views of trade unionism, and Davis discusses the 'tendency to regard women as victims rather than fighters' and its relevance to perceptions of the matchwomen.[38]

So did workers like the matchwomen really get a raw deal from posterity because of their sex?

In 1963, E. P. Thompson published the seminal 'Making of the English Working Class', with which he sought to '. . . rescue the . . . obsolete hand-loom weaver, the "Utopian" artisan, from the enormous condescension of posterity.' An admirable aim: however, all historians would probably recognize the scenario shown in an old cartoon, in which an esteemed, deceased, historian reclines on a cloud in heaven, surrounded by admirers, when he suddenly notices a devil tugging at his sleeve. 'I'm sorry, sir', says the devil, 'but I'm afraid you'll have to come with me. The revisionists have just got around to you.' As unassailably important as Thompson's work seemed, in 1988 Joan Scott highlighted the problematic status of women in the book. She argues that Thompson's understanding of class as an analytical concept is extremely, if unintentionally, 'gendered', and that his very success in bringing the lives of England's first industrial working class to the centre of the historical stage only emphasizes the lack of importance given to the roles played by its women.[39] Ten years previously, Eric Hobsbawm had frankly admitted that criticism of the neglect of women by labour historians was not only justified, but also applied to his own work.[40]

The 1960s and 1970s had seen the advent of a new generation of feminist historians. Sheila Rowbotham's *Hidden from History* provided a new analysis of patriarchy as the ultimate disposer of women's labour, and the work of Barbara Taylor, and Scott and Tilly, was equally illuminating in exploring industrialization and its effects on both labour and the family.[41]

However, the conflict between the classic Marxist view of the centrality of class as the supreme interpretative concept, and the desire to accord an equal importance to gender, remained problematic.

In addition to tensions between Marxist and feminist historians, there were also debates between women's historians and historians of the family. Feminist historians tended to see the family as the 'centre of women's oppression' reflecting the patriarchal order of society, and so often sought to study their public, rather than private, lives; understandable, given the dearth of such previous research.[42] There were further divisions between oral and feminist historians on the type of research which should be carried out on working-class women.[43]

Debates about the validity of 'gender' rather than 'women's' history became heated in the 1980s, with gender historians expressing the past as a 'history of *genders*', and also trying to move beyond the perceived acceptance of the dominant (male) view in the very concept of 'women's history', as an entity somehow apart from the mainstream. As Gisela Block has written, 'Women's history concerns not half of humankind, but all of it . . . it is no less problematic to separate the history of women from history in general than to separate the history of men . . . from the history of women.'[44]

If the two were to be united, and the concept of gender developed as a legitimate category for historical analysis, it would be necessary to re-examine ideas about what was historically significant, and to accept the vital importance of context: a person's understanding of gender would always be shaped by their own culture and times. It was also important that masculinity be understood as a concept. [45]

From the 1980s, the academic popularity of Marxism began to wane. Feminist historians looked for a new theory that would '. . . enable (them) to articulate alternative ways of thinking about . . . gender', as Joan Scott put it. Scott was herself a well-known convert to post-structuralism, which holds in part that the meaning of words and texts are not intrinsic or rigidly fixed but open to interpretation. Scott also took issue with Gareth Stedman Jones' widely respected deconstruction of British labour history, *Outcast London*, for its failure to correct the continuing lack of significance accorded to gender as an important analytical category. (*Outcast London* makes no mention at all of the matchworkers' strike).

Several groundbreaking works in the 1990s have addressed the continuing neglect of gender: Anna Clark's 1995 *The Struggle for the Breeches: Gender and the Making of the British Working Class* seeks to integrate gender into the analysis of class formation, and illustrates the 'gendered' strategies which working-class men and women developed to cope with the 'sexual crisis' resulting from industrialization. Clark has been criticized by some for an emphasis on male working-class rhetoric and 'insufficient attention to women's agency';[46] however, I found her analysis of gender and class illuminating and well-written.

Deborah Valenze's *The First Industrial Woman* takes issue with traditional histories of industrialization, with their emphasis on the deeds of 'great men' as transformatory factors. She shows that industrialization, far from giving women increased wages and independence, in fact gave some working-class men superficial economic autonomy (through the mostly male trade union movement and new adaptations of labour), while women's work was ideologically and remuneratively devalued – a process aided by the 'surplus army' of women workers.

Ellen Ross' *Love and Toil: Motherhood in Outcast London* (1993) emphasizes the centrality of motherhood to the lives of working-class Victorian women, and presents gender not as a fact of nature, but an ever-evolving set of relationships between working-class men and women, involving conflict and compromise.

Once patriarchy was no longer seen simply as the sole reason for the oppression of women, more attention was focused on this view of gender relationships as complex and ever-shifting.

The late nineteenth and early twentieth centuries were notable for periods of particularly intense conflict when 'gender divisions hardened'.[47] This means that the matchwomen's story was accordingly played out against the background of increasing hostility towards women in the workforce, and the demand for a 'family wage' (to be paid to the male 'breadwinner'). It has been argued that during this period working-class men effectively colluded with the bourgeoisie, seeing male solidarity as more important than their class identity.[48] Many of the negative attitudes about the place and capabilities of women – whose remnants persist to the present day – were either strengthened or established at this time. This made it seem even more implausible that the matchwomen – very young, poor, 'casual' and female workers (as well as mostly Irish) – could be capable of organizing their own strike. Although Annie Besant was female, she was not, to most Victorians, a 'lady', having transgressed against the feminine code of behaviour on a multitude of occasions. She was also from an educated middle-class background, and an active free-thinker and socialist. For these reasons, her leadership of the strike could be made to fit the ideological framework, as well as the conventions of traditional history where, as Joan Kelly has argued, individual women are occasionally allowed some of the limelight, but 'largely as exceptions; those who were said to be as ruthless as, or wrote like, or had the brains of men'.[49] As will be shown in Chapter Five, those who disliked Besant, including Beatrice Webb and Emmeline Pankhurst, tended to use her supposedly 'unfeminine' appearance and behaviour to castigate her.

As Jane Lewis states, it may never be possible to ascertain to what extent Victorian women really accepted the domestic ideology of the period, and the male 'breadwinner' model of respectable family life.[50] Though this ideology conflicted sharply with the actual experience of most working-class women in East London, we cannot be sure what it meant to them. It may have been dismissed, or adapted, or retained as an ideal; equally, the working-class notion of the 'respectable' was not necessarily adopted wholesale from the bourgeoisie. The oral history work of Elizabeth Roberts among working-class women in Barrow, Lancaster and Preston suggests that some women may have felt sympathy, not condemnation, for those who were obliged to work full time for financial reasons (however, this was based on a small and regional sample, and it is of course dangerous to project 'modern' desires for independence through work on to Victorian women, unless or until good primary evidence proves the case).[51]

Margaret Pember Reeves used a wider sample for 'Round about a pound a week', and found only a small number of married women who said they had taken on paid work. However, as Roberts points out, very different answers might have been given had the question been framed differently, to include paid work *inside* the home. Many women would have taken in washing or lodgers, or worked as childminders, common forms of 'self-employed' homework.

'Sweated' women's work for employers was also often carried out in the home – for example, matchbox-making and fur-pulling. In such cases, women may have underplayed the extent to which they worked either because the lines between the private, domestic sphere and the public world of work were blurred; or because they were affected by the notion that not working was a mark of respectability in a woman, particularly once she had married. Roberts found that over 40 per cent of her sample had taken on part-time work at some time in their married lives.

This was a further obstacle to my search for descendants of Bryant and May workers. It had to be considered possible that not all descendants of matchwomen would necessarily be aware of the fact. Working at Bryant and May's was apparently regarded by the matchwomen's contemporaries as a source of stigma because of the poor wages and conditions: those who had to work there, certainly before the strike, had been regarded by some as 'the lowest strata of society'.[52]

This idea may have been deeply ingrained, and prevented some women from talking about it to their children. Among those whose stories I have been able to trace, one did not know her grandmother had worked at Bryant and May until after her death, and this may have been common.[53]

As previously mentioned the search for autobiographical material by the matchwomen has been unsuccessful so far; even the percentage of matchwomen able to write is uncertain. Strike committee member Mary Driscoll, for one, never had the opportunity to learn. It also seems to have been the case, as Jonathan Rose has suggested, that working-class women were less likely to think their lives worthy of recording than men.[54] It is presumably also true that, with both domestic and work responsibilities, they simply had less time and opportunity.

Lack of primary evidence, and an implicit acceptance of the ideological framework which posits Besant as strike leader and lessens the event's significance to labour historians, are therefore two possible reasons why the matchwomen's story has never been re-evaluated.

The historian Anna Davin threw light on a further possibility during an interview. Davin and Sheila Rowbotham were, from the 1970s, members of the groundbreaking History Workshop group, which did so much to establish working-class 'history from below'; however, they still had to fight to get the inclusion of women in the historical account taken seriously. Davin recalled that, after one meeting, a women's history session had been suggested – and this was greeted with waves of derisive male laughter.[55] As a result of this struggle for academic credibility, Davin said that she and like-minded historians researching women would have chosen to research 'anything but the bloody matchgirls!'[56] This was partly because a wealth of research into working-class London meant other areas had been neglected, but also, significantly, precisely because the story was such a cliché of female activism. It was regarded as having been included in labour history for the wrong reasons – either simply because it was a colourful and appealing story, or in a purely tokenistic way because of the gender of the strikers. Either way, it was the last thing with which a female historian struggling to establish academic authority, and to be taken seriously by her peers, would want to associate herself.[57]

The very fame of the matchwomen, in other words, has damaged their credibility.

All of these factors, including the tensions and divisions between groups of historians, appear to have conspired to prevent the light of history from being shone upon the matchwomen, their true role in their own dispute and their crucial familial ties to the 1889 dock strikers.[58] Anne Stafford alone posits a possible connection between matchwomen and dock workers in her excellent history of New Unionism, *A Match to Fire the Thames*, in which she imagines the women proudly telling the story of their victory to husbands and brothers who worked on the docks. However, she has not confirmed this with the use of census or family records.

Despite Stafford's work, and much primary evidence that the matchwomen and dockers were strongly connected, in 1985 E. H. Hunt was still able to conclude, unchallenged, that the matchwomen were not only led by Besant but had not influenced the dock strike. While Hunt admits that in the climate of the time 'a single domestic victory [could] play a catalytic role', he goes on to argue that the Bryant and May strike could never have been such a victory: 'The Bryant and May strike in the summer of 1888 probably came too early to have this effect and the matchgirls themselves were probably too unlike the workers who had the best prospect of becoming successful "new unionists".'[59]

Unless Hunt regards gender as an absolute divide, it is difficult to understand how he could have reached this conclusion. The primary evidence of journalists like Charles Dickens and social researchers like Beatrice Webb shows that contemporaries acknowledged connections between the two groups.[60] My research has confirmed this, uncovering evidence about the women who formed the strike committee, and showing that the vast majority lived in dockside areas with dockers as friends, neighbours and relatives. Census work has further established this.

Research in the archives at the Docklands Museum has also revealed that dockers' strike leaders acknowledged a debt to the matchwomen: newspapers reported that, on at least two reported occasions, John Burns urged mass meetings of his men to 'stand shoulder to shoulder. Remember the matchgirls, who won their fight and formed a union.'[61]

That Burns simply said 'the matchgirls' without any further explanation, and not, for example, 'the match girls from Bryant and May who went on strike last year ...' shows how familiar he assumed all of his vast audience to be with the women and their victory.

Despite all of the available evidence, the matchwomen's story still resembles a relic from another age in the style of its telling, preserved in historical amber and little changed since 1888. Amongst recent works, John Charlton provides a socialist re-evaluation of New Unionism in 'It Just Went Like Tinder' (the title taken from the matchwomen's own words about the strike) – it is thoroughly researched, and Charlton has clearly gone back to primary sources. He notes the matchwomen's probable Irish heritage, but stops short of exposing the canard of Besant's leadership. [62]

Suzanne Fagence Cooper's *The Victorian Woman*[63] aims to 'explode the myth of passive Victorian women and ... [record] the daily struggles of working women',[64] but again repeats the traditional misapprehension of a strike led by Besant.

Influential historian Simon Schama's recent *History of Britain 1776–2000* contains several entries on Besant, the one concerned with the period of the strike running to more than three pages. Events are once again focused on Besant: 'A few days [after publication of 'White slavery in London'] a delegation of the girls came to their Fleet Street office to tell Besant and Burrows they had been threatened with dismissal unless they signed a document repudiating the information contained in the article. Instead they had gone straight to the *Link* with their story. A strike committee was formed . . .'[65] This version appears to have been taken straight from Besant's autobiography, which differs from her account in the *Link* in implying that this was the first she knew of the threats, with no reference to any other source. Schama fails to emphasize that the women had not just gone straight to the *Link* 'with their story' – they had already walked out on strike.

Once again, history has been careless with the facts of the strike.

THE MATCHWOMEN'S LIVES AND TIMES: CONTEXTUAL MATERIAL

Because of the lack of biographies and autobiographies of matchwomen, I had to rely on sources that deal with the lives of Victorian working-class women, and in particular those in the kinds of communities the matchwomen would have known, to give context to their lives.

Anna Davin's *Growing Up Poor* is a comprehensive study of nineteenth-century East End childhood, based on 20 years of oral history interviews. The book challenges modern ideas about what it means to be a child, and about child labour.[66]

Dr Davin generously allowed me access to her personal notes and archives, and lent me the manuscript of Cohen and Fagan's *Childhood Memories Recorded by some Socialist Men and Women in their Later Years*, which was helpful in demonstrating that even very poor working-class families were sometimes more politically active and aware than some scholars credit.[67] Marc Brodie's relatively recent doctoral thesis, entitled 'Politics stirs them very little: Conservatism and apathy in the East End of London 1885–1914',[68] backs this up, and directly challenges Gareth Stedman Jones' analysis of working class political activism in *Outcast London*.[69]

As well as the work already cited by Mary Davis and Sarah Boston, Ivy Pinchbeck's classic *Women Workers and the Industrial Revolution* (1981) emphasizes the particular misery caused to women by the transition from agricultural to industrial society.

Unequal Opportunities,[70] edited by Angela John, also contradicts Marx's prediction in *Capital* that industrialization would 'create a new economic foundation for a higher form of the family and of relations between the sexes', showing that instead women had to contend with the double bind of juggling home and work.

Pat Thane's chapter on 'Late Victorian Women' in *Late Victorian Women*[71] traces the development of 'The Woman Question' and the responses to it from Victorian male society and trade unionists.

Jane Lewis and Elizabeth Roberts' work has previously been mentioned, and also provided insight into working-class women and work during the period. Papers given by Mary Davis, Gerry Holloway and Sheila Rowbotham at the

'Women: Fighting for Rights at Work' conference in 2005 have also supplied useful contextual material.[72]

William Fishman's *East End 1888* provided much useful detail on the development of the East End, its poor population and its 'sweated' trades. Fishman's extensive knowledge of the streets of Victorian East London, its housing, sanitation, employment and culture, and his challenge to patronizing and sentimental views of its inhabitants, greatly assist in the construction of a picture of the type of life a matchwoman might have known. He devotes a useful chapter to East End women and children.

Tom Mann's *Memoirs*, William Kent's biography of John Burns, Terry McCarthy's comprehensive history of the Great Dock Strike and works by and about Ben Tillett have all given valuable insight into working-class trade unionism of the period and perceptions of it, and the way in which 'New Unionism' made mainstream society consider the lives and problems of London's working poor.[73]

On the debate on 'New Unionism' and the extent to which the term is a valid one, Robert Gray's *The Aristocracy of Labour in Nineteenth-Century Britain*[74] provides an excellent summary of academic debate on the subject, and the extent and significance of divisions within the Victorian working class. On the same theme, Roger Penn's *Skilled Workers in the Class Structure*[75] provides a thorough empirical study of the development of the nineteenth-century labour movement, including earnings differentials and intermarriage between supposed different sections of the working class.

Lynn Hollen Lees' seminal *Exiles of Erin* provided valuable insight into the lives of the London Irish community, of which many matchwomen and dock workers were members, and the way in which individuals' lives, politics and neighbourhoods could be shaped by the sense of 'Irishness'. Lees argues that the perception of Irish identity in this community could be sustained for several generations following migration.

THE SEARCH FOR THE MATCHWOMEN

Although the names and addresses of 712 of the strikers are recorded in the strike fund register – the original document is held at the TUC archives – previous sources have not speculated about the individual women's histories. It seemed that no attempt had ever been made, for example, to discover the identities of the first woman dismissed by Bryant and May, or the handful first interviewed by Besant for 'White slavery in London'.

I first conducted an extensive search of current resources, as it was just possible that such evidence already existed, but had been overlooked. I began my search with oral history resources. I approached the archivist of the Raphael Samuel Archive, and met with its director, Dr John Marriott, who told me that there was nothing relating to matchwomen in this archive. I next contacted historians who have conducted considerable oral history studies, including Paul Thompson and Dr Anna Davin. Mr Thompson, who conducted a national survey of life-story interviews on life in Britain before 1918, has deposited his archive in Brunel University's working-class autobiographies section, but I could find no material relating to matchwomen within it. When contacted by email, Mr Thompson confirmed that he knew of no material that could help me.[76] I then met with Dr Davin, who has extensively researched the lives of East End women and has a vast resource of oral history, to which she generously allowed me access. She was able to provide me with one brief but wonderful eyewitness account of the matchwomen by a Poplar resident, and much useful contextual material.[77]

I also sought the advice of Professor Jerry White, an expert on working-class life in London. Though not aware of any obscure archives I might have missed, he was generously encouraging of my search, and his own work contributed to my understanding of working-class London.

I studied entries at the National Sound Archive at the British Library, but as detailed found only one reference to the matchwomen, in the music collections: a recording of an East London contemporary of the women remembering a song they had sung during the strike.[78] I contacted Roy Palmer, who had made the recording, to see if he had further information: he didn't, but kindly gave me permission to copy and transcribe the tape. The information it contained, and the interesting path down which it led me, is detailed in Chapter Six.

Other resources used in the search for such material included the Warwick Modern Records Centre, the British Library, the Bryant and May company archives, the Theosophy Archives in Cardiff and the Theosophical Society in Chennai, India (Theosophy was the belief system which became so central to Annie Besant's life after the strike, and she ended her life in India). I also contacted the Society of Friends, as Bryant and May had been prominent Quakers.

There was always the possibility that any of the above could have held some useful evidence, but after more than a year of research on this, it was starting to look unlikely that any more oral history or any autobiographical material was going to turn up.

It was clear that I needed to change tack. One option was to try to trace and interview descendants of the matchwomen. This was an unusual route to take in an academic study, but began to seem increasingly justified. Aside from my own interest in the 'real' matchwomen, I felt history had for too long denied them an identity outside their working one, leaving many questions unanswered. Had the women all died young, of 'phossy jaw' or some other horror associated with industry or poverty? Or had they gone on to become mothers and grandmothers, and if so what, if anything, had they told their families about their lives and the strike? I also felt it was time to provide some counterweight to the proliferation of biographies of Annie Besant (of which there are at least twenty, as well as two autobiographies and numerous writings on aspects of Besant's work), remarkable as she was. As I had already discovered Bryant and May's list of suspected 'ringleaders'[79] at this point, I used this as the basis of my research.[80]

Clearly, the ideal interview subjects would be those who had known women on the list. However, my chances of finding them or indeed anyone who had known the 1888 strikers, seemed slight. If family members could even be located so many years later, they were likely to be great-grandchildren, and unlikely to have known their matchwomen forebears for any significant length of time, if at all. There might be any number of descendants who were not aware of any connection with the women: aside from the passage of time, we know that working at Bryant and May in the late nineteenth century was a low-status occupation, and perhaps not something to talk about freely.

However, I went ahead, aware that this might also conceivably be the closest any researcher could now get to the women of 1888, and that time was necessarily of the essence.

Taking the strike fund register as a starting point and attempting to track families to the present day through census records was, as expected, a considerable undertaking, with inherent difficulties. The census was not, after all, intended to help genealogists and historians. Certain TV shows which trace family histories can make it seem like a magical key guaranteed to unlock the past; but it's important to remember that the Census was designed only to provide basic demographic information for parliament. Any census only gives a 'snapshot' of inhabitants present in a particular house on a particular night; the quality and accuracy of the information provided by nineteenth-century censuses has also been questioned.[81]

A further complication to my census work was that, while we obviously think of the matchwomen *as* matchwomen, they might not have identified themselves as such, making it harder to find them by stated occupation. They may have done matchwork for only for short periods, or intermittently – working for Bryant and May was not a long-term career option for most, but something which would be picked up and dropped according to circumstances. It could also be seasonal work, with women swapping match manufacture for hop- or fruit-picking or jam-making in the summer months when trade was slack.

As I would discover, match factory workers might switch to matchbox-making at home, or vice versa, again according to their circumstances. Former factory workers might take on homework once they had married and/or became mothers. The established problem of married women's under-reporting of their employment due to the dominance of Victorian domestic ideology applies here too: there may have been 'undercover' matchbox-makers in any given street who did not report their work to the census enumerators; it is equally possible that some women described simply as 'box makers' may have been matchbox-makers.[82]

A further problem in tracking this particular group of families down the centuries was the sheer mobility of poor East End families surviving through casual employment.

Some were able to keep the same family home for years, but for others frequent moves from street to street or neighbourhood to neighbourhood were a fact of life, in search of better living and working conditions, or in flight from creditors or unpayable rent according to fluctuating finances; the 'moonlight flit' is a firmly entrenched part of East End history.[83]

While scholars usually suggest that urban migration during this period was exceeded by, and generally occurred over shorter distances than, that of rural communities, it has also been established that women were generally more migratory than men, particularly on marriage.[84] Marriage can, of course, also change a woman's surname at any point in her adult life, sometimes more than once.[85] We know too that Victorian East Enders tended to move out of the area if they managed to make enough money to do so, often to the new suburbs which developed alongside the railways, or further afield to areas like Hertfordshire and Essex.[86]

I expected that all or any of these factors might hamper my attempts to trace the families of strikers forward from 1888.

The second level of my research would be an analysis of connections between dock labourers and matchwomen. In order to select 'typical' matchwomen's streets to study for closeness to docks or for dockworkers in residence, I first analysed the strike fund register and selected a sample of the most frequently occurring addresses. I then attempted to locate these streets both in the closest census to the strike, the 1891, and on what I felt were the best available street maps of the period, those in G. W. Bacon's *Ordnance Atlas of London and Suburbs*, which dates from 1888.[87] I encountered several immediate difficulties: handwriting on both the register and the census records can be difficult to read, and the spelling in both documents arbitrary, as if based on the phonetics of what recorders heard. On the strike fund register, for example, Tidey Street is frequently spelled *Tidy*. The surnames and addresses of two sisters, who lived together, are rendered differently.[88] One frequently occurring street could not be conclusively located on either the census or Bacon's map: 'Blomfield Street' appears several times on the register, always with the same spelling, but does not appear in census records or on street maps, although there are *Bloomfield* roads and streets. (Charles Blomfield was Bishop of London from 1828 to 1856, and it seems that roads and streets named for him were habitually misspelled: the poet A. E. Housman's letters confirm that a more salubrious 'Blomfield Street', where a friend of his lived, was generally spelled 'Bloomfield' in 1894.[89])

Bacon's atlas has its own peculiarities too: some small streets are not listed in the index, but close examination, which often had to be done with a magnifying glass, shows them to be present on the map. Obviously, in order to know roughly where to look for them, an approximate location was essential, so if roads could not be found in Bacon, I used the resources of the Charles Booth Archive at the London School of Economics to try to locate them, with some success. Streets which were unnamed, or unclear, on Booth's own maps might still be mentioned in his survey notebooks, and by reading the account of his route the closest streets to them could often be located.

I was eventually able to locate four 'recurring streets' from the register on the 1888 street map, and so assess their closeness to the docks and dockside communities. To further assess neighbourhood and familial ties between the two groups, census records for each street were then studied, and occupational data on all the inhabitants examined. Each incidence of dock workers and matchwomen in residence was recorded. As a result of this, I was able to establish that matchwomen and dockers lived closely together in a remarkable number of cases.

Initial attempts to trace families of the five women on Bryant and May's list through the census proved time-consuming and expensive, as predicted, with a charge made per record viewed at the Family Records Centre. I therefore decided to attempt to contact descendants more directly too, through the media and local history societies. Publications would obviously need to appear in the right area or areas, but if course I couldn't be certain which these were: the grandchildren or great-grandchildren of East Enders could be living anywhere in the country – or the world. Furthermore, I obviously wasn't in a position to 'pick and choose' the newspapers and other publications that would carry my letters and articles: they would decide whether my research was of any interest to them.

I made initial appeals for information and descendants through BBC Radio London and two local papers, the *East London Advertiser* and the *Herts Advertiser*, but these were not particularly successful. Large feature articles were more likely to attract attention, and I managed to place these in the *Irish Times*, the *Irish Post*, two trade union papers (the Transport and General Workers' Union paper, *Record*, and the Communication Workers' Union paper, *Connect*), and the Whitechapel History Society's journal.[90]

The Irish papers were chosen for two reasons: first because I knew that many of the women or their parents would have been Irish or of Irish descent (along with many of the dockers), giving an angle which might interest them; and secondly because both are high-circulation papers, giving me access to a large readership. The *Irish Times* has worldwide circulation and is also published online, while the *Irish Post* is a weekly newspaper for the Irish in Britain. Some of the matchwomen's relatives could have returned to Ireland in search of their roots as its economy improved; or grandchildren in England and elsewhere might still consider themselves Irish enough to take the Irish press.

However, although I received some interesting and very supportive feedback from readers of these articles, and some indirectly useful information in letters and telephone calls from readers, contact with the grandson of an 1889 dock striker – who had indeed moved back to Ireland – was as close as I came to the matchwomen. Writing the articles was also necessarily quite time-consuming.

Much more successful was a series of public lectures in the East End of London and Hertfordshire.[91] It was through these that I eventually met all of the four subjects whom I would interview in depth. I doubt I'll ever forget the moment when Joan Harris, my first interviewee, pointed to a photograph of the women on strike and said 'I think that's my grandmother.'

Two other descendants came forward at talks too, and in the end I was lucky enough to be able to interview descendants of three members of the Matchworkers' Union committee, and of two of the women whom Bryant and May had listed as likely 'troublemakers'.

The information provided by my interviewees was fascinating and valuable. All were grandchildren rather than great-grandchildren, and provided supporting evidence to prove the connections, as well as documentation on their grandmothers' lives and personal photographs. Two had known their grandmothers extremely well and for a number of years. All were excellent interview subjects, possessed of good recall and knowledge of East End history (one is a local historian). Two remain living in the East End, and one has moved out to Essex.

Their grandmothers had all been working for Bryant and May in some capacity at the time of the strike: one, who was very young at the time, was making matchboxes at home but, as already suggested, this did not mean that she was cut off from the factory: box-makers had daily contact with Bryant and May, and the woman in question had known a number of the factory hands, later joining them at work in Fairfield Road. Her reminiscences also indicated that 'outworkers' sometimes made up their boxes inside the factory itself.

The other two grandmothers worked directly in the factory in 1888 and, most significantly, were among the list of five supposed 'ringleaders' compiled by Bryant and May foremen at the time of the strike. All the interviewees were able to provide me with good evidence about the women's lives, personalities and connections to the East London dockers and to the Irish community, and of 'family lore' regarding the strike and its conduct.

One of the three had identified strongly with the Irish 'rebel' tradition. Another of the women had died shortly before her grandson was born, but had told her children that she had been one of the leaders of the strike, and this was passed on to her grandson and granddaughter. This appears to be confirmed by primary evidence: I subsequently discovered a report in the *Star* newspaper which describes a woman of the same name and physical description who spoke at strike meetings, and whom the newspaper called 'one of the leaders of the strike'.[92] She may even have been the first woman dismissed by Bryant and May, who inspired the strike in the first place: newspaper reports state that this individual worked in the Victoria factory, as did the grandmother in question.[93]

The evidence provided, though necessarily anecdotal, will be shown to be a further component in supporting the concept of a self-organized strike. The three women in my sample are remembered as resourceful, tough, loving women who grew up to become matriarchal figures within their families. Two of the three were unofficial community leaders to some degree; one was the woman entrusted to lay out the neighbourhood dead and to act as unofficial midwife to new arrivals, and the other was often fetched for help when there was any 'trouble' in the area. The third went from abject poverty to owning two shops, which would have given her a certain status in the neighbourhood – particularly in a poor area, when shopkeepers were the arbiters of who could and could not receive the crucial credit or 'tick'.

None of the women bore any resemblence to the helpless waifs of popular lore.

Oral history sources, however, have their own 'problems and pitfalls'[94] which have to be taken into account in their use. Much has been written by both proponents and detractors of the genre on issues of accuracy, objectivity, the relationship between interviewer and interviewee, and the very nature of oral sources: can they, for example, strictly be called 'oral' once they have been turned into written testimony by scholars, and how much are they changed in the process?[95]

There has also been considerable debate about 'non-interference' on the part of the historian.[96] The Italian oral historian Allesandro Portelli has questioned the possibility of ever achieving this; the value of any exchange in which the subject provides only 'brute facts' which the historian then transforms, at his or her desk and out of sight of the interviewee, into 'a monologue of sophisticated ideas that the informant never hears about'.[97]

Others agree that what takes place in interviews is essentially a collaborative process. Clough *et al.* stress the importance of a true 'conversation' between fieldworker and informant, as opposed to 'monological method', to achieve a beneficial collaborative exchange.[98] Benison draws attention to an often overlooked factor: that such an exchange flows both ways, and that oral history does and should change the *historian*. As an academic, he said, 'theory poured from my lips ... I made generalisations about the lives of tens and thousands of people ...', but only when he undertook oral history fieldwork did he fully comprehend the complexity of the reality behind the theory.[99] There is no question that not only my hypotheses, but my understanding of the Victorian East End and the matchwomen's living and working conditions, were transformed and enriched by the testimony provided by my interviewees. There are many historiographical references, for example, to the East Enders' summer occupation of hop-picking, which served as the closest thing to a holiday many would know. My interviewees were able to confirm that this was another experience which connected matchwomen and dockers. Beyond this, they also enabled me to imagine the lively journeys from East London to the hop-fields, with everything but the kitchen sink (including one matchwoman's own bed, which she insisted on bringing along) strapped to the cart; the sound of rain on the tin roofs of the hop-pickers' shacks; and the little girl who, unlike the rest of her family, absolutely loathed the whole experience, trying to shelter among the hop plants in a thunderstorm, wishing she was back in the East End.[100]

This is a great strength of oral history: in providing engrossingly personal human stories it brings history vividly to life in a way that is democratic and accessible to all.[101] This does not, of course, mean that the usual rigorous controls can be put aside: in fact, accuracy is a central and all-permeating issue concerning such sources.

Portelli writes that oral history brings an uncomfortable awareness of the 'elusive quality of truth', but this is as much an advantage as a problem: it 'allows and permits' greater attention to subjectivity, and what Hawthorne has called the 'truth of the human heart'.[102] Thorough fact-checking is vital to both complement and balance these 'truths'. In the case of this study, the matchwomen themselves had not dwelled endlessly on their work for Bryant and May or the strike in their later years: as Gwen Etter-Lewis writes, women's narratives are more likely to be characterized by 'understatements, rare mention of personal accomplishments and disguised statements of power'.[103] It was in the checking of interviewees' testimony against official documents (such as census records and marriage certificates, and also some more unusual ones, like a twenty-year-old article written by museum archivists), that I not only obtained the names and addresses of all members of the matchwomen's strike committee, but confirmed that two interviewees' ancestors (two grandmothers and one great-aunt) played central roles in the strike.

In this way, as Portelli writes, accuracy and subjectivity are 'neither apart nor antagonistic', but each provides the standard against which the other is meas-ured.[104] It should also be noted when considering the accuracy of oral sources, as against written, that the latter form can be equally problematic: government and labour movement records of women's involvement in trade unions after 1850, for example, are known to be unreliable and incomplete.[105] In the specific case of the matchwomen, the historical version which this study has sought to examine and interrogate has proved to be flawed and highly subjective itself, and in fact largely based on the partly explored and often misquoted writings of one source, Annie Besant.

Accepting that the usefulness of any source depends upon the information the historian is seeking,[106] interview testimony which answers questions about the strike can only be valuable. Beyond this, it has also provided an opportunity to discover what the matchwomen and their lives were like, in the words of people who knew them. It has been argued that we impoverish historical writing if we do not attempt to connect in some way with women's 'inner and outer lives'.[107] In doing so here we can at last provide a corrective to these women's current historical position as a nameless, powerless mass of 'matchgirls' awaiting external direction. They are revealed instead as women who were personally powerful as individuals, mothers and members of their community. If they had not read theories about the position of women and the working classes, they certainly 'knew all these things in practice',[108] and remained as capable of standing up for themselves and their loved ones in their personal lives as they had been when Bryant and May sacked one of their friends back in 1888.

In conclusion, it is hoped that this book will build upon the tradition of the writers cited, who seek to examine history from the perspective of the working class, and also to integrate the complex interplay of class and gender into that account. It is my contention that the matchworkers' strike has been interpreted in a way which undervalues it; that their victory helped to inspire the 1889 dock strike; and that the orthodox version which denies the women's agency survives in part due to ideological bias concerning gender and class issues.

1

Angels in the House and Factory Girls

In October 1888, three months after the end of the matchwomen's strike, a letter arrived at the Bryant and May factory, signed 'John Ripper'. The author threatened to 'pay a visit' to the company's female employees, detailing what would then occur, in brief but brutal terms.[1] The writer claimed to have been provoked by the matchwomen's threats to *him*: they had apparently been heard loudly discussing 'what they would do' with the already notorious murderer plaguing their streets, if they could just get their hands on him.[2]

Since that August, five women had been murdered in the East End, resulting in a general panic; but according to the letter-writer the matchwomen had reacted with anger, not terror. There was probably an element of bravado in this but equally, there can't have been many women hoping for an encounter with one of the most infamous criminals of the age, even if it was with the intention of returning his violence with their own in order to defend their neighbourhoods.

No matchwomen ever did fall victim to 'Ripper', and the letter itself may well have been a hoax. The picture it presents of the women at first appears inauthentic too. These fierce, fearless characters seem far removed from the 'matchgirls' who had come to national attention three months earlier. Although hundreds of them had downed tools *en masse*, press accounts generally portrayed them as victims, not militant strikers, and certainly not women capable of menacing murderers. Exactly whose victims they were – their employers, or Annie Besant and the socialists – varied according to the newspaper's political perspective. That someone was or had been exploiting them was, however, not in doubt.

Even Besant's accounts encouraged this view. She had first met the women when interviewing them for her thundering exposé of Bryant and May which would be published in her political paper, the Link. The piece, with the sensational title 'White slavery in London', resulted from a discussion of the company's low wages and large profits at a Fabian Society meeting in June 1888. The 'slaves' Besant describes seem touchingly childlike: exploited by their employer and half-starved, but still, poignantly, trying to make the best of life. One 16-year-old matchmaker, Besant wrote, earned so little that she had to exist on 'only ... bread-and-butter and tea' for every meal; still, she spoke with 'dancing eyes' of her monthly treat, a 'proper meal' in a café where 'you get coffee, and bread and butter, and jam, and marmalade, and lots of it'.[3]

Besant calls her a 'child', and that is how she sounds: an innocent abroad, in fact very like the best-known, if fictional, matchgirl of the time. By 1888, Hans Christian Andersen's *Little Match Girl* had been an established nursery favourite for decades. In it, a 'poor little girl' roams the darkening streets of an unnamed city on New Year's Eve. She is bare-headed and -footed despite the freezing weather, but does not dare go home to her violent father until she has sold all the matches she carries in a bundle: she has been out all day, but so far sold nothing at all. She sees Christmas lights in the houses she passes, and is tormented by the smell of roast goose from their kitchens. Finally she succumbs to cold and hunger. Dying on a street corner she meets her death bravely, comforted by a vision of her dead grandmother, which comes to her in the light of the matches she strikes one after another in a vain attempt to find warmth, who carries her grandchild up to heaven in her arms.[4]

Despite being translated from the Danish, the story's heroine is a perfect example of the kind of poor girl the British Victorian establishment found acceptable: honest, virtuous and accepting of her lot, meeting her fate with resignation – and with absolutely no talk of workers' rights.

I believe that the orthodox version of the Bryant and May strike which commentators and historians have been retelling ever since owes as much to this sentimentalized view of the poor as it does to reality. It is tempting to hear echoes of Andersen's story in the traditional version of the matchwomen's. There is a confusion of fact and fiction in the way the real women are generally portrayed – as passive victims, not of a cruel father but of powerful employers who had also failed in their paternalistic duty. The real matchwomen are also supposed to have been 'saved' by a woman, though Besant took them out on strike rather than to their Eternal Reward. Though we know her name, the matchwomen themselves remain as nameless as the little girl in the fairy tale, archetypes rather than flesh-and-blood women.

Notwithstanding the forward march of historical thinking over the past century and the numerous revisions it has brought in its wake, the story has changed remarkably little in its essentials since the late 1880s. It seems to me that a kind of historical vicious circle has been at work here: because the strike's true significance has not been realized, it has not been thought a suitable subject for really serious academic scrutiny; and precisely because it has not been subjected to such examination, important facts about it, which would have increased its significance to labour history, have been overlooked.

Neither the 'people's history' school, nor those with a particular interest in restoring women – especially working-class women – to the historical picture, have succeeded in rescuing the matchwomen from what E. P. Thompson famously called the 'enormous condescension of posterity'.[5] In fact, it seems that the very trajectories of 'women's history', and tensions between it and other developing strands, have actually contributed to the failure to re-evaluate the matchwomen's strike, or to see in it anything worth re-evaluating.

A proper examination of the evidence makes it impossible to continue to believe that Besant led it. Not all of this evidence is difficult to come by; in fact, as we will see, it includes Besant's own accounts. Because of the assumed relative unimportance of the strike, it is often written about in passing; as we have already seen, few labour historians have carried out fresh research on it, relying instead on existing accounts and so reproducing erroneous assumptions about how the strike happened. What is more puzzling is that some writers who have clearly looked at original evidence which includes confirmation that Besant did not orchestrate events, continue to assert that she did.

How and why such learned sources came to overlook this evidence is important in itself, and is one of the central mysteries which we must try to solve. Something beyond carelessness must be at work here: a deeper ideology moving below the surface, which has concealed and distorted the truth even when it is in plain sight. The real matchwomen whose lives and experiences I have been able to uncover were far from the helpless victims of popular imagination, crushed underfoot by a powerful employer until rescued by their philanthropic 'betters'. The reality is more complex; and far more interesting. Why and how it has been hidden, not from, but actually *by* history for more than a century, is a story in itself; and it begins with Victorian ideas about the proper place of women.

'ANGELS' V. 'FACTORY GIRLS'

Whoever was behind the 'Ripper' letter of October 1888, there were certainly many in what was only now beginning to be called the 'East End' (or the 'Worst End', in contrast to the West London 'Best'),[6] and throughout the country, who found something threatening in the prospect of working women like the matchworkers.

It has been said that 1780 to 1830 was the period that created the 'industrial bourgeoisie'. By the mid-nineteenth century not just industry, but industrial *capitalism*, had undoubtedly triumphed. New equipment had harnessed the power of steam, eventually enabling mass production. Fortunes could be made, if not overnight, then certainly with speed for those who had capital to invest and entrepreneurial spirit. Real, and swift, social advancement too was now within the grasp of successful industrialists, who were almost exclusively male.

For women in general, industrialization, while it also changed the way they lived in many respects, was more likely to represent a 'dreary experience' than positive progress.[7] With the associated changes to economic and social relationships came a bitter struggle over gender divisions and work. Debates about the role and place of women in society, the 'woman question', were far from new, but resurfaced with a vengeance with the industrializing of production, and the social upheaval which resulted from it.

There is a wide literature from outside the working class on the ideology of domesticity, by proponents as well as opponents; but a paucity of auto-biographical accounts which tell us how working women, particularly those of the matchworkers' class and communities, responded.[8] Women's labour was needed in ever-increasing quantity to fuel the British industrial 'revolution'. All but the most affluent of women had always worked in some fashion in any case: in the previous century it had been said that 'only a fool will take a wife whose bread must be earned solely by his labour and who will contribute nothing towards it herself'.[9]

The new mills and factories, however, were very different propositions from the old cottage industries and family workshops, in which a woman's labour could be seen as little more than an extension of her household chores, untroubling to the *status quo*. Now, women were working outside the home, and their wages, however meagre, were paid directly into their own hands. Here was a potential threat to relations between the sexes: what wife would respect her husband's authority when she was no longer dependent on him for housekeeping money, and what daughter submit to a father's control when she had the wherewithal to set up home on her own? Worse, working-class women with money in their pockets might be lured by the same temptations that the middle classes frequently berated their menfolk for submitting to: what was now to keep them from the low company of music halls and pubs, and the evils of drink, rowdiness and promiscuity? The last was a particular preoccupation of Victorian society, and there ensued much fevered speculation about the sexuality, real or imagined, of women of the working classes. Welcome or not, the new figure of the 'factory girl' strode onto the public stage, and began to occupy a particular place in nineteenth-century fiction and media. She was always a 'girl', never given the dignity of maturity no matter her actual age, and her portrayal by mostly male and middle-class journalists and commentators would reveal many of the fears and preoccupations of the unquiet Victorian subconscious.

The removal of women from the workplace and their 'return' to the domestic sphere (whether or not they had in reality ever exclusively inhabited it in the first place) began to be seen as a palliative for all manner of social ills often laid at the door of the poor: insobriety, neglect of children, lack of 'social purity', and the overall degeneration of their race. During the century, a powerful consensus formed on the necessity of returning working-class women to the home, uniting disparate groups whose concern with the conduct of these women's lives derived from very different motivations, but all of whom hoped to effectively render the term 'working-class woman' obsolete.

It was such ideology which laid the ground for the matchwomen's struggle, and was at least as responsible as their class for the dire working conditions which underlay it.

In order to properly understand the strike and its impact, then, we must consider the effects of burgeoning domestic ideology on society at large – and therefore on disparate groups, including the journalists who covered the strike and the male leaders of the established labour movement – and how it coloured the way in which the strike and its main actors were viewed.

Because of it, both 'sides' in the struggle (that is, their employers and the middle-class socialists who would publicize their cause, rather than the women themselves, who were not then considered to constitute their own 'side') had tactical reasons for wanting to present the women as waifs, victims – anything but the dreaded 'factory girls'. This is crucial to an understanding of the ways in which the strike and the strikers have been both celebrated and misrepresented over the years.

'ANGELS' AT HOME

While the world outside the Victorian home was changing rapidly, new, idealized notions of femininity sought to ensure that within it dwelled a 'relic of the past discordant with the future'.[10]

As many commentators have warned, it is unsound to try to build an understanding of a society on its didactic literature. Matthew Sweet, for example, points to Victorian political and social advances, and offers the Married Women's Property Act and census records showing a one-third female workforce, in defence of the period's attitude to women.[11] Sweet traces our stereotypical conception of 'Victorian values' back to Lytton Strachey's famous 'poison pen-letter to the past', *Eminent Victorians*.[12] Whoever cast the first stone, Sweet is certainly right that the trend for heaping opprobrium on the Victorians for class, gender and race oppression, sexual repression and general hypocrisy has not always been empirically based: hence the apparently unshakeable belief in the mythical covering of piano legs for reasons of propriety.

However, it is undeniable that this was a period when the social standing and influence of the industrial bourgeoisie increased exponentially, to the point where it was powerful enough to become the 'hegemonic class', whose values eventually suffused and dominated the whole society.[13] In establishing an identity of its own which would distinguish it from both the working and landed classes, the new class rejected the aristocratic idea that a man could only be considered a 'gentleman' if untainted by the need to work for a living, asserting instead a strong work ethic and belief in the nobility of labour. However, one patrician ideal was embraced with enthusiasm: that of the 'lady of leisure' devoted – if not confined – to the private world of home and family. It became a mark of social standing that a man's wife and daughters should not have to seek employment: a 'decent' woman's place was now most definitely in the home. Lack of occupation of its womenfolk became a defining characteristic of the successful and respectable nineteenth-century family. 'Respectability' was the 'favourite description of the leading virtue of the age',[14] and a particular straitjacket for women, encompassing everything from their sexual morality to their dress and household management. The woman, whatever her class, who lost her 'reputation' might also lose the protection and support of her family, class and community, with disastrous consequences.

For the 'leisured' woman, life was highly circumscribed, and often anything but leisurely. Her supposed *raison d'être*, and often her only chance of setting up an independent household away from her parents', was to make a 'good' marriage with a financially as well as romantically suitable husband, like any good Jane Austen character before her. She must continue to please him in order to maintain her status: if her husband deserted her, she might be left destitute; even if he died, she had no automatic right to the custody of her children. Should she be unhappy or mistreated, she could not, until the latter half of the nineteenth century, apply for divorce – only men could do so.[15] Even within marriage, she was a legal 'non-person'[16] incorporated into the identity of her husband under the laws of coverture: a *femme covert* was a dependant, as much as an under-age child was.[17]

In reality, only in the most exceptionally affluent families could women truly aspire to anything approaching idleness.[18] The middle-class wife was expected to serve as an adjunct to her husband's life in the commercial world, ensuring that his domestic life was satisfactorily ordered, providing a pleasant haven after the hurly-burly of work; a contrast and a respite from *real* life, which took place outside it, rather than having a vivid existence in its own right.

The maintenance of this idyll was hard work for many middle-class women. A woman was supposed to be first and foremost a devoted wife and mother, too occupied with the concerns of home and hearth to have much to do with the world outside her own walls – and certainly not engaged in anything as sordid as the selling of her labour. This is not to say that she wasn't expected to work hard – even middle-class married women with servants could find their days fully occupied in the management of the household and family, frequent entertaining and possibly some 'good work' for church or charity – as long as she did so for free.

So 'Leisure for women became an indication of status just when the bourgeois man elevated the dignity of labour against the indolence of the aristocracy and of the poor.'[19] A further irony was that many bourgeois husbands would not have gained a position where they could denigrate working women *without* working women: female labour had been the backbone of the industrial 'revolution' which had made so many new fortunes.[20]

Queen Victoria, surrounded by a brood of children and elevating wifely devotion to an art form which not even her husband's death could interrupt, became an icon of domestic femininity, notwithstanding that this particular 'housewife' also presided over a powerful empire in her spare time.

Another powerful model for cloistered womanhood would be found in the deceased wife of a poet. Coventry Patmore's poem, *Angel in the House*, gave a name to the archetype of perfect femininity, gaining immense popularity and 'a permanent place among the Home Books of the English People'.[21] The 1854 work is a paean to a wife so utterly and selflessly devoted that it might be supposed – perhaps even hoped – that she was purely fictional; however, she was evidently inspired in part by Patmore's first wife, Emily. It has been suggested that Patmore was in fact employing parody in this work.[22] Emily Patmore was apparently a woman of high and lively intelligence in life; however, her widower's poem gives every appearance of suggesting that self-sacrifice to the point, to modern eyes at least, of masochism, was the authentic badge of womanly love:

> Man must be pleased; but him to please
> Is woman's pleasure; down the gulf
> Of his condoled necessities
> She casts her best, she flings herself.

The 'angel in the house' paradigm became well established, and so ideologically powerful as to be still regarded as something of a rod for the back of womanhood well into the next century: in 1931 Virginia Woolf wrote a bitterly funny essay about the vital necessity of 'Killing the Angel in the House' in order to liberate women from her repressive spell.[23]

What woman has not fought her own battle with the same 'phantom' of domestic concerns which distracted Woolf from her writing, whispering sweetly but insistently in her ear of all the feminine duties she was neglecting. 'Though I flatter myself that I killed her in the end', she wrote, the struggle was severe: it took much time that had better been spent on learning Greek grammar; or roaming the world in search of adventure.'[24]

The phrase 'Angel in the House' itself perfectly expresses many of the pre-occupations of the age. If the ideal woman was a kind of 'angel' then by definition she was not strictly human but a celestial higher being, presumably above earthiness and earthliness – and, most definitely, human sexuality. Rather than an individual, she was a kind of personification of goodness, and closer to God than her menfolk, with a duty to keep them on the moral straight and narrow, 'sent below to teach our erring minds to see'.[25] Unlike her biblical counterparts, the domestic angel's first concern was not the wider world but her own home: it was from her voluntary immurement within it that much of her purity derived. Free from the necessity of involvement in the commercial world, she was protected from contamination with the sinful world outside her walls.

In his 1840 play *Money*, Edward Bulwer-Lytton satirized the education and aspirations of the typical Victorian society girl, as described by her father:

> I ... never stuffed your head with history and homilies; but you draw, you sing, you dance, you walk well into a room; and that's the way young ladies are educated nowadays, in order to become a pride to their parents and a blessing to their husbands – that is, when they have caught him.[26]

Lytton has been described as 'a representative Victorian' in that his literary work illustrated – and indeed, it has been claimed, actually influenced – the thinking and preoccupations of the age.[27] His early work has been credited with inspiring the ideological turn from Byronic Romanticism to the 'moral earnestness of Victorian Social Reformers', and his later writing with inspiring the Theosophical movement, to which Besant would devote her life after the matchwomen's strike.[28]

However, Lytton's private life could also serve as an illustration of the gender politics of the period. Born into an aristocratic family, he became interested in the Reformist cause as a young man, and entered politics in order to advance it. He was disinherited when he married, against his family's wishes, Rosina Wheeler, a noted Irish beauty and daughter of Anna Wheeler, the adherent of Mary Wollstonecraft and influential writer on women's rights. For all that *Money* lambasted the restrictions placed on Victorian women, and for all Lytton's supposedly progressive politics, he would have Rosina committed to an insane asylum in 1858. She had failed to behave in a suitably forbearing and feminine manner on the breakdown of her marriage, instead embarrassing Lytton and threatening his political career with loud public complaints of his treatment of her, which she occasionally appeared at his hustings to deliver.

If Lytton condemned, at least in theory, the idea that a woman's biology alone defined her destiny, the popularity of the concept only increased as the Victorian period progressed. There was nothing original, either, in the invocation of 'nature' and the 'natural' order of things to justify the subordination of women; elements of nineteenth-century ideas on a woman's place can be traced back through millennia of Western thought. Aristotle, in his treatises *On a Good Wife* and *The History of Animals*, argued that woman was defective by nature: an incomplete version of man, whose lowly station was therefore inevitable and appropriate.[29] More than two thousand years later, the idea was back in fashion, encouraged in part by Darwinistic biological determinism and the popular pseudo science of eugenics.

What, then, of the middle-class women who did not marry and would – or certainly should – therefore remain childless? Society reserved particular opprobrium for 'spinsters', regarding them as women who had 'failed in business'. 29 The mid-1800s saw much debate on the 'problem' of these 'redundant women', whose number was then estimated at 750,000 and rising. The journalist W. R. Greg joined the debate on the best use to which this human surplus should be put, in his piece 'Why are women redundant?'. Greg quite seriously proposed that the bulk of unmarried British women be transported to countries like America, Canada and Australia, where men outnumbered women. Those who remained should be obliged to take lessons from high-class prostitutes in how to attract and please a man.[31] Unmarried women were in a double bind: if they tried to overcome their supposed redundancy by searching for meaning in their lives and financial security of their own, they found that few professions were regarded as suitable for the respectable woman.

Women did, of course, vociferously question their position. The celebrated campaigner, Josephine Butler was eloquent on the subject of the rights of women, who should be given 'the work of healers, preachers, physicians, artists, organizers of labour, captains of industry, &c . . .'.[32] However, she also expressed views which paralleled the 'angel of the house' stereotype, condemning women who were too strident in the cause:

It cannot be denied that a just cause has sometimes been advocated by women in a spirit of bitterness. Energy impeded in one direction, will burst forth in another; hence the defiant and sometimes grotesque expression which the lives and acts of some few women have been of the injustice done to them by society. This will cease, and while it lasts, it ought to excite our pity rather than our anger.[33]

There is little to distinguish these comments from age-old stereotypes of feminists as shrill, sexually frustrated 'spinsters'. Harris reminds us that women who wanted a public role at this time often had to 'cloak themselves in a quite exaggerated degree of modesty and outward trappings of acceptable femininity',[34] and there may therefore have been some tactical element to the use of the language of 'separate spheres' by women like Butler; however, her activism was also informed by a staunch Christianity and concern for public morals.[35] Butler did, however, admit the hostility and apathy of men towards the women's movement: 'Prejudice is slowly dying out, but indifference remains. Educated men who can help, who would help if they knew the need, have not yet learnt that need.'[36]

Autobiographical as well as fictional writings betray the palpable sense of frustration felt by middle-class Victorian women whose talents and ambitions were suppressed by the restrictions of their lives: Florence Nightingale's cry – 'Why have women passion, intellect, moral activity . . . and a place in society where no one of the three can be exercised?' – echoed the feelings of many.[37]

Socially 'useful' work among the poor was one allowable outlet for such women in an age which embraced *gravitas* exemplified by philanthropic work.

Historians like E. P. Thompson have divined in this a defensive, rather than altruistic, motive: paraphrasing Mary Shelley's remark that after the French Revolution 'every man felt the necessity of putting his house in order', Thompson concluded that the fear of class revolt inspired 'most men and women of property [to feel] the necessity of putting the houses of the poor in order'.[38]

More immediate practical considerations, such as outbreaks of cholera in poor areas, also worked to concentrate the minds of middle-class neighbours, appealing to both altruism and self-interest. State legislation too began to encroach on areas of what had previously been its citizens' private lives, with the likes of the 1870 Elementary Education Act. Teaching was slowly becoming an acceptable profession for women, also sending middle-class women into working-class areas. The standards they upheld and imposed, with an emphasis on cleanliness and respectability, were often those of the class from which they came. In addition, the school curriculum reinforced notions of biology as destiny: for girls there was a great emphasis on practical skills like needlework, which was considered essential; indeed, potential women teachers had to show themselves to be competent needlewomen.[39]

The enthusiastic attentions of middle-class women to their working-class sisters, whether through paid or unpaid work, were often based on a belief that 'women could always reach across the class barriers and help each other'.[40]

However, with an ideological assumption, however unconscious, of the superiority of their own values, many middle-class investigators found themselves 'repelled' by the disorder of urban working-class life, and set out to remake it in the image of their own notions of what was right and respectable.[41]

Helen Bosanquet, the social reformer who would be a leading figure in the Royal Commission on the Poor Laws, was typical in her belief that 'The great problem with this class is how to bring them to regard life as anything but a huge chaos. The confusion which reigns in their minds is reflected in their works.'[42] Bosanquet and her contemporaries saw the male breadwinner model as the most stable, and accordingly criticized working-class mothers who worked for neglect of their children.

Some historians have asserted that middle- and working-class women shared a 'female' consciousness which overrode class; others, that class was always a major dividing line between middle-class teachers and benefactors and their subjects.[43] Much primary evidence from both classes, including interviews conducted for this book, seems to confirm the latter view: one matchwoman's granddaughter remembered that, though her grandmother refused to feel inferior as a person to an aristocratic woman who did 'good work' in her neighbourhood and indeed became friendly with her, she was nonetheless acutely aware of their different stations in life; another confirmed that the gulf between 'toffs' and ordinary East Enders was keenly felt, but that it was their educated status, rather than their social position, which was respected.[44]

In any event, by the 1880s the belief was that the benefactors, even if delicately reared women, should go *to* the poor, rather than the other way around. The angels were thus required not only to leave the house, but their entire milieu, to experience life as it was lived in the nation's slums and rookeries. Those whose well-shod feet encountered for the first time the streets of East London would not always be prepared for what they found in the 'City of Dreadful Night'.[45]

THE MAKING OF THE 'EAST END'

> He turned . . . into the familiar Whitechapel Road, and walked on past the flaming gaslights of the costermongers, the public houses and the street hawkers. An old woman offered him pig's feet; a newspaper man shouted the last ghastly details of a murder, tipsy men and women rolled past him singing East end songs . . . He caught sight of the slum lassies in a public house, and listened at the door as they argued. Turning away he stumbled over two half – naked street children who were waiting for their drunken parents. A woman with a sickly infant on her breast asked him for money to find a night's lodgings.[46]

So the novelist and social reformer Margaret Harkness guided her readers through the dark streets of the East End in 1889. The images of women she presents – drunken 'slum lassies', mothers who cannot or will not provide for their children – reflect the growing concerns of wider society, which were fed by the 'travellers' tales'[47] emanating from the 'mysterious East', now virtually a world apart from 'respectable' London. Similar social divisions were replicated across the industrialized country as those who profited from industrialization built what Annie Besant called their 'mansions and pleasure grounds' on the labour of those who inhabited 'reeking slums within the sound of factory bells'.[48] However, the most sensational and shocking tales of inequality emanated from London, which, with its burgeoning press and closeness to centres of political power, was well placed to attract national attention.

If the spectre of social revolution was haunting the Victorian bourgeoisie, contemporary accounts suggest that the wraith of the 'factory girl' – loud, brash, and probably physically and morally degenerate – was stalking them too. She seems to have personified a number of the fears of the unquiet Victorian subconscious, as well as offering a convenient scapegoat to those who disliked the idea of women's presence in the industrial workforce under any circumstances. In East London, where Bryant and May had become the largest employer of 'unskilled' female factory labour, she was typified by the matchwoman.

London had, of course, always had an 'eastern quarter', but not until the 1880s did it acquire an 'East End'.[49] Who coined the term isn't known, but soon its citizens had been ascribed a collective identity, as 'East Enders', which put them beyond the pale. As a contemporary journal noted: 'A shabby man from Paddington, St Marylebone or Battersea might pass muster as one of the respectable poor. But the same man coming from Bethnal Green, Shadwell or Wapping was an "East Ender"; the box of . . . bug powder must be reached for, and the spoons locked up.'[50]

It was said that even some who lived close to the East End could not locate it on a map; it began to seem as foreign to respectable London as the souks of Baghdad – dangerous and lawless but somehow thrilling, especially from a distance. 'I have seen the Polynesian savage in his primitive condition,' wrote T. H. Huxley, 'before the missionary got at him. With all his savaging he was not half so savage, so unclean, as the tenant of a tenement in an East London slum.'[51] (Annie Besant would later point out that the 'savage' probably had standards of living actually superior to those of an East End pauper.[52])

Polite society had an insatiable appetite for sensational reports from this mysterious land, but it preferred them first filtered through the middle-class consciousness of the intrepid journalist, social reformer or missionary who was essentially 'one of them'. What remained was cleansed of the worst of the dirt and grit of reality for popular consumption, and there was no shortage of accounts to satisfy the demand.

It was partly an accident of geography which had led to this part of the city being metaphorically cast adrift from the rest. Surrounded by water on three sides,[53] it was an obvious location for the docks which were first established in the eighteenth century. Routes designed to connect them directly to the City of London, like the Commercial Road, followed, and so began the radical reshaping of the East End.

Construction of the ultimately unprofitable St Katherine's Dock alone displaced 11,300 people, and destroyed ancient buildings. In 1840 the London and Blackwell Railway built train lines through Poplar and Stepney with a spur line to Bow: the building of four miles of track meant the demolition of almost 3,000 existing homes.[54]

Industrial change brought social change in its wake. New factories were first established around the Isle of Dogs, and new industries forced some of the old into decline. The second wave of industrial expansion in the 1860s and 1870s, and the development of steam trains, lead to an exodus of more affluent workers away from increasingly grimy and soot-encrusted East London, out into the newly flourishing suburbs. The railways also made the area accessible to outsiders searching for accommodation and work; it became a centre of immigration and also, with the collapse of traditional industries like shipbuilding and silk-weaving and the concomitant unemployment, casual and sweated labour.

The gentry's exodus from the East End left behind was described by the writer John Henry Mackay as 'a hell of poverty. Like an enormous, black, motionless kraken, the poverty of London lies there in lurking silence and encircles with its mighty tentacles the life and wealth of the city and of the West End.'[55] The East End proper consisted of mazes or narrow streets and alleyways often ending in the so-called rookeries, described by reformer Rev Samuel Barnett, a founder of Toynbee Hall: '. . . rabbit warrens, mainly topsy-turvy one-storeyed, leprous, grey bricked hovels . . .'[56]

The middle and upper classes were unable to ignore the plight of the East End's 'outcasts' for long. Insanitary living conditions led to repeated outbreaks of cholera – 10,000 people died in one epidemic in 1866 alone[57] – and became a national scandal.

Charles Dickens was among the voices warning the middle classes that 'unless they set themselves in earnest to . . . amend the dwellings of the poor, they are guilty of wholesale murder'.[58] Middle- and upper-class consciences were temporarily stirred at such times, and funds flooded into charities for the poor and destitute. However, seventeen years later the *Pall Mall Gazette*'s publication of Andrew Mearns' *The Bitter Cry of Outcast London*, with its devastating reports of conditions in the East End, still shocked: 'South Kensington awakened to the fact that there were some two or three million people in the brick and mortar wilderness beyond the Bank of England, many of them in woeful distress.'[59] Mearns revealed lives of unimaginable horror:

> Every room in these rotten and reeking tenements houses a family, often two. In [one] room a missionary found a man ill with small-pox, his wife just recovering from her eighth confinement, and the children running about half naked and covered with dirt. Here are seven people living in one underground kitchen and a little dead child lying in the same room. Elsewhere is a poor widow, her three children, and a child who had been dead thirteen days . . .[60]

In 1884 the *Pall Mall Gazette* warned that the extreme poverty in London's East

End was 'a great danger to the Commonwealth'.[61] For various reasons, not least the fear of violent social unrest, the condition of the urban working classes became a matter of national concern. It became 'quite the proper thing to do to go down East',[62] and charitable missions and settlements were established.

So the middle and upper classes began to return to the quarter they had abandoned, but now in the persons of philanthropic volunteers and officers of the state. From the 1860s the voluntary visiting and inspection of the homes of the poor became a popular middle-class activity, particularly among women, paving the way for what has been called 'the invasion of the working-class family'.[63] Volunteers included 'superfluous' single women revolting against their supposed redundancy, who 'made middle-class homes for themselves in the slums and happily set about to untangle the lives of overworked mothers, teenage girls, and children'.[64] (Annie Besant herself returned to the East End to work among the people, after her marriage ended in acrimonious separation.)

How different from the home life of the respectable woman (to say nothing of her dear Queen) was that of the East End factory girl, many commentators seemed to feel: the bulk of the historical material available on their lives is often redolent of the class and gender judgements of 'respectable' society, and there is a paucity of objective biographical accounts. Because of the strength of the very ideologies which will be discussed here and the way in which they affected notions of class and gender, the individual lives of women like the matchmakers were not regarded as of great interest beyond the contribution of general information for social investigation literature. Some use of prescriptive literature and material by middle-class commentators is unavoidable in writing about working-class women such as the matchworkers.[65]

THE FACTORY GIRL AND HER CRITICS: PERCEPTIONS OF WORKING-CLASS WOMEN

If, as has been said, the Victorians had three female archetypes, the 'symbolic triad' of 'ideal mother/wife . . . celibate spinster or . . . promiscuous prostitute',[66] it is significant that there was no place for the working woman even in their stereotypes; though in practice, working-class women working outside the home, particularly alongside men, risked classification as prostitutes.[67] Patricia Johnson, after studying representations of working women in Victorian 'social problem' fiction, concluded that authors and readers actually found it more acceptable for characters to be prostitutes than factory hands.[68]

Women industrial workers were in fact nothing new: cotton mills had been the first to draw upon the labour of very young women and children, more than half of whom were under 14, as a source of cheap labour early in Britain's industrial 'revolution'.[69] By 1838 only an estimated 23 per cent of workers in textile factories were male,[70] though women earned around half of the male wage even in trades like this which they dominated. Such areas of production, closely allied to domestic life, had long been accepted as 'female', and continued to be so: as the French aphorism expressed it, 'Wood and metal are man's work, family and fabric are woman's.'[71] Pinchbeck quotes the medieval belief that 'the virtuous woman ... seeketh wool, and flax, and worketh willingly with her hands ... maketh fine linen and selleth it'.[72] Even after industrialization women remained highly concentrated in areas such as textiles, clothing and food manufacture.[73] The first president of the Society of the Employment of Women (the both aristocratic and male Earl of Shaftesbury) summarized views on 'suitable' female work in 1859: 'The instant that the work becomes minute, individual and personal; the instant that it leaves the open field and touches the home; the instant that it requires tact, sentiment and delicacy; from that instant it passes into the hands of women.'[74] Shaftesbury's words express the Victorian *desire* that women's work should be 'feminine', rather than the reality: the work of scythe-wielding agricultural women workers, or those who laboured in mines and heavy industry, was hardly 'delicate'.

Labour reports began to expose the reality, and to fuel moral panic. The new factories were portrayed as dens of vice, and female workers as sexually promiscuous. The mixed-gender nature of many workplaces, and the fact that women engaged in hot or dirty work were inevitably not formally, or even fully, dressed was emphasized, with illustrations calculated to shock – or to titillate – polite society. Some reports demonstrated what appears to be an almost obsessive curiosity towards the sexuality, real or imagined, of the working-class woman.[75] A mining commissioner in 1842 employed surprisingly overwrought language in what was after all an official report: '[A]ny sight more disgustingly indecent or revolting can scarcely be imagined than these girls at work. No brothel can beat it.'[76] (What research he had carried out in order to draw this comparison he does not share with us.)

The process of industrialization had been generally disruptive to female labour, displacing women workers and dislodging them from their traditional crafts and industries. This was true for male workers too, but whatever status women workers had managed to attain in an always unequal labour market, was frequently lost as men began to encroach upon their territories, driving them into increasingly segregated and poorly paid employment.

Some commentators have argued that working-class women gained financial and practical independence from employment in the new factories and mills; others, like Ivy Pinchbeck, acknowledge the grimness of initial conditions while still seeing it as a first step to greater leisure and freedoms.[77] Marx felt that large-scale industry might 'create a new economic foundation for a higher form of the family and relations between the sexes'.[78]

However, most of the evidence available seems to suggest that poor working-class women gained little from the transition, at least initially, but the 'freedom' to enjoy low wages and miserable living and working conditions. The segregation of female labour increased as public concern over women's employment grew. As industrialization gathered pace, women's opportunities in the labour market contracted, particularly if they were married or older. Women were seeking work in increasing numbers but often encountered bitter hostility from male workers and the organized guilds and unions. Pre-existing gender divisions of labour were also perpetuated by capitalist employers, who simply incorporated them into new systems of production. As Johnson points out, the often-used designation 'working men' denied the true make-up of the factory workforce and left women 'disembodied sources of cheap labour'.[79] Casual workers like the matchwomen had little hope of ever achieving financial and social advancement, or even security, through work. Though not all workers categorized as 'unskilled' and 'casual' were women, very few women workers did not fall into these categories: their horizons were therefore limited from the start. Regardless of the level of experience and skill attained by a Bryant and May matchmaker, she would still be regarded as the 'lowest strata of society'.[80] Many men endured appalling working conditions too, but at least had more opportunity to join a union to fight against them. Large-scale attempts to organize women workers, on the other hand, usually came from outside the labour movement, from organizations like the Women's Political and Provident League – at least before the 1880s.[81]

Industrialization by no means spelled the end of homework – hand-finishing of factory-produced goods was often done in the home, as were other ancillary tasks like matchbox-making. However, this was far from a cosy domestic alternative to the factory: Bryant and May used the sweated labour of married women and young children for matchbox production in particular, and their dreadful conditions were exposed in *The Bitter Cry of Outcast London*:

> We go in at a doorway . . . and find a little girl twelve years old. 'Where is your mother?' 'In the madhouse.' 'How long has she been there?' 'Fifteen months.' 'Who looks after you?' The child, who is sitting at a table making matchboxes, replies, 'I look after my little brothers and sisters as well as I can.'[82]

Homework was 'the No Man's Land of the industrial world. Here treads not the foot of the labour agitator, for the home-workers are composed largely of "casuals" . . . no organising secretary of any trade union, however enterprising, would waste time or effort in inducing them to join its ranks'.[83]

However, the factory became the primary place of employment for many women, and criticisms of women who persisted in working began in earnest: the stark choices they faced often conveniently ignored. Women like the matchworkers may have loathed their jobs, and preferred not to work at all; they may have been glad to contribute to the family purse in any way they could; they may have enjoyed the workplace camaraderie and independence from their family. For many, however, the struggle for bare survival was so intense it must have precluded the luxury of thinking about work as anything other than a necessity, and the interviews conducted for this study suggest that this was the view of at least some of the matchwomen, whose employment options were limited and generally unappealing. As the radical writer George Sims noted of women engaging in dangerous work at minimal wages: 'Why do [they] not refuse? Because they would be discharged. There are always hundreds ready to take their place. The struggle for bread is too fierce for the fighters to shrink from any torture in its attainment.'[84] The shadow of the workhouse also loomed large after the introduction of the New Poor Law in 1834.

Choices were therefore few, and perhaps fewer still for the women of the East End: though domestic service was a major employer of women nationally, evidence suggests that 'East End' women, especially those of Irish origin, were thought too 'rough' by many employers – they evidently returned the compliment by disliking the constraints and limitations of 'service'.[85] There were then a variety of casual and 'sweated' jobs, performed either in factories or at home, or sometimes a combination of the two.

Violence among such women was another of the shocking aspects of their behaviour to 'respectable' Victorians, if not, perhaps, just a little titillating too: it was a favourite topic of social investigators. A drawing in the *Illustrated Police News* from just after the matchwomen's strike showed a group of factory girls, dressed to at least the nines in elaborate hats and curls, attacking a hapless policeman.

The illustrator could have had the Bryant and May women in mind: but not just because they were prepared to come to blows if the occasion demanded. Frances Hicks noted that 'factory girls always have girl-mates', and that they were ready to look out for one another in times of trouble.[86] The matchwomen too were known for existing in relative harmony, enjoying each other's company both in and out of work, and, like the women in the illustration, travelling in lively gangs, with their own particular sense of style: 'Dress is a very important consideration with these young women. They have fashions of their own; they delight in a quantity of colour; and they can no more live without their large hats and huge feathers than 'Arry can live without his bell-bottom trousers. They all sport high-heeled boots, and consider a fringe an absolute essential.'[87] However, when disagreements did arise between the women, the local police had evidently learned not to get involved: '[The matchwomen] fight with their fists to settle their differences, not in the factory for that is forbidden, but in the streets when they leave work in the evening. A ring is formed, they fight like men and are not interfered with by the police.'[88]

One Poplar resident remembered the matchwomen's toughness, but also that it was usually employed in self-defence: 'These matchgirls . . . all wore long hatpins, and if anyone interfered with them they did not hesitate to retaliate with these horrible long hatpins.'[89] Two of the matchwomen's grandchildren, interviewed later in the book, remembered the importance in their grandmothers' worlds of being able physically to protect themselves and their daughters from assault: to be able to 'chase men away from the family women'.[90] Another East Ender confirmed:

> Many of the women could fight like men, yet unlike men. Not for them the leading with the left and crossing with the right. For them it was grabbing the hair and tearing the blouse. Many a time I saw women still fighting with their blouses hanging in ribbons round their waists, and great chunks of hair in their hands.[91]

However, it suited the Victorian mood to see such unfeminine behaviour as resulting from the corrupt influence of factory work, rather than the harsh realities of poor women's lives.

MOTHERHOOD

Harsh they unquestionably were: premature death from the direct or indirect results of poverty was a distinct possibility. Newspaper reports show that even women in regular work died of starvation, and there is much primary evidence that women deprived themselves in times of crisis so that their husbands and children could eat.[92] Death during, or from the complications of, childbirth was also particularly common for the poor: the physical stresses of the average of ten live births which British women experienced at this time, combined with poor nutrition and living conditions, took an inevitable toll.

Should they and their children survive, the separation of work and home life and the long shifts of industrialized work made the care of infants extremely difficult for working mothers. As a contemporary observer noted: 'a married woman with a small child, a single mother, or a sibling with child-care responsibilities could not leave the factory to supervise the child. Once the factory gates closed, she remained locked inside until the evening bell.'[93]

A small number of day nurseries were established in factory districts, but they were too few and, for many working mothers, too expensive to address the problem. Mothers often had to stop breastfeeding almost immediately, and feed their babies instead on 'pap', a mixture of bread, water and sugar, or diluted cows' milk which, without proper pasteurization, might contain harmful bacteria.[94] Otherwise, only working mothers allowed out for a lunch break could continue to nurse, as Engels noted: 'Women often return to the mill three or four days after confinement, leaving the baby . . . in the dinner hour they must hurry home to feed the child . . . and what sort of suckling that can be is also evident.'[95]

Marx's view was that 'modern industry, in overturning the economical foundation on which was based the traditional family, and the family labour correspondingly to it . . . had also unloosened all traditional family ties.'[96] Engels, however, seemed to suggest that working women were in themselves the problem:

> The employment of women at once breaks up the family; for when the wife spends twelve or thirteen hours every day in the mill, and the husband works the same length of time there or elsewhere, what becomes of the children? They grow up like wild weeds; they are put out to nurse for a shilling . . . a week, and how they are treated may be imagined . . . That the general mortality among young children must be increased by the employment of the mother is self-evident, and is placed beyond all doubt by notorious facts.[97]

Such infant mortality rates among the working poor increased the barrage of criticism of working mothers. It was estimated that in 1899, the most impoverished areas of Liverpool had an average of 509 infant deaths per 1,000 and that, taking the nation as a whole, **one half** of all children of farmers, labourers, domestic servants and artisans would die before their fifth birthday. This compared to one in eleven children of the landed gentry.[98] Before the advent of vaccinations, children of all classes were at risk from diseases like diphtheria, scarlet fever and polio, but those born into crowded and insanitary conditions were most vulnerable. Scandals over infant mortality rates only increased the barrage of criticism directed at working women.

'FALLEN' WOMEN AND DEGENERATION

As we have seen, 'factory girls' were frequently accused of unfeminine, immoral or even amoral behaviour; and these ideas arose not just from their class and upbringings, but also specifically from their employment.

The criticisms levelled at them by their social 'betters' were often as contradictory and illogical as the domestic ideology from which they sprang. Women workers were seen as a threat to social order because they failed both to be controlled, and to control: as daughters they were too independent of parental (particularly paternal) authority; and as mothers and wives, they neglected their proper role as the moral centre of the home, keeping children and husbands both literally and metaphorically clean and healthy, and away from temptation.

Both the fact that they earned money, and that they earned so little, were Fretted over by commentators. Some were convinced that the 'factory girl's' wages were a dangerous currency, which would drive factory women to the 'paths of vice which we have it on the highest authority are always the most easy of access'. Women with the resources to be free of male constraint might reject the domestic sphere altogether for the venal pleasures of city pubs and music halls. Others were concerned about their lack of money – not necessarily because of the injustice and exploitation involved, but because this might lead them into moral danger, and specifically the great Victorian 'social evil' of prostitution, so frequently condemned from the pulpits: the 'ghastliest curse which haunts society, which is steadily sapping the very foundations of our morality . . .'.[99]

Annie Besant herself, in her famous exposé of conditions inside the Bryant and May factory, 'White slavery in London', evoked the double-edged Victorian fear of both the sexuality and the sexual vulnerability of the factory girl, arguing that the matchwomen's poverty wages could drive them 'on the streets': three euphemistic words which were universally understood. What social campaigner Josephine Butler condemned as the 'double standard of morality' that existed in Victorian society was a significant factor in the criticisms of working-class women:

> Worldly and impure men . . . think . . . they can separate women into two classes – the protected and refined ladies . . . and those poor outcast daughters of the people whom they purchase with money before returning to their separate and protected homes.[100]

There is an implicit understanding of the interplay between class and gender in Butler's words. The users of prostitutes described are clearly middle and upper class, and are making cynical use of the doctrine of 'separate spheres' to sexually exploit working-class women while still retaining a 'good' woman to return to. The separation of their wives' lives from their own allowed such men a good deal of licence with little risk of disgrace. However, Butler also reinforces some of the tenets of domestic ideology in asserting the superior goodness of women, and their moral duty to men:

> Men are driven away at an early age from the society of women … and thus they have concocted…a wholly different standard of moral purity from that generally existing among women … Women are guilty also in this matter, for they unfortunately have imitated the tone and sentiments of men, instead of chastening and condemning them; and have shown, too often, very little indeed of the horror which they profess to feel for sins of impurity.[101]

Samuel Heming's section on prostitution in Mayhew's *London Labour and the London Poor* portrays prostituted women as more sinning then sinned against, so corrupted by their experiences that they have 'become brutal'.[102] Little allowance is made for the brutality, sexual and otherwise, frequently experienced by working-class women, on the factory floor and the street: Annie Besant found that match factory foremen sometimes beat the workers, and primary evidence also suggests that sexual assault was not uncommon.

Heming, however, sees his 'fallen' women as at fault even while admitting the abuse they suffered. He offers one young woman's story as a 'condensation of the philosophy of sinning' rather than the tragic tale of a victim.[103] She sought to explain herself to Heming: 'You folks as has honour and character, and feelings, and such can't understand how all that's been beaten out of people like me, I don't feel it …' In this woman's mind virtue was clearly associated with class, but in the sense of nurture rather than nature: finer feelings were a luxury which secluded gentility could preserve, lost by too much exposure to harsh reality – they were, in other words, a false construct. As in Butler's work, most of the literature on prostitution at this time assumes that all prostitutes were working class, plying their trade in darkened slum streets away from 'respectable' homes. Little acknowledgement is made of either 'high-class' prostitution, or the parallels between this and the purely financial marriages which societal pressures led some 'respectable' women to contract.

Indeed, notions of the eminent corruptibility of the working-class woman strongly contradict Victorian concepts of the purity of the 'angel in the house'. If poverty can so easily bring a woman to what was then considered sin, what price the universal woman's 'naturally' moral nature? If virtue was to be understood as an innate female quality, then this must apply to all women equally. If it only applied to those virtually confined between four walls, this implies either that experience of the 'real' world could corrupt them, or that they must be segregated to prevent them from seeking out sinful pleasures. In either case, the assumption is deeply contradictory.

Theories of 'urban degeneration', popular in the latter part of the nineteenth century, seemed to confirm the worst fears of those opposed to working women. The effect of life in city slums, it was believed, was weakening the race. As Alfred Marshall wrote, the 'London Poor ... will tend to drink for excitement; they will go on deteriorating; and as to their children, the more of them grow up to manhood, the lower will be the average morality of the coming generation.'[104] These ideas gained widespread support and credibility through the 1880s and 1890s, with the support of eminent figures like Charles Booth. At a time when the pseudo science of eugenics was gaining popularity, not just among the political right but among socialists like Shaw and, later, H. G. Wells, it was feared that nothing short of degeneration of the race might result from living in city slums. In 1885, former surgeon Sir James Cantlie delivered a lecture entitled 'Degeneration amongst Londoners' in the capital. He described two 'specimens': a 19-year-old man, small in stature, 'whose grandmother was Irish' and whose face was 'mottled, pale and pimpled. He squints rather badly. His jaws are misshapen ... Solemnity great.'[105] A young woman 'of similar pedigree' was described as having 'a red scrofulous aspect. Solemnity marked.'

The aristocracy, on the other hand, were the epitome of *mens sana in corpore sano*: '... those whom luxury had upset have died out, and we are blessed ... with a race of men and women capable of resisting ... effeminacy and sloth'. While conceding that lifestyle might play a part in the disparity, and that mechanized work was particularly unnatural for the human frame, the speaker concluded that the difference in health between the two groups largely resulted, not from good food and accommodation which one enjoyed and the other markedly did not, but from fresh air and healthful exercise exemplified by 'shooting, riding ... yachting and such like'. He accordingly proposed a programme of cycling and lawn tennis for working-class Londoners.

'A ROUGH SET OF GIRLS': PERCEPTIONS OF THE MATCHWOMEN

The matchwomen did not escape the opprobrium heaped on working-class women in general. In his influential poverty surveys of London, Charles Booth judged the match-women, in a phrase redolent of lofty respectability, to be 'a rough set of girls'.[106] Booth judged them 'rough' not just in their class, but in behaviour too: in keeping with the factory girl stereotype they could be 'scandalously undecorous'. Certainly the matchworkers were a boisterous and unmistakable presence on the streets of East London,[107] where they caused some alarm: one observer noted that 'decent folk' did not care to be out of doors when the matchwomen came off shift.[108]

There is a sense that their refusal to 'know their place' was a factor in the irritation they caused: their subordinate position in the labour and gender hierarchies should have led them to be humble and meek, not to hold their heads up and look their betters in the eye: who did they think they were? One observer noted the matchwoman's 'insolent confidence': '. . . she cheeks her employer and laughs at passers by . . .'.[109]

The women's supposed collective morality was also weighed in the balance. Despite the affront they sometimes caused to the middle classes, they escaped the most serious condemnation that could be made of a Victorian woman: Booth judged them 'not bad morally', and QC and magistrate Montagu Williams also noted that 'there is not nearly the amount of immorality among them that one would imagine'.[110] However, despite that very faint praise, Williams had some complaints:

> With regard to the match girls who, to use a vulgar expression, are on their own hook – that is to say, who have detached themselves from their families, if they have any – I am bound to confess they are not the very best of girls. But what can be expected, seeing the way in which they are compelled to live? I am sorry to say that there is a considerable amount of drunkenness among them, though they are not often brought up on that charge before the magistrates presiding at the East End Courts. On looking over the statistics of my cases at Worship Street, I find that there were only about half-a-dozen charges of the kind over a period of several months.[111]

Williams found their language shocking, but didn't hold them entirely responsible for it: 'It is scarcely surprising that they should repeat the oaths and vile language they hear almost every day of their lives in public-houses, music halls, and dancing rooms, not to mention the so-called East End "clubs" . . .'[112] Their sociability seems to have been a problem: the matchwomen simply enjoyed themselves too much, and in all of the wrong ways, for middle-class tastes. Montagu Williams again:

> Match girls come out very strong on a Saturday night, when any number of them may be found at the Paragon Music Hall, in the Mile End Road; the Foresters' Music Hall, in Cambridge Road; and the Sebright, at Hackney; The Eagle, in the City Road, used to be a favourite resort of these girls, and in bygone summers dancing on the crystal platform was their nightly amusement. They continue to be very fond of dancing, but they are even more attached to singing. They seem to know by heart the words of all the popular music hall songs of the day, and their homeward journey on Bank holidays from Hampstead Heath and Chingford, though musical, is decidedly noisy.[113]

It is hard to imagine Mrs Coventry Patmore and her friends after a night out 'irritating . . . quiet-loving citizens' by 'singing at the top of their voices the chorus of "Ta-ra-ra Boom-de-ay", or "Knocked 'em in the Old Kent Road"'[114] in the fashion of the matchwomen: the latter's behaviour, in short, bore remarkably little resemblance to the quiet dignity expected from the 'angel of the house'. Williams felt their lack of domesticity was a far-reaching problem: 'Their home life is not so bright, and the cause for this is not far to seek. They can sing a good song, or dance a break-down with any one; but can they wash clothes, or cook a dinner? Alas! neither the one nor the other.'[115] (Exactly what a 'break-down' was I have yet to discover, but I'm sure it was worth seeing.)

Despite their apparent lack of marriageable qualities, Williams noted that the women were 'eager to marry, and did so very young'. Once again the choice of their preferred husbands is telling: 'Many a match girl of sixteen marries a dock labourer or factory hand no older.' The result of these marriages was not always happy: 'Very often one of these poor creatures, a month or two after marriage, has applied to me for protection against her husband.' However, Williams' sympathy lay with the men who had, presumably, threatened or beaten their wives: '[The husband] has very likely worked hard, and never failed to take his earnings home to his "missis", as he calls her; and yet, night after night, he has returned to a dirty and neglected fireside, and found no dinner and no wife awaiting him.'

However, Williams also admitted that not all matchwomen's marriages were as unhappy as domestic ideology dictated they should be:

> ... the marriages of the match girls do sometimes turn out well, and I think that such a result is somewhat surprising. With so many temptations around them, with so much vice in their midst, and with so many troubles in their lives, it is really astonishing to see the great affection these young people entertain towards one another.[116]

It's noticeable that even once married the matchworkers are still 'girls'. It was, as Lewis writes, always the fate of the factory 'girl', to be presented as perpetually immature, just as middle-class 'spinsters' of the period were 'old maids' regardless of age.[117]

In most accounts the matchwomen are portrayed as both literal and metaphorical children, with accordingly marginal involvement in their own dispute. No consideration has been given to readily available evidence that they included older women among their number, as indeed the factory and education acts stipulated that they should, and that some were married. This is not a problem from which male groups of workers tend to suffer: many of the dock labourers who began the celebrated 1889 strike would have been young too, but are not referred to as 'dock boys'.

Though many matchworkers were of course young, maturity is a relative and complex concept, and was viewed differently in the matchwomen's time and place. The oral evidence gathered by historians like Anna Davin and Jane Lewis, as well as from my own interviewees, shows that 'children' were often proud to be considered old enough to go out to work in their early teens or before, both because they wanted to contribute to the family purse and because of the adult status which this conferred.

That the women are always 'matchgirls' in contemporary accounts is not unexpected; that it is still the most common epithet used by today's historians, after all the works that have been written on the politics of linguistics, is perhaps more telling.

I have decided to generally refer to the workers as 'matchwomen', for all of the reasons stated, and in an attempt to free them from their usual image, which is too easily confused with that of Hans Christian Andersen's helpless 'Little

Match Girl'. They were working women, and the implications of immaturity and helplessness – traits with which both primary and secondary accounts have been all too ready to associate them – have, as we shall see, little to do with the reality of their lives.

I was interested to find myself being taken firmly to task for this decision, however, when speaking to a group of largely male socialist historians about the women in 2004. My questioner thought I had called them 'women' through ignorance of their youth, and had apparently not considered the linguistic aspect.

In the course of this book we will uncover the real lives of the women who struck against the powerful and well-connected gentlemen in charge of Bryant and May; and seriously consider, for the first time, how they saw themselves.

Most of the accounts we have of them concerns only what others thought of them, and it is this which has so distorted the historical record, concealing the obvious truth of what happened on the streets of the East End in the summer of 1888.

We have seen that as factory girls the matchwomen were judged 'rough and rowdy', but that their judges were middle- and upper-class observers espousing, whether consciously or unconsciously, all the class and gender preconceptions of polite Victorian society. Not only were they the wrong sort of women from what was, to middle-class commentators, the wrong area, but they also had the wrong heritage, being largely of Irish descent: although Victorian art would come to celebrate a romantic image of Irishness, what Booth called the 'Irish cockney' remained a figure of disdain.[119] This all amounted to a disreputable 'roughness', and must have presented something of an image problem for those, like Besant, who would seek to elicit publicity and sympathy for the women's cause. Besant wanted to enlist support from those who had the power to sway Bryant and May: their middle- and upper-class shareholders, the press and the government. This was not going to be achieved by showing the strikers as a 'rough set of girls': but it transpired that the problem presented by the first two words had its solution in the last one.

It was in the interests of both the political right and left that the matchwomen be associated with childlike 'good' working women; more 'little matchgirls' than 'factory girls'. Besant and the Fabians could gain greater public sympathy for waif-like victims who had been mistreated by an exploitative employer and needed to be 'rescued' by the actions of the middle classes (both middle-class socialists, and Bryant and May's shareholders and customers). In 'White slavery in London' Besant therefore presents certain aspects of the women's characters and not others, deliberately or subconsciously slanting her report to make them more appealing – which meant more passive and more victim-like.

Meanwhile, it also suited Bryant and May and the political right to portray them as the innocent dupes of the socialists. Any implication that these might be tough young 'factory girls' who had no qualms about fighting for what they thought was right was disadvantageous to both sides, who squabbled over the rights and wrongs of the strike quite above the heads of the matchwomen themselves.

The continuing willingness to identify the Bryant and May women with the 'little matchgirl' stereotype has ensured their continuing celebrity. However, I believe that it has equally ensured that the strike continues to be seen by many as an interesting and colourful 'aside' to British labour history at best, rather than a seminal event. How could such innocents have struck, on their own initiative, a blow against a hugely successful cartel, as well as against the class and gender norms of their time?

Despite the lack of straightforward autobiographical accounts, there are sources which can be of value in trying to determine what working-class women themselves thought of the boundaries of feminine 'respectability'. Jane Lewis has employed the so-called 'maternity letters' of the Women's Guild to great effect, and historians like Anna Davin, Raphael Samuels and David Vincent have worked to fill the gap with some invaluable oral history collections. While there is not yet a sufficient body of primary material for a conclusive analysis of the extent to which working-class women accepted domestic ideology as valid, these are sources which grant us some valuable insight. They show that notions of 'respectability', expressing aspirations and concerns about individual standing within the community, were prevalent among poor London women in the late 1800s.[120] 'Everyone', said one, 'knew the boundaries between rough and respectable', and this included the matchwoman Mary Driscoll, according to her granddaughter: 'A couple of doors down from us were the Pitaways, who to my Nan's mind were not really respectable – although, of course, *we* were!'[121]

Factory working women like the matchmakers, though looked down upon by others, could still be respectable within their own lights and those of their immediate community. The grandchildren of three of the strikers I have interviewed for this book confirm their grandmothers' lack of shame at their lowly status, but also their awareness of it. Their deliberately upright bearing, and their belief that they were the equals of anyone, may have been partly a deliberately defiant reaction to this, or equally a sign of their genuine pride in themselves and their matriarchal status – and the respect they received from their neighbours and families.[122]

There were a multiplicity of subjective definitions of respectability, adapted to reflect working-class life; for example, money was not necessarily an indicator of respectable status, though clothes and furnishings had to be as 'good', or at least clean, as possible. Because working-class women usually had to work, this was obviously not used as an automatic disqualifier from respectability among the working classes. However, some forms of work were more respectable than others. Matchbox-making, for example, was considered 'not respectable' by some working-class women, perhaps reflecting the low hierarchical position of Bryant and May's factory workers, but not by those who did it. Women in domestic service apparently looked down upon match factory workers as well as matchbox-makers; but the reverse was also true, as many East End factory workers disliked the loss of independence which being 'in service' entailed.[123] Homework like matchbox-making was usually regarded as lower in status as well as pay even than match factory work, but one matchbox-maker interviewed in Bow proudly declared that she preferred her lot: 'She is an independent girl, who is not inclined, as she says, "to work under anybody".'[124]

In the matchwomen's East End, the esteem in which a woman held herself was a further important factor in the ever-shifting sands of attributed respectability: the reputations of the more self-assured could survive occasional, or even frequent, forays into non-respectable behaviour if they successfully 'fronted it out'.[125] As will be shown in later pages, for matchwomen Mary Driscoll, Martha Robertson and Eliza Martin (later Best), hard drinking and occasional physical fights were part of life. There were suggestions that two of them may have had lovers after marriage; but although the realities of their lives were far from the original template of the 'angel in the house', this did not affect their absolute authority as heads of the family, or within their communities, where both Best and Robertson were the women to whom neighbours would turn in crises, to bring babies into the world as well as to lay out the dead. Driscoll went on to be a shopkeeper, a position of some status in itself in working-class neighbourhoods, as it carried the ability to give or refuse 'tick' (credit), so vital to the lives of the poor. Their grandchildren could not remember, nor imagine, anyone ever challenging the respectability of these three great East End matriarchs.

Research has shown that working-class women like these were, however, strongly affected by the 'rough–respectable' dichotomy, and quickly learned the appropriate categorizations.[126] They quickly learned that as adult women they would be expected to embody the respectability of their family. It has been suggested that a working-class woman's domestic skills and pride in her home mirrored male artisans' pride in their skilled status, and certainly it was equally vital to the survival of the family. The burden of cooking and general domestic duties generally fell heaviest upon the women of the family, regardless of whether or not they worked, although there are plenty of accounts of men who cheerfully rolled up their sleeves and cooked and cleaned too. A woman's ability to balance the family's budget, keep in with shopkeepers to get credit, and produce nutritious meals out of more or less nothing, could literally mean the difference between life and death for her children.

Some girls chafed against the demands and limitations which respectability placed on their childhoods, noting that the 'rough' children with whom they were not supposed to mix seemed to have a lot more fun and freedom.[127]

There may have been direct links to domestic ideology in the designating of children as 'rough' or 'respectable': a mother working long hours outside the home would obviously find it harder to closely monitor her children's behaviour. Girls seem to have been especially likely to reject the restrictions of femininity if not constantly checked: many recalled their hatred of being trussed up in girls' clothes and shoes, when trousers and boots allowed so much more freedom. Some longed to play outside with local boys, but by the late 1800s and early 1900s the demands that girls be clean, tidy and decorous often ruled this out.

Davin notes that 'the zest with which octogenarian ex-tomboys recall those years is striking. "Oh, I was a terrible tomboy I'm afraid!" is always said in a celebratory tone, not an apologetic one . . . a contradiction which suggests the transition to conformity may have been reluctant.'[128] However, the very use of the word 'tomboy' does, of course, suggest an acceptance that they were transgressing conventional notions of correct gender behaviour.

We cannot know for certain where the working-class conceptions of respectability came from, and to what extent they were internal rather than influenced by middle-class ideology transmitted by the 'invaders' of middle-class homes. There are some examples of working-class women refusing to give up their notions of respectability despite middle-class urgings. Working-class London mothers were criticized for their insistence on spending time cleaning, and especially in whitewashing their doorsteps, to them an important yardstick of respectability which the middle-class observers saw as a pointless consumer of time – which would be better spent caring for children.[129]

More research is needed in this area and it must be considered that, as Gray concludes, working-class respectability 'is not just a passive reception of middle-class indoctrination', but something altogether more complex.[130]

One of the matchwomen's grandsons grew up around the Bryant and May women, who were his grandmother's friends to the end of her life, and frequent companions on what they called their 'beanos' (day trips, often to the seaside and usually involving a fair amount of drinking). He summed up the thorny issue of gender and class stereotyping succinctly:

> The matchwomen were very strong characters, all of them that I knew, very efficient and strong. They stuck together like a big family, and kept their own families going in hard times with their strength of character. They were great ladies – I know people from the outside might have laughed at that because they weren't what they would have called 'ladies', but to us they were. They were East End ladies.[131]

CONCLUSIONS

In the matchwomen's story issues of class cannot be separated from those of gender. Their strike took place against the background of extreme gender conflict in the workplace, and it has been argued that the effects of this conflict both contributed to the strikers' exploitation and motivation, and coloured contemporary and historical accounts of their actions.

The 'return' of women to the domestic sphere, whether or not they had ever exclusively inhabited it in the first place in reality, was being offered as a palliative for all manner of nineteenth-century ills often laid at the door of the working poor, from the lack of 'social purity' to insobriety, neglect of children, and the overall degeneration of the race. A powerful consensus had united behind the banner of 'domestic ideology', uniting disparate groups whose concern with the conduct of these women's lives arose from vastly different motives.

Such ideology was at least as responsible as the matchwomen's class for the dire working conditions which caused the strike, and for the ongoing refusal of history to accept that they really did strike autonomously, and from genuine grievance. Few at the time believed – or wanted to believe – the working classes capable of helping themselves. Even Engels thought that 'nowhere else in the civilised world are the people less actively resistant, more passively submitting to fate . . . than in the East End of London'.[132]

Working-class women were supposed to be doubly kept 'in their place' by their dependant gender role as well as their social position – any sign that they could overcome both restraints would have posed a serious threat to the established order. To the public and the media, the fact that the matchworkers were young women who both worked and went on strike in contradiction to dominant ideas about women's roles and nature, added to the 'novelty' and picturesque nature of the strike, and so to the high level of publicity, which in turn aided the women's victory and renown.

Because the matchwomen fell short of the Victorian domestic ideal of woman-hood, those seeking public sympathy for the women's cause may have chosen, as a tactical move, to portray them as helpless waifs rather than militant workers, thus avoiding the negative connotations of the 'factory girl' stereotype; equally, the effects of the dominant class and gender ideologies of the day may have affected the way in which even sympathetic outsiders saw them. The mythical 'matchgirl' image, though a colourful one which has held public interest, has also distracted us from the reality of their strike. If fame were the only measure of historical importance, therefore, their gender could be said to have worked in their favour: their name arguably resonates more today with the average non-historian than those of the gas workers or even the dock strikers.

However, it is the contention of this study that gender has been a hindrance to serious analysis of the strike, and directly contributed to misconceptions about it which have led some to conclude that the matchwomen's reputation is, as Paul Thompson writes, 'exaggerated', and their continuing acclaim largely undeserved.[133]

It is problematic for students of the strike that the many and various accounts of events from the media and other commentators do not come from the matchwomen themselves nor, usually, from people of similar backgrounds. We must be aware that prevailing domestic ideology affected disparate groups at the time, from the journalists who covered the strike to the male leaders of the established labour movement, and also affected the way in which the strike and its main actors were viewed, as we struggle to catch glimpses of the real women through their accounts.

Despite the lack of autobiographical material from the matchworkers them-selves or women like them, by exhaustive use of the full range of contemporary sources as well as through the recollections of those who knew the women, we are able to get closer than ever before to the real matchwomen and their lives. The picture we then see is so different from the conventional one that we cannot doubt the role of ideology in hiding it from view for over a century.

2

Haunted by the Woman Question: The Victorian Labour Movement and Woman Workers[1]

From the mid-1880s, a revival of interest in socialism in Britain was attracting widespread attention. In a foreshadowing of the 'reds under the beds' scares of 1950s America, sections of the press saw malign socialist influence everywhere, so that when the matchwomen struck, *The Times* quickly attributed the action to 'those pests of the modern world'.[2]

Historians, in their continuing assumption of Besant's leadership, have essentially concurred with this view. When East End dock workers struck the next year, socialist influence really was an important component, though this has never been used as an argument against the importance of the dispute, as it has with the matchwomen's.

However, a proper examination of events, and the beliefs and motivations of the main actors, exposes major flaws in that theory, not the least of which is clear evidence that the strike in fact caught established labour and socialist movements completely off guard; nor was it as initially welcomed by either as we might expect.

In order to understand the reasons for the surprising reality behind the myths about the strike, we need to further examine the development of ideas about Victorian working women, and the 'woman question', which would trouble trade unionists and socialists alike throughout the century and beyond.

'A LACK OF QUALITIES IN WOMEN': TRADE UNIONS AND FEMALE WORKERS

While some histories may give the impression that the matchwomen's strike represents the entire history of women and trade unionism, records actually show female workers coming together to fight exploitation since at least the eighteenth century. The textile industry, one of the first to industrialize, was dominated by women workers, and had a particular reputation for female militancy. It boasts the first recorded all-female union, which was formed in 1788, exactly a hundred years before the matchwomen's strike, among Leicester hand-spinners. The union was 18,500 strong at its peak, and had marked Luddite sympathies.[3]

Women and children also supported the 1818 Salford cotton-spinners' strike: one Elizabeth Salt wrote pro-union pamphlets, and observers were shocked by the degree of class antagonism expressed by the women, such that their own middle-class supporters were forced to cross the street to avoid being barracked.[4]

Women cotton workers themselves also struck in 1808 and 1818. It is important to understand that working men had not always sought to drive women out of the workplace as unwelcome economic competition, but had at times joined with them in the fight against exploitation. In Manchester, women were admitted to the Spinners' Union and drew strike pay from it – though they were later expelled. Male and female spinners fought together for equal pay in Glasgow in 1833.[5]

Women without unionization – and therefore without strike pay – needed considerable courage, or desperation, to take action against their employers. Militancy among women was seen, as one commentator remarked ironically, as 'more menacing to established institutions even than the education of the lower orders',[6] and punished accordingly. There is at least one example of an employer having his striking women workers arrested and sentenced to hard labour.[7] Even if not defeated legally, women strikers were often simply 'hungered back' to work.

Women made vital contributions to the major political movements of the first half of the nineteenth century, fighting alongside men throughout a period of almost continuous class struggle from the French Revolution to Chartism. Robert Owen, who had been influenced by the writings of Mary Wollstonecraft and favoured women's emancipation, was a driving force behind the Co-operative and Communitarian movements of the 1820s and 1830s. Communitarian women actively campaigned for equality, believing that only a socialist society could deliver it.[8] Owenites made common cause with early 'feminists' (though the word was not current until the 1890s).[9] Anna Wheeler and her daughter Rosina, the unfortunate wife of Edward Bulwer-Lytton mentioned in the previous chapter, lived according to Communitarian principles for some years. Women in the Co-operative movement openly challenged the 'double standard' of dominant sexual morality, and developed models of Co-operative associations for women workers.[10]

The all-inclusive Grand National Consolidated Trades Union (GNCTU) was established with Owen's assistance in 1833 and, though short lived, had a considerable female membership and self-organized women's branches including the Lodge of Female Tailors.[11] At its height in the 1830s the 'Grand National' may have had as many as half a million members. It declined during the slump in union activity after the deportation of the 'Tolpuddle Martyrs', six farm workers from the Tolpuddle in Dorset who were sentenced to seven years' transportation in 1834 for taking an oath of solidarity. Employers took advantage of fears of political unrest to launch an attack on trade unionist workers. Nonetheless, the GNCTU left its mark.[12]

Women continued to be active in the Chartist movement, as they had been from its beginnings in 1837. However, the 'Charter' itself called only for universal *manhood* suffrage. Joan Scott has argued that this masculine definition of citizenship rendered female participation largely irrelevant:[13] Chartists would employ the rhetoric of domestic ideology with the intention of uniting working-class men and women behind it, but with the eventual result of 'excluding women from most forms of work and politics'.[14] All across Europe, there was a great escalation in women's political activism in the years leading to 1848, the great 'Year of Revolutions' when, de Toqueville wrote, 'those who had anything were united in common terror'. Tens of thousands would die in uprisings, from the *Risorgimento* in Italy to the revived revolution in France.

However, the setbacks and reverses that followed saw the waning of Chartism in Britain, and marked an especially negative turning point for British women: the labour movement would virtually turn its back on women workers for the next three decades.[15] In spite of this, the 'woman question' could not be ignored, and trade unionists largely chose to answer it in the language of domestic ideology, causing lasting divisions through the entire working class.[16]

We have seen that as women and children moved into previously male areas of work following its mechanization, generally as cheap labour, male hostility to 'factory girls' grew. Adopting the rhetoric of 'separate spheres' allowed working men to suggest that the return of the woman to hearth and home was entirely in her interests, a reclaiming of her natural position: accordingly, a group of potters in 1845 appealed to 'maidens, mothers and wives', warning them that mechanized work was their 'deadliest enemy', and would destroy their 'natural claim to home and domestic duties'.[17] Striking Kidderminster carpet-weavers in 1875, however, did not sugar-coat the pill. When their employer hired women at a lower wage-rate to inveigle the men into accepting a pay-cut, threatening letters to the *Englishwoman's Review* accused the women of stealing men's jobs and warned that they 'might very likely get their brains knocked out'.[18] (The *Review* responded that 'even the tiger suffers his tigress to hunt in the same jungle'.[19])

The mid-nineteenth-century union movement had developed in a piecemeal fashion, and never adopted an overall ideological position on women's equality and unionization, which left it vulnerable to the vicissitudes of dominant social theory.

In spite of economic realities – most women worked because they had no choice – unions began to emphasize that they should not be in the workplace. The records of one union meeting at this time show that whilst those present condemned the 'wickedness' of their exploitative employer which was making 'poor women the enemy of poor men', their solution was not to recruit women, but to petition their employer against hiring them.[20]

In 1875, seven years after the founding of the Trades Union Congress, Henry Broadhurst, secretary of its Parliamentary Committee, declared that it must aim to 'bring about a condition . . . where (our) wives and daughters would be in their proper sphere at home, instead of being dragged into competition for livelihood against the great and strong men of the world'.[21]

A growing skill divide in the nineteenth-century workplace reflected a gender divide, both indirectly and directly. Workers were defined, often arbitrarily, as skilled, semi-skilled or unskilled. 'Custom, practice and prejudice',[22] rather than logic, often determined the divisions: cotton-spinning was poorly regarded and paid when spinners were female, but became the best-paid work in the industry when men took it over.

Skilled-worker status was usually achieved through apprenticeships, which were controlled and limited by the unions. The majority of female workers had no opportunity of supplying anything other than 'unskilled' labour – their skills were either undervalued, or insufficiently scarce. There were some exceptions: certain exclusively female trades like dressmaking and millinery were acknowledged as requiring a degree of skill, but places on apprenticeships were few, and hours and conditions at work still long and unhealthy.[23] There were women too in sections of male 'honourable trades' (working as 'closers' in shoemaking, for example, or sewers in book-binding), but they were rarely able to join unions, and still worked for lower wages than the men.[24]

In general, apprenticeships, described as working men's first line of defence of their 'property in skill' when women's employment became an economic threat, were closed to women.[25] The 'property in skill' of artisans like the weavers, for example, was eroded by the Napoleonic wars. As men were pressed into, and then returned from, service in the wars, the labour market was alternately starved of and glutted with workers. In times of labour shortage the use of female labour, often from within weaving families, had been a necessity: the weavers well understood the plight of the women who were forced to take work at low rates of pay. However, during periods of labour influx, the overall response from the textile trades, as from the male union movement as a whole, was not to organize unskilled and female labour but to organize *against* the incursions of women through strikes, petitions to employers, and the lobbying of parliament.[26] Anna Clark imagines a meeting by a group of organized weavers in Glasgow in 1809, 'leaving their wives and children toiling over looms' as they meet to discuss whether or not women should be admitted to their union.[27] She sees the increasing association of skill with masculinity as deliberately constructed, an invention of the mid-nineteenth-century 'fight' against female workers.[28] At this point, working men were gaining a consciousness of their exploited position in the workplace just as employers were starting to try to replace them with cheap female and child labour. If they were not able to compete economically and were not willing to show solidarity with the competition, working men had to promulgate the idea that their labour was so superior in quality that it alone justified a higher expenditure on wages.

In time, the idea that masculinity was a prerequisite of skill took root so deeply that even the supposed champions of women workers were unable to see beyond it. By extension, women could be blamed for their own low wages and poor conditions, and both the Women's Trade Union Association and Women's Industrial Council would ultimately conclude that women's inferior position in the labour market resulted from the 'inefficient and untrained quality of their work'.[29] This led the two organizations to argue for the technical, but also domestic, training of young women, campaigning to train them as children's nurses 'to provide an opening for remunerative work and fitting them for their future lives as wives and mothers', effectively surrendering women once again to the strictures of domestic ideology.[30]

Here, women's own organizations joined much of Victorian society in using the concept of skill to make women themselves, rather than the unequal system in which they laboured, responsible for their suffering.[31] The idea would prove extraordinarily persistent: in 1986, historian Elizabeth Roberts offered a surprising commentary on the elderly women she interviewed about their working lives from 1890 to 1940:

> The final irony about married women's work in textile areas is that while women believed they had to work because their husbands' wages were low, what they did not realize was that by working they were helping to keep those wages low.[32]

While the neighbours, brothers or fathers of women like the matchworkers faced equally grim working conditions, job insecurity and low wages, for the men class and economic circumstances, rather than gender, dictated their situation. The decay of traditional East London industries had led to widespread destitution, and a vast 'residuum' of unemployed men, forcing thousands to join the desperate 'call-ons' at the docks. However, there was an opportunity, however slight, for some of their number to join the ranks of the 'dock royalty' – the permanently employed elite who enjoyed comparatively high pay and status. But there was no match factory royalty. Though some matchwomen earned more than others, as this was piecework, skill and speed alone dictated the 'take-home' wage. The highest paid, regarded with awe by the others, were four women earning around 13 shillings: many earned 4 or less.[33] A skilled male manual worker could expect to earn on average of around 40 shillings a week at this time.

The ideological victory of the concept of 'separate spheres', and all that went with it, had resulted from a long and sometimes hard-fought battle over ideas of sexual morality, the sexual division of labour, and gender itself: what it meant, or should mean, to be a man or a woman in the nineteenth century.[34]

It has been argued, too, that the failure of radical politics to address working-class women's concerns was an important factor.[35] Barbara Taylor has further suggested that as the overall economic situation worsened, working-class women were simply placed in too weak a position to challenge the *status quo*; that they were, in other words, forced to accept the 'trade-off' of personal freedom for such male protection as marriage might offer.[36]

Though the concept of 'separate spheres' was hugely divisive for the working class, it was ironically offered as a force to unite it.[37] Adopting the domestic ideal protected working-class families from the intense bourgeois criticism of their morals and domestic lives. The ideas of Malthus came into play too, with their conclusion that poverty was a direct result of uncontrolled population growth. Even working-class advocates like Francis Place, who directly rejected the Malthusian idea that poverty resulted from population growth,[38] advocated birth control and early marriage as a route to social improvement – though from the perspective of limiting the labour supply and freeing up workers' time and energy to concentrate on political reform.[39]

So the labour movement began to argue for the transformatory power of the 'family wage' on the working class via the calm, ordered homes and domestic lives it would create. Those women who argued against it could be conveniently accused of putting gender before class, the stick also used to beat women in socialist organizations who advanced arguments for equality.[40] Trade unions also, conveniently, claimed that women were 'bad trade unionists', impossible to organize or to keep organized, either too selfish to understand the need to defend their sisters, or too 'feminine' to be up to stand up for themselves. The *Trade Unionist* opined: 'The short sentence "organise the women workers" simply bristles with difficulties . . . the lack of qualities in women of self-reliance, independence and self-government, their greater timidity, home cares, and many like objections.'[41]

As we have seen, it has been argued that men in the labour movement knew that they were not acting in the interests of their class, nor simply responding to the exigencies of capitalism, in defending domestic ideology and the 'family wage' campaign. Rather they were making a conscious choice purely to maintain their labour price, which would lead to the marginalization of women workers and long-standing divisions in the movement on gender lines.[42] Specific and widescale attempts to organize working women would not now be made until the 1870s, and even then it would largely be left to women, and often those from outside both the labour movement and the working class, to make them.[43]

LADIES AND WORKERS: ORGANIZING WOMEN

Generally, then, the movement for women's rights developed in isolation from the main body of radical politics after 1848. The tensions and misunderstandings between the labour and women's movements left each to develop separately, and contributed to their failure to properly encompass issues of class and gender, weakening the potential and integrity of each. This ideological muddle was equally evident in women's trade union organizations, which displayed in their early days a peculiar mix of 'feminism, trade unionism and middle-class attitudes'.[44] The national leaders of women trade union members in the nineteenth century would tend to be middle-class women – if not men.[45] This has led to debate about whether major organizations of working-class women in the nineteenth century constitute genuine trade unionism, or just an extension of middle-class 'rescue' work. The line was further blurred when organizations like the National Union of Working Women (NUWW) organized 'mothers' meetings' of working-class women where, as one unenthusiastic attendee noted: 'Ladies came and lectured on the domestic affairs . . . in the workers' homes, that it was impossible for them to understand.'[46]

In 1898 the peculiar incident of Millicent Fawcett and the Bryant and May women seemed to confirm the divisive effect of class even upon supporters of working-class women. Fawcett was prominent in the NUWW and the National Union of Women's Suffrage Societies (NUWSS). The NUWSS officially supported Clementina Black in her work of campaigning for low-paid women. In July 1898 the *Star*, still a champion of the matchwomen, published an article claiming that Bryant and May continued to subject their workers to unsafe levels of phosphorus exposure. It named the firm's shareholders – who included Fawcett. She wrote to the company to ascertain the truth of the allegations and Gilbert Bartholomew, the managing director, invited her to visit the factory. He seems to have easily convinced Fawcett with his protestations of innocence and care for his workforce, whose own 'ignorance' or negligence he blamed for any incidences of necrosis.[47] Fawcett was then taken to meet some of the women in their dining rooms, which had been established as a condition of the strike settlement. They apparently professed themselves entirely happy with their working conditions, and were in complete agreement with their employer that it was 'yer own fault' if necrosis developed, as it resulted from poor hygiene.[48]

Fawcett accepted what she was told without question, and rounded upon those campaigning against Bryant and May with extraordinary vehemence. It does not seem to have occurred to her that the workers were likely to have been coached, or threatened, and may not have been speaking freely. Bryant and May were certainly capable of bullying their workers to cover up cases of necrosis, as the mother of Cornelius Lean, who later died of it, discovered. The company told her that if she called in outside medical help, her son's sick pay would immediately cease.[49] Fawcett's willingness to side with the employer, despite clear evidence, reported in the *Star's* article, that they had concealed at least 17 cases of necrosis and 6 deaths, is telling.

Though class was clearly a complicating factor, it is difficult to ascertain the exact extent to which it hampered attempts to organize women workers. As with the historiography of the matchworkers' strike, the story of the organizations which attempted this is invariably told through the lives and actions of individual leader figures. There are some notable exceptions, like factory worker Aida Nield Chew, who asserted working-class mothers' right to economic independence, and was active within the NUWSS and Women's Trade Union League (WTUL).[50] We know about Nield Chew's life and work because she kept her own record, later edited by her daughter and published, but it is a rare example.

Certainly class and gender issues were acknowledged to have affected from the outset organizations like the Women's Protective and Provident League (WPPL), established by middle-class bookbinder Emma Paterson in 1874. Paterson had become secretary of the Women's Suffrage Association in 1872, but left on her marriage the following year. During a visit to America, she was impressed by the work of women's unions such as the Female Umbrella Makers' Union, and on her return wrote to *The Times* advocating the organization of women.[51] Paterson established the WPPL along with feminist supporters and social activists like the Fabian Isabella Ford. The league's aim was to gradually establish unions, trade by trade, in all industries where women worked. These unions would be single-sex,

as Paterson believed women were disadvantaged by mixed unions – like those in
the cotton trade where they were accepted as members but on an unequal basis
to men, and denied access to decision-making.

In 1874 the WPPL backed a successful strike by unorganized women weavers
in Dewsbury, Yorkshire, and the next year they began to assist with the building
of a number of small unions among female bookbinders, upholsterers, and
dress-, shirt- and collar-makers in London.[52] Thirty trade associations were
established between 1874 and 1886, although with limited objectives and success.
The league generally adopted a 'unitary' approach to industrial relations in
its early years, promoting co-operation between workers and employers, and
emphasizing financial membership benefits rather than militant action as the
surest provision against want.[53] This position resulted largely from Paterson's
belief that middle- and working-class women were united by their gender, and
that the more affluent would help their poorer sisters to fight male oppression
– an incomplete understanding of the operation of class and the inevitability of
class antagonism under capitalism.

Although Paterson appealed to working-class women for their ideas and
opinions, the league's first conference was apparantly more a 'meeting of
Christians, feminists and philanthropists' than of workers.[54] The leadership of the
WPPL generally believed that the uniting factor of gender would override class
divides between them and the women they sought to organize. However, there is
evidence that, as with the NUWW, some working-class women found the league
somewhat patronizing in attitude, and remote from their concerns.[55]

This is not to say that none of its members understood the interlinking of
class and gender oppression. Isabella Ford for one argued that women could not
be fully emancipated under capitalism, and socialists should support the cause
of women and vice versa: 'The Socialist movement, the Labour movement, call
it which you will, and the Women's movement, are but different aspects of the
same great force which has been, all through the ages, gradually pushing its way
upwards, making for the reconstruction and regeneration of Society.'[56] From
a landowning family, Ford had joined the Fabian Society in 1883 soon after
its formation, and in 1885 helped Paterson to form a Machinists' Society for
tailoresses in Leeds as part of her campaign to improve the pay and conditions
of women in the textile industry in the area. However, the league ultimately
failed to make common cause with working women to the extent it had hoped,
and its views on class created suspicion among male trade unionists, who were
unconvinced that this was genuine trade unionism.[57]

This problematic relationship produced apparent *non sequiturs* such as the
opposition of the WPPL, which campaigned against women's long working hours,
to legislation which would reduce them, while the TUC, though often hostile to
working women (as well as to the WPPL), supported it. Although Paterson
supported the establishment of the Factory Inspectorate and the appointment of
female factory inspectors, she opposed the struggle for protective legislation on
economic grounds, arguing that although she was of course against long hours, this

reform would only worsen women's earning potential and career opportunities in the short term. Paterson's position divided opinion within the league.

The matchwomen's strike, when it came, also failed to 'shake [the league] from its lethargy'.[58] Its committee members sent a message of 'full sympathy' to the strikers and asked its members to boycott Bryant and May's products, but also voted to take 'no active part' in the stoppage itself, though the issue divided its members.[59] However, the league noted the matchwomen's active recruitment work among other East End women workers. Members of the Union of Women Matchmakers asked the league to contribute to a meeting they wanted to hold for women in local jam, sweet and pickle factories, whom they hoped to persuade to unionize.[60] A league supporter provided tea and cake and the league itself probably found the venue: but it was the matchwomen who had led the way. The next year the league talked to Bryant and May matchbox-makers about unionizing: they noted that the women were enthusiastic about doing so if the difficulties of organizing homeworkers could be overcome; and that '[t]he husbands of many of them are members of the Dock Labourer's Union'.[61]

In 1889, at the height of New Unionism, Isabella Ford helped to establish the Leeds Tailoresses' Union and was elected its president in 1890. Ford supported the long and bitter, Manningham Mills strike of 1891. She retained her interest in women's rights, and became active in the suffrage movement. Meanwhile, the established labour movement continued to argue that women did not make good trade unionists; that they were expensive to organize because of the cost of paid volunteers; that they were not valid members of the workforce in the first place, because they should be at home, or because they really *wanted* to be at home, and were only waiting to marry in order to return there.[62] When middle-class women began to appear at annual trade union congresses to voice the concerns of working women in the late 1870s, Henry Broadhurst had them excluded because, he said, he doubted the wisdom of sending women to congresses where 'under the influence of emotion they might vote for things they would regret in cooler moments'.[63]

As Rowbotham and Harris both suggest, personal psychologies added to political complexities in making individual reactions to class and gender issues unpredictable, regardless of the overall ideology of the organization in which they operated.[64]

The lack of harmonious interaction and exchange of ideas between women's organizations, socialists and the labour movement in the nineteenth century was to the detriment of all parties, leaving the first to develop without a coherent policy on class relations, and socialist groups and the labour movement to harbour sexism and misogyny.

Working women's organizations were accused of being shaped more by a handful of charismatic but ultimately philanthropic middle-class 'Lady Bountifuls' than by the demands of working-class women themselves.[65] Their leaders were often women of Annie Besant's milieu: middle class and politically aware with a social conscience, but, like Besant, no syndicalists; indeed it has been argued that 'in some respects their ideology of organizing women put a brake on the women who applied to join unions, ran strikes and entered the labour market, as well as being a shaping force for women's trade unionism'.[66]

Although the 'cult' of the leaders of women's organizations has too often obscured the agency of rank and file members, it cannot be inferred from this that the latter were merely passive bystanders – rather that, once again, more work is needed to recognize the actions of the many rather than the few.

'STRIKES OF GIRLS': HISTORICAL TREATMENT OF WOMEN'S MILITANCY

The failure to develop a 'doubled vision' which encompassed gender as well as class oppression is not confined to the Victorian past.[67] It has been said to have caused 'gender blindness' in the work of the 'mainly manly Marxist greats' of British labour history, and in the genre in general.[68] While women are present in, for example, E. P. Thompson's *The Making of the English Working Class*, they appear as individuals rather than members of classes, and play little part in the 'making'.[69]

As Boston discovered, even those with a good grounding in labour history believed that when it came to women and trade unions there was little worth recording.[70] In fact, as Davis shows, use could have been made of considerable contemporary evidence: there is in fact much documenting of the preponderance of women in the industrial workplace, not least in the work of both Marx and Engels.[71]

The overlooking of women's part in the labour force and movement has, then, made a lasting and negative impact upon British labour history. Even today, Davis argues, despite sustained criticism of the neglect of 'the female half of the human race' and Hobsbawm's statement of the justifications for it, labour historians have tended to either 'carry on regardless, colonize the area (e.g. suffrage history) or merely make a passing genuflection'.[72]

It is the contention of this book that such 'gender blindness' was responsible for misperceptions of the matchwomen at the time of their strike, in spite of the fact that some of their contemporaries, like John Burns and Tom Mann, recognized their contribution. However, the fact that the matchwomen have not been 'rehabilitated' with changes in the understanding of their role suggests that such prejudice may be an ongoing facet of labour history. To advance this theory, recent research on two other strikes by mostly female workforces will also be examined, in which both the effects of gender prejudice among the strikers' contemporaries, and their mistreatment by labour historians, have been convincingly exposed by modern researchers.

The 'Black Country Strike'

The 'Black Country Strike' was in reality a series of strikes and demonstrations in the metal industries in Birmingham and the West Midlands in 1913, by unskilled male and female workers. Research by C. and W. Staples in 1999 focused on one particular strike, part of this 'great unrest', among metal workers at a Kenrick and Sons' factory in West Bromwich.

Kenricks had dramatically increased their use of low-paid female labour in the years up to 1913, and apparently engaged in deliberate 'deskilling' to further cut costs. Because trade unionism had been minimal among unskilled Kenricks workers before 1911, they presumably anticipated little challenge. However, a strike began on 7 April 1913 among 100 workers, 'mostly "factory girls" fed up with pitiful wages, dirty and dangerous working conditions, and mistreatment by their "masters"'.[73] By the afternoon they had been joined by an equal number of workers from another of Kenricks' factories, and by the middle of the week all of their 1,200 workers were out. During the strike, local newspapers described the female strikers' grievances: 'The girls are typical factory workers, their ages ranging from 14 to over 30, and among them a general feeling of dissatisfaction appears to exist with regard to the rates of pay prevailing.'[74]

At the beginning of the strike, the desire for equal rates of pay for equal work, as well as a fixed minimum wage, was advanced by the workers themselves, but not by the Workers' Union (WU), which negotiated on their behalf. Tom Mann had established the union, for both sexes, in 1910. Two weeks later, after 'considerable ruckus at the negotiating table, at the factory gates and in the streets', agreement was reached: male rates of pay were set at 23 shillings and women's at only 12 shillings. This was nonetheless hailed as a victory for the workers, as unions won the right to organize at specific factories.

However, as the terms agreed not only failed to challenge the exploitation of low-waged women, but also suppressed women's militancy in the industry for some years, the Staples argue that this could equally be seen as a victory for the employer, and that the WU's refusal to challenge gender discrimination only reinforced the 'sex caste system' operating in the workplace.[75] Despite the WU's 'progressive' policy of welcoming women into the workplace, it subordinated them once inside: '[Once the women were] shaped in ways that did not pose a threat to male supremacy, then the men could be re-enlisted to "protect" them, and in doing so re-assert male authority.'[76] Sheila Lewenhak has also written of the settlement that reframing the conclusion as a victory conceals the reality of an example of 'men's determination to secure wages for themselves, even at the expense of women co-workers'.[77]

Gender ideology has, the Staples argue, played another role in framing the conventional version of the Black Country Strike in general. Seven years after it ended, Lord Askwith, the 'industrial peacekeeper' who held senior positions on the Board of Trade and was chairman of the Industrial Council between 1912 and 1913, reflected on the strike – and drew an interesting parallel:

There suddenly occurred a flare in the Midlands which spread rapidly through Birmingham and the Black Country, directly involving about 50,000 operatives in boiler and bridge works, tube works, railway carriage and wagonworks . . . and thousands of workpeople indirectly in various industries. The principal claim was for a minimum wage of twenty-three shillings a week in Birmingham and the Black Country, but the strike commenced with the small beginning of some girls at Dudley saying that they could not live any longer on the wages paid to them. **Just as years ago the London match-girls had started the London dock strike, so these girls lit the torch which fired the Midlands** [my emphasis]. The men followed suit in factory after factory.[78]

As the Staples point out, Askwith was able to accept that women were at the centre of the Black Country Strike, 'one of the most significant strikes of the tumultuous "unrest of labour" that shook England between 1910 and the start of World War One'.[79] Deborah Thom's 1986 account of the Black Country disputes concurs with Askwith's, asserting that much of the unrest took place among women and that during it:

> Women did join unions in greater numbers than before, they went on strike more frequently, they were more often to be seen on the public platforms of the labour movement. But it is not true to say that this was women catching up to men. There were specifically female characteristics to the unrest. Women were much more likely to take strike action . . . [and] to attempt a public display of . . . their grievances.[80]

However, in 1985 historian Hugh Clegg disputed this in his *History of Trade Unions Since 1889*: 'it is a flight of fancy to ascribe the origin of the stoppage to a strike of some girls at Dudley' who 'lit the torch which fired the Midlands', with the result that 'women joined the strike in large numbers, adding their demand for a 60p minimum wage to the men's claim . . .'.[81] Clegg offers no evidence for his dismissal of Askwith's evaluation and is, the Staples argue, forcing the women strikers 'back in their assigned, marginal, place in British Labor history',[82] whether consciously or not.

By reframing history to exclude or devalue the actions of such women, say the Staples, 'Clegg and company repeat, rather than critically analyse, the particular, partial and masculinist way in which the English working class was organized.'[83] They attribute this failing in traditional accounts of the strike to the fact that these were inevitably 'written on top of patriarchy' and so do not, and are perhaps cannot, expose the discrimination at the heart of the case.[84]

The Melbourne Tailoresses' Strike
The 1882–3 tailoresses' strike in Melbourne, Australia, also provides interesting parallels with the matchwomen's.

In December 1882, 300 women clothing workers walked out on strike in protest over a cut to their piecework rates. The tailoresses had protested before, in the 1870s, and this had led to criticism in the press. One newspaper advised the women that, if they had had enough of 'half starving at a trade',[85] they would be better off entering domestic service than making a public fuss. It helpfully added that a more respectable livelihood would have the added advantage of increasing their chances of making 'a happy settlement' – i.e. marrying – which must of course be their ultimate goal. The media complained that women like the tailoresses 'liked the large liberty of the factory, where they can wear what they please and find time to flirt with whom they like', flaunting their 'mistaken love of liberty' and 'unwillingness to submit to any restraint'.[86]

This, too, was a strike of 'unskilled' female factory workers, and also confounded perceived gender norms. The left-wing media of the day hoped that the strike would draw attention to the evils of sweated labour, but still persisted, in familiar fashion, in referring to the strikers as 'helpless girls'[87] who should place themselves 'entirely in the hands' of the Trades Hall Council (THC), the Australian equivalent of the Trades Council.[88] As we will see Bryant and May do in their turn, the employers at the Victoria Clothing Company expressed public irritation and bewilderment at their employees' behaviour, claiming there had previously been 'such a good feeling'[89] between the parties. However, recent research by Danielle Thornton for the University of Melbourne has highlighted an important difference: the tailoresses themselves were interviewed decades after the strike, meaning that in this case there is a record of the strikers' motivations and intentions at the time of the dispute.

Until its centenary the strike received little detailed attention in labour history, being – like the Bryant and May dispute – mostly the subject of 'fleeting mentions' in general histories, and then 'only as a catalyst for broader developments' in the labour movement.[90] Accounts have also stressed the role played by the male trade unionists of the THC, though Thornton has found that this is open to question, and obscures the role that the women themselves played in the strike. Not until the 1980s did historians begin to consider that responses to the strike had been conditioned by gender, and to recognize it as 'part of an ongoing challenge to traditional notions of femininity'.[91]

Unlike the Bryant and May case, historians generally accepted that the women's initial walkout was 'spontaneous', but one THC representative claimed that the women immediately approached the council's male trade unionists for assistance. This has been generally accepted as correct, and so the emphasis has been placed on the THC's role in 'rescuing' and organizing helpless women who had, almost by accident, found themselves in dispute. Thornton challenges this, proving that the date given for this supposed approach cannot be correct, and furthermore that the THC's detailed records of the period made no mention of any such approach. Thornton argues that evidence suggests that the women in fact held out for a week, and that the THC finally approached *them* to offer help (which was accepted), only after the strike became a *cause célèbre*: 'the chief topic of conversation among the working classes'.[92]

Key participants in the strike were interviewed in the 1920s, not by historians but by an industry paper, the *Clothing Trades Gazette*. This rediscovered testimony, together with that given to a Royal Commission, provides a compelling account of an action begun and continued by women who were well aware of the significance and consequences of their actions, in pursuance of clear aims.

Ellen Creswell, who would propose the formation of a union at the first mass meeting, had thirteen years' experience of the clothing trade and a personal record of industrial militancy, having been sacked from a previous job for trying to organize a union. She testified that employers were engaged in a relentless attempt to drive down wages and a 'cat-and-mouse' struggle with their workforce, for whom 'collective protest was their only weapon'.[93]

Helen Robertson recalled that she and four other tailoresses had reached a point where they were 'sick of being treated like animals', and resolved to start a union.[94] It is not known how many of these women also had prior experience in this area but, as Thornton argues, their organizational skills make this a strong possibility. They had to act covertly in order to protect their jobs, on one occasion fly-posting several factories with handbills for a meeting, on another organizing a rally to the parliament buildings, all the time fearing discovery and dismissal. They succeeded in forming a union, which Robertson remembered as the 'starting point of our improvement'. Robertson remained active in the Clothing Trade Union throughout her life, and was the first woman to be elected to its executive in her sixties. Interviewed at the age of 74, she said that her only wish was that she could be 'forty years younger, so that I could get properly into the fight for a long time to come'.[95]

The strikers also testified that they were particularly determined to succeed because they knew that defeat would have given the signal for other employers in the clothing trade to drop their prices in line with the Victoria Clothing Company's. The strike eventually spread to around six hundred workers at thirteen of the company's factories. A union was formed, and the strike finally resolved in March 1883. The employers accepted the workers' list of piecework rates – though in reality they soon began to undermine them by the increasing use of homeworkers. However, in spite of this the strike is recognized as having presented a 'radical challenge to conventional femininity',[96] demonstrating a shift away from perceptions that the labour movement was a 'man's movement', and representing an important instance of 'women workers moving from merely seeing themselves as sharing a common experience of exploitation with their workmates, to collectively and self-consciously engaging in political action'. The strike would become a 'reference point for subsequent generations of female union activists'.[97]

CONCLUSIONS

There is a clear parallel between the way in which history has dealt with women's trade unions in general and the matchworkers specifically. There is the same historical 'blindness' to the significance and contribution of all but a handful of supposed leaders: just as Besant dominates accounts of the Bryant and May strike, so the histories of the leaders of these women's organizations obscures the experiences and agency of their wider membership.

Any alliance between such organizations and the wider labour movement in the nineteenth century would prove 'problematic. Underlying it was, and still is, the vexed question of the relationship between class and gender . . . between feminism and socialism.'[98] Late-twentieth-century theorists seek to avoid the expression of patriarchy and capitalism as separate entities, seeing the former as a facet and product of material circumstances. However, work still remains to be done in the search for a fully conceptualized 'doubled vision' of the operation of class and gender which overcomes the limitations of political language and understanding.[99] Historiography lacking such underlying theory has ensured that what survives is the history of the figureheads of women's unionism rather than of the rank and file, and of these leaders' estimations of the female workforce, often as weak and undisciplined before the imposition of order from outside.

The motivations of historians who continue, in the light of all the evidence, to deny or downplay women's militancy is equally problematic; it has been contended that part of the explanation lies in the 'gender blindness' of British labour history, in which the experiences of working-class women have continually been excluded from the mainstream. The examples of the Black Country Strike and the Melbourne Tailoresses' Strike clearly demonstrate the operation of gender ideology in representations of female action. The Black Country Strike was acknowledged by participants to have been significantly female in character; but, as the Staples' research has shown, subsequent labour historians made determined efforts to devalue the female contribution. However, Askwith freely acknowledged it at the time, 'Britain's chief industrial peacekeeper', freely acknowledged it, using the matchwomen's strike as a reference thirty-two years after its end – and asserting that the Bryant and May action had 'started the London dock strike'.[100]

I believe it is now more important than ever that we remember these women's lives and contributions, and consider the way in which history has concealed them. British labour history seems to be under increasing threat from revisionist attempts to overturn its progress. Even as previously unpalatable a topic as Victorian imperialism has undergone something of a rehabilitation in the works of historians like Niall Ferguson,[101] who has called for a 'new liberal imperialism' modelled on it.[102] Scholars like Amanda Vickery have also attacked 'women's historians' for their portrayal of the experiences of Victorian women, suggesting they ignore 'positive comments' from women who either did not find themselves rigidly confined within the domestic sphere, or found such lives 'enriching'; though she cites no specific examples of this from primary sources.[103] The purpose of 'separate spheres' theorizing was, in Vickery's view, a preparation of the ground for a 'feminist assault on public institutions',[104] by 'countless historians' who 'follow Engels' and his 'preoccupation with the idea that women were infinitely better off before the coming of commerce'.[105] Groundbreaking 1930s historian Ivy Pinchbeck is named as one of these, rather bizarrely given that she is one of the more positive modern writers on industrialization, seeing it as ultimately beneficial to women.

As recently as 2009, historian and television presenter David Starkey revealed what the *Guardian* called a 'deeply misogynistic view of the past and his fellow historians'.[106] Starkey attacked 'usually quite pretty' female historians who sought to 'feminise' history': their work, he said, was the historical equivalent of Mills and Boon: "If you are to do a proper history of Europe before the last five minutes, it is a history of white males...and to pretend anything else is to falsify." Dr Starkey presumably exempts his own works on Elizabeth I and the wives of Henry VIII from this charge.

In the 1890s, after the matchwomen's strike, labour organizer Margaret McMillan wrote:

> A new feature . . . was the stir and murmur among women. Overworked mothers and wives, young girls too and older women who were unmarried, and living by their own labour, at factory and workshop, wakened as from sleep and began to conceive new hope and purpose.[107]

It is important that we defend the experiences and achievements of such women, and the history of working people like them, against not just the 'enormous condescension of posterity' but of new fashions in history which seek to deny them.

3

Life, Work and Politics in the Victorian East End

This chapter will consider the probable significance of the matchwomen's action and victory, not to outside observers, but to the women themselves and their communities.

If, as I believe, the Bryant and May women took deliberate, independent action against powerful employers, then they were acting outside conventionally understood class and gender roles in doing so. East End 'factory girls' were not supposed to be capable of serious, and effective, industrial militancy: as we have seen, the established labour movement generally thought women too self-interested and preoccupied with 'home cares', if not too lacking in intelligence, to make good trade unionists, let alone successful strikers.

In this chapter we will look at the home lives of East End women, their roles in their families and communities, and what they felt about respectability, work and a woman's place – in contrast to what middle-class writers thought they should feel.

As far as possible, given both our historical distance from events and the comparative rarity of working-class accounts, we will consider whether the women of the East End were more than just passive recipients of bourgeois 'domestic ideology', and whether their backgrounds themselves played a role in events, shaping the gender and political perspectives which may have informed the strike.

It has never previously been thought possible that the strike might have been influenced by the matchwomen's own political opinions, rather than those of Besant and her milieu. However, it is notable that when the Melbourne tailoresses discussed in the previous chapter were interviewed years after their strike, they admitted to strong political motivations – though these were not credited at the time. The present chapter will consider whether this might also have been true of the matchwomen.

While the matchworkers and their fellow East Londoners were by no means alone in their industrial rebelliousness in the late 1880s, the East End's geographical and social context increased the propensity of their actions to attract publicity, and therefore to inspire and influence others. The reasons for the considerable political and media attention focused there around this period will accordingly be considered.

'WORST END TO BEST END' – EAST LONDON AND SWEATED LABOUR IN THE 1880S

When the matchwomen walked out of Bryant and May's factory, they could not have known that they would be walking on to a national stage. The East End of the 1880s, however, had become an ideal arena in which to play out a struggle of rich versus poor, workers versus industrialists; there was also a perfect audience of supporters in situ, waiting to cheer the strikers to the echo. This may have contributed to the idea that the strike was essentially 'staged' – deliberately organized from the outside for wider political purposes at a critical time and place in the nation's political history.

London was the nation's political centre, and East London at this time 'the greatest homogenous working class area accessible to the House of Commons by popular demonstrations', as Sylvia Pankhurst neatly put it. Pankhurst understood that the establishment of a movement here, in 'that great abyss of poverty', could serve as 'a rallying cry to the rise of similar movements in all parts of the country'.[1] It was no coincidence that she chose to establish the East London Federation of Suffragettes, which would have great political importance as an organization embracing otherwise excluded working-class women.

The lives of those women and their families had already attracted national attention. East Enders were living under conditions which exemplified the exploitative nature of industrial capitalism, repeatedly held up to the rest of Victorian society as a 'Dreadful Warning' by writers and commentators including Dickens, Mearns, W. T. Stead and Besant herself,[2] assisted by a flourishing newspaper industry.

Taxes on newspapers had been abolished in a series of reforms from the 1850s, which 'liberated' the press and made daily publication feasible for the first time.[3] A proliferation of new local and national papers, and an expansion of the political press, resulted. By the time of the Bryant and May strike, newspapers like the *Star* (owned by the Irish nationalist T. P. O'Connor during the 1880s) were therefore both willing and able to bring their readers day-by-day coverage of events, giving an important momentum to the progress of the dispute.

The House of Lords Select Committee was in the middle of its enquiry into sweated labour at the same time, reporting between 1887 and 1890, and the media made much of its often disturbing findings. Writers like W. T. Stead – famous for a series of articles on child prostitution, the 'Maiden tribute to modern Babylon' – were pioneering a 'new journalism', highly sensationalist in style but politically serious in content,[4] and well suited to the struggles of exploited young matchwomen.

Completing the picture was a flourishing socialist revival in and around the East End. Though Marx and Engels' *Communist Manifesto* had been published in London in 1848, their work was only beginning to be widely read in Britain in the early 1880s, around the time of Marx's death. It influenced societies like the Social Democratic Federation (SDF), established in 1884. The Fabian Society was founded the same year. Some kind of social revolution was beginning to be widely dreaded, or looked for – in either case, was starting to seem a viable proposition. We have already seen that socialist influence was beginning to be divined everywhere by some sections of the press, so that when the matchwomen struck, *The Times* quickly attributed the action to 'those pests' the socialists.[5]

Both the place and time of the matchwomen's strike were, it will be argued, factors in its ability to influence other workers. The East End provided, as Barbara Harrison put it:

> ... a point of identification for issues around women workers, the linking of health and work and ideas about remedy at the national level. National issues were played out on East London terrain ... because of actual living and working conditions here, and also the way these issues and related aspects assumed symbolic importance in the popular and political imagination.[6]

So it would prove with the Bryant and May strike, and the New Unionist movement which would follow it.

'Sweating'

East London would become stigmatized as the home of the disreputable poor, and also of casual and 'sweated' labour. 'Sweating', as defined by the House of Lords Select Committee, was work with one or more of three characteristics: below-subsistence wages, excessively long working hours, and 'an insanitary state of the houses in which the work is carried on'.[7] Sweating was by no means a new feature of the late Victorian period, being well established for several decades before the select committee enquiry into it; but it would prove to have made its transition into new industries, as well as continuing to thrive in the old.[8] The Sweating Commission was a result rather than a cause of the extent of re-awakened concern about sweating, and popular concern about it at this time can only have contributed to the ability of the matchworkers' strike to capture the popular imagination. Although the committee did not publish its final report until 1890, the national press followed its sessions on a daily basis; as will be shown, one such piece aroused initial Fabian interest in Bryant and May.

In previous decades the sweated woman worker had been regarded by society at large as more to be pitied than censured. Those involved in the manufacture and finishing of clothing, the 'seamstresses', were seen as the paradigmatic 'sweated' workers, and contemporary representations tended to portray them as martyrs, in the mode of Andersen's 'Little Match Girl'. In fact Sheila Rowbotham has pointed out the resemblance between mid-nineteenth century paintings of such women and religious iconography, particularly before the popularization of photography.[9] Certainly one of the best known, Elizabeth Blunden's *A Seamstress: the Song of the Shirt* (1854), shows a romantically pale young shirt-maker with her hands clasped in prayer, on her knees by her work-table in a dark, dirty London room, eyes heavenward. Blunden was inspired by Thomas Hood's poem *The Song of the Shirt*, published in *Punch* in 1843:

With fingers weary and worn
With eyelids heavy and red
A woman sat, in unwomanly rags
Plying her needle and thread –
Stitch! stitch! stitch!
In poverty, hunger, and dirt
And still with a voice of dolorous pitch
She sang the 'Song of the Shirt'.[10]

As we shall see, it was earlier in the same year that *The Times* published an exposé of the exploitation of needleworkers which made use of the emotive 'White slavery' theme Besant would later employ to such effect.[11]

However, economic and social unrest would radically alter public perceptions of sweated workers and the 'casual poor'. The years 1874 to 1887 saw an overall national decline in wages, with sweated workers, always at the bottom of the heap, particularly badly hit.[12] By the mid-1880s the country's philanthropists and social reformers were increasingly focused on their plight, with the usual combination of genuine outrage at the suffering of so many, and fear of the consequences. From 1883 the press was full of dire warnings of imminent revolt. In 1884 the *Pall Mall Gazette* warned that such extreme inequality was 'a great danger to the Commonwealth'.[13] Appreciation of some of the economic injustice of the situation was displayed by *The Times* later that year, when it commented that 'The old relation of capital and industry ... has not succeeded in giving satisfaction to one of the two parties (i.e. labour) to the transaction.'[14]

In 1885 the Industrial Remuneration Conference of trade unions, employers, politicians and economists met to consider the matter – but arrived at little in the way of solutions. At this stage the only plan seriously considered was the break-up and removal of the London residuum – land reform was proposed which would allow its members to be settled on farms at a safe distance from the capital.[15]

In February 1886 economic depression was at its height and extreme temperatures had caused exceptional distress in outdoor trades. A meeting on 'free trade' led to a supposed riot as the fury and despair of the crowd had spilled over into Pall Mall. *The Times* considered the situation more dangerous than in 1848, reporting that the West End had been 'for a couple of hours in the hands of the mob'.[16] Rumours were rife throughout the capital that this 'mob' was on the march; the gates of Downing Street were shut, and troops confined to barracks. Potentially adding to both the fear and guilt of the more affluent classes was increasing evidence that casual and sweated labourers were not the shiftless, demoralized 'roughs' of popular stereotype, but that men and women were working themselves sometimes literally to death in East London docks, homes and factories, so close to the affluence and luxury of the West End.[17]

In 1887 both the Board of Trade and the *Lancet* carried out their own investigations into sweating, with the latter focusing on the London tailoring trade. In early 1888, MPs representing East London constituencies urged the government to take action, and the House of Lords established its select committee. As investigations would show, a large proportion of sweated workers were female; apart from the construction industry and dock labour, the select committee would concentrate almost exclusively on women's work, and take evidence concerning 646,880 female workers. The Royal Commission on Labour, established in response to New Unionism, would also request special reports on women workers, and publish three of these in their findings, including Clara Collet's 'Statistics of Employment of Women and Girls'.[18]

When the matchwomen's strike came soon afterwards, the women were therefore both chronologically and geographically well placed to attract maximum attention. The matchwomen would provide journalists and social campaigners of all political persuasions with a convenient personification of the *zeitgeist*, ensuring constant coverage which would spread the news of their strike and its victory.

WORKING-CLASS POLITICS IN THE 'EAST END'

Secondary Accounts

If Annie Besant and the Fabians did not plan or lead the matchworkers' strike, and the workers themselves were solely responsible for their actions, then we must, for the first time, consider the motivations, and the possible intentions, of the true leaders. Even if theirs had been a straightforward strike over pay and conditions, rather than one with a wider political agenda, this would not lessen the importance of the matchwomen's actions or their victory as an example to others. It could still be argued that the matchwomen deserved a far more prominent place in the history books: as Bosio has proposed, 'the history of the working class should not be limited to their history of the leadership of the major unions and parties, but should rather include all their organized and spontaneous forms of expression'.[19] However, from the extremely limited reports we have of their words at the time come hints at a potential degree of politicization which historians have generally ignored, and which runs counter to traditional suppositions about the political apathy of the poorest casual workers.

As will be shown, the matchwomen supposedly recognized Annie Besant from 'socialist platforms', so they must have attended political rallies; indeed, it would be surprising if a fair number had not done so, in the atmosphere of mass demonstrations around socialist and Irish causes that categorized the East End of this period.[20] A note which they later wrote to Besant spoke of an interest in, and desire to attend, more political meetings. This is not to suggest that all, if any, of the matchwomen had necessarily read Marx cover to cover, or at all. However, as Rosa Luxembourg argued, 'activity itself' is an excellent tutor: workers who acted out of frustration at their exploitation were essentially educating themselves politically by so doing. We will see in subsequent chapters that the matchwomen had traditions of militancy which stemmed from, and possibly heightened, their sense of solidarity and of their place in the labour hierarchy.[21]

It is, on reflection, rather surprising that it has never before been seriously considered that the matchwomen – or at least a proportion of them – might have responded to the message of socialism which they had obviously heard. However, that is not the received wisdom. Casually employed, sweated workers like the matchwomen were supposed to be the despair of socialists and trade unionists alike, owing to their 'poverty-induced apathy towards political solutions'.[22] Any political sentiments they did have were meant to be reactionary in nature, and crudely expressed, as evinced by 'occasional, violent displays of support for populist calls for Protectionism, Imperialism and . . . opposition to Jewish immigration'.[23]

Orthodox accounts of politics in the East End after 1848 and before the 1889 dock strike tend to focus in detail on the views of a minority of its inhabitants. The socialist groups which have been so well studied represented only a minority of East Enders, and membership was generally highest among the middle classes and men from the more affluent sections of the working class. By contrast, the politics of the 'casual poor' are portrayed as akin to those of the mob. Pelling, Stedman Jones *et al.* assert that when the working class was in retreat, it would turn to fragmentary sectional interests rather than class unity as a means of defence, supporting them with violence if necessary. This echoes, presumably unintentionally, the arguments of Victorian socialists from outside the working class, comparing to Annie Besant's assertion (*after* the matchworkers' strike) that 'women workers and unskilled labourers' were the 'unorganised mobs' responsible for many of the defeats of the 'disciplined army of unionists'.[24]

On analysis such views are problematic. To Stedman Jones, these men and women were 'ignorant, inarticulate and unorganised', and pre-industrial in their attachment to sectional trade interests, 'unlike the artisans'.[25] One of the bases for this conclusion is the sectionalism of their unions prior to 1889. Leaving aside the contradiction inherent in demonstrating the apoliticization of a group – manifesting partly in a tendency to be ununionized – with a critique of its unions, Stedman Jones' categorization of non-organization as a fault on a par with 'ignorance' ignores the realities of life at the bottom of the labour hierarchy. We need only look at the furious reaction of Bryant and May to their workers' disobedience to understand the reserves of courage, and levels of solidarity, needed to organize from such a disadvantaged position. In addition, as debate on the existence and political implications of the 'labour aristocracy' demonstrates, unions of the 'unskilled' are by no means the only ones open to charges of sectionalism prior to 'New Unionism'.

Stedman Jones' arguments for both the innate conservatism and violence of the politics of the poorest 'casuals' in East London are also open to question. He has interpreted the events of February 1886 as evidence of willingness to 'resort to riot', and of support for right-wing causes, on the part of this group. He also exposes their political inconsistency, if not stupidity, in immediately abandoning the first demonstration to march with the socialists as John Burns and his party came along waving the red flag,[26] like children helplessly following the Pied Piper.

In fact, as Marc Brodie's research has demonstrated, contemporary accounts show that the crowd supposedly supporting the Trafalgar Square speakers on trade protectionism were by no means united in doing so. The 'London United Workingmen's Association', which was putting the case was in fact a bogus 'front' organization, working in conjunction with employers' groups; but even with the probable element of staging which could be expected in such circumstances, their audience was by no means wholly receptive to their arguments.

Stedman Jones has the crowd mindlessly agreeing with the free traders one minute, and 'riot[ing] the very same afternoon under the banner of socialist revolution'.[27] However, both *The Times* and the *Daily News* reported that even before the SDF came on the scene with its counter-demonstration, the listeners had been quite able to state their own contradictory political views, expressing 'a great mixture of opinion', and strongly opposing attempts to agitate them through nationalist sentiments: 'any allusion to ... the subject of emigration met with an unmistakably impatient hearing' from the genuinely unemployed workers present.[28] One speaker, a former Conservative candidate, met with such a hostile reception that he was unable to speak. If those present were really representative of what Gidley calls the 'lumpen masses' and 'roughs', this does not support one of the key assumptions about that group's politics, that they were easily swayed by such popularism.[29]

Brodie further questions the numbers and status of those actively engaged in rioting, which Stedman Jones proffers as demonstrating the lack of proper pre-revolutionary socialist discipline.[30] Given that Annie Besant and John Burns were part of a group who made repeated attempts to forcibly break through a police cordon on 'Bloody Sunday' later that year, it seems that some definition is required of acceptable behaviour on such occasions, and whether or not this depends on the class or celebrity of those engaged in it.

Brodie also challenges Stedman Jones' conclusions about the Conservatism of the East End poor based on electoral information, citing Garrard's findings on the below-average levels of voter registration in the area.[31] Stedman Jones cited inner constituencies which were dominated, though not completely monopolized, by Conservatives. The constituencies which surrounded this inner core, however, had a quite different political history, showing variations in electoral victors or, as with Poplar and Whitechapel, remaining solidly Liberal. Furthermore, Conservative victories frequently relied upon the turnout of a limited but very stable vote, but Liberals had to mobilize an innately 'progressive' electorate which often abstained from voting at all.[32] Brodie argues that it was the more affluent sections of the working classes, and not the 'casual' poor, who were more likely to vote Tory. These more 'respectable' men were also the most likely to have and to exercise the franchise.

'DREAMERS OF THE MOST ROMANTIC DREAMS': POLITICS AND THE WORKING CLASS

Recollections of Working-Class Socialists

We have, as yet, only limited proof of the politics of the matchwomen themselves. However, first-hand accounts from other working-class men and women of the time can help us to a greater understanding. A self-produced typed manuscript, never published, of the recollections of working-class socialists of their childhoods in London, casts an alternative light on perceptions of political apathy among the poor. Hymie Fagan, a key activist in the British Communist Party in the 1940s and 1950s, recorded their memories for this little-known collection, which includes his own recollections. Though the men and women interviewed were born after the matchwomen's strike, some offer insight into the political views of their parents and their peers, who would presumably have been of, or close to, the matchwomen's generation. They also include insights into the politicizing effects of Irish heritage, also relevant to the matchwomen, as will be thoroughly examined in Chapter Eight.

Minnie Bowls, born in 1903, was the granddaughter of an East End docker, and grew up in relative poverty. Her father was an active socialist, and she remembered going with him to socialist meetings on Sunday mornings, becoming a reader of Robert Blatchford's left-wing weekly the *Clarion*, and later the *Daily Herald*, and joining the Clarion Cycling Club.[33] Her father's beliefs, she recalls, were reinforced by his own reading, and enthusiastically passed on to his children: 'He began to read to us when we went to bed – Blatchford's *Merrie England*,[34] Bellamy's *Looking Backward* . . . etc. – and when mother called up to him to let us get to sleep I remember his reply that "What I'm telling these children will do them as much good as sleep."'[35] He would take the entire family on 'Sunday jaunts to the Oval' [where socialist meetings were held].[36] Her father's socialism deepened as he read ever more widely and gave himself the education that the school system had not. His eyes were opened to social injustice on many levels: Bowls remembered that 'one of the main points of his indignation was the unequal position [of women] in society. So from this time on all the children had to have Ellis, my mother's maiden name, in their names.' She recalled her father's gift for communicating his ideas:

> . . . later on when there were four or five of us, our Sunday morning outing became a discovery of London. He showed us all the beautiful buildings, art galleries, cathedrals etc., and on the way home . . . he would point to the working class hovels and say, 'Never forget. The men who built those palaces I showed you this morning, themselves live in these tumble-down slums.' We never forgot – we all joined the Communist Party.[37]

Bowls later went to work in Crosse and Blackwell's factory, and felt the equal of anyone because she was 'Mr Bowls' daughter'. Her father had instilled confidence and a sense of pride in themselves in his children, and Minnie was emboldened rather than intimidated by the fact that her mother had been in service in the house of the owner, Mr Bell: 'I expect my mum had made his bed and dusted his sideboard.'[38]

John Gibbons was initially politicized by his upbringing in Ireland, recalling the bones of famine victims 'still piled high in our time' (the beginning of the twentieth century) within the walls of nearby Burrishole Abbey, where Father Manus Sweeney, hanged for his part in the 1789 rebellion, were buried. His grandmother never forgave a local family who had been involved with the 'crowbar squads' who accompanied the RUC in the 1880s, de-roofing farm cottages and evicting the residents. His evenings were spent with his family 'reciting and singing ... old Irish ballads and telling the fireside chronicles of Erin's wrongs all the way from the Elizabethan, Cromwellian and William of Orange plantations to the 1798 Boys of Wexford and to the hanging and beheading of that most romantic of all Irish patriots, Robert Emmett'. Emmett was hung, drawn and quartered in Dublin in 1803, for leading an uprising against the English. His famous speech from the dock, although made some hundred years earlier, was, said Gibbons, 'in my time ... and much to my delight, always recited during the fireside gatherings. It ended with the unforgettable words: "When my country takes her place among the nations of the earth, then, and not till then, let my epitaph be written." This, then, was the heady romantic brew which we schoolboys ... imbibed day by day ... Given this atmosphere, how could we not be dreamers of the most romantic dreams. We found ourselves envying Emmett and the men of '98 who had ... the good fortune to ... fight for and go to the scaffold for their country's cause.'[39]

Hymie Fagan himself remembered the excitement that general elections brought, and marching round the East End streets 'singing election songs for Liberal candidates'.[40]

Examples from the autobiographical collections of Rose, Vincent and Burnett also confirm that even the poorest members of the working class were, despite numerous obstacles, passionately interested in education and 'self-improvement', that great 'Victorian working-class ethic' – and not, as Stedman Jones argues, completely cut off from the wider world by 'their poverty, their hours of work, their physical exhaustion, and their lack of education'.[41]

Rose cites the example of Mary Smith, the daughter of a shoemaker, born in 1822, who read widely, including the work of Pope and Shakespeare, going on to campaign for suffrage and write on politics for local newspapers.[42] F. W. Jowett, later a pioneer of the Labour Party, read widely as a millworker. Robert Blatchford, whose tract *Merrie England* sold two million copies in Britain, including one to Minnie Bowls' family, was himself the son of an impoverished dressmaker. He grew up reading Dickens and the Brontës, and was convinced the working classes could be politicized by the classics. Rose's findings show that working-class readers were well able to 'read between the lines' of the most Conservative reading-matter, finding something to enjoy and relate to rather than being blindly influenced by their author's politics. While Walter Scott was attacked by radical papers for his Conservatism in the early nineteenth century, still his working-class readers were able to detect or infer subversive elements: socialist activist Walter Hampson decided that Rebecca in *Ivanhoe* was in fact voicing a 'satire on chivalry', and A. Jackson of the Communist Party thought Scott was 'a shocking old Tory . . . [but] . . . No radical could be more unsparing than he of the mere "aristocrat"'.[43]

Despite their many competing responsibilities, which lead to their attendance at school suffering more than that of their male peers, poor working-class girls were equally fascinated by learning: '"Slum girls" were frequently ordered to get their noses out of books and attend to their chores.'[44]

THE STREETS WERE ALL ALIVE – EAST END LIFE AND COMMUNITY

There is, of course, no such thing as a 'typical' East End life or childhood. However, the recollections of people who could have been the matchwomen's friends, neighbours or relatives help to provide context, and throw some light on the makings of the matchwomen's famous solidarity. They can help us to establish whether the women and dock workers, who lived in the same areas, would have been likely to know each other well enough to have identified with each other and keep up with developments in each other's lives and work, or whether, as Hunt believes, the matchwomen were 'too unlike' workers such as the dockers to have influenced them.[45]

Arthur Harding was born in 1886, and his mother made matchboxes for Bryant and May, among other jobs. His account of his life gives us some idea of the conditions faced by these workers, many of whom would have alternated between factory and homework, and have been the friends and relatives of the 1888 strikers; boxmakers would later support the strikers with donations out of their own pitiful wages, showing how closely they identified with the factory workers:

> Our home in Keeve's Buildings was very crowded. The floor being the drying ground for the matchboxes, there was no room to move about. The matchboxes had to be spread out to dry and you couldn't afford to tread on them. I used to be put in a box outside the door or sent out into the street with my sister Mighty. My mother monopolized the table with the paste for the matchboxes . . . there was no room for you inside . . . Immediately you got home from school at four o'clock you were naturally a wee bit hungry. But mother would be busy at the table, and the floor was covered with matchboxes . . . directly I got in she would say 'Get out'. Sometimes she would chuck me something to eat – she would give me perhaps two slices of bread and put it on a saucer and . . . I'd eat it on the street.[46]

In this way the pressure of parents' work meant that East End life was especially communal and sociable for the children. 'Indoors' often meant 'no amusements . . . no books and no games, nor any place to play the games should they exist . . . wet holidays mean quarrelling and mischief and distracted mothers'.[47] The appeal of the streets outside was therefore strong, and many children virtually lived there, using home 'merely as a base'.[48] East End children played together 'on landings, stairs and balconies, in hallways and passages' in their tenement blocks. The streets themselves offered numerous excitements: 'mud-pies, wells, bricks, lamp posts to which ropes could be attached as temporary swings'. Carts and toboggans were made from soap boxes, and these served a practical purpose too: for girls especially, play had to be fitted around caring for younger siblings, and little ones could be both contained and transported about in these home-made conveyances.[49]

From the 1860s, social reformers like Octavia Hill campaigned for more open spaces for children to play in. Temple gardens were opened for children for a few hours every day in 1870s, as were some churchyards: swings were erected in 'Itchy Park', the old graveyard of Spitalfield's Christchurch. Those who lived some distance from these open spaces would travel a long way to, for example, Victoria Park in Hackney, where there were bandstands, lakes and open-air speakers – including political and socialist speakers. It was a two-mile trek from Whitechapel but many children recalled making the trip, either hiring carts and prams for the youngest or again employing the home-made variety.[50]

Early bedtimes might suit parents who had to be up in the early hours for work, as well as increasingly being part of 'respectable' culture, but in many neighbourhoods children had freer rein and went to bed late. Bedtime might be 'when the public houses close . . . the hours before that are the liveliest of the twenty-four, and they swarm about undisturbed until then'.[51] Children would be fetching beer to take home until late: 11 p.m. was not an unusual bedtime, according to evidence given to the Committee on Children's Employment in 1902.[52] Saturday was often the latest night for Whitechapel children, because of their own casual work in the late markets, and even visits to the music hall. The middle classes looked on with disapproval, and worried about the risk of 'racial degeneration' from lack of sleep.

In reality, in overcrowded homes an early bedtime did not necessarily guarantee much sleep, with the coughing of the sick, the noise of mothers working through the night, babies crying, and outside the noise of 'wife-beatings, the return home of drunken men and women . . . midnight flittings, and the incessant barking of a number of dogs chained up'.[53]

Shared beds caused more restlessness; and the other inhabitants were not only human. Several East End accounts recall sleep lost to the biting of bed bugs, and also the black beetles which were the constant companions of poor East Enders: Bill Jones remembered that 'It was a nightly occupation for my brothers and me, awakened by bites, to chase the bastards up the wall.'[54] Matchwoman's granddaughter Joan Harris remembered these same beetles infesting the home of her grandmother Mary Driscoll in Parnham Street near Limehouse Cut,[55] and there are accounts of some Londoners even sleeping outside to escape them as late as the 1920s.[56]

However, oral history accounts make clear that despite material conditions, the East End was not solely a place of bleak despair. For all the horrors of overcrowding, and its inevitably destructive effect on family bonds, many people, even while recalling clearly the privations of their childhoods, also remembered the comfort of close family and community ties. Several remembered that when they first had the opportunity to sleep in a bed on their own, they missed the comfort and warmth of their siblings, and felt lonely.[57] The freedom and independence of the poorest children was actually envied by their middle-class peers: an East End vicar's daughter remembered that after her bedtime, all kinds of fun was being had tantalizingly close by: 'outside the street lamps [were] burning brightly . . . the children yodelling piercingly to each other from one street corner to the next – lucky children who never seemed to have to go to bed'.[58] The vicar's daughter, by contrast, never saw a star until she was five years old, not having previously been allowed out after dark.

Although the average working-class home was not 'conducive to the domestic scenes envisaged in the domestic ideology',[59] middle-class observers could not fail to remark on the confident friendliness of the large troupes of working-class children who made the streets their own, and they concluded – with some surprise – that 'the poor use their children well and . . . this treatment is extended to the children of others'.[60] The fact that this was considered noteworthy speaks volumes about the prevailing wisdom.

So much communal experience gave young East Enders a good knowledge of entire neighbourhoods beyond their immediate streets. They knew large numbers of their inhabitants very well: who could be counted upon to tolerate children's games and high spirits, and who was best avoided. Mothers would try to watch other people's children as well as their own: one East Ender remembered her mother calling out to a neighbourhood child and saving her from an attempted abduction by a stranger. Neighbours would often take each other's children in for a time when new babies arrived. Childminding might be provided by neighbours on a more regular basis – neighbours might in any case often be relatives of some kind. Davin has found that in settled neighbourhoods 'ties of blood or marriage could link almost anyone in the street'.[61]

Bill Jones remembered the community's defiance of authority in the shape of the police, and recalled that there were 'places where the police only patrolled in pairs'.[62] From what he tells us, this seems sensible on their part:

> [Brick Lane] was a wild, and sometimes violent, place in those days. Hardly a Saturday night would pass without a riot call being issued at the Old Street Police Station down the road. [We would see] the lads and lassies just put out of the pubs, laying into the police. Law and order would only be re-established when the number of heads cracked by the police grew too many to bear.[63]

This marked lack of respect for the constabulary was confirmed by Hymie Fagan, who remembered that the police didn't risk solo patrols in Spitalfield either.[64] However, Jones cautions that an element of *braggadocio* could be involved in the building of such fearsome neighbourhood reputations: 'the story that a policeman had his throat cut, and his head placed over a drain . . . to let the blood run out, was probably a tale put around . . . to prove how tough the district was'.[65] The 'probably' may not have been completely reassuring to the local officers, however.

GIRLHOOD AND WOMANHOOD IN THE 'EAST END'

According to contemporary stereotypes, young East End women like the matchworkers should have been either helpless, waif-like drudges, wild 'roughs', or brazen 'factory girls' displaying wanton sexuality. None of these allows for the responsible, competent maturity which both primary accounts and, to an extent, material necessity, suggest must have been prerequisites for young working-class women in the East End and throughout the country at this time.

Childhood ended very early for the poor. It was taken for granted that older children, particularly girls, would care for younger brothers and sisters for much of the day, even if they were scarcely more than infants themselves. As one East End woman recalled, 'I never seemed to have a baby out of my arms after I was six.'[66] They would sometimes take baby siblings to their mothers' workplaces to be suckled in lunch breaks: a district nurse was amazed to witness very young girls carrying 15-lb babies 'for more hours than a strong man would like to hold an equal weight with similar care'.[67] Sometimes neighbours' or relatives' children added to the workload. The Communard refugee Jules Valles noted of London in the 1870s that he saw big sisters 'being mother' everywhere, on doorsteps with babies in arms.[68] However, as Davin points out, the term 'little mother' implies a middle-class interpretation: not all of these girls were taking on a mother's role or preparing for their naturally ordained futures, but merely doing another necessary household chore.[69] Nor was it only a female task: the *Girls' Own Paper* in 1881 published an article on baby care intended for the use of both sexes, using the term 'little nurses' with deliberate inclusiveness.[70]

Such childcare duties were often a cause of absenteeism from school. By 1871, legislation had made it compulsory for children between 5 and 10 to attend school at least half-time, but little provision was made for the young students' smaller siblings: charity-run crèches were few and far between. Children were allowed to be 'half-time' to combine work with schooling, where their wages were seen to be essential to the home: Bryant and May made enthusiastic use of such half-timers during the 1870s and, as we will see in the next chapter, in fact complained that the school board 'refused to give half-time certificates for children who have attended school under ten', when the company thought 8 'a very good age' for working.[71]

Arthur Harding's sister Mighty frequently missed school altogether, between going to and from Bryant and May's factory to collect and drop off matchboxes and materials for her mother, shopping, childcare, washing, and running errands. Inspectors regarded truanting by girls as far less serious, if a problem at all: Miss Hicks, a 'school visitor', concluded in 1890 that boys 'ought never to miss an attendance, unless there is not an elder girl in the family'.[72] Daughters of parents in 'irregular work', for example with fathers seeking employment in the docks, had particularly erratic attendance.[73] If girls could attend at all, it was hard for them to be punctual with all that they had to accomplish before lessons began. They might have to dress and feed several younger children and see them to their own schools. A worker at a Stepney crèche used to watch one little girl set out every morning with 'an infant she was hardly able to carry' in her arms, then, having dropped the baby off, walk a mile or more back to Whitechapel to collect a toddler, who still needed to be carried much of the way to its own school. The crèche worker eventually found the girl an old pram in sympathy.

The school curriculum was limited even for those who were able to get there, and in particular for girls. Religious overtones were strong, even in non-sectarian Board schools,[74] and there was an emphasis on duty and acceptance of one's station in life. Lambeth School in 1896 taught 'minding baby', 'punctuality', 'tidiness', 'how to light a fire', and 'cleanliness in homes'. Girls began their domestic training in infant classes with needlework and knitting drill (boys had been taught needlework too, but from the 1870s drawing was deemed more suitable).[75] Schoolchildren made the transition from unisex 'infants' to 'boys' and 'girls' schools at the age of 6; and some astute observers condemned the way in which 'the little rift between the sexes is extraordinarily widened by simply teaching one set of catchwords to the boys and another to the girls'.[76] This was, however, deliberately done; there is evidence that working-class children were considered insufficiently modest by nature to mix innocently with the opposite sex.[77] Playgrounds were also segregated, and this imposed separation soon did its work in creating peer pressure: 'It was an unwritten law that boys and girls should keep apart, and unless a boy had a sister in the same school he acted on the assumption that girls did not exist. If he displayed any interest in them he was regarded as a "sissy" by his schoolfellows.'[78] Meanwhile, a girl seen walking with a boy was 'not quite nice'.[79] The difference in the syllabus too became more marked after the transition from infants, and only female teachers taught female pupils from this point.[80]

Moral and social control of working-class women was a clear, if tacit, aim of education at this time: George Sims noted approvingly that women in the 1880s who had benefited from compulsory education were 'a race apart' from their older peers, defining this superiority in terms of domestic ideology: 'These young women . . . live in a better way; their room is tidier and cleaner, there is little coquetry in them; and they have a sense of shame which renders them excellent service.'[81]

When science was first introduced to the syllabus in the 1880s, it was for boys alone. However, when a course of experimental science lectures was given to girls in specific schools, girls were shown to be both interested and adept. It was grudgingly admitted that they might find science useful after all – but mostly where it could be applied to their domestic tasks.[82]

Until the 1870s it was common for working-class children to start working at 6 or 7; a parliamentary enquiry in the 1860s found them employed in domestic manufacture and in workshops, street selling, in service, and running 'errands'. Certainly matchwoman Martha Robertson was, her grandchildren relate, working by the age of 6 in 1888, making matchboxes at the Bryant and May factory as well as at home.[83]

Most working-class children would certainly be working in some capacity by 11 or 12, even when there was no pressing financial necessity. Their parents generally regarded this as good training for future life[84] and, as interviews for this book have illustrated, girls and young women seem to have understood and accepted their responsibilities from an early age. In some cases they positively looked forward to the opportunity to help out financially, as well as to the status and independence that 'earning their keep' would bring.[85]

Gender divisions at work were imposed from the outset. Street labour markets in the East End included one for girls and boys from about 9 to 16, where children were hired by the week; girls were hired primarily for childcare, boys for general labour.[86] Daughters leaving school might be expected to stay at home to help with the running of the household before looking for work, and then to pay most of their wages into the family 'kitty'. An alternative to factory work for women was domestic service as nursemaids or maids of all work; but East End or Irish women were, as we have seen, apparently less sought after by employers, so had little prospect of 'good' places in affluent households. Jewish families, and those in more socially mixed districts, were more accepting. In poorer districts, young women might be taken on in lodging houses or pubs if they looked strong enough to be good 'workhorses'.[87] In any event, daughters would usually remain within the bounds of the family economy at least until their own marriage.

To the middle classes, what was most disturbing about the children of the poor was their independence. They failed to be sufficiently 'childlike' according to idealized Victorian notions of childhood: 'Precocity had been an admired quality 50 years before but ... in the prevailing ideology of the nineteenth century precocity and sharpness were unnatural, even dangerous, and a working child, still more an independent one, was a contradiction.'[88] Surveys and investigations into children's labour were carried out by 'those whose own experience and definitions of children were middle-class, whose acquaintance with other views was limited and rarely sympathetic, and who took for granted the superiority of their own ways', and who accordingly saw all child labour as exploitative.[89]

Working-class awareness of this perception increased difficulty in collecting data: a 1902 committee found that 'a 13 year old with an unemployed father reckoned she spent 61 hours a week at housework and making matchboxes with her mother: her parents would only admit to nine'. Girls' work in particular often defied precise categorization, as the line between work and 'chores' was often blurred.[90] Even when not required to attend school or work, girls' domestic duties were immensely time-consuming:

We had the table and on the shelf there was the salt box, the knife box and the boot box. They all had to be scrubbed. Outside the back yard where the sink was – scrub 'em ... The toilet was wood – that had to be scrubbed ... And then you got brick dust and a board and you sprinkle the brick dust on there and you got to do the knives. Knives and the forks and spoons – all had to be done. That was your morning's work.[91]

Charles Booth recorded that all the work done at his own East End lodging house was done by a 13-year-old girl, the 'drudge' for parents who 'drank and never did a thing'.[92]

WOMEN'S NETWORKS AND CULTURE

Gender therefore determined much of the pattern of working-class women's lives from childhood into adulthood, preparing the ground for the female networks and solidarity which would later sustain them when they had families of their own. Mutual aid among numerous poor communities has been well documented, and London was no exception. Poor Law administrators recorded well-established networks of reciprocal favours in the 1870s:

> Indeed . . . what amounts to interchange of charitable assistance among the poor in London is not uncommon . . . they assist each other to an extent which is little understood . . . It is scarcely possible to conceive a form of charity which combines so completely its highest reciprocal benefits, with the absence of mischief so frequently incident to almsgiving. As long as one person has anything to share, they are willing to share it. Hungry children given meals, simple and rough as it may be, but the starving can always secure help from their neighbours in distress, for the poorest never know when their turn to starve may not come.[93]

As mothers, 'women's dual role as financial manager and moral guide cannot be underestimated. She acted within tight financial and social constraints . . . she was . . . limited by her actual physical environment, her home'.[94] In Ratcliffe Dockland women working in a bottle factory organized their own crèche to benefit a workmate serving a six-month jail sentence for fighting, providing two shillings a week so that her two children could be cared for.[95] Women also worked together to defend one another against male violence: when men arriving home drunk were thought likely to 'attempt to molest'[96] their daughters, their mothers would first try to lock them safely in a room or, if this was not possible, 'pass the girls over the back walls for the neighbours to look after them until the husband had slept it off'.[97] Women could use violence in each other's defence as well. One of the 'best fighters' in Bill Jones' street near Brick Lane was 'a quiet friendly woman who went about her business until a drunken bully . . . provoked her into defencing [sic] some helpless woman in the street'.[98]

Women helped each other in a variety of ways, often with great tact and sensitivity:

> Mother used to say to me, 'Poor Mrs Somebody next door, she's got no food in the house.' So mother used to have a good old nourishing stew, and she used to cook it in a big saucepan with a handle both sides. And I was the one to take it in to Mrs Somebody next door . . . and one day mother never had enough for her neighbour. And four o'clock came and she said do you think you could give me some food? She says, 'The children

have got nothing', and Mother felt so ashamed, she said she would always buy sufficient in future for the person next door. You didn't count the cost, you just did this . . . This is how the poor would help the poor.[99]

In Irish communities, neighbours would commonly contribute money for funeral expenses, if the deceased's kin could not raise sufficient funds themselves. Neighbours loaned money and kitchen utensils, helped orphans to find jobs and lodging, and attended wakes and weddings. Newcomers were given a corner of a room in which to sleep, and were helped in their search for work.[100]

This is not to suggest that the East End was a nirvana of female mutual harmony and altruism. Life could be bleak for women who were, for one reason or another, not on good terms with neighbours: they might be refused help, though their children would usually be assisted regardless. Women could have more dramatic fallings-out too, and as we have seen, physical fights were not uncommon.[101]

CLASS AND GENDER CONSCIOUSNESS

The matchworkers, then, may well have grown up among female solidarity and networks; but is it possible that this had any political implications for their later actions? 'Few things,' in the words of John Foster, 'are more difficult to establish than class consciousness.'[102] However, as more recent debate has shown, one of these 'few things' is *gender* consciousness. As we have seen, much work by feminist historians initially centred on an all-encompassing women's culture; but, it was subsequently argued, an overemphasis on the bonds of womanhood belies the operation of race and class oppression.[103] We have seen that the work of Victorian 'social feminists' like the leaders of the WTUL, who saw gender as an absolute unifying factor, tended to fall at the hurdle of class division, and that whatever their political convictions 'few middle-class white women denied themselves the power derived from their class positions and racial status'.[104] The relationship between Besant and the matchwomen, as the re-examination in Chapter Six will show, was by no means an equal one.

While feminist historiography has demonstrated the importance of gender in the emergence of industrial capitalist relations, serious consideration has only comparatively recently been given to the interplay of gender and class consciousness.[105] Sian Moore's study of women workers in Bradford from 1780 to 1845 has shown that working-class culture and networks remained tenacious in the face of industrialization, merely adapting and finding different forms in the new mills and factories, and that female networks were particularly 'central to industrial communities', both in and out of the workplace.[106] Much oral history work confirms this;[107] the question is whether such ties between women can be seen as feminist consciousness of a kind. Moore cites several studies demonstrating the vital contribution of pre-existing female networks to working-class struggles, where 'women's militancy, informed by sexual segregation within the workplace and the household and community, was the basis for strike action'.[108]

Women's culture has, however, been used to reinforce as well as challenge the sexual *status quo*. In her work on women's collective action in Barcelona, Temma Kaplan used the term 'female consciousness' to conceptualize action centring upon gender rights and social concerns. Kaplan argued that though this was an ultimately conservative force, it could still 'promote a social vision incorporating radical political implications', and could in fact have revolutionary consequences in its politicization of social networks.[109] Ardis Cameron has also demonstrated that close bonds between women have been extremely beneficial in providing a ready-made basis for collective action, helping to maintain solidarity during strikes and ultimately promoting class consciousness.[110]

CONCLUSIONS

As we have seen from contemporary accounts, the matchwomen's solidarity was legendary in the East End, and it was by no means untypical – one of the clichés of the fearsome 'factory girl' was that she travelled in close gangs. The Bryant and May matchwomen's solidarity extended from the workplace to the community, and vice versa: the strike register and my interviews have shown that sisters and mothers were often employed together, and that many of the women were from the same neighbourhoods. We now know too that there was no absolute divide between matchbox-making outworkers and in-factory workers: the two jobs were interchangeable for many women according to their circumstances, adding an extended group of women to this protective circle.

This solidarity was no doubt increased as the women united against the brutality of the foremen, the terrible conditions of their work, and the apparently low esteem in which outsiders generally held them. Interview evidence, which will be presented in Chapter Nine, bears out the strength of the ties between matchwomen and their friends, female relatives and neighbours. Martha Robertson, for example, socialized until the end of her life with women she had worked with at Bryant and May. These kinds of experiences are replicated in working-class accounts from other communities. Whether they can be considered a form of 'gut-reaction' gender and/or class-consciousness is another matter. As Moore writes, women's protest cannot be assumed to always result from class, gender or feminist consciousness.[111] However, traditions of class and gender solidarity can only have benefited the striking matchwomen: the spontaneous downing of tools by virtually the entire workforce in defence of one workmate is something which no amount of political reading could necessarily have induced.

4

Liberals and Lucifers: Bryant and May and Matchmaking

INTRODUCTION

Bryant and May's power and success as a company was a significant factor in the level of fame and influence attained by the matchwomen's victory. In terms of industrial impact, a strike in a match factory is obviously a different proposition from an all-out stoppage on the London docks, through which much of the wealth of the British Empire passed. The latter could quickly affect the national economy, adding considerably to the strikers' bargaining power – and despite the uncompromising stance of the dock company, this would prove to be the case in 1889. The economic importance of the industry involved would seem to strengthen the dock strike's role as the catalyst for New Unionism.

Not only was match production considerably less vital than dock labour, but Bryant and May's was far from the only matchmaking firm in London – or even in Bromley-by-Bow. Bell's, the first match factory to be established in Britain, was in such close proximity that Annie Besant would urge consumers to buy their matches when boycotting Bryant and May. However, the matchworkers had strengths to play to beyond economic 'muscle'. Matchmaking may not have been crucial to the British economy, but the government of the day considered Bryant and May, as exporters as well as producers, so important that it would delay a ban on white phosphorus specifically to protect their interests.

Bryant and May's irresistible rise from Quaker grocers to the powerful and ruthless cartel they had become by 1888 is an interesting one. Their attitude to their workforce and the high esteem in which they were held by the establishment would also prove to be important factors in the strike.

BRYANT AND MAY: HISTORY AND REPUTATION
The Matchwomen v. Bryant and May

At the time of the strike, Bryant and May were at a peak of status and influence. They were a household name, newly registered as a limited company and already producing enormous dividends for their shareholders, many of whom were establishment figures such as clergymen and Liberal MPs. Bryant and May was not just one of many firms turning out an insignificant everyday item. It had become such a key player in both the British domestic and export markets that it could influence government legislation. Its director, Wilberforce Bryant, had obtained an elevated social position by 1888, and was a close associate of leading political figures of the day.

The firm was a huge employer in the East End, and the largest for female 'casual' labour in the area – as were the docks for men. By the time of the strike they had become a large cartel; my research has found that while Bell's, the company Besant proposed as a preferable source of matches, retained their own name, the majority of their business had in fact been absorbed by Bryant and May by 1885.[1]

The matchwomen had also attained their own place in the public conscious-ness. The popular perception of them as waif-like 'little matchgirls' could, as we have seen, be usefully employed to portray them as helpless victims. Accordingly, the conscience of Victorian society could be pricked into feeling the need to help them, without the fear that such innocents would threaten the *status quo* by trying to help themselves; reform could keep the spectre of revolution at bay. Their apparent weakness was therefore a strength, and the press and establishment responded more warmly and protectively to the matchwomen than to the less 'safe'-seeming dockworkers, whose strike provoked initial panic.

Even those sections of the press which disapproved of strike action *per se* did not, generally, attack the women themselves for their action, preferring to accept Bryant and May's line that Besant and her cohorts had manipulated them. The matchwomen were almost always portrayed as victims, be it of Bryant and May, 'the socialists', or economic forces. The women's apparent vulnerability, contrasted with Bryant and May's power and affluence on the one hand or the supposed manipulativeness of the socialists on the other, lent their struggle the fairy-tale quality of an archetypal struggle of good against evil.

This was a gift to an expanding and sensation-hungry press and, beyond Besant's own efforts, guaranteed the women almost constant publicity. Workers in the East End, the rest of London and beyond would have followed the progress of the strike in the newspapers. Contemporary observers have pointed out how well informed East End workers were:

> No statement appears in print about themselves or those they know, without it being quickly passed round to all . . . Many cannot read, but what does that matter? The news is soon read to them in little groups . . .[2]

Bryant and May's benign public image also contributed to the shock caused by the strike. They were a trusted brand, associated with British and imperial confidence, and undoubtedly the country's premier matchmaking company; their products were ubiquitous. Shock at the dichotomy between the company's public image – which as we will see was carefully constructed – and the reality of their workforce's lives, was a further factor in generating publicity.

All of these factors contributed to making their defeat at the hands of women supposedly from the 'lowest strata of society'[3] a significant and galvanizing event for other workers from their community and class.

PHOSPHORUS AND THE EVOLUTION OF THE MATCH

In Victorian homes, principally lit by candles or gaslights and heated by coal fires, matches were essential, and accordingly important to the domestic market. Without them food could not easily be cooked, water heated, or lamps and candles lit. Portable devices to produce a flame had been in use since the Saxons' tinderbox. Marco Polo reported seeing what sound like matches in use in China in the 1200s; but the long evolution of the matches made at Fairfield Road did not begin until the discovery of phosphorus in 1669. In 1680 Irish physicist Robert Boyle made a striking device consisting of a piece of coarse paper coated with phosphorus and a small wooden 'tinder' tipped with sulphur. Small tinderboxes were designed for portability.[4]

In 1805, a French chemist created the ancestor of the modern match, the 'Instantaneous Light Box', introduced to England in 1815. This consisted of a small wooden splint coated with chlorate of potash paste and sugar. The devices were ignited, not entirely safely, by dipping into a bottle of sulphuric acid and asbestos; on withdrawal, they would burst into flame. Some time after this, a London shopkeeper named Heurtner invented the 'Vesuvian match', consisting of a cartridge containing chlorate of potash and sugar and a glass bead of sulphuric acid. In 1827, English chemist John Walker developed the friction match, by coating the end of a stick of wood with a mixture of potassium chloride, gum Arabic, starch, and antimony sulphide. He called these 'Congreves' after William Congreve, inventor of a rocket system used by the British Artillery. While considerably less deadly than the rockets, Congreve matches were a potential fire hazard, having a tendency to scatter blazing fragments from the head, and consequently were banned in France and Germany.

Walker did not patent his invention, and his match was improved upon, renamed the 'Lucifer' and patented by a competitor, Samuel Jones. The first Lucifers carried a warning against inhaling the gases: 'Persons whose lungs are delicate should by no means use Lucifers.'[5] However, the Lucifer was such an apparent improvement on what had gone before that Herbert Spencer deemed it 'the greatest boon to mankind of the 19th century',[6] an impressive claim in an era of progressive invention. Jones' were the first matches to be sold in cardboard boxes of a size and shape not dissimilar to the modern matchbox.

William Smith, in *Morley: Ancient and Modern*, recalled: '... a friend of ours in Leeds tells us that in 1831 he was in Keswick, and was shown a very great curiosity, a box of matches ... The ... price was 2s. 6d.'[7] If Smith's friend was correct, then matches were an expensive item, costing the equivalent of around £6 per box today.[8]

In 1831, French chemist Charles Sauria introduced the modification which would ultimately cost the lives of untold numbers of matchworkers,[9] substituting white phosphorus for sulphide of antimony. This made the matches even easier to strike: they could be readily ignited on any hard surface, eliminating the necessity of carrying around a matchbox with a striking strip. This added to their popularity, as they could easily be shared; servants, for example, could purloin one or two matches from the household stock and take them up to their rooms to light fires and candles, without having to buy a whole expensive box for themselves. This convenience was a definite selling point, as one contemporary source noted: 'Working men, day in, month out, prefer to have a match in hand that will strike anywhere: on their trousers, the nearest lamppost, or even the hand – than one which necessitates the presence of a box.'[10]

Journalist George Augustus Sala recorded that by the 1850s the walls of the typical London lodging-house were 'covered with the marks left by Lucifer-matches rubbed against them for ignition'.[11] However, white (also known as yellow) phosphorus would prove no boon at all to one section of mankind, the matchworkers, due to its toxicity. Even those who did not develop the full-blown symptoms of the horrendous industrial disease the matchwomen called 'phossy jaw' suffered to some degree from working in the poisonous fumes. The grandchildren of East Enders who lived near the factory recall tales of the glowing piles of fluorescent vomit which marked the Bryant and May workers' homeward routes at the end of each shift.[12]

Matchmaking in Britain was centred on London, Gloucester and Birmingham, and Liverpool. The first British match factory was established in Bromley-by-Bow by Charles Bell. It produced a type of phosphorus-tipped 'Lucifer'. There were 25 match factories in Britain by 1897, employing 4,152 people, of whom 2,015 were adult women, and 1,067 girls aged 14 to 18.[13] The industry was dominated by a small number of firms, of which Bryant and May worked steadily to become the principal by the 1880s through the steady acquisition of its rivals.

Because only a small outlay of capital was required to establish a match-making works, and the manufacturing process was relatively simple, there were also a number of small-scale ventures, like Lewis Waite's in Bethnal Green:

> . . . a very small place, employing about six men and eighteen boys. It consists of two small sheds, one a mere lean-to, the other a cart hovel. The latter is, I should say, judging by the eye, about 20 by 11 feet only, with no ventilation whatever. The door is at one end, and the only window close by it. This place serves for both dipping room and drying room, as well as for mixing and heating the sulphur and the phosphorus composition.[14]

BRYANT AND MAY AND 'PHOSSY JAW'

No retelling of the matchwomen's story is ever complete without mention of the horrors of 'phossy jaw' or 'the phoss'. It has become inextricably bound up with the history of the strike and of Bryant and May, and would become a significant factor in damaging Bryant and May's reputation in 1888. This association was something that the company continued to resent for a surprising length of time. Their archives show an extraordinary sensitivity on the subject as recently as 1966, in advance of the first performance of the musical *The Matchgirls*, which contained a song called 'Phosphorus'; Bryant and May wanted all references to the company removed, and their solicitors were finally obliged to tell them that 'we have to realise that phossi [sic] jaw and the strike are part of the industrial history of this country'.[15]

On examination of what was known about 'phossy jaw' at the time of the strike, however, it begins to appear surprising that this could ever have become the case. Phossy jaw should not have become part of the industrial history of Britain at all, given that it was both well known and preventable. The disease had been officially recognized fifty years beforehand, by the Viennese medical profession in 1838, seven years after match manufacture had been established in Vienna.[16] Charles Dickens referred to it as well known in his 1852 article 'The evils of matchmaking' in the journal *Household Words*. John Bristowe, later president of the Medical Society of London, presented a series of reports in 1862 'On phosphorus poisoning in match manufacture' to the Public Health Department of the Privy Council.[17]

Bryant and May also seem to have been aware of the disease: a copy of the relevant issue of Dickens' journal is lodged in the company archives, and the anarchist journal *Freedom* claimed in 1888 that it was the company's practice to conceal rather than prevent it: 'Directly a woman appeared with a swollen face, the foreman ordered her to have her teeth drawn on pain of dismissal. One pregnant woman refused, fearing miscarriage from the shock. She was instantly turned adrift.'[18] The condition was clearly well known in Britain at the time of Bryant and May's establishment, even to very small workshop manufacturers like Lewis Waite's: Waite said that although he had

> worked himself for 17 or 18 years, as a dipper for 10 or 11 years . . . it never caught hold of his teeth. It does of some people. The dipping is the worst part. Never finds the work hurt his people. 'It's not in these places that the harm is done; it is in those great places. They make more in an hour than we do in a day.'[19]

One of Waite's dippers, William Lovell, commented that he could 'see his dress shine in the dark'. However, he had 'had no toothache for seven or eight years', although the inspector noted that he was 'not a healthy looking man'.[20]

Ingestion of just a small amount of white phosphorus caused nausea and vomiting.[21] Those poisoned initially fluoresced.[22] The effects of full-blown poisoning were horrific: beginning with toothache and influenza-like symptoms, with some swelling of the face; the pain then spread to the lower jaw, although the upper jawbone could also be affected. The gums and cheeks eventually developed 'putrid abscesses'[23] which produced evil-smelling pus, making it difficult for even loved ones to remain for long in the presence of a sufferer.[24] Disfigurement and sometimes a painful death resulted, with inflammation of the brain resulting in convulsions, and haemorrhaging from the lungs.[25]

The number of deaths which phosphorus poisoning caused are hard to calculate, at least before compulsory notification of such deaths began in 1895; even after this point it seems that Bryant and May, at least, failed to report illness and fatalities. Not all phosphorus-related deaths were in the matchmaking industry, however: phosphorus was widely used in suicides and abortions; of 147 known deaths during the period 1882–92, 92 were suicides.[26] There was a marked decline in fatalities from phosphorus poisoning after 1895, but Barbara Harrison points out that fatality is not necessarily the only, or even best, indicator of the effects of a chemical's toxicity: phosphorus would have produced 'considerable morbidity and disability which ... went unrecorded'.

There had in fact been a safe alternative for decades: the 'safety' match, which had been patented in Sweden in 1855, used red phosphorus. These could only be struck on the special strip on the outside of their box.[27] After the 1888 strike, Bryant and May would protest that they would actually prefer to switch to the manufacture of these matches, but could not do so because of the continuing popularity of the 'Lucifer'. The government repeatedly backed them in this, to the extent of vetoing the Berne Convention banning the use of white phosphorus specifically because of the detrimental effect this might have on Bryant and May's profits.

Fewer than half of the workers involved in match production were likely to have been directly exposed to phosphorus, and because of strict sexual division of labour fewer female than male workers tended to be involved in what was even then regarded as the most dangerous process: 'dipping'. In the workshops, wood was sliced into small pieces, each of which would eventually become two matches. These were heated on an iron plate and dried. A machine then attached these dried 'splits' to frames, which were dipped into the phosphorus paste, then removed from the frames, cut into 'singles', and boxed.

Even with increased mechanization, 'dipping' still tended to be done by hand. 'Dippers' were usually male, and frame-workers, boxers and 'cutters-down' usually female; but as Barbara Harrison writes, 'the effects [of phosphorus fumes] were rarely able to be segregated given the structural conditions in most nineteenth-century factory buildings'.[28] In fact, women were disproportionately represented in cases of phosphorus poisoning, according to official figures. Harrison has examined the incidence of cases among male and female matchmakers to explain the preponderance of women sufferers. Dental health was linked to the development of the disease, as the poisonous particles could enter the system through carious holes in the teeth; and Bryant and May's dentist had recorded that 'the older females have the worst teeth', which was apparently 'typical of lower-class East End women'.[29] He was also aware that the women, in particular, went to great lengths to hide symptoms of toothache even from the dentists, partly from fear of dental treatment itself, but mainly because they knew toothache meant immediate dismissal.

Nor were 'cutting down' and boxing as benign as they sounded. One of the first female factory inspectors recalled

the awkward scramble of arms and hands of a crowd of girls working at feverish speed to cram the handful of matches into boxes which, when overfull, flared up and were cast upon the floor, the fumes and smoke rising into one's nostrils.[30]

The boxes themselves were generally made by homeworkers, the lowest in the matchmaking hierarchy. As Davin notes:

> Disregard of the convenience or needs of the homeworker was an integral part of the way in which the exploitative relationship was maintained. She always had to be reminded of her individual insignificance to recognize that it was a favour to be given the work which so many sought, to be fearful of giving offence.[31]

Homeworkers were supposed to be invisible. At his tailors, the diarist A. J. Munby noticed at his tailor that the homeworking women returning finished garments such as trousers had to slink away when customers appeared, as if unfit for respectable eyes. He witnessed one tailor keeping a woman waiting while he discussed a new suit with a client – completely forgetting her presence. He finally noticed her 'still standing there, on the mat by the door, meek and silent, holding the bundle in her thin arms. "You had better go," said the young tailor in his lordly but not unkind way.'[32]

Many East End families were engaged in box-making in their own homes for Bryant and May, which was space-consuming and miserably paid work. In his evidence to the Factory Commission, Wilberforce Bryant would claim that a woman working at home could earn 10 to 12 shillings a week; he became rather evasive when asked how many hours' work a day this would entail, however, finally settling on 'not more than 10', which he would have known was the maximum the law allowed.[33] However, Emilia Dilke of the Women's Trade Union League (WTUL) found evidence of average earnings as low as 7 shillings for an 84-hour week.[34] Home matchbox-makers were, however, at least safe from phosphorus necrosis.

The 1864 Factory Act singled out matchmaking as a dangerous trade because of the disease, and banned the eating of meals in workrooms; by the 1870s the Chief Factory Inspector believed that 'necrosis has entirely ceased',[35] presumably because of under-reporting and concealment by employers. Bryant and May's case shows that little precaution was being taken against the disease. Testimony from women factory inspectors in the late nineteenth century describes sufferers who were living as social outcasts due to the odour and disfigurements:

> In a certain town I dug out cases of men and women, hidden away in the slums – piteous cases they were. One woman had completely lost her lower jaw; a young girl at earlier stages was constantly in great pain while her suppurating jawbone was gradually decaying.[36]

The 1895 Factory Act made it a requirement that every case of phosphorus poisoning be immediately notified to the Factory Inspectorate, and also to the certifying surgeon. In 1898 a government report backed Bryant and May's refusal to abandon white phosphorus, on the basis that a ban on 'strike-anywhere' matches would only lead to an increase in imports of foreign matches.

In 1891, the Salvation Army opened its own match factory in protest. The 'Darkest England Match Company' was established in Old Ford, East London, close to Bryant and May's Fairfield Works. General William Booth named the company after his 1890 work, *In Darkest England and the Way Out*, in which he outlined his philosophy for the assistance of the 'sinking classes'.[37] Using only red phosphorus, and paying workers twice as much per gross as Bryant and May, the factory was soon producing six million boxes a year.

William Booth organized conducted tours of MPs and journalists around his 'model factory', and also took them to the homes of sweated workers who were working eleven and twelve hours a day producing matchboxes for companies like Bryant and May. However, the matches produced were more expensive than others available, and this and the introduction of substitutes for white phosphorus matches by other match companies meant the 'Darkest England' factory finally had to close in 1901.

THE COMPANY

Francis May and William Bryant were Quakers, like a number of the employers who rose to prominence during the nineteenth century – for example, the founders of Clark's, Rowntree's, Lloyd's and Cadbury's. British law from the seventeenth century onwards restricted the professions which Quakers could enter, excluding the military, clergy, medicine and the law, and making business one of the few acceptable alternatives for middle-class Quaker families. Quaker businesses' reputations for fairness towards both customers and workers had undoubted commercial benefits. Confectionary heir Adrian Cadbury said in 2000 that Quakers had been so successful in trade 'because they were trusted . . . [Cadbury's] . . . were the first shopkeepers to put the price on their goods at which they intended to sell it. This was regarded as extremely unfair commercial practice by our competitors.'[38]

It remains a source of some discomfort to the Society of Friends that Bryant and May, a firm with Quakers at its helm, should have become by-words for exploitation.[39]

William Bryant was the son of a starch- and polish-maker from Devon. He and May, a tea dealer, set up in business as general merchants in 1839. Originally they imported matches from Carl and Johan Lundstrom's match factory in Sweden, but when Lundstrom's became unable to meet the growing British demand for safety matches, May took out a British patent in 1855 on a design based on Lundstrom's specification.

In 1861 Bryant and May leased the Fairfield Works at Bow, which was not purpose-built but consisted of three former factories, including a crinoline manufacturers' and one used by the British Sperm Candle Company. Initially the company continued to use splints imported from Sweden, and also continued to import and distribute some of Lundstrom's matches until 1902. The 'Fairfield Works' was divided into three different buildings: the centre and top workshops, the Victoria factory, and the Wax and Box Stores and Patents. Including homeworkers and workers at other locations in East London, an 1876 visitor recorded that Bryant and May employed around 5,000 people in total, making them a significant East End employer.[40]

Early reports of life inside the factory appear to indicate a reasonably happy workforce, with the caveat that such reports inevitably emanate from 'establishment' figures – either government commissioners or middle-class journalists – and not from the workers themselves. Inspectors from the Children's Employment Commission, who visited Bryant and May shortly after their leasing of the works, appear to have talked to some of the workers in passing, and apparently found no evidence of health hazards; indeed, white phosphorus matches do not seem to have been used in production there at all, although this may have been because the factory was not fully completed:

> These are spacious, airy works, with much open ground all round . . . There is nothing unpleasant or objectionable here. The manufacture carried on here differs from that at other places inasmuch as no common phosphorus or other offensive ingredient is used . . . The works, too, are only just established, and only partially completed. All the processes, with the exception of mixing the composition and drying the materials when dipped . . . are conducted in a long shed-like building, cut into compartments by wire caging. When a larger portion of the building is ready, the boys will work in a part cut off from the girls by a party wall, and separate closets and washing places are being provided for each . . . Along the wall are pegs, each with a number on it, on which the children and others hang their bonnets, coats, etc . . . Altogether this seems a very nicely conducted place. The children appear very happy and contented, and seem without exception much to prefer their employment here to that in other Lucifer manufactories, in which most of them seem to have been engaged more or less before. They give various reasons, mostly that this work is 'not so nasty', 'has no steam', or that they can earn more or are better treated here.

It is also notable that meal breaks, taken away from the workrooms, were provided, at least at lunchtime: 'Just as I arrived, one o'clock, a bell rang, and the children rushed out as if from school; I was there when they returned at two.'[41]

This account strongly contradicts Annie Besant's reports of conditions endured by the matchwomen 20 years later; yet the firm was still in family hands in 1888. These disparate accounts appear hard to reconcile. This is not a matter which has been remarked upon by previous commentators, but it is an important one; if the workers really *were* more reasonably treated than Besant had stated, this would add weight to the idea of a strike which was forced upon them from the outside to satisfy middle-class political ambitions, rather than one generated by the workers themselves in response to genuine exploitation. Having studied the company's history, I believe the latter explanation provides an answer.

While Francis May was apparently a 'mild-mannered and kindly' man, Bryant and, in particular, his four sons, Wilberforce, Arthur, Frederick and Theodore, were far more 'forceful and determined' characters.[42] Once Bryant had persuaded May to allow his sons to become involved in the business, the formidable Bryant faction had little difficulty in gradually sidelining May. When William Bryant died in 1874, the eldest of his four sons, Wilberforce, took over the directorship. In discussions with the Society of Friends I have discovered that their researchers regard William Bryant's death as the point at which the firm veered sharply away from liberal business practices: 'William Bryant's sons ... did not follow their father's Quakerly concerns ... Francis May ... was sidelined.'[43] Two of the brothers, probably Wilberforce and Frederick, who would become the main players in the firm, appear to have rejected the Quaker religion and converted to Anglicanism. Their motivations are unknown, but it is possible that this could have been something of a good 'career move' at a time when Quakers still suffered from discrimination and were excluded from the inner circles of the British establishment.[44]

By 1884 Arthur had died, but Wilberforce, Frederick and Theodore remained in senior positions and, with £300,000 capital, set the business up as a limited company in the same year.[45] Had they not done so, they might never have come to the attention of Besant and her 'comrades'. It was the massive shareholder dividends which first brought them to socialist notice, and not simply the poor treatment of their workers, although it will be shown that this mistreatment had been well known in the area for many years.

Local firms Pace and Sons and J. S. Hunt were now absorbed into the new company, and Wilberforce and Frederick established as chairman and managing director respectively. Under the brothers' stewardship, the company would become ruthlessly competitive, and both economically and politically powerful. They increased the output of the factory by installing new machinery, and began to pay close attention to the company's public image, investing heavily in advertising and assiduously courting the press.

The firm expanded widely throughout the next few decades, taking over numerous smaller matchmaking concerns, enabling it to force down wages and maximize profits. By 1876 Bryant and May was the largest British employer of matchworkers.[46]

Records in the company archives show that Bryant and May made inroads in the American market from 1883. In 1885, they took over Bell's matches and its four factories. Increased output enabled them to make forays into the Indian, Australian and Far Eastern markets. By 1888, they had become so dominant that they were able to pay wages which were lower than they had been a full 12 years earlier; as Besant would report:

> [they] have ... aimed at a monopoly which would enable them to trample on their workpeople unchecked. They have ... succeeded in gradually lowering wages, until a woman, fifteen years in the trade, who used to earn from 16s. to 20s. a week, took on her last pay 5s.6d.[47]

The effects of this were palpable: Besant saw that the older women, who had been earning better wages while growing physically, were in much better condition than the young girls on poverty wages in 1888.[48] Bryant and May claimed to be paying 10 to 12 shillings a week to 'steady' workers in 1876, but the 1888 strike register shows many workers earning 4 shillings (equating to around £12 today)[49] or even less. The highest paid workers, according to Besant regarded with awe by the others, were four women earning 13 shillings a week.[50] A skilled male manual worker at this time could expect to earn on average around 40 shillings a week.

By this means Bryant and May were able to make the price of their matches, as William Morris noted in the *Commonweal*, 'so cheap that the public buy twice as many as they want and waste half',[51] in contrast to match prices in earlier years. A catalogue from 1896 shows the company producing numerous different types of match under the Bryant and May brand, including the patriotically named 'Crown' and 'Victoria'.[52]

The company exercised rigorous control over their workers' behaviour as well as their wages, through the system of fines imposed by the male foremen. Workers had to pay for faulty work and were forced to reimburse the company for accidental 'burnts', matches that had caught fire during the production process.

By the 1880s, Wilberforce Bryant had attained significant social status as well as a personal fortune. In 1887 he purchased the vast Stoke Park estate as his private residence, and spent thousands of pounds improving it. He entertained extensively there, with prominent members of the Liberal Party, with whom the company was at pains to build strong ties, among the guests. Bryant would eventually be invested as Sheriff of Buckinghamshire.[53] Bryant's status and connections were significant factors in the strike: papers like the *East London Advertiser*, owned by businessmen, would prove simply unable to comprehend that 'gentlemen' industrialists would knowingly have exploited their workforce, even when reluctantly forced to accept that justice was on the workers' side.[54]

By the time of the strike, then, Bryant and May might have felt themselves virtually unassailable, with what Besant would call their 'monster profits', and the protection of friends in high places. Such was their confidence that they had been flouting factory legislation in at least two respects for many years, as we will see.

Certainly their first response to Besant's opening volleys in her exposé 'White slavery in London' would be aggressively confident and choleric, as will be discussed in a following chapter; Bryant appeared to be infuriated that Besant should have the temerity to attempt to challenge him, rather than troubled by the challenge itself. The firm immediately threatened Besant with libel action, and actively courted publicity, although they must have known very well that her assertions were substantially correct. They perhaps assumed that, if legal threats did not silence Besant immediately, their tight control of their workforce and the economic situation in the East End meant that Besant's 'witnesses' could be prevailed upon to deny her. Her article could then be dismissed as no more than politically motivated troublemaking. Here the company made a drastic miscalculation, underestimating Besant and, crucially, their workers.

Their overconfidence is perhaps understandable; they had worked hard and successfully in wooing journalists and social commentators to establish a strong reputation as good and caring employers, no doubt trading on the residual trust inspired by the first Bryant and Francis May's more liberal business practices.

In 1876, the writer W. Glenny Crory was gathering material for his *East London Industries*, and the company made the most of the opportunity to be favourably presented. Crory was escorted around the factory by Bryant himself, and by the end of his visit had been strongly convinced that rumours of the firm's oppression of its 'labourers'[55] were false. Without speaking to any of the 'labourers' himself, Crory wrote: 'probably few of the calumnies afloat in East London are more baseless than this one'. In fact, said Crory, Bryant and May were 'real benefactors' to the community, where 'employment of women and girls, at once wholesome and remunerative, is a desideratum'. As to dangers to health. 'There is . . . so small a quantity of phosphorus, even in common matches, that there is not the slightest danger to health in working any of the processes of manufacture . . .'[56]

It is interesting to note that, even in an area hardened to labour exploitation, there was discontent about the treatment of the matchworkers by Bryant and May twelve years before Besant and the Fabian Society decided to boycott them.

However, the working poor of the East End had little or no influence over the establishment, which continued to favour Bryant and May. The company was given official endorsement as a 'model' employer for others to emulate by the 1876 Factory Commission. While it is impossible to know whether Wilberforce Bryant's public relations efforts and growing political power had any influence over the commission, the verbatim transcription of his evidence undeniably shows that he was treated with extreme courtesy and leniency. It also reveals an employer with, to modern eyes, astonishingly little concern for his workforce, who does not feel any need to disguise that lack of concern. Bryant's expectation that the commission will be in sympathy with him and his interests as an employer, is manifest in his decision to use his appearance as an opportunity to protest that legislation is standing in the way of what might have been considered the fullest exploitation of his workers, rather than to cover up that exploitation.

Bryant begins his testimony by stating that he is unhappy about the operation of the 'half-time system', under which he has been legally obliged to allow his child labourers to attend school: 'the School Board insist upon their own half-time rules as against those of the Factory Act, enabling us to employ children above eight, and the School Board refuse to give half-time certificates for children who have attended school under ten'.[57] He complains that the School Board have brought prosecutions, not against the company but against some of his employees' parents, which have made them 'so frightened . . . they would not run the risk of allowing their children to work'.[58] Bryant says that he thinks eight is 'a very good age' for children to start working in the factory, because 'it is not work that these children do, it is play for a considerable time; it is simply learning from the experienced hands; just helping them, and seeing how it is done'.

The chairman, Sir James Fergusson, demonstrates the commission's favourable view of Bryant and May during his extremely gentle questioning about phosphorus poisoning: 'With regard to the sanitary question, of course your works have been mentioned as being in a particularly good state in that respect, as you have always taken measures to prevent the peculiar bad consequences that come from matchmaking?'[59] Bryant claims that his factory is using greater quantities of chlorate of potash than phosphorus at this time – possibly a disingenuous statement as the Lucifer match, as we have already seen, contained both substances in different proportions.

As to incidences of what the commission calls 'jaw disease', Bryant is either deliberately evasive or indifferent:

> We had one case, I think, of a child, and I think there was one of a young woman, although I forget whether we had two; but they had worked in small places before they came to us; the disease was not contracted in our factories at all.[60]

As phosphorus poisoning could quickly result from exposure, and Bryant and May dismissed those displaying any symptoms, we can assume that they would not have hired workers who already had the disease. It must then have developed after the commencement of employment at Fairfield, so Bryant cannot state with certainty that it was contracted elsewhere.

Bryant's casual attitude to his workforce in appearing not to know the number, or even the ages, of those affected by phosphorus, is borne out later in the proceedings when he is unable to give anything like an exact figure for the number of workers in his employ: he says that he 'does not have the memorandum'[61] and eventually hazards a guess that about a thousand work in the factory, and a further two thousand are homeworkers making matchboxes. It is obvious, however, that Bryant does have thorough knowledge when it comes to the law as it affects his business practices; he knows exactly what his and the School Board's obligations are in regard to child workers. It could therefore be assumed that the illegal fines and lack of meal breaks, which Besant reported in 1888, were knowingly imposed. The same commission to which Bryant gave evidence in 1876 confirmed that 'Lucifer match making' was one profession where 'meals should not be taken by protected persons in rooms where such manufacturing processes are carried out as they are likely to cause injury to the health of those partaking of food therein.'[62]

The factory was certainly an unsafe and unpleasant place to work by 1885, when the first recorded strike over phosphorus necrosis took place; and much earlier into Wilberforce Bryant's directorship according to the local 'rumours' reported by Crory.[63] However, in December 1887, seven months before the successful strike, *Cassell's Saturday Journal* published a feature article on Bryant and May which found no fault with their practices. It seems likely that Wilberforce Bryant had once again given one of his personal tours of the works.

According to *Cassell's* the 'girls' were found to be 'very industrious and remarkably well-behaved' (remarkable only if one was unaware of the dominance of the foremen), and to look generally 'strong and healthy'. The piece is accompanied by a line drawing showing ten robust-looking young women 'cutting down' matches. All appear to be well dressed in smart, unpatched clothes and boots, and sporting fashionable hairstyles. They are in enormous contrast to the seven malnourished-looking young women in the famous 'strike photograph'.

Whoever represented the management's views to *Cassell's* portrayed them as much more sympathetic to their workers than we know was in fact the case. Their journalist saw matches accidentally catching fire: 'Every now and then in different parts of the room are seen a puff of smoke and a flare as a box of matches takes fire in the hands of the packer.'[64] *Cassell's* were told that this was 'an unavoidable occurrence. The burning box is thrown into a receptacle provided for the purpose, and nothing is thought of it.'[65] This reasonable attitude would no doubt have come as a surprise to the packers, who were accustomed to being reprimanded and fined over 'burnts', and is a clear example of Bryant and May's success in manipulating the press and concealing the true state of workplace relations.

Certainly they were powerful enough for Bryant's personal attentions to seem flattering: 'The firm may now be said to be almost without a rival in England. Match factories in various parts of the country have been bought and amalgamated with Messrs Bryant and May, and upon their firm the whole of England and many of the colonies have virtually to rely for their supply of matches.'[66]

Wilberforce Bryant may be assumed to have been the sole interviewee in that he is the only director mentioned in the piece, apart from his late father, who is mentioned as the company 'founder' – in the singular. No mention whatever is made of Francis May, confirming the Society of Friends' view that Bryant deliberately sidelined the Mays.[67] The firm's high-handed confidence would also be evident when Bryant and May dipper Cornelius Lean died from phosphorus necrosis some years later. Lean had been treated appallingly by his foreman, who would not allow the sick man's mother to collect a 'medical order' (authorizing his absence) on his behalf, forcing him to get out of bed and present himself at the company's offices. His death, which came shortly after that of Caroline Hawkins, also a Bryant and May employee, raised questions in the Houses of Parliament, and Home Office proceedings resulted.

During the course of these proceedings it was discovered that Bryant and May had failed to report a 'long list' of cases; at least 17, according to the *Daily Chronicle*'s report of the proceedings, and Lean's death at least was 'not a case where the firm could say that it was through carelessness or inadvertence that they had forgotten to report the case'.[68] Even after Lean's death the firm tried to mislead the factory inspector, claiming that his was the first and only case of phosphorus poisoning which had ever come to their attention.[69] This was overwhelmingly disproved and the firm was fined £25 9s.

By 1888, then, Bryant and May were both extremely important to British trade and, as William Morris noted, 'extremely respectable'.[70] The extended Fairfield Works was, and its façade remains, a vast and imposing structure towering over the neighbourhood. Perhaps their bravado in the face of strike action resulted in part from the high standing which they enjoyed. They continued to escape censure in some sections of the press even after the strike, as William Morris noted in *Commonweal*: 'It is curious to see how the capitalist press have straightaway set their backs up, and set to work to whitewash the . . . firm.'[71]

The *Daily News*, for example, found no fault in the company itself; the matchwomen were seen as simply caught up in the inevitable march of progress:

> These poor people are really the victims, not of any exceptional greed or hard usage of Messrs Bryant and May but of that steady onward rush of the great industrial machine, whose course is directed not by the needs and welfare of those immediately beneath its wheels, but of the community at large for generations to come.[72]

However, not all of the 'capitalist press' was sufficiently behind the company for Wilberforce Bryant's liking, and he would later attack *The Times* for peddling 'lies'.

Bryant and May held out, rejecting the efforts of Besant, criticism in the media, and attempts at negotiation by the London Trades Council, until political pressure was brought to bear; the daily processions of thousands of matchwomen through the street and to parliament, and the resultant publicity, were evidently becoming an embarrassment to august Liberal politicians among their shareholders, who were seeming to be guilty of hypocrisy in espousing liberalism while supporting oppression.[73]

CONCLUSIONS

On first consideration, matchmaking does not appear to be an essential industry in which a major strike could paralyse the country's economy. However, this is not the only indicator of industrial significance. By 1888 Bryant and May were considered Britain's premier matchmakers, and were also considerable exporters, as we have seen.[74]

Given Bryant and May's powerful standing in both the area and the country at large, the local community must have regarded the rebellion of their workers as particularly brave, or even reckless, and awaited the outcome with bated breath; this in turn would have made any victory against such a force all the more noteworthy and celebrated, and therefore more likely to inspire others to action of their own. Added to the women's position within the East End and the London Irish community, and their links to the dock workers, it is argued that this ensured their victory would be a celebrated and influential one. The site of the dispute was significant too: as Harrison has argued, such events in East London at the time 'assumed symbolic importance in the popular and political imagination'.[75]

To outsiders, the possibility that such a rebellion had really taken place at the behest of poor working-class 'casuals', and women to boot, was so far outside the realms of what was expected of them as to be incomprehensible. However, a subtle reworking of events made it possible to believe that the women had been 'made' to come out by others who, though socialists, were at least educated and middle class. In this way the strike could be accommodated within accepted norms of class and gender behaviour. Either Besant or Bryant and May could be cast as the villains of the piece, representing archetypes of the socialist as '*eminence grise*' and '*agent provocateur*', the puppet-master of the easily led poor, or the employer as greedy and ruthless 'fat cat'. In either conception, the matchwomen are the innocent victims of others, and can be cleared of all suspicions of blame and unfeminine behaviour. Indeed, in obeying the instructions of their 'betters' without question the women could be considered to be behaving as poor working-class women should, and even something as active as taking strike action can be re-imagined as passive.

However, the memoirs and oral history work discussed above show that there was far more vibrancy within working-class politics, even among the poorest and supposedly most ignorant workers, than has previously been accepted.

5

The 'Notorious' Annie Besant: The Strike Leaders Reconsidered

INTRODUCTION

This chapter will work towards an understanding of what actually happened in the period before the matchwomen's strike, using contemporary media accounts and the witness of those who were present.

An understanding of the politics of Annie Besant and the Fabian Society is crucial to any reconsideration of events. As we have seen, Besant's 'White slavery in London', was and still is frequently quoted. However, neither this famous article itself, nor the actions and beliefs of its author, have ever been subjected to detailed analysis, nor their compatibility with industrial militancy assessed. Besant's motives in bringing the matchworkers out on strike have neither been questioned, nor even considered. In the great mass of writing on her, I have been unable to find anything beyond an implied connection between her being 'a socialist' and her desire to bring about a strike.

George Bernard Shaw was, according to Sidney Webb, the architect of Fabian policy. A prolific diarist and eyewitness to the strike, it was he who introduced Besant to the Fabian Society. His writing and journals will accordingly be scrutinized, as will those of the Webbs, for evidence relating to the planning and execution of the strike, and to key Fabian attitudes towards strikes among workers like the matchwomen. Besant's life before the strike will also be considered, to demonstrate her status and fame in 1888, important factors in the rewriting of events so that they revolved around her alone.

BACKGROUND TO THE STRIKE

Annie Besant: her Life and Politics

The story of the matchworkers' strike has, for 120 years, principally been told through the accounts, and therefore from the perspective, of the one observer whose name has become inextricably linked to it. Annie Wood Besant was born in the East End of London, within, as she proudly said, 'the sound of Bow Bells'.[1] Though never particularly prosperous, her parents were middle class, educated and intellectual. Besant left the area as a young woman, but returned to it in 1873 on the break-up of her marriage and quickly established herself as a writer, journalist and social activist in a variety of causes, including women's rights and secularism. She would be mentioned in the writing of Engels, Sylvia Pankhurst and George Bernard Shaw, among others.

Besant was already well known in political circles and beyond before her involvement with the matchwomen. In 1885 Edward Pearse, an early member of the Fabian Society, wrote of one of its meetings in London, that it was 'memorable because it was attended by Mrs Annie Besant, then notorious as an advocate of Atheism and Malthusianism, the heroine of several famous law cases'.[2]

Besant's controversial atheism had not been lifelong. In her autobiography she described herself as an ardent, imaginative child, greatly attracted by the dramatic, romantic aspects of religion. Poring over the lives of Christian martyrs, she had lamented having been born in a time when 'no suffering for religion was practicable'.[3] She spent her childhood days in enjoyably grisly daydreams, in which she too was being 'flung to lions and burned at the stake'. She later attested to more prophetic imaginings too, in which she saw herself 'preaching some great new faith to a vast crowd . . . and [becoming] a great religious leader'.[4]

Despite the early death of her much-loved father, Besant's childhood was generally secure and happy, and she had a close and affectionate relationship with her mother which lasted until the latter's death. In spite of this, she was temperamentally at odds with her parents' rejection of religious enthusiasm as 'unbalanced and unbecoming'. Politically, though, she initially shared their 'decorous Whiggism', accepting the belief that 'the poor' should 'be educated, looked after, [and] charitably dealt with', with the politeness that she, as a lady, owed to all.[5]

Besant's journey towards radicalism began when she met William Prowting Roberts, a lawyer and close associate of the Chartist leader Feargus O'Connor. She soon made the first of many swift ideological conversions, towards the more socialist conception that the working classes were 'the working-bees, the wealth producers' who had 'a right to self-rule, not looking after; . . . to justice, not to charity'.[6]

Her induction into Irish affairs came through watching Roberts defend the 'Manchester Martyrs', five Fenian men of whom three were publicly hanged in 1867. This made a deep impression on Besant, who would later declare that 'three quarters of my blood and all of my heart are Irish'.[7]

Also in 1867 Annie became engaged to Frank Besant, a Church of England clergyman, almost by accident. She had innocently spent some time with him on a church mission in the spring, and this had been enough for a young man with rigorously traditional ideas about female behaviour to infer a romantic attachment. Besant reluctantly reconciled herself to the marriage with the idea that she could find opportunities for usefulness and self-sacrifice to the Church as a vicar's wife.[8]

From such inauspicious beginnings began a disastrous marriage. Annie's loving upbringing had not prepared her for any of the duties of conventional Victorian wifedom: sexually innocent, she found the physical side of the relationship a tremendous shock and affront. Perhaps with a more congenial partner her early married life would have been less traumatic, but her incompatibility with her husband on every level quickly became evident. Frank Besant's bewilderment as he unwittingly struggled to make an 'angel in the house' out of one of the least suited women in England for the role, can readily be imagined. As his wife wrote, she was 'accustomed to freedom, indifferent to home details, impulsive, very hot-tempered and proud as Lucifer', in all 'a most undesirable partner to sit in the lady's arm chair on the domestic rug by the fire'.[9] Eventually his frustration led, according to his wife, to violence. The Victorian battle of the sexes was fought in the Besant household for several unhappy years, with Annie staving off her unhappiness in her marriage and the tedium of vicarage life by devoting herself to her two beloved children, a boy and a girl. She also began to go out into the parish, and in doing so witnessed the terrible suffering of poor agricultural workers, at this time struggling to establish their first trade union, which would be led by Joseph Arch, the former plough boy who would become an MP.

Eager for intellectual challenge and companionship, Besant eventually befriended a group of religious freethinkers, and began to write on the subject. To her husband, this was a humiliating betrayal. The inevitable separation came in 1873. Besant had to leave behind her son, at her husband's insistence. This caused her great pain, as would his later successful suit for custody of her daughter. Once they were old enough to choose, both children would return to live with their mother.

Annie became increasingly well known and, to the Besant family, ever more a blot on their name, which she would nonetheless retain to the end of her life. Her brother-in-law was Walter Besant, also well known for his work among the East End poor. He wrote about their lives, and even about the matchwomen; but managed to do so without ever mentioning his sister-in-law's name.

On her separation, Annie moved back to the East End of London, and made her first public speech, on the political status of women.[10] She quickly embraced 'unmitigated atheism',[11] after her first meeting with Charles Bradlaugh, later a Liberal MP,[12] then president of the National Secular Society, and an extremely controversial figure who 'terrified the middle classes'.[13] He had refused to swear the parliamentary traditional oath on the Bible on becoming an MP, which caused a scandal. On the question of the poor, Bradlaugh was strictly reformist, adamantly 'against any form of class struggle', and boasted of having 'crossed swords with Karl Marx' at the time of the Paris commune, writing: 'we do want that the poor shall not increase in misery [but] we do not want a Commune in England'.[14]

AN 'OBSCENE LIBEL'

Besant and Bradlaugh achieved joint notoriety over the affair of the Knowlton Pamphlet. The pair had been working on access to birth control and sex education for working-class women. The whole premise, as well as the deeper motivations, of middle-class intervention into the birth rates of the poor is questionable: this was a time when eugenic theory was finding widespread popularity. However,

Besant's writings do not reveal any conscious agenda beyond the desire to give women exhausted by constant reproduction some control over their own fertility. Her 1893 autobiography rails against the inadvisability of sending women into marriage hampered by sexual ignorance, using her own experience as an example, so it can be inferred that she was acting out of empathy as well.

The controversial pamphlet was written in the 1830s by the American physician Dr Charles Knowlton. Influenced by the theories of Thomas Malthus, the 19th century economist who argued that unchecked population growth would outstrip the world's ability to feed itself, Knowlton published a guide to birth control rejoicing in the title 'The fruits of philosophy; or the private companion of young married people'. It was uncontroversial until a Bristol bookseller evidently decided to try to move a few more copies by adding some salacious drawings.

Besant and Bradlaugh shared a publisher for their own political works, and he had, apparently by chance, bought a stock of the pamphlets for distribution. Held responsible for what was considered an immoral work, the publisher was prosecuted in 1877. The perceived immorality stemmed from the nature of the advice contained within, rather than the supplementary drawings; Besant and Bradlaugh were accordingly dismayed when the publisher pleaded guilty rather than contesting the case. They decided to print some copies of the pamphlet themselves, expecting to be prosecuted and thereby gain the opportunity to debate the right of the poor to limit their families. As Besant stated in her autobiography:

> Our position as regarded the pamphlet was simple and definite; had it been brought to us for publication . . . we should not have published it, for it was not a treatise of high merit; but, prosecuted as immoral because it advised the limitation of the family, it at once embodied the right of publication.[15]

Besant and Bradlaugh printed and prepared to sell the copies themselves, and first resigned their posts at the National Secular Society, so that it would not be affected by any subsequent publicity. They delivered copies to the Chief Clerk of the Magistrates at Guildhall, the City Police Office and the Solicitor for the City of London, and announced the date and time of the proposed sale.

Though deliberately courting attention, Besant was not without trepidation: she understood that her reputation could be ruined by association with an 'obscene' publication. Warrants were issued her and Bradlaugh, and they were arrested on 6 April. In mid-June, the trial commenced before the Lord Chief Justice of England and a special jury, with the defendants representing themselves. The Lord Chief Justice advised acquittal from the outset, calling the prosecution 'ill advised' and the defendants 'two enthusiasts who have been actuated by a desire to do good'.[16] He gave a detailed statement on population control, which can only have been music to Besant's and Bradlaugh's ears.

All present felt the case was already won; however, as Besant said, they had failed to take into account the 'religious and political hatred'[17] against them, encouraged by sections of the media: a leading journalist for *The Times* was in fact a member of the jury. When a verdict was reached, the pamphlet was declared to be 'calculated to deprave public morals', though the defendants were personally exonerated from any 'corrupt motive' in publishing.[18]

In sentencing, the judge attempted to avoid a penalty by asking Besant and Bradlaugh to undertake not to sell the book again; they would not, and were accordingly sentenced to six months' imprisonment and substantial fines.

Thanks to some accomplished legal manoeuvring by Bradlaugh, the verdict was subsequently quashed and no prison time served, but the case had established Besant as a political celebrity. The media had greatly enjoyed the spectacle of an attractive young woman, estranged from a clergyman spouse, on trial for obscenity with a close male friend of scandalous repute; no wonder that the Fabians would be so struck by the attendance of the 'notorious' Mrs Besant at her first Society meeting eight years later.

Besant joined the Fabian Society in 1885. She and George Bernard Shaw began a complicated, somewhat intense and sometimes romantic friendship. Besant was, or so Shaw felt, singularly lacking in the humour on which he prided himself: he, she wrote, was 'one of the most brilliant of Socialist writers and most provoking of men'.[19] Besant's report of one encounter shows the scope for misunderstanding which their different personalities allowed. Shaw described himself to Besant, on their first meeting, as a 'loafer': a humorous acknowledgement that he did not have to resort to gruelling manual labour. Besant took his assessment at face value, however, and 'gave an angry snarl' at him in a piece in the *Reformer*, only to find that in fact

> ... he was very poor, because he was a writer with principles and preferred starving his body to starving his conscience; that he gave time and earnest work to the spreading of Socialism, spending night after night in workmen's clubs.[20]

She apologized, and was self-deprecating enough to recount the tale in her autobiography, but also revealed that she felt 'somewhat injured at having been entrapped into such a blunder'.[21] When Besant's natural earnestness and Shaw's teasing wit collided, some mutual incomprehension was perhaps inevitable.

Besant established political 'halfpenny weekly'[22] the *Link*, with the assistance of fellow journalist and friend W. T. Stead, editor of the *Pall Mall Gazette*, in early 1888. Herbert Burrows would later join Besant at the paper, contributing 'some noble articles' to it, and the pair formed a close association that would eventually lead both back to religion.[23] It was, of course, the *Link* which would expose conditions at the Bryant and May factory, 23 June. The saga began at a Fabian meeting on 15 June, when Clementina Black addressed the group on the subject of female labour and exploitation in the East End. Black suggested the formation of a Consumers' League, whose members would undertake only to buy goods produced without 'sweated' labour. In the discussion which followed, H. H. Champion drew attention to the low wages paid by Bryant and May, and the contrast with the enormous dividends enjoyed by their shareholders.

Champion produced statistics showing the huge increase in share value from £5 each (presumably four years previously when the company was first listed on the stock exchange) to £18 7s. 6d. He then proposed a motion, seconded by Burrows and carried *nem con*, stating that:

> This meeting, being aware that the shareholders of Bryant and May are receiving a dividend of over 20 per cent, and at the same time are paying their workers only 2¼ d. per gross for making match-boxes, pledges itself not to use or purchase any matches made by this firm.[24]

Champion had been the editor of the Social Democratic Federation's paper *Justice*, but was dramatically expelled from the SDF the year before after clashes with H. M. Hyndman. Though he joined the Fabians, Champion was disappointed by the Society's unwillingness to work towards the formation of a working-class party.

In considering Besant's reputation as the leader of the Bryant and May strike, it is instructive to consider Champion's reservations, and what we know about her and her Fabian colleagues' political attitudes, particularly concerning the organization of 'unskilled' female workers.

FABIAN AND SDF POLITICS

Much has been written about Besant's life, in her many and various incarnations as fervent Christian, secularist, atheist, Malthusian, socialist, Theosophist, and advocate of Indian independence; no wonder that one biography of her should have been entitled *The First Five Lives of Annie Besant*.[25] Most biographical writing on Besant is straightforwardly narrative and uncritical; not all contains any reference at all to the matchwomen.[26]

Had the strike indeed been the result of deliberate Fabian machinations, it is likely that the copious writings of Besant, as well as other prominent Fabians like Bernard Shaw and Beatrice Webb, would contain some explanation of their tactics, and indeed some celebration of the strike's success. Were the Fabians some kind of early syndicalists, seeing the strike as a stepping-stone to a general strike and revolution? If so, the match industry would seem a curious place to start. Matches were an important product, but as we have seen there was no overall monopoly in their production and the lack of them would seem unlikely to lead to civil uproar. Perhaps, then, Besant and the Fabians merely hoped to unionize the women: this would have made Bryant and May a better choice of target, as they were a major source of 'casual' employment in the East End. However, detailed study of sources which accept Besant as having lead the strike shows that they offer no evidence, or even speculation, as to her motivation for having done so.

Bryant and May, and papers like *The Times*, certainly promulgated the Besant-led version of events, blaming the socialists, the political 'pests of the modern world',[27] for the strike, but it is hardly to be wondered at that either should prefer this explanation. It is far more surprising that scholars of all political persuasions continue to let it stand unquestioned. Even a relatively cursory study of the political scene in 1888 demonstrates that Besant would have been acting against the grain of the majority of current socialist and labour movement thinking, and therefore taking an enormous risk, if she had in fact brought over a thousand of the poorest casual labourers out on strike that summer. Besant's close association with Charles Bradlaugh had ended in 1884 as she prepared herself for another of the swift ideological *volte faces* which were a feature of her early career. As the Social Democratic Federation's paper *Justice* remarked, 'Mrs Besant feels it necessary to turn Socialist but does not want anyone to tell her so.'[28] Nonetheless, Besant did become a member of the Fabian Society, in 1885 according to her autobiography. (Secondary sources give differing dates for this, and also contradictory accounts of her membership of the SDF: various sources say she was already a member in 1888, or joined in 1889.[29] The Fabian Society's own record of their executive committee shows her as an executive member from 1886 to 1890, so the two memberships must have overlapped.[30] Besant's autobiography mentions her close work with the SDF, but not her formally joining the federation.)

The Fabian Society and the SDF were both founded in 1884, and were among the most important of the various socialist groups established in the 1880s.[31] The Fabian Society was, at least at the outset, closer to a middle-class 'discussion group' than a revolutionary party in the mould of the SDF or the Socialist League.[32] Initially it had no specific policy, but from 1886 to 1887 Sidney and Beatrice Webb and Shaw began to evolve a reformist version of socialism advocating the gradual permeation of the Liberal party and existing political institutions, to effect change through legislative means rather than revolution.

The Society had little interest in trade union activities, and indeed 'discouraged the formation of independent working-class organizations to the point of sabotaging them'.[33] It would continue to draw its membership largely from the educated middle classes.[34] Though its membership was never large, it did include a higher proportion of women than that of the SDF or, later, the ILP.[35]

Among Shaw's prolific writing are some clarifications of the political positions of this architect of Fabian policy. Despite the practical assistance he gave to the matchwomen's strike fund, acting as clerk on at least one occasion, Shaw's views of trade unionism and industrial action are uncompromising: 'Trade Unionism is not Socialism: it is the Capitalism of the Proletariat.'[36] In any case, he wrote, it would be very difficult to organize most workers into united unions: 'they live too far apart', and 'in some callings there are such differences of pay and social position that even if all their members could be brought together they would not mix'.[37] Shaw's views on strikes are somewhat choleric: on a country 'ravaged by strikes and lockouts' he writes:

> Between six and seven hundred battles a year, called trade disputes, are fought; and the number of days of work lost to the nation sometimes totals up to ten million and more. If

the matter were not so serious for us all one could laugh at the silly way in which people talk of the spread of socialism when what is really threatening them is capitalism.[38]

This was not an unusual position for a British socialist of this period: in *The Historical Basis of Socialism* H. M. Hyndman also wrote about strikes as a waste of financial resources.[39] *Justice* would famously rail against the dock strike during its course, with editorials stating that 'a strike is only guerrilla warfare for small results'.[40] This could have been overlooked given the efforts of individual members – Lewis Lyons was much involved in organizing sweated workers – had *Justice* not redoubled its attack once the dock strike was won, asking if 'such a ridiculous mockery of success was worth a month's starving and misery'.[41] 'The point,' as Crick writes, 'is that to observers *Justice* was the official organ and Hyndman the federation's chief spokesman'.[42]

Once the matchworkers' strike had begun, Shaw was personally involved in the distribution of the strike fund, and kept a detailed daily diary during this period. He confirmed his attendance at the Fabian discussion meeting on 6 July, the evening of the day in which the matchworkers had first apprised Besant of their strike, as will be shown. Shaw records that the theme of the meeting was 'Prospects of Art under Socialism', and makes no mention of the matchwomen in this entry. Indeed he makes no reference to them until 14 July, so it does not appear that the strike was an all-consuming issue for the Fabians. It is likely that Shaw would have recorded it if it were, as his diaries were a very thorough record of his daily activities – however mundane, as these entries for days when the strike was taking place demonstrate:

7th July

Whilst I was at breakfast Mrs Adams the charwoman fell on the steps and broke or badly bruised her rib. I had to take her to hospital and thence to her house in cabs . . . the events of the morning put me out of sorts.[43]

8th July

. . . When I got home I took a big tea.
Ginger Beer 2d
Bread and Cheese 10d[44]

Shaw does give an insight into how the strike fund register was compiled on 14 and 21 July, at Charrington's Hall:

14th July

Meet Mrs Besant and Bland [presumably Hubert Bland of the Fabian Society] at Cannon Street Station to bring down the strike money to the Bryant and May girls. Found Bland waiting at Cannon Street. Headlam [Rev Stewart Headlam, later of the Fabian Executive Committee] and Mrs Besant came in a cab and picked us up. We went to Charrington's Hall in the Mile End Rd., where we found Oliver and Hobart of the [Social Democratic] Federation. The girls came in at noon and the work lasted until past 15 [Shaw's rather individual way of noting time, using the 24-hour clock] . . . Charlotte Roche[45] . . . took some photographs. I went as far as the Temple with her on the way back and got out there with Bland and Mrs Besant. We went into Fleet Street to wash our hands.[46]

The next reference to the strike is on 16 July:

Wrote to Beale, the Liberal candidate, about the Bryant and May business . . .

The strike fund was again distributed on the 21st:

Call at 63 Fleet Street at 13 to bring the strike money down to the Charrington Hall with Mrs Besant. Payment to begin at 14 and-a-half. Mrs Besant and I found Burrows, Massingham [*probably H. W. Massingham, the assistant editor of the* Star, *who would be appointed to the Fabian Executive in 1891*]. W. Clarke was waiting for us besides Wallas [*Clarke and Wallas were both prominent Fabians*] who acted with me as cashiers. Wallas came home with me and had tea.[47]

This is all Shaw has to say about the strike, and he gives no indication that he had been expecting it, nor that it was orchestrated or desired by his organization. Had the Fabians planned the strike with some kind of syndicalist aim (leaving aside the contradiction with their avowed aims and policies), this would have been the potential beginning of a social revolution, and there is no doubt that Shaw, with an eye to posterity, would have devoted far more attention to it.

Two years after the matchwomen's strike, the Fabian Society published a collection of essays on its beliefs by its leading lights, to which Besant contributed. Her essay is particularly instructive on the Fabian model for social change: she states her preference for the 'vast changes wrought by evolution' to the 'transient riots which merely upset thrones and behead kings'.[48] She detailed the Fabians' plan to work through 'Mr Ritchie's gift' (County Councils, instituted in 1888 by Conservative Chancellor Charles Ritchie, through the Local Government Act). The Fabians, she wrote, would 'convert the electors and capture the county councils', and through them slowly begin what Bernard Shaw in the same volume called the 'gradual transition to Social Democracy'.[49] The entire volume of essays makes only one passing reference to trade unions: Besant remarks that the union minimum will initially be a suitable guideline for wages.

In 1892 Sidney Webb still regarded trade unions as capable only of narrow protectionism: 'The trade unionist can usually only raise himself on the bodies of his comrades.'[50] Five years later a Fabian leaflet confirmed that their anti-revolutionary standpoint had not changed either, warning against 'revolutionary doctrines' and 'class war instead of the give-and-take bargaining between Capital and Labour to which England is accustomed'.[51]

So, nowhere in their writings do Shaw, the Webbs or indeed Besant write about the matchworkers' strike as an intended result of Fabian influence, which would be a strange omission if this had in fact been the case since it would clearly have ranked among its most notable achievements.

As has been shown, the Webbs only touch upon the strike in their history of trade unionism; in her diaries of the period, Beatrice Webb does not mention it at all, though there are several detailed references to Besant in other contexts, and not all are positive: Webb initially opposed suffrage and evidently disliked the type of independent woman she believed Besant personified.[52] Webb's sharply expressed views about Besant, like those of Engels, who would accuse Besant of being influenced more by the men she loved than her own convictions, illustrate the difficulty of getting feminist ideas to penetrate 'socialist parties, where men rarely saw women as equals'.[53] The SDF, for example, might have been expected to make links with the developing suffrage movement, being 'avowedly Marxist'.[54] In fact, E. Belfort Bax, the 'philosopher of the movement', was an avowed and unchallenged misogynist and author of 'The fraud of feminism'.[55] The anti-feminist views of such leading SDF-ers were widely and frequently expressed, and given considerable oxygenating publicity, for example in editorials of *Justice*.[56]

It is of course unsound to judge organizations purely on the basis of their leaders' opinions. The general interpretation is that the SDF as a whole was unsympathetic to feminist thought,[57] and certainly more so than the ILP:[58] this was certainly Sylvia Pankhurst's view, based on Bax's and Hyndman's opposition to women's suffrage.[59] However, George Lansbury supported suffrage while still an SDF member, and later worked closely with Pankhurst's East London Federation of Suffragettes.[60]

In fact, despite socialism's rhetoric of universal emancipation, the 'Woman Question' still 'haunted socialist politics' as a whole, with none of the main groups at this time able to satisfactorily exorcize it.[61] The Question was often reduced to one of 'sex versus class', female socialists being frequently dismissed with an instruction to wait until the overthrow of capitalism, which should automatically end sex oppression, rather than risk derailing the socialist project with 'side issues'. This did not go unchallenged: Margaretta Hicks of the SDF wrote that this would be 'worse than waiting for heaven. Unless we do something and say something now we shall be dead and buried before any improvement is made.'[62]

The SDF established women's groups from the 1890s, though these had more to do with branch social activities than the empowerment of female members.[63] Not until the 1900s was real energy devoted to forming national socialist women's groups, in response to fears that the socialists would lose members to the burgeoning suffrage campaign.[64] The Fabians formed women's groups from 1908.[65]

Aspects of the 'Woman Question', including married women's work, would continue to be divisive: even feminists often assumed that if a woman had married she would retire from the workplace, discounting working-class women who could not afford, and women of any class who did not want, to give up their wages.[66] Even socialists with working-class origins like John Burns tended to blame infant deaths on 'bad mothering', which included mothers working.[67] The nature of politics in socialist groups, 'gendered in theory and practice', inevitably served to 'marginalize women and their concerns'.[68]

Among the chief Fabians, not only Webb but also Shaw expressed conventional views on women: 'the most important and indispensable work of women, that of bearing and rearing children and keeping house for them'. On working-class women, Shaw opined that

> most of the hungry, left to themselves, would be quite as helpless as plutocrats ... A woman may be a very good housemaid; but you have to provide the house for her and manage the house before she can set to work ... Ask them to manage a big hotel, which employs dozens of housemaids, and ... you might as well ask the porter at the Bank of England to manage the Bank.[69]

(Ironically, Shaw was a patron of the Cavendish Hotel in London,[70] which was famously owned and run by former domestic servant Rosa Lewis. Lewis became known as the 'Duchess of Jermyn Street', and would later be immortalized in the BBC's historical drama *The Duchess of Duke Street*.[71])

Such opinions add to the problematic nature of the belief in the Fabians as architects of a show of militancy by women, which conflicted with accepted gender roles. Not until the burgeoning of the suffrage campaign would Fabian policy begin to demonstrate an understanding of the need for women's financial independence: even then, it would also propose state measures which would essentially intrude into the private lives of working-class families, denying them the privacy so sacrosanct to the middle-class home.[72]

Besant and Militancy

One of the most perplexing aspects of my research has been the discovery of the extent to which Besant's true views on militancy and trade unionism have been 'hidden from' – or, perhaps, 'by' – history, despite the multitude of sources which reveal them. The most striking example occurs in the very same issue of the *Link* containing the eternally quoted 'White slavery' article. On the next page, Besant criticized attempts being made to organize unskilled casual workers in general – and related this to the Bryant and May women in particular:

> How could a union be formed among the girls of Bryant and May, mentioned in another column? Suppose a union was formed, and the girls went on strike: the foreman would simply announce that so many hands were required at so much an hour, and their doors would be besieged within hours.[73]

Trade unionism might, she wrote, 'teach [women] comradeship and stir up social feeling, and improve their business faculty, and brighten their lives in many ways; but raise their wages – no'.[74]

It is surprising that scholars should have so consistently ignored such statements, and the light they cast upon Besant's supposed role in it.

After the matchwomen's strike Besant published her book *The Trade Union Movement*, making no mention whatever of the matchwomen, and praising New Unionism on the grounds that 'when it desires change it will use the ballot box instead of the strike', and control 'women workers and unskilled labourers, the two unorganized mobs which have hung round the disciplined army of unionists and have lost them many a fight ... unions [were] hampered by the crowding ranks of cheap and unorganized labour'.[75]

Years later, when living in India as a Theosophist leader, Besant would applaud the government's actions in ordering troops to open fire on the participants in a strike there, opining that 'A Government's first duty is to stop violence; before a riot becomes unmanageable brickbats must inevitably be exchanged for bullets in every civilized country'.[76]

Besant and Theosophy

Theosophical beliefs were, in essence, diametrically opposed to support for industrial militancy. As we shall see, Besant's involvement in the movement was not a much later development, but had already begun during her involvement with the matchwomen.

Theosophy was a 'new age' occultist philosophy, the invention of Russian émigrée Madame H. P. Blavatsky. It drew on palmistry, spiritualism, paganism, magic and various aspects of established religion, and gained widespread popularity over the next decades. There are still 36 Theosophical 'lodges' in Britain today, and Societies in America, Canada and India, and Besant is still hailed by some as a great leader and heroine of the movement.[77] Theosophy shared with traditional Victorian morality a central belief that the poor deserved their fate. In the case of Theosophy, this was within the context of reincarnation; as Besant herself would state, sickness, deformity and poverty were regarded as the results of past 'evil and cruelty'[78] in previous incarnations, being punished in the present.

As a result of this final conversion, Besant lost what one biographer called the 'magnificent strength of her compassion',[79] which had perhaps always informed her socialism more than deeper political analysis. She herself admitted in her autobiography that she had always known that socialism would be only a brief stop on the road to personal fulfilment, not a lifelong commitment: she describes herself at the time of the establishment of the *Link* as already 'marching toward Theosophy': 'How deeply this longing for something loftier than I had yet found had wrought itself into my life, how strong the conviction was growing that there was something to be sought to which the service of man was the road ...'[80]

In fact Besant must have already been aware of Theosophy at the time of the strike, and well along the road to conversion. Herbert Burrows, her close 'comrade' and, by some accounts, partner, was already so deeply involved in it that the strike fund register, which was compiled in his bound notebook, bears the insignia of the Theosophical Society above his monogram. Engels, in an 1891 letter to Kautsky, suggested that it was he who drew Besant into Theosophy through their relationship:

> Do you know Mother Besant has joined the theosophists of Grandmother Blowatsky [Blavatsky]. On her garden gate ... now is in big gold letters: Theosophical Head Quarters. Herbert Burrows has caused this by his love.[81]

Although he had some respect for Besant's writings, Engels had accused her before of following 'the religion of the man that has subjected her' in her changing political beliefs.[82] This may have been coloured by the fact that he never forgot her early opposition to socialism. As de Tollenaere notes, the accusation of male influence was one which had been made against Besant since she first deserted Freethought for socialism.[83] Shaw agreed that she was a woman who could change her political colours with breathtaking speed: '[she] came into a movement with a bound, and was preaching the new faith before the astonished spectators had the least suspicion that the old one was shaken'.[84]

However, the idea that each new enthusiasm stemmed from a romance, though repeated by modern biographers,[85] should be treated with some caution: it is unlikely that a man whose political and spiritual beliefs altered, however quickly, would be accused of being influenced by his girlfriends. Besant was an intelligent woman stimulated by new ideas, and was surely equally influenced by women like Clementina Black, as she was later by Madame Blavatsky; but she was no more immune to prejudiced assumptions than the matchwomen would be. Besant herself, in her autobiography, remembered such an accusation being thrown at her in the course of a political debate, and commented that '[t]he moment a man uses a woman's sex to discredit her ... the thoughtful reader knows that he is unable to answer the arguments themselves'.[86]

Burrows himself regarded Theosophy as something he and Besant had arrived at together, writing in the spring of 1889 that:

> Beset with problems of life and mind that our materialism could not solve, dwelling intellectually on what are now to us the inhospitable shores of agnosticism, Annie Besant and I ever craved more light. We had read The Occult World, and in bygone years we had heard – who had not? – [of Madame Blavatsky] ... the woman whom we afterwards learned to know and to love as the most wonderful woman of her time.[87]

Besant's closest colleague at the time of the strike, who has as much claim to have 'led' it as Besant, was, then, not only a member of a political organization which did not believe in unionizing casual labour, and not only opposed to women's rights, but in fact deeply committed to a 'religion' which believed that social inequality was the natural order of things and resulted from moral failings – whether in this life or in previous incarnations. Though Burrows would remain secretary of the matchwomen's union after Besant withdrew, this combination of beliefs would make him an unlikely *agent provocateur* of a strike by women like them; and some of these beliefs were not only shared by Besant, but became the foundation of her life and work.

'White Slavery In London'

The Fabian meeting on labour and exploitation in the East End was held on 15 June, and here Besant 'resolved to personally investigate [the] accuracy'[88] of Champion's statements concerning Bryant and May's wages and profits. She went shortly afterwards – the next day, according to some accounts – to the Fairfield Road factory. As the women began to leave work for the day, Besant approached a handful of them and obtained details of wages, working conditions and the fines which the company imposed upon workers.

The title of Besant's subsequent exposé was well chosen, and calculated to provoke outrage, laden with meaning which would not have been lost on her readers. In its first and most straightforward application, the term 'white slaves' had been a staple for decades for those railing against not just 'sweating', but factory production in general; the term was employed by both the media and various prominent individuals. Richard Oastler, the Tory manufacturer and prominent factory reformer, received national attention when he used the term 'Yorkshire slavery' to protest about the condition of child labour, in a letter to the *Leeds Mercury* in 1831. A year later Oastler gave evidence to the Committee on Child Labour, again employing the metaphor: 'The demoralising effects of the system are as bad, I know it, as the demoralising effects of slavery in the West Indies.'[89] The metaphor had great resonance at a time when there was heated debate on the subject of the literal slave trade. Britain would pass the Abolition of Slavery Act in 1833, and therefore felt some moral superiority on the issue, which increased consternation when the term was later applied to its own working men and women.[90]

In 1843 *The Times* published an article about London needlewomen, often seen at the time as the archetypal 'sweated' female workers, entitled 'White slaves of London'.[91] Similar in structure to Besant's later exposé, the piece berated the 'proprietors of several establishments at the eastern part of the metropolis' for their exploitation of young women workers, who were compelled to work 18-hour days in order to survive, earning six shillings in a 'good week' – though even this low and 'precarious' wage was higher than that of some matchwomen almost half a century later.[92] Shortly afterwards, the *Manchester Guardian* warned against the too-frequent application of the term 'white slaves' to British workers, regardless of their condition, noting that it had 'found much favour in the eyes of the Oastlers, Trollops, O'Connors, and other traducers of the manufacturing system', but that its use in this context 'furnishes the abettors of slavery in the United States with an argument which they very readily fling in the teeth of those Englishmen who speak in favour of its abolition'.[93]

By the time of Besant's article the term had lost none of its sensationalism, and, indeed, gained a new facet. The sexual behaviour and morality of young working-class women had become a preoccupation of Victorian society, and three years before Besant's article her friend W. T. Stead, editor of the *Pall Mall Gazette*, had whipped up a furore over the supposed 'white slave' trafficking of young English girls for sexual purposes. This scandal had come to light in

1879 when Alfred Dyer, a publisher of religious pamphlets, began to investigate rumours that English women and girls were being kidnapped and smuggled abroad. Although his enquiries into these claims were inconclusive, Dyer's associate Josephine Butler then became involved, publicly stating in 1880 that girls as young as 10 were being forcibly immured in foreign brothels. A select committee was established as a direct result of her claims, reporting in 1882.

When the resulting Bill proposing the raising of the age of consent to 16 was shelved, Stead, seemingly at Butler's suggestion, staged the kidnap and transportation to Paris of a young girl to show that at the very least, it could be done.[94] His resulting series of articles, 'The maiden tribute to modern Babylon', appeared in July 1885 and caused a national scandal. The age of consent was raised within weeks, by August 1885, and the whole affair would have presumably still been relatively fresh in the minds of Besant's readers.

Finally, it is possible that Besant also intended a jibe at Bryant and May's chairman, *Wilberforce* Bryant, who had been named in homage to the great anti-slavery campaigner William Wilberforce. His was the kind of legacy with which Bryant and May would have been pleased to be associated, as prominent Liberals who had recently erected a statue to William Gladstone near the Fairfield Works. Besant adroitly exposed this dichotomy between public perceptions of the company and the reality in the theme and headline of the piece. In it she not only compared 'Messers. Bryant and May' to slave owners, but concluded that their workers were ultimately *worse off* than slaves: slave owners were obliged to provide food and housing, far more costly per capita than the expenditure on wages at Fairfield Road.

Besant began her piece by emphasizing the magnitude of the gulf between the matchmakers' wages and the 'monstrous dividends' of Bryant and May's shareholders.[95] She then attempted to show at what cost to the workforce these profits were made: 'Working days begin at 6.30 a.m. in summer . . . work concludes at 6 p.m. This long day is performed by young girls who have to stand the whole time.' A 16-year-old piece-worker earned '4s. a week[96] and lives with her sister, employed by the same firm, who earns good money, as much as 8 or 9s. a week'. Out of her earnings, 2s. is paid for the rent of one room; 'the child lives only on bread-and-butter and tea, alike for breakfast and dinner, but related with dancing eyes that once a month she went to a meal where "you get coffee, and bread and butter, and jam, and marmalade, and lots of it"'.[97] Occasionally, this same girl related, someone would 'stand treat' so that she could go to 'The Paragon' – presumably the Paragon Music Hall in the Mile End Road, which according to contemporary Montagu Williams was popular with matchwomen.[98] This seemed to be the 'sole bit of colour' in her life.

Bryant and May's habit of imposing arbitrary fines on the women, as penalties for supposed misdemeanours, increased their financial hardship: 'The splendid salary of 4s. is subject to deductions in the shape of fines; if the feet are dirty, or the ground under the bench is left untidy, a fine of 3d. is inflicted; for putting "burnts" – matches that have caught fire during the work – on the bench 1s. has been forfeited, and one unhappy girl was once fined 2s. 6d. for some unknown crime.' Some departments even inflicted fines for talking, and 'If a girl is late she is shut out for half the day . . . and 5d. is deducted out of her day's [wages].'[99]

Besant also heard much about what the women called their 'pennies', deductions that had aroused a particularly deep sense of grievance. It appeared that Bryant and May had been stopping this amount from the box-fillers' wage packets to pay for the labour of young girls who fetched and carried work for them. This service had long since been dispensed with, but the deductions continued.

Some of the foremen were evidently threatening figures who physically mistreated their workers: the women interviewed spoke of 'one, a gentleman of variable temper, [who] clouts [them] when he is mad'.[100] Aside from the apparent threat of physical abuse, matchmaking was potentially hazardous in itself, and made more so by the company's attitude:

> One girl was fined 1s. for letting the web twist around a machine in the endeavour to save her fingers from being cut, and was sharply told to take care of the machine and 'never mind your fingers'. Another, who carried out the instructions and lost a finger thereby, was left unsupported . . . while she was helpless.[101]

Conditions at Fairfield were made more dangerous still by the failure of the company to provide employees with a separate area in which to eat. Food was not provided either, so it was left to their workers to bring with them each day whatever could be spared from their homes, probably plain bread, which they then 'ate in the rooms in which they worked', as they told Besant.[102] This meant that highly toxic phosphorus particles settled on the food: 'Fumes from the phosphorus mix with their poor meal and they eat disease as seasoning to their bread.'[103] This put the women at risk of phosphorous necrosis. The women were clearly aware of this risk, but presumably could scarcely avoid it, as not eating would have made the long hours of physical labour impossible to sustain.

The matchworkers were so dependent on their wages that they would attempt to conceal the toothache and swollen faces which could signify phosphorus poisoning, in order to carry on working: potential sufferers were often sacked. Unmarried women who got 'caught' (pregnant) were also liable to be sacked, and so were workers held responsible for any accident resulting in loss of revenue: the frame-workers, for example, were dismissed if their matches caught fire. All in all, Besant concluded, 'chattel slaves' would have been better off, and their upkeep 'would have cost considerably more than 4s. a week'.[104]

The piece written, Besant personally telegraphed the directors to inform them of its contents in advance of publication on 23 June. In doing so, she must have been expecting, and perhaps courting, a litigious response.

The Bryant brothers who were then in control of the firm had some reason to be concerned by Besant's indictment. As outlined previously, management practices had changed considerably in recent years, particularly, according to their workforce, 'since they was made a firm',[105] (became a limited company).

After that the women complained that deductions and fines worsened and 'we never get all our wages'[106] The powerful cartel that Bryant and May had become had no compunction in driving down wages either, so that rates in 1888 were lower than those paid ten years previously, and Besant could see that the girls who had grown up on lower wages were noticeably smaller and more frail.[107] The Commission on Sweated Labour had recently heard some damning evidence about their employment practices, and though they had issued vehement denials, and fought off such criticisms before, they did not have a total monopoly on match production. There was therefore a real possibility that negative publicity could undermine sales and affect shareholder bonuses, particularly worrying for a relatively new limited company.

Besant's article actively encouraged the public to boycott their products until or unless better conditions prevailed at Fairfield Road: 'let us strive to touch their consciences, i.e. their pockets, and less us at least avoid being "partakers in their sins" by abstaining from using their commodities'.[108] Her deft portrayal of the matchwomen as pitiful, poverty-stricken children, unaware or uncomplaining of their exploitation and still struggling bravely to make the best of their harsh lives, was calculated to elicit enough sympathy to make such a boycott feasible.

Study of the legislation then in force also suggests that Besant may also have been accusing Bryant and May, not simply of unjust treatment of their workforce, but of actual illegality on two counts. Under the 1831 Truck Act, employers were obliged to pay the full agreed wage and not impose any condition as to how any part of the wage should be expended: this would have applied to deductions like the 'pennies' to which the matchwomen referred – deductions instigated by the company to pay for young girls who had carried out work for the box-filling women, and continued in spite of the fact that the carriers had been dispensed with.[109] The 1863 Royal Commission on Children's Employment had invest-igated 'Lucifer' matchmaking among other areas of noxious production, and concluded that women and children in such trades should not eat in any room where production was carried out: this was later incorporated into the Factory Acts legislation.[110]

'White slavery' was, then, an unquestionably clever and calculated piece of journalism. Historians have concluded, more or less solely on the basis of it, that Besant's intention had been to bring the women out on strike.

Few sources make reference to the chain of events prior to Besant becoming involved with the matchwomen, which has added to the impression that she was their sole champion and strengthened her association with them. In fact the first to publicly decry Bryant and May's business practices in the 1880s was the Reverend W. Adamson, vicar of Old Ford, a parish in which many matchwomen lived. Adamson gave evidence to the House of Lords Select Committee into the sweating system in 1888, telling the committee about the exceptionally low wages paid by Bryant and May.[111] The company responded furiously, suggesting that 'the Revd. Adamson ought to be locked up for three months for making assertions simply based on hearsay'.[112]

It seems to have been this which first brought the matter to the attention of the London socialists – not the Fabians, but the SDF, who published the reverend's statements in *Justice*. Annie Besant had been a reader of this paper since 1884, by her own account: despite the rivalry and ideological differences which separated the Fabians and the federation, and indeed all of the socialist groups, individual members clearly kept a close eye on each other's work, and also associated freely together.[113] She may therefore have been aware of the Bryant and May case before the 15 June meeting, though if so she made no reference to it anywhere.

What is clear from Besant's account of the meeting is that, although we infer from secondary sources that it was then and there that Besant formulated the strike plan, the discussion in fact centred purely on the financial rights and wrongs of the case. Clementina Black, the speaker that evening, was at the time secretary of the Women's Trade Union League (WTUL), and had developed the idea of organized consumer action against exploitative employers. To this end she had compiled a list of 'fair' employers for the benefit of both ethically concerned customers and women workers seeking employment. She was also considering forming a Consumers' League to widely publicize these findings. It is likely that when those at the Fabian meeting discussed what should be done about Bryant and May, Black's expertise in such matters would have influenced debate, and she would almost certainly have favoured a consumer boycott. This seems to be confirmed by Besant's repeated calls for such a boycott, not just in 'White slavery' but repeatedly in the *Link*, and, as will be shown, at a mass meeting even after the strike had begun.

Besant's plan to go to speak to the women at Bryant and May's and obtain details of wages and fines echoes the 'scientific' approach to the reform of working conditions practised by Charles Booth, and for many decades by Beatrice and Sidney Webb, Fabian colleagues of Besant. Black and the WTUL and Women's Industrial Council (WIC) would also spend twenty years collecting such data as a strategy in itself, in order to compile reports like 'Married women's work',[114] which could be used to lobby government.

When Besant left the meeting, I believe she had little more in mind than a brief visit to Fairfield Road as preparation for an article which would embarrass the company and give weight to a consumer boycott, rather than agitating the workforce to cause a strike. This accorded with the known *modus operandi* of those present at the meeting, and Besant's Fabian colleagues. It is confirmed by Besant's retrospective statement of her intentions in her autobiography, written five years later: 'to obtain lists of wages, of fines, &c'.[115] She makes no mention of having had any desire to lead the women in industrial revolt, merely commenting that the piece was published 'and [we] called for a boycott of Bryant and May matches'.[116]

Neither does Besant, or any subsequent source, appear to have realized that she was, in fact, talking to the wrong group of workers. Champion's motion to boycott Bryant and May, passed at the Fabian meeting on 15 June, in fact concerned the pay of the *matchbox* makers, who usually worked in their own homes and not in the factory. Besant does not appear to have become aware of this until the strike was well under way, and she became aware that 'The worst suffering of all was among the box-makers, thrown out of work by the strike, and they were hard to reach. Twopence-farthing per gross of boxes, and buy your own string and paste, is not wealth, but when the work went more rapid starvation came.'[117] The evidence on Besant's visit to Fairfield Road, then, suggests a hastily conceived idea: whatever her intentions, she did not at this stage think detailed prior research or planning necessary.

It was only in her autobiography that Besant first revealed that she was not the only person who went to Fairfield Road, or interviewed the women. The traditional image of the courageous lone woman waiting at the enemies' gates, promulgated by so many commentators, has probably added to the popular appeal of the story. There is in fact a hint in parentheses in 'White slavery in London' that Besant did not act alone: though she writes about what happened in the first person singular, Besant also reveals that '(The figures quoted were all taken down by myself, in the presence of three witnesses)'.[118] The women themselves would not have been considered 'witnesses'. Besant's autobiography reveals that one of the three was probably Herbert Burrows, though the identities of the other two can only be speculated upon – perhaps W. T. Stead, perhaps H. H. Champion: it would seem logical that those who were present at the Fabian meeting might have volunteered to go to Fairfield. Besant gives no further details, making just this one reference to the fact that no fewer than four people had gone to Fairfield Road that day. The fact that there was more than one, and possibly four, Fabians present also strengthens the likelihood that the original plan devised at the meeting – to collect details for an article – would have been adhered to, leaving little room for Besant to spontaneously develop the maverick intention of leading a strike, even had she wanted to do so.

Still, most historians continue to favour the romantic idea that Besant acted alone; Burrows is rarely mentioned, and I've found no source which refers to the mysterious 'three'. With a slightly different emphasis, and if Burrows had also put his name to 'White slavery', the whole affair could therefore just as accurately have gone down in history as the story of 'Herbert Burrows and the matchgirls'. Perhaps, however, it would never have achieved the same level of celebrity if that had been the case – the concept of an attractive, cultured and rather notorious woman striding into battle like a Socialist Joan of Arc, leading a ragged army of matchwomen, being a more colourful and sensational one.

Burrows remained involved throughout: his name first appears with Besant's on letters to the *Star*, *Echo* and *Pall Mall Gazette*, appealing for money to help three girls who had been put out of work by Bryant and May, and after that continues to appear in this way on various correspondence with the media and notices and pieces in the *Link*.[119] He was listed as one of the five speakers at a protest meeting which should have been held on 22 July (had not events overtaken it) to 'protest against the tyranny of Messrs. Bryant and May': a meeting which, however, was planned only after Bryant and May had begun to intimidate workers. A protest meeting was more compatible with the tenets of Theosophy, with which Burrows and Besant were already involved and which was arguably incompatible with strike action.[120]

Although Besant had ensured that Bryant and May were aware of her findings well before publication, it was not until 26 June that she and her colleagues distributed copies of the *Link* outside the Fairfield Works: this was three days after publication. If the article was supposed to light the touch-paper for a strike, they would presumably have wanted the women to read it without delay to keep up momentum. However, the women were only now given the opportunity to see what had been written about them. This may indicate that the socialists saw contact with the workers as of secondary importance to the main work of engaging with the company and its shareholders.

Nor were Besant and Burrows, as might be expected, either privately or publicly holding tactical meetings with other Fabians, or representatives from the factory, to arrange the orchestration of a strike. From all accounts, this distribution of papers was only the second time they had had any face-to-face contact with the workers themselves.[121] It was certainly a public gesture likely to further annoy the employer, but as there is no record of any serious conversation between matchwomen and Fabians, it seems unlikely to have assisted with the practical organization of a strike. As will be shown below, Besant and Burrows were going about their business as usual, rather than prioritizing the Bryant and May affair as if expecting momentous events to follow.

The Days Before the Strike

As a result of Besant's article Bryant and May were, as she may have calculated, stung into a hasty retaliation. Director Theodore Bryant went on the offensive, telling the media that he had always paid good wages; working conditions were excellent; and relations with the workforce had been harmonious until Besant's interference had 'upset [their] minds'.[122] He announced his intention of suing Besant for libel if she did not immediately withdraw her allegations, and repeated this in a telegram to Besant in which he roundly denounced her article as 'a tissue of lies' and 'twaddle'.[123]

Besant was not intimidated: in fact she invited Bryant to carry out his threat in the next issue of the *Link*, confident that 'the statements are true ... and [the company] fear the publicity that such a suit would give to their shameful treatment of the helpless girls they employ'.[124] By threatening legal action, Bryant may in fact have played into Besant's hands: she knew from experience that a court case could be turned to her advantage. During the 1877 trial for obscene libel, conduct of her own defence had enabled Besant to use the trial as a forum for her political message with her remarks duly reported in the national press, giving extensive publicity to her cause. Besant may have envisaged doing the same again, and could probably have called on some heavyweight testimony in the current case, perhaps from Clementina Black, and also make use of the House of Lords Select Committee's recent damning evidence of Bryant and May's employment practices.[125]

The *East London Advertiser* on 30 June expressed the general view that a case would result. The *Advertiser* tended to take the employers' side during the dispute, publishing interviews with the Bryants and writing critically of the strike and the strikers, who it argued had been influenced by Besant. The following item seems to have been informed by the employers, whether directly or indirectly:

> An interesting action is likely to occupy the attention of the Law Courts shortly. A week or so ago . . . Mrs Besant published . . . a scathing article regarding the conditions under which, she alleged, work was carried on by the girls employed in the large match factory of Messrs Bryant and May . . . The article proceeded to denounce the action of partners in the firm in the matter, and challenged a denial . . . We understand that Mr Bryant has been advised by his solicitors that the article affords good grounds for an action for libel, and . . . no alternative remains now but for the question to be fought out in the Law Courts.[126]

There would, however, be 'No sign . . . of the legal attention threatened in such hot haste by Mr Theodore Bryant;[127] as Besant noted in her autobiography, 'it was easier to strike at the girls'.[128] The company had evidently lost little time in attempting to intimidate the women. Besant recorded in the *Link* on 30 June that she had been called out of an anti-sweating meeting 'on Wednesday night' (i.e. 27 June, four days after the publication of 'White slavery in London') by a friend, who 'came to me from Bow with the news that Bryant and May's factory was in a state of commotion, and the girls were being bullied to find out who had given me information'.[129] The foremen had left pre-prepared statements in each work area saying that Besant had lied in her article, and that the women were happy in their work. Below were blank pages where the women were ordered to sign: but when the foremen returned to collect the papers, each found that 'it offered to his angry eyes a white unsullied surface'.[130] Some time later, the women themselves put a letter through her door confirming this.

If we assume Besant's transcription to be accurate, then this is a rare example of the women's own words: 'Dear Lady,' the letter began, 'you need not trouble yourself . . . you have spoken the truth. We will not sign . . . we hope you will not get into any trouble on our behalf.'[131] The 'Dear Lady' greeting implies that the relationship between Besant and the women was formal, and had not bridged the social divide. The letter gives no impression that the women regarded Besant as their leader; rather, they knew of Bryant and May's threats to her and wanted to reassure her that they would stand by her. It is also clear that Besant was not in regular touch with them, as they wrote: 'We hope you will let us know if there are any meetings.'[132] As there had been no meetings specifically to discuss the women's situation and none were planned, it can only be assumed that they were here referring to the mass political meetings which were a feature of East End life at this time. We know that matchwomen had attended these before, and that some of them had even recognized Besant from the speakers' platform of previous occasions.[133]

Besant did not reply to this letter. Nor did she take any follow-up action in the women's defence beyond publishing details of it in the *Link*, when she wrote that the letter's meaning had not been clear, though from her own quotations it appears perfectly comprehensible.[134]

CONCLUSIONS

History has placed Besant firmly at the forefront of events in the matchwomen's strike and, by a continuing reliance on her own accounts of events, has not questioned whether this position is merited; or would even have been sought by its incumbent. In fact, even a fairly cursory study of Besant's beliefs and writing brings some inconsistencies to the fore – a more detailed examination shows considerable opposition to the kind of strike the matchwomen would undertake, by the type of workers who undertook it.

That history has so strenuously overlooked such evidence is noteworthy in itself. Besant's celebrity was almost certainly a factor in obscuring the reality of events in favour of the almost fairy-tale neatness of the orthodox version, in which a famous leader and political heroine 'saves' the poor exploited matchwomen. However, her very renown should have mitigated the continuation of such myths by providing much detailed evidence of her life and thought.

The latter is also true of other key Fabians such as Shaw and the Webbs: their journals clearly show that they were anything but preoccupied with the strike which was supposedly of their making. In fact, as the modern preface to Beatrice Webb's own history of the Co-operative movement makes clear, 'trade unionism was not of much interest to the Fabians, a subject which had also escaped the notice of the writers of the Fabian essays, a strange omission, seeing that Annie Besant, the leader of the matchgirls strike, was one of them'.[135] 'Strange' indeed: virtually incomprehensible, if the conventional version were correct.

British labour history has memorialized Besant as a socialist, atheist, and trade union leader. However, this represents a transitory period in a life which can be read as a typically *fin de siècle* search for meaning by someone who had, to paraphrase G. K. Chesterton, 'stopped believing in God and started believing in everything'. When Besant turned her back on socialism, she did so with a speed and completeness which must make the depth of her commitment to it questionable. Besant was without some form of religious belief for only fifteen years of her long life (she died at 86). Her mother, at the end of her own life, would remark: 'it has been darling Annie's only fault; she has always been too religious'.[136]

Besant herself made clear her intentions in regard to the matchwomen, or rather to Bryant and May, in the *Link*: a boycott of their products to 'touch their consciences, i.e. their pockets'. This was a logical tactic: Besant knew that their shareholders would apply pressure if the boycott were successful. Furthermore, she knew that many were politicians and 'gentlemen of the cloth': reputations and, by extension, careers could be damaged by suggestions that they profited from the suffering of sweated workers. Besant knew from her own unhappy experience how Victorian clergymen would react to any attempt to stain their honour.

Besant was an exceptional woman in many ways, and what she proposed was still courageous: she was almost certainly prepared to risk trial for libel with all the strain and invasions of her privacy that would come with it. However, applying pressure through boycotts, and negative publicity which would hopefully affect shareprices, was essentially a middle-class solution to a working-class problem, and certainly very different from an all-out strike.

'One Girl Began': The Strike and the Matchwomen

INTRODUCTION

In this chapter I will reconstruct the days of the strike in detail, using first-hand material but avoiding too heavy or uncritical a reliance on Besant's own accounts. In order to prepare for this I first constructed a 'timeline' of events by mapping carefully- analysed primary accounts onto a calendar of the crucial days. Once a clear chronology is established, and misleading and inaccurate information weeded out, the true causes and significance of the strike begin to come to the fore.

I will then look at what is known about the matchwomen and industrial relations before the strike, to help us to understand it as an event which grew out of the women's working lives, rather than as an aberration forced on them by outsiders. This will prepare the ground for the detailed evidence in subsequent chapters of those who, it will be argued, were the true leaders of the strike.

CHRONOLOGY AND CAUSES

Attempting to understand, and to pinpoint chronologically, the exact start of the strike proper is complicated by a variety of conflicting reports. For example, the *Star*, in a report published on 6 July, states that the strike 'began yesterday', i.e. 5 July. However, the same article quotes the women as saying that they all 'left work then and there' as soon as the first worker was dismissed; and correspondence in the *Star*'s letters pages shows that this was probably on 2 July.[1] An interview with Wilberforce Bryant, on 3 July, ran as follows:

Q: What is the cause of the strike?

A: Why, a girl was dismissed yesterday; it had nothing to do with Mrs Besant. She refused to follow the instructions of the foreman, and as she was irregular anyway, she was dismissed.

Q: Is it not very unusual that all the girls should strike because of one?

A: Yes, but I've no doubt they have been influenced by the twaddle of one.[2]

The *East London Advertiser* quoted the works manager, a Mr Rix, as saying that he believed 'some outside influence has been brought to bear on the girls', and that '[a] few days ago sensational bills were posted near the factory'. This is the only reference I've been able to find to these 'bills', so it's hard to assess the accuracy of this.[3]

The *Star* reporter who spoke to the women and observed their strike meetings was adamant that they told him they went out because one girl was dismissed, and did so immediately. The reporter noted the presence at the meeting of 'a pale little girl in black . . . who had caused the strike by refusing to sign the paper . . .'.[4] Conflictingly, another matchwoman told the reporter that 'we would have come out sooner only we wasn't all agreed'.[5] On 4 July, the *Star* published company secretary William Carkett's response for Bryant and May, denying Besant and Burrows' claims. Only one girl had been dismissed, he wrote, and this had 'no connection with the cause your correspondent suggests'.[6]

Besant's journal, however, suggested that not one but three women were sacked: 'On Wednesday the three girls went crying to the friend at Bromley who is good enough to act for me, saying they had "got the sack".'[7] This also brings another date, 4 July, into play, though this was not necessarily the date the women were actually dismissed.

Besant's tone is rather jarring here: 'went crying' seems to imply childish behaviour. The entry also shows that the women chose to approach not Besant herself but the unnamed 'friend' (whose identity has not yet been discovered: Burrows lived in North London, or at least did when addressing letters as secretary of the Matchworkers' Union shortly afterwards).[8]

Had Besant been actively agitating for a strike, here was a potential trigger: it might be expected both that Besant would have shown more enthusiasm for it and that the women would have gone straight to her, rather than to the unnamed friend, whose identity I have yet to discover. It would also seem logical to expect that Besant would have remained in frequent contact with them so that they would not have needed to 'go crying' to anyone. In fact it can be deduced from Besant's own accounts that the socialists had not communicated with the matchwomen since the distribution of the *Link* on the 26th. Besant wrote that the women had been kept on slack work for a week, and then given their week's wages and turned out, 'with a sneering quote from [her] article'.[9] The three were promised that they would not be left unsupported, and Besant's friend seems to have given them some money to tide them over. However, Besant's later autobiography stated that they had been urged by the Fabians to go back to work if they could, at least to collect wages owing. This again contradicts Besant's account that they had been paid to date and then 'turned out'.

Adding to the confusion, in a letter to the *Star* published on 3 July Besant reported that the three had been discharged on 2 July. In the *Link* on 7 July Besant gives another apparently contradictory account, saying that one girl was sacked, not officially for speaking to Besant but for refusing to carry out her duties; her colleagues were not fooled and 'promptly seeing the reason of her punishment, put down their work with one accord and marched out . . . the rest of the wood-match girls followed'. More followed later that day until 'some 1,400 women in total'[10] were out.

In any event, Besant's next move concerning the sacked women was to propose a public meeting more than two weeks later, on 22 July. She wrote that she hoped nothing further would come of it, and that Bryant and May would be sufficiently cowed by the 'commotion' to 'feel that they had better try to undo some of the wrong inflicted',[11] and that would be the end of the affair. Until then, she continued to press the idea of a boycott and the shaming of company shareholders, and to this end shareholders' names were next published in the *Link*. Many were clergymen, and Besant capitalized on this. Referring to hair loss caused by carrying heavy wooden pallets on the head, she wrote:

> Country clergymen with shares in Bryant and May draw down on your knee your fifteen-year-old daughter; pass your hands tenderly over the silky clustering curls, rejoice in the dainty beauty of the thick shiny tresses. Then like a ghastly vision, let there rise up before you the pale face of another man's daughter . . . [who] shows a head robbed of its hair by the constant rubbing of the boxes, robbed thereof that your dividends might be larger, Sir Cleric . . . shame on you who so long as silence can be kept, do not care whence comes your gold; shame most of all on you who preach love and purity from your pulpits.[12]

The company archives show that this did indeed have an effect on Bryant and May: despite public assertions about the fairness of their wages, behind the scenes the directors were frantically writing to other local manufacturers to enquire about their wage rates, no doubt hoping for some ammunition to throw back at Besant and her allies. At least one reply which survives brought bad news: Clarke, Nicholls and Coombs Confectionary Works Ltd, of Hackney Wick, paid its workers, depending on age and experience, 9, 10 and 15 shillings a week.[13] However, while Besant and the company were involved in disputes over financial matters, events at the factory had now moved beyond the control of either. The walkout had begun.

FIRST DAYS: A NEW TIMELINE

In order to attempt to understand the events of the strike, we have seen that we have first to pick our way through a maze of conflicting reports. A new timeline was necessary to pull everything together into the most logical and credible sequence of events.

We must first consider the evidence for who was sacked and when. Several reports– one from Besant, two from the employer, and two from the *Star* – mention one woman being dismissed. The *Star* reporter was unique in interviewing the women themselves while the strike was going on, and quoting them in what are apparently their own words, so these accounts have been given some credence. However, Besant also mentions the dismissal of three women, in some detail.

It seems certain that in late June, around the 27th, the foremen put around the paper refuting Besant's claims. Besant says so, and the *Star* independently corroborates it. Either all or the majority of the women refused to sign it. The foremen then continued to apply pressure in various ways. Three women were 'kept slack' (given so little work to do they could not make their usual wages).

It is here that one of my most valuable pieces of new evidence comes into play. Bryant & May's own 'ringleaders' list. I have not seen this source mentioned in any other history, but it's extremely significant that the firm themselves believed all along that the strike was an 'inside job', despite while publicly blaming Besant. The five women on the list were those the foremen felt were those most likely both to have been among Besant's interviewees *and* to have begun the unrest.

Those named are Alice Francis, Kate Slater, Mary Driscoll, Jane Wakeling and Eliza Martin.

I've been fortunate enough to have traced Eliza Martin's and Mary Driscoll and her sister Margaret's descendants. Martin and Driscoll worked in the Victoria factory where the strike seems to have begun. As will be shown in Chapter Nine, Eliza Martin's version of events, handed down from her to her son and then her grandson Jim Best, was that she and her friends had begun the strike, and she maintained this throughout her life. There is, as we will see, some subsequent evidence which seems to show Eliza to have been an active participant, indeed a possible leader, of the strike.

Among the five names may have been the three women 'kept slack' and/or sacked, and the one dismissed. If the three women were not directly sacked, given the casual nature of their employment they may have simply been kept so short of work that they had to to seek financial help from the socialists. This would explain why the strikers told the *Star* that they had walked out after the dismissal of one girl, not three.

In the week after 'White slavery . . .', the pressure was stepped up by the employers. It would make sense for this to have begun on the first day of the new working week, Monday 2 July. One woman had been singled out to be made an example of, perhaps because she had 'form' for standing up for herself and her workmates. When she would not sign the paper she was dismissed, either that day or the next day, on the pretext of 'refusing to cut the matches into half cuts'.[14]

The interview with the works manager in the East London Advertiser – owned by businessmen, subtitled 'the Conservative Journal for the East of London', and thoroughly pro-employer in the early days of the strike – gave a different account of the process the worker allegedly refused to carry out:

> Mr Rix . . . states that the strike was really brought about by the summary dismissal of one girl yesterday morning . . . She had been instructed by an overseer to fill boxes of matches in a particular way, according as the machine cut them. The reason assigned for this order is that the condition of the atmosphere at the time and its effect upon the chemicals used in match-making rendered this direction a mutual advantage to the firm and to the girls, in as much as it prevented what is technically known as 'firing' and therefore stopped undue waste . . . This particular girl refused to obey and she was dismissed.[15]

From Rix's long-winded account it is easy to understand why the matchwomen suspected foul play. The claim boils down to a worker suddenly refusing to put matches in a box in the approved way, which stopped them 'firing'; but gives no reason why she should suddenly have done so. It was obviously a regular part of the work, and since the women were fined for 'burnts', not in her own interests to disobey. In any case her colleagues felt this to be a trumped-up charge to conceal the real reason for dismissal, and left work in support of her.

If the structure of the Fairfield Works is considered, then there may not in fact be any contradiction between the quoted accounts stating that 'all' of the woman's colleagues immediately walked out, and those which suggest only some did not because initially 'we wasn't all agreed'.[16] The now-demolished Victoria factory, where the strike seems to have begun (the *Star* stated that the young woman sacked worked here,)[17] stood in the centre of the site. The other workers were in separate buildings: the 'Centre and Top Centre Works', 'Wax and Box Stores' and 'Patent factory'. These may have functioned like four separate factories. The strike fund register shows a strict dividing line between them, listing workers' names under four separate headings: it will also be shown that the union committee comprised three elected women from each 'factory'.

Therefore it is possible that all of the women from the Victoria building walked out immediately, some time during the morning of Monday 2 July, but that there was some pause before the news was communicated to the other buildings. Rather than going home or seeking out Besant there and then, the Victoria workers told the *Star* that they stayed around the factory gates until the lunch break. They waited for the workers from the other sites to come out, told them what had happened, and persuaded them not to go back after the break.[18] The Centre and Patent workers seem to have been next out,[19] and the majority of workers to have followed by the end of the day, though possibly some came out the next day, 3 July. The *East London Advertiser*'s account speaks of the women 'march[ing] out of the factory in two batches'.[20]

Bryant and May alleged to the *East London Observer* that the minority of male workers, who seem to have been regarded as quite separate from the main workforce and mostly worked as dippers, did not strike, but ceased work only when they ran out of matches to dip.[21] However, the strike fund register shows they drew strike pay, and it might be thought that their female colleagues who oversaw the payments would have had something to say about that had they actively broken the strike.[22] Equally, it seems likely that Bryant and May, having been so suddenly deprived of their workforce, would have put whoever was left to other work as well as dipping, to at least keep production going. The male workers might therefore have simply taken a day or two to follow the women out.

Bryant and May had clearly not bargained for this mass rebellion. Their first response was not the angry defiance they would later adopt, but an offer to immediately reinstate the sacked woman, but it was too late: 'the spirit of revolt against cruel oppression had been aroused'.[23] The women immediately widened their demands and declared that they would not go back until other conditions were met too, including the reinstatement of their 'pennies'.[24] Reports in the *Star* show that the women immediately and effectively organized themselves. The paper's reporter attended their lively and very well-attended picket line, which was in action by 8 a.m. on the second day of the strike, showing the commitment of the strikers. Present were vast crowds of matchwomen, looking: 'just like the girls that one reads about in a story of outcast London, clad in old, worn out, faded jackets, or in ragged shawls and bedraggled skirts, with their heads covered with old brown or black straw or felt hats battered into every conceivable shape, they made indeed a strange gathering'.[25]

Once the reporter had recovered from the 'strange' sight of poor women looking poor, he spoke to them and found that they confirmed the truth of Besant's article.[26] This is the only opportunity history affords to get close to the original strikers' immediate feelings about what had taken place, albeit through the 'middle-class filter' of the *Star*'s reporter. They confirmed the truth of the factual statements in the *Link*, and stated that they had walked out because of the dismissal of one of their number by the foreman, upon which 'the other girls followed suit and stopped work'.[27] The workers in the Centre and Patent factories had been next.[28]

The women told the *Star* that they had then selected six of their number to go as a deputation to meet with the company directors. This is not mentioned in any subsequent source, but apparently took place on the first day of the strike. The deputation consisted solely of matchwomen, with no outside support, so the women were clearly not intimidated by their employers. We do not know who these women were, but it seems possible at least that they may have included the five 'troublemakers'. Clearly Bryant and May did not meet the demands of the women, and 'the girls were in a great state of excitement and refused to resume work'.[29]

The *East London Advertiser*, despite initially backing the employer, confirmed the scale and vibrancy of the walkout, giving the highest estimate of numbers: '1,500 females . . . once outside, made a noisy display for a little while and then repaired to Bow Common . . .'[30] By 6 July the *Star* reported the 'whole factory lying idle'. The directors were threatening to draft in workers from their Glasgow factory to replace the strikers, and were quoted as saying they would not 'have back' all of the original workforce even if the strike ceased immediately.[31] A mass meeting was held at the factory gates and the *East London Advertiser* reported that the women had attracted much attention: '. . . eleven hundred employees paraded the streets in the neighbourhood of Bow on Thursday and Friday. A large number of police are stationed in the neighbourhood.'[32]

The strike must presumably have been under way for some days to allow for the drafting in of such a large number of police, supporting the suggestion that the bulk of workers were out by 3 July. Not only did local reporters know about it by the 6th, but Lewis Lyons, militant activist for the tailoring trade, had also heard the news. Lyons came down to the factory and attempted to address the crowd, only to be heckled by one of the Bryant and May managers, a Mr George Hicks, who shouted: 'It's a lie.'[33] Lyons was arrested for obstruction, and a crowd of matchwomen surged around the arresting officers, marching in solidarity to the police station with Lyons 'singing popular sings and cheering'. They then 'marched in procession to Mile End Waste', where a mass meeting was held: organized, it would seem, completely spontaneously by the women themselves. A further meeting was arranged for the next day.

Lyons was later bailed.[34] This was not a new experience for him: by coincidence, as Besant mentions in her autobiography, one of her first duties on joining the Fabians was to become involved in their efforts to stand bail for 'workingmen' arrested during the protests over the banning of public assemblies. Besant's first 'bailee' was none other than Lewis Lyons. So those known to Besant and from the same political circles were in attendance on the 6th: but she herself was not.

6 JULY: APPROACH TO BESANT

With the aid of the timeline it can be proved that accounts which imply, or directly state, that when the women walked out Besant and the Fabians were ready and waiting, are incorrect.[35] The chain of events detailed above already make this unlikely, showing that Besant could not possibly have predicted the strike and been ready and waiting to rally the strikers, because it resulted not specifically from her article, but from management's actions. There was a meeting between Besant and the strikers: but a close reading of the evidence makes it clear that this occurred much later than generally assumed. Besant reported what transpired in the *Link* on 7 July. This was a Saturday, and her account states that the meeting had taken place the previous day, i.e. Friday 6 July.

A deputation of around one hundred of the striking women had met with Besant, but she makes clear that they had decided of their own volition to seek her out: Besant was not expecting the women when they arrived at her offices, near Fleet Street in the City of London.[36] She had been working in an upstairs room when someone came up to tell her that the deputation had arrived. She confessed herself nonplussed by their arrival: she had no idea why they were there – because, as quickly becomes clear and is central to the arguments of this book, she did not know that the strike had begun two days previously.

Accordingly, Besant's first concern was that the women were blocking the pavement below, causing 'serious inconvenience'.[37] She sent down a note via a third party, asking them to move, and then, following 'a little puzzled delay', agreed to see a small deputation.[38] Three women, whom Besant describes only as 'respectable', were ushered in and informed her of what had happened. Besant does not indicate whether they included any of the women she had initially interviewed.

Only now did Besant become aware of the strike. Even now the women did not directly ask her for help: Besant writes that they implied that they wanted her assistance 'by look and gesture rather than by word',[39] in keeping with representations of shy, helpless 'little matchgirls'. However, prior events suggest these were women capable of saying what they meant. They had not been shy about asking for guarantees of financial assistance, should these be needed, before agreeing to be interviewed for the *Link*.[40] They had already sent a deputation to their employers, and organized a picket line and mass meetings. Probably they were hoping for advice of some sort; it would have been an obvious and sensible tactic for a group of strikers with no union support to use their contacts and approach Besant, perhaps the most influential middle-class person they knew who might help them. However, their awkward meeting hardly paints a picture of strikers communing with their leader, and Besant shows none of the jubilation of a socialist who has just successfully brought about a planned and hoped-for walkout. The meeting ended with Besant dismissing the three women with no more than a 'cordial handshake' and a 'promise to think what could be done'.[41]

In Besant's 1893 autobiography, as part of an account of the strike which lasts less than a page in total and places the author firmly in the foreground, Besant gives another account of this meeting. This too demonstrates her lack of prior knowledge of the strike, and her bewilderment at the deputation's arrival:

> I couldn't speechify to match-girls in Fleet Street, so asked that a deputation should come and explain what they wanted. Up came three women and told their story: they had been asked to sign a paper certifying that they were well treated and contented, and that my statements were untrue; they refused. 'You had spoke up for us,' explained one, 'and we weren't going back on you.' A girl, pitched on as their leader, was threatened with dismissal; she stood firm; next day she was discharged for some trifle, and they all threw down their work, some 1,400 of them, and then a crowd of them started off to me to ask what to do next.[42]

These revelations have further implications: for one thing, they show that Besant had not been monitoring the situation at the factory, despite having received at least two warnings about bullying at the factory, and being aware of the victimization of the three women. This does not mean that Besant had abandoned the women, but that she had not wavered from her initial plan to pursue the company through the media, without the involvement of the workforce.

In the Link article the day after her visit from the strikers, Besant actually expressed dismay at the action the women had taken. She disassociated herself from the strike by expressing the view that the women should have allowed a few of their number to be dismissed, but should not have taken strike action in support of them, for financial and practical reasons at least: 'We could have managed to maintain, till they got work, a few discharged for giving information, but we can't support 1,400 women.'[43]

There were, in other words, no plans or funds in place to assist with the strike which conventional accounts suppose Besant had been planning since mid-June. Besant also stressed, in a paragraph header in bold type, that **The girls will go back to work**,[44] if only some of the illegal deductions are stopped; no mention was made of the reinstatement of the sacked woman. On the same page Besant continued to press for a legal solution ('Why not prosecute Bryant and May?')[45] to resolve matters.

So, even after the strike had begun, Besant held to her view that strikes by casual workers were imprudent. She went about her business as usual: The *Star* reported, in an item unrelated to the strike, on the Fabian meeting on 'Art under Socialism', on the evening of 6 July, also referred to by Shaw. The report shows Besant to have been one of the key, and presumably pre-arranged, speakers. The meeting is reported in detail: Shaw and Oscar Wilde made contributions; but nowhere is it recorded that Besant made a reference to the strike, and the *Star* does not at this point connect her in any way with the strike that they are so keenly following.

It is tactically surprising that Besant should not have used this opportunity to at least mention the strike, if not suggest that the meeting be given over to discussing it. As so many of her comrades would have been assembled anyway, this would have been a perfect time to plan a strategy for the raising of much-needed initial funds, and future meetings. The fact that Besant gave her speech as scheduled, with no mention of the strike, suggests either that she considered it should not take precedence over the theoretical discussions of the evening, or that she was still taken aback at the news and unsure of how to proceed.

7–18 JULY

The next day found the matchwomen busily publicizing their cause. The *Star* reported that on 7 July 'over 300 of Bryant and May's work girls held a meeting on Mile End Waste this morning'.[46] Again there was an interest in the distinct fashions of the matchwomen, which seem to have been a virtual uniform and badge of identity: 'They wear long, plain black jackets ... ponderous earrings of yellow metal'. Despite obvious 'physical degeneration due to their social environment', the women were 'in good spirits, warmly welcoming the speakers who came to address them'.[47] The women's efforts at drawing attention to their plight had borne fruit: news had clearly spread through the neighbourhood and beyond, and some political figures 'turned up and orated', being 'too energetic propagandists not to utilise' the opportunity.[48] Annie Besant, however, was again absent, and this was clearly the women's own meeting.[49] Local police, who obviously knew the matchwomen and their traditions of solidarity well, told the *Star* that 'no girl will dare to commence work while the mass of others remain out. They will have it taken out of them if they do.'[50]

The *Star* recognized the importance of the strike, calling it 'this female revolt against the iron rule of wages'.[51] What it did not do, now or at any time during the strike, was mention Fabian orchestration; and as their assistant editor was an active member of the society, the paper had every reason to loudly trumpet this if it had been the case. By 9 July the newspaper was calling it 'The match girls' strike', and reporting that 'thousands of people' were at the next meeting at Mile End Waste, 'for the affair has created enormous sensation in the neighbourhood'.[52] Several speeches were given by the matchwomen themselves, detailing conditions in the factory and their reasons for striking.

Now comes the first reference to Besant's presence: she spoke at this meeting, but still fell short of the stirring oration we might expect from a strike leader. She urged no solidarity action, but continued to request a boycott of Bryant and May's products. Furthermore, she specifically disassociated herself from the women's actions:

> With regard to the charge that we instigated the strike – although it is a matter of no importance – we beg to say that this statement is absolutely false, nor were we, as asserted, near the factory on the day it commenced.[53]

Besant herself gave a later account of this mass meeting in which she implied that she had had a hand in its organization.[54] *Justice* carried an alternative claim that its own Harry Hobart had arranged it, having previously visited the women at Bow, and making no reference to any involvement by Besant, though confirming that she spoke at the meeting. Besant in turn makes no reference to Hobart in any of her accounts. It should be remembered that the strikers had already arranged a number of activities for themselves by this stage.[55] At another mass meeting on the same day, in Regent's Park, a resolution was passed for a widespread boycott of Bryant and May's products. Bryant and May now stepped up their media offensive, repeatedly asserting that the women had no genuine grievances. To counter their claims, Besant issued a statement to the press giving further evidence of fines and low wages, and an account of the bullying which had led to the strike.[56]

Besant's old friend Charles Bradlaugh MP raised questions in parliament, and a deputation of 56 matchwomen marched there in person to meet with three other MPs, on 11 July. Their deputation apparently brought 'cabs and buses to a standstill',[57] simply because of the novelty of such poor people appearing in procession outside the East End. The women answered the MPs' questions with 'quick intelligence, directness and frankness', telling them that they were made to pay for their own materials out of their meagre wages.[58] In an adroit and dramatic gesture, one of their number suddenly swept off her bonnet to show her bald scalp, the hair worn away by the constant pressure from the wooden pallets she had to carry on her head.[59]

On Friday 13 July the strike was the subject of a leader in the *Star*, which reported that shareholders were pressuring Bryant and May. The London Trades Council (LTC) had also become involved: though hitherto an organization which had 'shunned unskilled workers',[60] it agreed to lend support once approached, and a committee of matchwomen was formed to liaise with the organization. It has been suggested that the LTC may have been motivated not just by Victorian paternalism and shock at the women's conditions, but also by a desire to 'demonstrate to the socialists that they were experienced trade unionists who knew how to conduct themselves in industrial matters, and did not require help from outside political activists'.[61]

Certainly there is something of this tone in the remarks of LTC secretary George Shipton to a meeting of the council reported in the *East London Advertiser*:

> Mr George Shipton . . . said that he had written to Messrs. Bryant and May stating that
> it had been suggested that the London Trades Council, as experienced and unprejudiced
> workmen, should offer their services to try to bring about an amicable solution. He had
> received a most courteous reply from the firm which . . . stated that [they] were willing
> to receive a deputation of the London Trades Council.[62]

Despite such gentlemanly exchanges, no agreement was reached. The LTC
reported that 'the Firm will make no concession'.[63] If the workforce returned to
work immediately they would accept the majority back, 'except the ringleaders',
otherwise they would replace them.[64] However, the council did propose a levy
of all affiliated trade unionists should the strike continue, which, as the *Pall
Mall Gazette* pointed out, was an 'almost unprecedented event in the history of
labour',[65] and showed the action's deep impact. In 1890, the LTC would change
its rules to admit female delegates for the first time.

By 14 July around 600 of the women had gone fruit- and hop-picking, as they
were accustomed to doing in the summer months when the match trade was slack.
Besant noted with obvious relief that 'we haven't so many on our hands now'.[66]

The *Star* and *Pall Mall Gazette* had been collecting donations from their
readers, and the first strike pay was distributed on the same day. Donations to the
strike fund had been coming in steadily, so that 'not one of the six hundred hands
went away with less than four shillings'[67] when the first distribution took place.
However, an enjoyably vivid, though by no means pro-matchwoman, account in
the *East London Advertiser* showed that the women were collecting donations on
their own account, and continuing their protest in lively fashion:

> During the strike the principal streets and thoroughfares of East London, especially the
> Mile End Road, have been swarmed with the girls, who were generally accompanied
> by male members of the lowest orders. The [Mile End] Waste every morning has
> generally presented a strange spectacle of some 500 or 600 people lolling about doing
> nothing. Some of the girls marched up and down the streets soliciting coppers, and were
> quite willing to pour their tale of hardships into every sympathetic ear. On Tuesday
> morning, opposite the Earl Grey [public house], a vanload of pink roses drew up and
> it was presently surrounded by some 200 of the girls. The roses were flung into the
> street by the two men who had charge of the carts and it afterwards appeared that the
> roses had been sent down – by whom it did not transpire – to be worn by the strikers
> as badges.[68]

Among the Fabians in attendance at the registration for the strike fund and
distribution of official funds on 14 July were Sidney Webb, Graham Wallas and
George Bernard Shaw. The *Eastern Post* gives a rare insight into the way in which
Besant addressed the matchwomen at such meetings:

> The women, boys and girls were urged to . . . remain quiet, to give no cause for legal
> interference . . . Mrs Besant . . . explained to these poor girls that there were friends ready
> and willing to assist them provided always they behaved themselves . . .[69]

The women had been without money for several days at this point, and must have been experiencing hardship; but as one observer saw, their usual cheerful solidarity remained strong. The matchwoman was traditionally 'like wax when a fellow worker falls ill or a collection has to be made for a sick companion. She lends clothes and boots . . . she shares her last crust with a girl out of work . . ',[70] and this was no exception:

> . . . few people could fail to be touched by the way in which the girls were determined to stand together at all costs. 'I can pawn this for you', 'I'll lend you that', in every direction girls might be seen plotting how they could help one another on until Bryant and May gave them back their pennies.[71]

It was also decided at this meeting that the strike committee should go to the House of Commons to petition the MP for Glasgow, also a shareholder in Bryant and May, to stop the proposed 'Glasgow importation' of workers from the factory there.[72] Pressure on the company grew. Independent investigators Laurie, Rogers, Smith and Stevenson from Toynbee Hall examined Besant's original allegations, and sent their findings to *The Times*. Besant was vindicated, and further grievances uncovered:

> The fillers state that they used to receive 1s. 11d. for filling 100 frames and now receive 10d. for filling 100 coils, but they cannot fill twice as many in the same time, owing to the frequent breakdown of the machine. They also complain that they have to pay 6d. for brushes to clean the machine. The brushes have to be renewed every six months or so. The packers complain that 3d. is deducted from their weekly wage to pay for children to fetch their paper, and 2d. is deducted to pay the packer who has to book the number of packages, and such like, for the week. They also have to pay 6d. for stamps to stamp the package.[73]

Confronted with these findings, Bryant and May could no longer deny the existence of unjustified deductions. The *Star* published their humiliating climb-down:

> The directors admit the existence of the charges of sixpence for brushes, sixpence for stamps, and the payment of 2d. per week by the packers to one of their number for booking. At a subsequent interview the directors have admitted, after reference to their books, that the deductions of 3d. a week from wages of packers, as alleged by the girls and denied by them, is in fact correct.[74]

The company was discredited, and moving towards a position of compromise far removed from their initial hostile defiance. Political pressure was a factor, as the *Echo* noted:

> Messrs Bryant and May are well known Liberals and have . . . paraded their Liberalism before the world . . . more than one shareholder is a well-known member of parliament who in other matters profess to champion the cause of the poor and the oppressed. How could they meet their constituents with large dividends in their pockets, and with

vaunted liberalism on their lips, when their employees in the east of London existed on next to starvation wages?[75]

The company's directors finally met with a deputation of matchwomen and LTC members on 16 July. After prolonged discussion all parties agreed the following terms to be put to a full meeting of strikers:

1 abolition of all fines;
2 abolition of all deductions for paint, brushes, stamps &C;
3 restitution of 'pennies' if the girls do their own racking work, or payments by piece work of the boys employed to do it – (the result of this latter will be more than equal to the penny);
4 the packers to have their threepence;
5 all grievances to be taken straight to the managing director without the intervention of the foremen.

In addition the company agreed to 'provide a breakfast room for the girls so that the latter will not be obliged to get their meals in the room where they work', and to the formation of a union 'so that future disputes, if any, may be officially laid before the firm'.[76] The *Eastern Post* reported the meeting that followed: again, the substance and tone of Besant's remarks to the strikers is unexpected, and far more admonishing than congratulatory:

> [At] a largely-attended meeting in Mr Charrington's small hall . . . Mrs Besant . . . stated the result of the previous day's interview with the directors. She said the firm had suggested that if they were to concede the points demanded by the workers, possibly when the busy time came round the girls would again strike. Now, said Mrs Besant, I feel sure, I may say, you will do nothing of the kind, will you?[77]

By 18 July Bryant and May had ceded to all of the strikers' demands including the taking back of even those women regarded as 'ringleaders', and the *Star* was enthusing over the workers' 'magnificent victory'. The paper also recorded the last distribution of the strike funds, on 21 July. Bernard Shaw was again present, but while his diaries, as has been shown, offered no observations on the women as individuals, the *Star*'s reporter recalled that among the 700 workers present was a young woman called Eliza whom he described unequivocally was 'one of the leaders of the strike'.[78] Eliza and her companions on the committee evidently stood behind the table and checked entries, so were involved directly in the administration of the strike fund along with the socialists, and also made speeches.

Bryant and May, one of the most powerful employers in East London, had been defeated, but what were the directors' feelings about the situation in which they now found themselves? The *East London Observer*, which obviously had close contact with the directors, reported Frederick Bryant's grudging comments upon the agreement, which show the company still trying to save face by implying that, had they known about the women's grievances, matters would have been resolved – therefore trying to foist the blame on to the foremen.

1   We agree to abolish such fines as have existed, on the distinct understanding that any girl disobeying orders or wilfully destroying property should be discharged;

2   We find the total amount paid by the 75 work-girls concerned in the items of paint, brushes, and stamps in the six months ending June 20th last is £9 19s 2d., while the cost of these items to us is £31 9s 2d.

3   The principal spokeswoman of the girls asked that the rackers out should be paid by the piece instead of the day as now. To this we agreed, and we understand the girls have decided to continue the system . . .

4   We have always been ready to give our most careful attention to any complaints brought under our notice, but as a matter of fact there have been no complaints.

5   . . . It is stated that repeated complaints have been made to us that a separate room had not been provided for our workers to breakfast and dine in. This is a mistake. No complaint has been made at any time, but we are prepared . . . to give this matter our prompt consideration. We have but a friendly feeling towards our workpeople, and it is a source of great regret to us that they should have had to suffer through bad advice in the early stages in this strike.[79]

It is noticeable that, while still trying to present the directors as caring employers and more sinned against by a workforce with no genuine grievances, than sinning themselves, Bryant does not here imply that Annie Besant 'led' the strike, only that someone – presumably she – gave them 'bad advice in the early stages'. It is also obvious that the directors were genuinely negotiating with 'spokeswomen' from among the women themselves.

The Union of Women Matchworkers, which Clara Collet noted was the largest union of women and girls in the country,[80] was formed, with Besant as secretary. Burrows was appointed treasurer, which position he still held in 1893 when Besant wrote her autobiography – though she herself had by then moved on.

William Morris' *Commonweal* celebrated the victory:

. . . even people in such a wretched condition as these poor match girls can make themselves felt temporarily, and can help to swell the mass of opposition to the manufacturers' ideal, to wit, human machinery which will give not more, but less, trouble than the machinery of mere dead matter.[81]

The *Eastern Post* agreed:

One of the most important strikes that has agitated East London for a considerable time past has happily been brought to a close. The employees of Messrs. Bryant and May have been successful.[82]

Even the Conservative *East London Advertiser* had completely changed its tune. Though still looking at the strike from a business perspective, it now blamed management (though not the directors themselves) rather than the 'insane advice of Mrs Besant' and '[t]he Socialist leaders'.[83]

> Messrs Bryant and May have done the proper thing in making the concessions they have; but why were they not made before? . . . The inference that most people will draw is that a rich and powerful trading company have been declaring large dividends whilst the people, who had so much to do with making them, have been certainly not well paid and subjected to restrictions and penalties of a most harassing kind. We can quite believe that the directors have been imposed upon as to the true state of affairs by the foremen and forewomen. But that does not relieve them of their responsibility. It is the plain duty of gentlemen in their position to make themselves acquainted with the labour side of a concern in which so many hundreds of hands are engaged . . . The unpleasant impression remains that justice has been done only by reason of outside agitation . . . Certainly the lesson should not be thrown away upon other large employers of labour. Capital has its responsibilities, which cannot be shirked even when transformed into 'Limited Liability'.[84]

From the workers' perspective, the *Star* too clearly signalled its conception of the importance of what had occurred:

> The victory of the girls . . . is complete. It was won without preparation – without organization – without funds . . . a turning point in the history of our industrial development.[85]

In 1923, Mile End's Member of Parliament noted of the Fairfield Works that 'as a result of that fight it is now one of the model factories. Every person there is a trade unionist'.[86]

'THERE HAVE FREQUENTLY BEEN STRIKES . . .': THE MATCHWOMEN AND MILITANCY

We are left, now, with a very different conception of the strike; and also some unanswered questions about the continuing misconception of Besant's role.

The latter may have survived in part because it can be made to conform to a variety of conventional ideas without disturbing the ideological *status quo*. Victorian hegemony on gender and class would suggest that at least some contemporary commentators might have found a strike being led by one charismatic middle-class individual, albeit a woman and a socialist, less disturbing than one begun by poor working-class 'factory girls'. Historical tradition also dictates that women are 'allowed' to subvert gender norms and take leadership roles occasionally, but 'largely as exceptions; those who were said to be as ruthless as, or wrote like, or had the brains of men'.[87] Besant was certainly castigated for her lack of 'proper' femininity, and often by women: this underlay Emmeline Pankhurst's criticism of her personal appearance, as well as Beatrice Webb's breathtakingly harsh assessment of her as a woman 'unsexed by the loss of her child'.[88]

A Besant-led strike was also in keeping with beliefs of the day about the capabilities of working-class women like the matchworkers; it could be seen as an extension of the philanthropic work of middle-class women among the East End poor. It also conformed to the idea of popular protest as something whipped up among previously content individuals by 'agents of the left' (or right, depending on the persuasions of those in power). Female militancy, as we have seen, was then considered an enormous threat to the *status quo*.

Perhaps it is understandable that, on first assessment, even those on the left might have struggled with the idea that such young, poor women could successfully take on the might of Bryant and May: in terms of societal power, the workers were seriously outgunned by their employer. However, the women had their own strengths, and were not averse to using them. It is harder to understand, or justify, how and why evidence for this could have been so consistently ignored in order to make events 'fit' the myth.

The Match Tax Protest

In 1871, the matchwomen were joined by their communities in protests against a proposed match tax after Gladstone's Chancellor, Robert Lowe, committed what is now generally regarded as an epic blunder.[89] A levy was proposed of a halfpenny per hundred on wooden matches, British and imported, and one penny per hundred on vestas. The proposal was immediately unpopular, attacked by *The Times* as 'reactionary' and likely to affect the 'great number of poor children' employed in matchmaking and selling.[90]

Bryant and May's workers convened a mass meeting at the Victoria factory, passing a resolution 'unanimously amid great cheering' stating that 'we the match-box makers and employees of ... match factories, resist to the utmost of our power by all legal means the imposition of this cruel tax upon our labour'.[91] The workers met again the next afternoon to form a 'monster procession' intended to present a petition to parliament.[92] The marchers gathered in Bow Road, and set off in an orderly fashion, despite police harassment from the outset. At Mile End Road, battalions of police provoked them by roughly manhandling them into smaller groups, and there were running battles along the way to Westminster.[93] At Trafalgar Square a large force of police charged the march, seizing the women's banners and throwing them into the Thames. Stones were thrown 'freely, and ... not without effect' at the police, who retaliated with baton charges.[94] Despite this the marchers would not retreat, and several women managed to break through the cordons and recapture their petition.

The Times denounced the brutality of the police, who 'by their hard usage of match-makers and spectators converted what was before not an ill-behaved gathering into a resisting, howling mob'.[95] There were questions in parliament about the 'quiet and orderly number of poor match-makers' who were 'beaten with staves by the police'.[96] The furore around the march was a leading factor in the hasty dropping of the tax. Lowe had no alternative but to retreat; and Gladstone was obliged to take over and replace the abandoned indirect tax with another increase to income tax.

While their workers' opposition to the tax was clearly in Bryant and May's interests too, reports of the demonstration suggest that the procession and protest were the workers' own: they alone faced and resisted the police hostility. *The Times* observed:

> Those who made the demonstration were . . . working girls and working boys, a year or two into their teens, and beyond doubt of the working classes. They numbered several thousands, and were accompanied by men and women of their own class, without any mixture of the usual agitators.[97]

Bryant and May's only formal response to the proposal seems to have been to take a decision to pass the tax on to their workers in the form of deductions; this was true to form, and subsequent events show they would have had no qualms about doing so. It was perhaps knowledge of this decision which caused their workers to revolt.

Since Bryant and May were prominent Liberal supporters who set great store by their establishment connections, to the extent of erecting a statue to Gladstone during his second term, they may not have been willing to risk the displeasure of the government by openly opposing the tax.

The Matchgirls' Song

In the entire sound archives of the British Library there is only one brief piece of recorded oral history from an eyewitness to the matchwomen's strike. However, extensive research into it has suggested a tantalizing link between the strike and an ancient form of community justice sometimes used to expose employers' mistreatment of their workers. The recording was made by Roy Palmer, to whom I am indebted for copyright permission, as part of his project on traditional music in England. His interviewee, Samuel Webber, was 14 when he watched the striking matchworkers march through the East End. Due to the focus of the research, Palmer's interest is not in the strike *per se* but in a protest song that the matchwomen sang while marching through the streets. As the only known piece of oral history from an observer of the strike it has value in itself, and also provides a vivid image of the strikers in action from the perspective of a working-class East End onlooker.

The following is a full transcription of Webber's recollections:

> When [the matchgirls] went on strike, they walked from Bow Road all the way up Mile End Road, up Whitechapel Road, Leadenhall Street and straight through Trafalgar Square, and on the way through Leadenhall Street particularly they used to sing [sings, to the tune of *John Brown's Body*]:
>
> > We'll hang Old Bryant on the sour apple tree
> > We'll hang Old Bryant on the sour apple tree
> > We'll hang Old Bryant on the sour apple tree, as we go marching on.
> > Glory glory hallelujah . . .[98]

And so on. And while they were walking along the people in the offices overhead would throw coppers down and then there'd be a scramble among the girls to get these coppers up. That caused a bit of an interlude from the singing and when they picked up all the coppers on they'd go, singing and marching.[99]

While it is uncertain exactly when during the strike the march, or marches, took place, it is interesting to note that the route taken by the women on this occasion was the same as that taken during their demonstration against the proposed match tax in 1871, reminding us once more that these were old hands at protest. Even more significant is the confirmation the recording gives that those in the area could scarcely have failed to notice that the Bryant and May women had, very definitely, walked out.

'John Brown's Body'

While the brevity of the clip is frustrating, the information contained within it has yielded more information than at first appeared likely. The tune Samuel Webber is singing is clearly that of the song which became known as 'John Brown's Body', sung by Union troops during the American Civil War to commemorate the execution of the militant abolitionist John Brown.

Born in 1800, Brown's father had been an active abolitionist working for the American 'underground railroad' network which transported escaped slaves to freedom. Brown himself settled with his family in a black community founded in North Elba, New York, in 1849. Here he became convinced that only armed struggle could overthrow the slave system. In 1855 he moved with five of his sons to Kansas, with the aim of helping abolitionist forces to take over the area. When his house was burned down and one of his sons murdered, Brown moved to Virginia and established a refuge for escaped former slaves at the foot of the Blue Ridge Mountains.

From there in 1859 he planned a raid on a federal armoury at nearby Harpers' Ferry, and the capture of prominent local slave owners. This was to be the precursor to an uprising by men and women held as slaves in the area. The initial raid was successful, but within days Robert E. Lee and his troops had stormed the armoury, capturing Brown and killing two of his sons in the fighting which followed. The planned uprising never took place. Brown was tried and convicted of insurrection and treason, and hanged on 2 December 1859.

Three years earlier William Steffe had written a song for Methodist meetings, 'Say, Brothers, Will You Meet Us?' with the 'Glory, glory Hallelujah' refrain. This became popular, particularly in churches with emancipated former-slave congregations, and was used as a marching song at army posts.[100] Following his execution, Brown became a hero to abolitionists and African-Americans, prompting the addition of a new verse to the hymn:

> John Brown's body lies a-mouldering in the grave
> John Brown's body lies a-mouldering in the grave
> John Brown's body lies a-mouldering in the grave
> His soul goes marching on![101]

Union regiments, in particular the Twelfth Massachusetts, are credited with passing on the song as they marched south. Union soldiers appear to have altered the words in 1861, the first year of the Civil War, at the battle of Bull Run, inserting the name of the Confederate general to taunt the retreating troops: 'They will hang Jeff Davis to a sour apple tree.'[102] This is the first appearance of the 'sour apple tree' of the matchwomen's song, and according to some sources was introduced in response to Confederate troops' mocking version:

'John Brown's a-hanging on a sour apple tree . . .'

Julia Ward Howe, an active abolitionist, later composed an uplifting religious poem to fit the tune, which was first published in 1862, and became famous as the 'Battle Hymn of the Republic'.[103] The infinitely adaptable 'sour apple tree' refrain remained popular, though never officially part of 'John Brown's Body' lyrics: it has been continually used to attack particular individuals, whether well known or not, up to the present day.[104] In Britain the lyrics were incorporated into protest songs: there are records of 'We'll hang Anthony Eden on a sour apple tree . . . when the red revolution comes' being sung in the 1940s.[105]

This does not explain how the matchwomen came to be singing what seems to have been a verse from 'John Brown's Body' in the Victorian East End. There were, however, examples of solidarity between the British working classes and the American abolitionist cause, and therefore Union troops. One remarkable incident took place during the Lancashire 'cotton famine' in the first years of the Civil War. Because of the economic blockade of the southern United States, cotton workers in Britain lost access to raw cotton, and therefore their livelihoods, resulting in appalling hardship, starvation and death.[106] Nonetheless, the working people of Manchester met together at the Free Trade Hall in December 1862 to express their support for Abraham Lincoln and the northern states in their fight to abolish slavery. Lincoln would later commemorate their courage by commissioning and shipping to Manchester a statue of himself, which still stands there today.[107]

The Ceffyl Pren

I also uncovered a much earlier, European usage of the 'sour apple tree' refrain. The *ceffyl pren* was an ancient means of punishment in Wales, literally translating as 'the wooden horse', but encompassing a variety of practices used to punish those who threatened community harmony. Derived from an ancient Welsh law, *ceffyl pren* methods continued to be used, particularly by women, to enforce local justice, as well as to demonstrate political rebellion, up until the early twentieth century.[108] Many European countries had similar 'charivari' or 'rough music' traditions: E. P. Thompson has written extensively on these.[109] However, this account of the use of the *ceffyl pren*, which dates from the 1850s, shows why the Welsh rituals are of particular interest here:

Wooden horse: a ladder used as a stretcher in former years for carrying a person, tied thereon, around the district so as to expose them for some great sin, or disgraceful act which they had committed. The leading carriers were all masked so as to disguise their identity, and it was part of their programme to stick pins in the person tied on the wooden horse, as well as to torture them in other ways. It was the same in principle as the ducking stool of olden times, and was in later years replaced by a burning of a person's effigy, which consisted of an image made with a stick and old rags (a kind of Aunt Sally) which was saturated with oil or tar and then put fire to – the crowds around singing loudly, 'We'll hang old — on the sour apple tree', using the name of the person desired to be exposed.[110]

Crab apples had been grown in Wales for centuries – there are references to them as 'sour apples' in the Laws of Hywel Dda, transcriptions of ancient Welsh law which date from the thirteenth century.[111] The wood from the European crab-apple tree, *malus sylvestris*, was notably strong – a 'crab-apple cudgel' being proverbially hard – and popularly used in turning.[112] Perhaps the original 'wooden horses' upon which transgressors were 'hung' were made from this wood, explaining the singing of these words during the *ceffyl pren*. The militancy of Welsh women throughout the country's history has been 'almost proverbial',[113] as contemporary accounts demonstrate: 'reports on food riots, enclosure disturbances and attacks on bailiffs and other officials invariably attest to the commitment and vitality of female participation'.[114] Rosemary Jones has written about the increasing 'feminization' of the *ceffyl pren* throughout the nineteenth century, and credited the tradition with inspiring the 'Rebecca Riots' of late 1839 and the early 1840s, during which impoverished Welsh farmers and land workers attacked the toll-gate system, 'one of the tangible symbols of their exploitation'.[115]

'Beca' grew into a widespread and long-lasting movement, and has been called a 'rural version of Chartism': there was speculation that the Chartist Hugh Williams was its secret leader.[116] Historian George Rude has argued that the movement represented 'a remarkable example of the crowd acting upon its own initiative'.[117]

The *ceffyl pren* often ended with an effigy of the offender being ritually burned, shot – or hung, another possible explanation of the 'sour apple tree' chant. The rituals seem to have been initially used to enforce male domination – women judged to be 'scolds', or men thought too submissive to 'petticoat government', being the victims. This was generally believed to be the case with English 'rough music' too, as described in Andrew Marvell's 1667 poem:

> A punishment invented first to awe
> Masculine wives transgressing Nature's law
> Where, when the brawny female disobeys
> And beats the husband till for peace he prays . . .
> . . . the just street does the next house invade
> Mounting the neighbour couple on lean jade . . .

> Prudent antiquity, that knew by shame
> Better than law, domestic crimes to tame . . .[118]

However, as E. P. Thompson has shown, 'rough music' was not used solely to reinforce patriarchal order and morality, but also to punish those who threatened class and community solidarity: police informers and strike-breakers, for example.[119]

Jones argues that, as *ceffyl pren* traditions survived the shift to industrialization, so they became the increasing preserve of women excluded from established male forms of industrial organization.[120] Informal female networks played an important part in selecting the victims of the *ceffyl pren*, like the Rhyl policeman accused of adultery who was forced to resign from his job in 1857 after his effigy had been paraded through the town; or the Llangefni man tied to a ladder by neighbours after deserting his wife in 1887, in a procession which paused intermittently to 'allow the womenkind to wreak their vengeance upon him'.[121]

Jones notes a pattern in contemporary reports of the use of public shaming, where punishment of supposedly domineering wives began to give way to that of wife-beaters. In such cases, the vast majority of both instigators and participants tended to be female. At the peak of the Rebecca Risings in 1843, for example, 40 women in Pontarddulais surrounded the home of a man 'who was in the habit of rather ill-using his better half', led by a woman blowing on a horn.[122] They threatened to drag him to the river and 'duck' him unless he reformed immediately. From the middle of the nineteenth century such cases became more common, and the punishment of 'domineering' women increasingly rare.

Jones argues that, while women too continued to be the victims of such punishments, the *ceffyl pren* became an important sanction for the protection of abused working-class wives who could not always rely on the legal system. It also gave women an opportunity to defy violent male authority and demonstrate that they were no mere passive victims.[123]

The *ceffyl pren* also had its more overtly political uses, as demonstrated by its enthusiastic revival during the Rebecca Risings, when it was widely used against those believed to have been informants and collaborators for the authorities. The riots themselves took their combination of protest and theatricality from the *ceffyl pren*.

Ceffyl pren rituals could also 'serve as a guise for direct criticism of the ruling classes by, on occasion, providing a useful model for more widespread protest'.[124] 'Political' use of the tradition continued beyond the Rebecca period – in 1857 it was used by the 'wives of oyster-dredgers'[125] (who may well also have been dredgers themselves) to drive out an exploitative tithe collector, and extensively during the nonconformist 'Tithe War' of the 1880s and 1890s.[126] Even after the turn of the century, these traditions were used in trade union disputes: miners who had refused to join a union were paraded through the streets in wheelbarrows by 'amazons' in Maesteg in 1906.[127]

How the words associated with the *ceffyl pren* were transported to America to attach themselves to 'John Brown's Body' and then, possibly, back again to the East End of London, is not certain. The matchwomen were, however, using the older form of words in 1888, even if the tune was the American one. The American adaptations mention 'Jeff Davis' and 'John Brown', using full first and second names. The Welsh *ceffyl pren* version was 'We'll hang *old* so-and-so', and the matchwomen sang: 'We'll hang *old* Bryant on the sour-apple tree', and not 'William Bryant' or 'Mr Bryant'. There is no evidence of the 'old so-and-so' form being used in the USA, even in the present day. With so much migration into London there is certainly nothing to preclude some of the women being Welsh or of Welsh heritage.

It must be considered possible, at least, that in using this form of words the Bryant and May strikers were consciously acting out a 'public shaming' of their employers based on this ancient form of people's justice which was so strongly associated with women. This fits in with matchwoman Martha Robertson's summary of the motivations for the strike, as recalled by her grandson Ted Lewis in Chapter Nine, as an attempt to right a wrong, to expose an injustice perpetrated by Bryant and May, not just on them but on their families and communities. This strengthens the concept of a strike carried out by and for the workers themselves, born not out of external manipulation but a sense of genuine grievance and outrage, and utilizing the only weapons at their disposal – strength in numbers and community feeling – to expose the exploitative practices of Bryant and May.

The Statue

During the affair of the Gladstone statue, the matchwomen independently demonstrated their discontent against their employers, a full six years prior to Besant's involvement. In 1882 Theodore Bryant, a prominent Liberal supporter, commissioned the statue of William Gladstone, then Prime Minister for the second time, to stand on the Bow Road near to the factory, as it still does today. Evidently he instituted a compulsory deduction of a shilling from each worker's wage packet to pay for this grand gesture. He compounded his generosity by granting a half-day holiday so that the workers might witness its unveiling – unpaid. Not surprisingly, as the women would later tell Besant, on such terms they decided 'we don't want no holidays', but attend they did – with 'stones and bricks in their pockets':

> . . . they surrounded the statue – 'we paid for it' they cried savagely – shouting and yelling, and a gruesome story is told that some cut their arms and let their blood trickle on the marble paid for, in very truth, by their own blood.[128]

This incident lives on in the memory of the East End to such an extent that the statue is to this day frequently daubed with red paint, supposedly to represent the matchwomen's blood. At the time of writing the statue bears the remnants of the last incident: red paint is visible on the statue's hands. This has happened so frequently that the council are now reluctant to have it cleaned on each occasion, as they suspect it will immediately be repainted and 'it's very expensive to get it removed'.[129] As will be discussed in the following chapter, my research uncovered evidence from a matchmaker's descendant that the matchwomen themselves threw red paint over the statue after the unveiling, so this may be a sign of the lasting impressions – literal as well as metaphorical in this case – made by the women's protests.[130]

Previous Strikes

Independent strikes at Bryant and May are confirmed by media accounts in 1881, 1885 and 1886. The *National Reformer* reported that a strike in the autumn of 1885, to which Tom Mann also made reference in 'What a compulsory eight hour working day means to the workers', was over 'low wages and "Phossy Jaw"'.[131] With no union support or funding the strikes ultimately failed, but they showed the capability and willingness of the workers to take action on their own initiative.

Beatrice Potter (later Webb) reported for Charles Booth's survey that the matchwomen had

> always shown a remarkable power of combination. Those in the East End live near each other in Bow, Mile End, Stepney, Limehouse and Poplar. They are distinguished by a strong 'esprit de corps', one girl's grievance being adopted as the grievance of every girl. There have constantly been small strikes in the match factories of the East End.[132]

William Bryant's claim that relations with the workforce had always been good until socialist interference had 'upset [their] minds'[133] was therefore patently untrue: he must have been aware that there had been at least three strikes in the preceding seven years, but he too was prepared to jump on the convenient bandwagon of blaming socialist manipulation rather than admit that his workforce's genuine discontent had been building for years.

Nor was the 1888 strike anything like the last. After it, as a direct result of the women's victory, a dining room and social club, the Clifdon House Institute, was established in Fairfield Road across from the factory for the use of Bryant and May's workers. A leaflet from 1896 shows that Gilbert Bartholomew was the honorary treasurer.[134] In the same year Charles Booth interviewed its superintendent, Miss Nash: the full text of the interview can be seen in Booth's original notebook in the London School of Economics (LSE) archives. Miss Nash was evidently no great fan of the strikers of 1888, and ventured that the 'girls' at the time of the strike had been 'a terrible rough lot and decent people scarcely dared to go down the street when they were coming out of work'.[135] Just after the strike, 'relations between the girls and the firm were as bad as possible; none of the girls would ever say a good word about their employer, and small strikes on the most trivial matter were a constant occurrence'.[136]

The women had clearly not listened to Besant's admonishment that they should not go on strike again.

CONCLUSIONS

Previous chapters have presented considerable evidence that Annie Besant was an unlikely candidate for the leadership of a strike of sweated workers: the events of the strike itself confirm this. Besant herself stated her position with extreme clarity just days before the strike began, in the very issue of the *Link* which contained the famous 'White slavery in London', the article on which her reputation as strike leader largely rests. Any scholar who merely turned the page could find Besant dismissing as impractical and impossible the notion of unionizing 'the girls of Bryant and May'. It is extremely surprising that history has missed, or chosen to ignore, this glaring contradiction of reputation and reality, though in fact it is just one of many anomalies that have been passed over in order to maintain belief in the orthodox version of the strike.

There is no evidence in any of Besant's accounts that she planned anything beyond a consumer boycott, and considerable evidence that she did not. Furthermore, re-examination of the sequence of events of the strike has shown that Besant was not even aware of its commencement until some days later.

This chapter has argued that it was in fact management bullying, and not Besant's article, which brought the women out. The myth of external leadership survives in spite of the evidence against it. Even if Besant had wanted to cause a strike, she could not have predicted the behaviour of the employer which triggered the action. It is also puzzling that subsequent public references by Bryant and May to the 'ringleaders' of the action from within the workforce have not set alarm bells ringing with commentators, when the only 'ringleader' is supposed to have been Besant.

Besant's reaction on discovering the strike is also telling. It is understandable that she should have been initially dismayed to discover that such a large number of women were now without financial support. This is not a condemnation of Besant: her views on strikes were no more and no less enthusiastic than the wider socialist movement, and indeed the established trade union movement of the day. However, both her dismay and the fact that no funds were put in place confirm the erroneousness of asserting that she had planned the strike.

Primary sources also conclusively show that the strikers began their own lively and effective protests almost immediately: picketing, organizing mass meetings and deputations to the employer, and collecting money to support themselves. This, it transpires, reflected a tradition of industrial militancy at the factory.

The final question must be whether Besant's articles and strategies would have achieved much more than causing Bryant and May discomfort, without the women's action. Tom Mann, though a great admirer of Besant, thought not:

despite the efforts of 'kindly disposed persons' in publishing shareholders' names, he wrote that 'nothing brought any change for the better until the women and girls went on strike'.[137]

7

The Matchwomen, the Great Dock Strike and New Unionism

INTRODUCTION

1889 is generally agreed to be a hugely significant year in labour history. It saw the birth of 'a movement of the whole labour class against exploitation', writes Cole.[1] In the aftermath of the Great Dock Strike that summer, came what Harrison calls a 'truly massive advance in trade unionism', in which membership numbers increased from 750,000 in 1888 to more than 2 million by 1900.[2] Thompson agrees that the dock strike 'set off a whole series of agitations and strikes, the formation of new unions and the expansion of those already existing'.[3]

It was not just the numbers of new members, nor the increase in organization among workers designated unskilled and semi-skilled, which led to these unions being called 'New Unions' and the movement 'New Unionism'. There had been new unions among these groups of workers before, but now came an apparent ideological change which gave the unions of this period their historical significance. Prior to 1889, some established unions were so politically weak as to be only 'playing at Trade Unionism'.[4] After 1889 Hobsbawm has written:

> Ideologically and politically the union expansions . . . marked a sharp turn to the left, the creation of a new cadre of leaders and policy-makers – mostly inspired by various versions of socialism – and the association of the movement with an independent working-class political party and, after 1918, a socialist programme.[5]

Although subsequent historians have questioned the extent to which socialist involvement equated to real influence, key New Unionist leaders like John Burns, Ben Tillett and Tom Mann were active members of the Social Democratic Federation (SDF).[6]

For many historians then, the dock strike was the seminal event of New Unionism, while the Bryant and May action was only retrospectively important – a minor signifier of great events to come, which proved that 'it might be possible to organize even the poorest and most exploited groups of workers'; but of little significance in itself.[7] Accordingly, New Unionism is invariably dated from 1889 rather than 1888. Paul Thompson accepts that prior events, such as the organization at Beckton gasworks, played a vital part in the movement, but as we have seen, discounts the Bryant and May strike as 'relatively isolated' and 'given exaggerated publicity'. Thompson does not explain in what sense he believes the strike to have been isolated, nor provide supporting evidence, but he is presumably referring to the year which separates the two strikes. The perception of isolation may also relate to the matchwomen as a group of workers, also judged by Hunt as 'too unlike the workers who had the best chance of becoming successful new unionists' to have influenced them, and their strike 'too early'.[8] Certainly the matchwomen's gender set them apart from other New Unionists: Hunt does not reveal whether it is this to which he refers, and, again, he gives no evidence to support his argument.

Because of this prevailing view, while the matchwomen's strike is usually discussed within the context of New Unionism, it is also denied a true role in the movement.

This chapter will reevaluate the matchwomen's place in history, both introducing new evidence and looking afresh at established sources. It will begin to challenge the concept of the matchwomen's strike as 'isolated' in two ways. First, the 13-month period between the women's victory and the beginning of the dock strike will be studied, and patterns of industrial unrest noted, to discover whether the strikes were really separated by a cessation of struggle.

The Great Dock Strike itself will then be reconsidered. Though it has already been extensively covered in secondary sources, the account of it in this chapter has been compiled largely from primary sources, such as contemporary accounts, media coverage and the memoirs of its participants, largely researched at the archive of the Museum in Docklands. I felt that going back to original sources was justified in that commentators who were not looking for links between the dockers' strike and the matchworkers', and who had no specific interest in the latter, may have overlooked evidence linking the two.

BEFORE 1888: THE LABOUR 'ARISTOCRATS'

From the mid-nineteenth century, transport links improved so dramatically that amalgamations became possible between unions which had previously been organized on a purely local basis. The Amalgamated Society of Engineers (ASE) was formed in 1851, and provided an organizational, and ideological, template which others would follow. Membership was strictly limited to appreticed workers and subscription rates high, allowing for the employment of a core staff of full-time officials as well as the payment of sickness, accident, unemployment and death benefits to members. The ASE seems to have settled fairly quickly into a political moderation which made it more akin to an old Friendly Society than a radical union in the mode of the Grand National Consolidated Trades Union (GNCTU).[9]

The 'new model' period did not put an end to local societies, and even within national unions a high degree of branch-autonomy remained. Nor did all unions follow the ASE template, some preferring to maintain a separation between their trade and friendly society functions. However, trades like tailoring, woodworking and shoemaking followed the ASE's lead, in outlook if not in organizational structure. These new model unions are generally regarded as having been protectionist in outlook – concerned to preserve their members' labour price through the employment of apprenticeship and similar schemes, and so limiting the amount of skilled labourers who could enter their professions.[10] One miners' leader of the period expressed this simple philosophy of supply and demand with the maxim:

> When eggs are scarce, eggs are dear:
> When men are scarce, men are dear.[11]

The leaders of the key new societies, collectively christened the 'Junta' by Sidney and Beatrice Webb, set about

> transforming the 'paid agitator' into the trusted officer of a great financial corporation . . . enlarge[ing] the mental horizon of the rank and file . . . opening out to those whose vision had hitherto been limited to the strike and the tap-room, whole vistas of social and political problems in which they as working men were primarily concerned.[12]

The boom in 'skilled' trades such as engineering, printing and building, it has been argued, assisted the rise of an elite within the workforce. Morton and Tate have written that the increasing use of cheaper, unskilled female labour, in industries like textiles, also helped to give a 'more distinct and dominant place to highly-skilled male workers'.[13] Writers like Clark, Honeyman and Goodman, Pinchbeck, and Shoemaker and Vincent, however, argue that this new emphasis on 'skill' as a masculine preserve was deliberately constructed, and lead to the downward classification of work done by women to 'unskilled', though it might quickly be upgraded to 'skilled' if taken over by men.[14]

The 'skilled hands' continued to grow in both affluence and status, aspiring to a lifestyle closer to that of their bourgeois masters than of lower-ranking workers.[15] As George Potter, himself a prominent 'new model' trade unionist and editor of union journal the *Beehive*, noted in 1870:

> The working man belonging to the upper classes of his order is a member of the aristocracy of the working classes. He is a man of some culture, is well read in political and social history . . . His self-respect is also well developed.[16]

The term 'aristocracy of labour' became, and remains, current to describe this elite.[17] How much the development, and behaviour, of this elite tier affected the rest of the working-class has been highly controversial among historians. To some the 'aristocrats' put a break on industrial militancy, suborning their fellow workers into a period of compromise and collaboration with the employer. To others, their influence has been over-stated. Periodically as John Field put it, this debate 'smoldering quietly in the corners of British historiography' will 'once more burst into flames.'[18]

Morton and Tate have estimated that the 'aristocracy' represented around 15 per cent of workers, with the skilled but less affluent making up about 50 per cent, and including those classed as semi-skilled in the new mechanized industries, and also the highest-paid labourers (workers in industries regarded as 'unskilled' which nonetheless included workers with particular skills). Making up the remaining percentage were 'dockers, gas stokers, agricultural workers, building, railway and shipyard and "general" labourers, and a large proportion of the miners'.[19] The industries within which this elite predominated were unionized, and it has been argued that the aristocratic unions dominated the politics of the labour movement during the latter half of the nineteenth century

It is noticable that Morton and Tate make no reference to any groups of women workers in their classifications. The matchwomen would presumably have belonged in the last category, with other unskilled groups who would become central to New Unionism, such as the 'dockers, gas stokers . . .' and others. Women workers were largely excluded from the 'craft' unions, as they were from apprenticed work; and unions with protectionist stances were inclined to view the encroachment of female labour with hostility, seeing them as an economic threat. This made the self-organized victory of the matchwomen all the more unexpected and significant.

BEGINNINGS OF THE DOCK STRIKE RECONSIDERED
July 1888 to August 1889

As news of the matchwomen's victory spread, the dockers were among groups of workers who contacted the Union of Women Matchmakers to ask for advice on establishing their own organizations: as Besant, in her role as union secretary, noted: 'Then came a cry for . . . help from tin-box makers . . . aid to shop assistants . . . work for the dockers and exposure of their wrongs . . .'[20]

A wonderfully vivid WPPL report for 1889 noted that the matchwomen themselves responded enthusiastically to such requests, actively recruiting other workers. The report also highlights the prosaic, practical problems of trying to build a movement: the difficulties of booking reliable entertainment for meetings, and the exhaustion of the good ladies of the League in the face of the indefatigable energy, and appetite for cake, of the hundreds of working women who attended:

> Unions likely to be formed in London: Some members of the Match-makers' Union, convinced of the advantage of unionism, were anxious to spread the advantage to their neighbours in other trades and offered, if the League would arrange a meeting to distribute bills among the girls in jam, sweet and pickle factories. A lady interested in the League offered to give tea if a hall could be procured; and this tea took place on Wednesday, 19th. Several hundred girls and women belonging to the trades named were present, and the energies of those who were helping were severely taxed in distributing bread and butter, cake and tea. When the meal had been cleared away, the chair was taken by Herbert Burrows, and music and short speeches followed. The music seemed likely as late as the same morning, to be altogether absent, for a long chain of refusals and disappointments had left the league at the last moment absolutely unprovided with performers . . . Mr Baker's Irish songs were particularly delightful to his audience – among whom there was a strong Irish element.[21]

This report clearly shows the matchwomen themselves as active trade unionists engaged in secondary recruitment, using their political knowledge to approach the league for assistance. Besant is not mentioned; it is also interesting to once again note the 'Irish element'.

The next year the WPPL again noted the eagerness of matchbox-makers to unionize, emphasizing the women's 'intelligent' understanding of trade unionism and strong links with unionized dockers:

> Unions to be formed in London Shoreditch: A tea was given to which all women working in the match box trade were invited. Over three hundred came and during tea, Lady Dilke and Miss Routledge talked to them about the chances of forming a society. The difficulty to be contended against in organising the match box makers, does not consist in inability on their part to grasp the principles of unionism. The husbands of many of them are members of the Dock Labourers' Union, and they listen with intelligent interest to a discussion of the question of combination. They all however work in their own homes, their labour is unskilled labour and their children help with the easier portions of the work. The fact that matchbox-making is not carried on in factories, makes it specially difficult to induce the women to attempt combination, although the union is by no means looked upon as abandoned.[22]

In fact the first East End dock strike occurred not one year, but only three months after the matchworkers' victory. Ben Tillett, who had sought work on the docks after being made redundant, had become a vocal member of the Tea Operatives and General Labourers' Association, and was elected as its General Secretary in 1887. In that same year he published the pamphlet 'A dock labourer's bitter cry' (after Mearns' *Bitter Cry of Outcast London*) and exchanged correspondence with Besant.[23]

In October 1888 Ben Tillett led an unsuccessful strike at Tilbury Dock. The inspiration of the matchworkers was clearly shown in the speaker chosen to address the strikers: Tillett reported that, at his request, the then secretary of the matchworkers' union, 'Mrs Besant', came and 'spoke to 5,000 dockers'.[24] The next few months marked the beginning of a resurgence of working-class consciousness, with East London as its centre, and the eight-hour day and minimum wage its 'rallying call'.[25] There was a growing sense that, as one of the striking dockers would put it, 'If the working classes hold together, they can do what they likes.'[26]

The *Daily News* summed up the unsettling effect of recent events on established views of the working classes. Workers like the matchwomen and dockers were 'supposed to be struggling so hard for a bare subsistence that they would rather crowd each other out than help each other. We now see that this was a mistaken notion. The dry bones live and stand upon their feet – an exceeding great army.'[27]

An event largely ignored by secondary sources illustrates the widespread transmission of news of the matchwomen's victory, and its direct and immediate impact on unskilled female workers as far away as Ireland. I am indebted to Paddy Logue of the Derry Trades Council for the story of the Derry shirtmakers, who,

when the news reached them, contacted the local branch of the Boilermakers'
Union on their own initiative, asking to be allowed into membership.[28] The
boilermakers contacted the Derry Trades Council for advice, who in turn
corresponded with their London counterpart. As a result, Eleanor Marx went to
Ireland to advise them. She was the daughter of Karl and Jenny Marx, a founder
member of the Socialist League and extremely active within New Unionism.
Her life would end tragically in 1898, when she committed suicide by poison. At
the time of her visit to Ireland Eleanor was 34, and both her parents deceased.
She made a celebrated entrance into Derry, to be greeted by large crowds and
welcoming processions; afterwards the Derry Trades Council became only the
second to admit women and unskilled workers.[29]

An analysis of recorded strike action after the matchwomen's victory also
shows a definite upsurge of action, with *The Times* recording more than double
the numbers of strikes per quarter in the first half of 1889, after the match strike,
as in the first half of 1888, before the strike.[30] The list is not exhaustive: known
strikes among female cigar-makers in Nottingham and tin-box makers in London
in 1888 are not shown, and neither are the strikes by women workers at mills in
Kilmarnock and woollen weavers in Wakefield.[31] By the same token, there may
have been other short female strikes which were not reported.

STRIKES 1888 TO 1889[32]

Strikes in 1888
First Quarter:
Boot and shoe makers, Northampton
Colliery workers, Bolton
Colliery workers, Usworth
Iron shipbuilders, Middlesbrough
Jute spinners, Dundee
Total: 5

Second Quarter:
Coal miners, Silkstone Colliery, Yorkshire
Cotton workers, Blackburn
Steelworkers, West Cumberland
Coal miners, Wales
Shipbuilders, Tyneside
Total: 5

Third Quarter:
Bryant and May matchwomen, London
Cabmen, London
Chainmakers, Cradley Heath, Staffordshire
Cardroom hands, Burnley (strike averted)

Card and blowing room workers, Lancashire
Marine engine workers, West Hartlepool
Colliery workers, Durham
Cotton workers, Bolton
Steelworkers, Darlington
Forth Bridge workers, Scotland
Ironworkers, Aberdeen
Miners, Rhondda
Shipbuilders, Belfast
Shipbuilders, Liverpool
Iron and coal workers, Ebbw Vale (strike threatened)
Shipbuilders, Tyneside
Weavers, Leeds
Total: 17

Fourth Quarter:
Coal workers, Wales
Ebbw Vale coal workers
Coal workers, Rhondda
Engineers, Middlesbrough
Apron makers, Shropshire (strike proposed)
Dock workers, Tilbury
Hematite ironworkers, Workington
Coal workers, Yorkshire
Total: 8

Strikes in 1889
First Quarter:
Boilermakers, Southampton
Cotton workers, Bolton
Cotton workers, Blackburn
Ironworkers, West Coast
Cotton workers, Lancashire
Harbour workers, Seaham
Sailors and firemen
Seamen, Cork
Seamen, Dublin
Seamen, Glasgow
Tram workers, Cardiff
Shipyard workers, Wearside
Steelworkers, West Cumberland
Total: 13

Second Quarter:
Mill workers, Armagh
Army accoutrement makers
Boilermakers, Southampton
Ironmakers, Hull
Ironmakers, Leeds
Miners, Somerset
Miners, Bristol
Riveters, Clydeside
Seamen and firemen
Drivers, Cardiff
Tinplate workers, Worcester
Brewery workers, Stroud
Total: 12

Third Quarter:
Dock labourers, Clydeside
Shipbuilders, Clydeside
Nailers
Seamen
Tram workers, Cardiff
Dockers, London

1889: the Beckton Gas Works Dispute

In March 1889, a number of workers at the Beckton Gas Works were made redundant. Will Thorne, gas worker, secretary of the Canning Town branch of the SDF and later MP for West Ham, wrote that this and a number of 'slave-driving methods' employed by management had left the men 'almost prepared to go on strike, even though there was no union behind them'.[33] Thorne was eager to seize the moment: 'the time was ripe'.[34]

Thorne called in Ben Tillett for assistance and, together with William Byford, the proprietor of a temperance bar, the men formed an organizing committee. They held a mass meeting on 31 March, and a resolution in favour of forming a union was passed. On the first morning of what was to be 'the birthday of the National Union of gasworkers and general Labourers of Great Britain and Ireland',[35] 800 members were signed up.

Thorne noted that great popular interest in their activities spread: 'London was ablaze'[36] with talk of it, even in the first days when the union was still building and no demands had yet been put to the employer:

> News of meetings spread like wildfire, in the public houses, factories and works of Canning Town, Barking, East and West Ham, everyone was talking about the union.[37]

The union's activities were also being reported in national newspapers, which were 'curious to know what we wanted and what we were going to do'.[38] Thorne already knew, having given a pledge to his members at the union's inception to 'work and fight for the eight-hour day'.

Thorne and Tillett both stood for the post of General Secretary; Thorne was elected. The responsibilities of the post would cause him some anxiety, as he had had little formal education. Eleanor Marx was a friend and helped him with his writing and reading, which he said were 'very bad at the time'.[39] Every Sunday thereafter a series of 'Sunday morning crusades' encouraged men at other gasworks to join the union too, bolstering numbers to 3,000 within a fortnight. Against this background, the union began negotiating with the owners of the Gas, Light and Coke Company and the South Metropolitan Gas Company, which in turn owned the Beckton and Greenwich works respectively. The union quickly achieved a decrease from twelve- to eight-hour shifts, an extra shilling's wages per week, and one less shift per fortnight.[40]

News of this further victory over a powerful East End employer spread. In June, tram workers organized a rally and Annie Besant was called upon to address them. The atmosphere in the East End was now 'electric . . . A small dispute would be enough to cause a grand explosion.'[41]

It is interesting to note that the gasworkers' organization was a true case of 'socialists' encouraging a strike in accordance with their political beliefs; much more so than the matchworkers' strike of which this has so often been said to be the case. However, as with the dockers' strike to follow, the gasworkers' organization has never been subject to claims that outside political influence made it anything other than a genuine 'grassroots' stoppage. The matchwomen set the agenda for their socialist supporters rather than vice versa, and they provided a template for Thorne et al. to follow. The immediate attention of the national media on the gasworkers' activities must have been helped by the widespread publicity for, and public interest in, the women's strike.

However, Hobsbawm's detailed analysis of the gasworkers' organization in Labouring Men fails to give any consideration to this. Hobsbawm asks 'what [had] changed?' in a group previously believed to be incapable of strong organization.[42] In response he advances several theories, including socialist influence, for the signs of unrest which first became visible in 'the second half of 1888' – but he neglects to mention the matchwomen's victory.[43]

That news of the 31 March gasworkers' meeting spread so quickly and was of such interest to other Londoners, as vividly described by Thorne, is also noteworthy: a mood of similar but even greater excitement must have swept the area following a 1,400-strong strike only six months previously.

'LONDON ON STRIKE': THE GREAT DOCK STRIKE BEGINS

By the 1880s, casual and 'sweated' labour dominated the East End market. If Bryant and May was the largest East End employer of casual female labour, the equivalent for men was dock labour. The Port of London, comprising ten docks, was a massive employer: an estimated 150,000 families depended upon port work in the 1880s.[44] Fierce competition for work – 90 per cent of workers were casual – and a strict hierarchy had previously been bars to unity.[45] With thousands unemployed, competition to find even a day's work on the docks was desperate. Several times a day there was a 'call-on' for casual labourers at each of the docks. Henry Mayhew described the desperate struggle for a day's wage:

> As the foreman calls from a book the names, some men jump on the backs of others, so as to lift themselves high above the rest, and attract his notice. All are shouting. Some cry aloud his surname, some his Christian name, others call out their own names, to remind him that they are there. Now the appeal is made in Irish blarney – now in broken English . . . it is a sight to sadden the most callous, to see thousands of men struggling for only one day's hire, the scuffle being made the fiercer by the knowledge that hundreds out of the number there assembled must be left to idle the day out in want.[46]

On 14 August 1889 Ben Tillett was suddenly called to a dispute at the South-West India Docks, which had arisen during the unloading of the ship *The Lady Armstrong*. The men unloading the cargo had been working for five pence an hour on the 'plus' system, meaning that if they completed the job in less than the standard time defined by custom and practice, they could earn an extra halfpenny or penny per hour. In this case, however, the dock supervisor refused to pay the extra; so the men in turn refused to continue with their work.[47]

Tom Mann was present from the afternoon of the first walkout, summoned by Tillett, and he saw the inspiration of the matchwomen in what had occurred. Mann had first met Annie Besant, 'whose powers and courage I so much admired',[48] in 1885 when he was invited to address a Fabian Society meeting on the eight-hour day. Despite his admiration of Besant, his account of the match-women's strike does not give any suggestion that she had led them:

> The first considerable movement [of New Unionism] came from the women and girls employed at Bryant and May's Match factory at Bow. Kindly-disposed persons had written about the awful conditions under which the girls worked . . . Lists of shareholders were published showing that a considerable percentage of those were clergymen; but nothing brought any change for the better until the women and girls went on strike. This immediately attracted public attention, and Mrs Annie Besant . . . at once gave close personal attention to the girls on strike.[49]

Although he was at pains to praise Besant for her role, Mann's statement confirms several important points:
- that Besant's efforts were limited to 'middle-class' methods like trying to embarrass the company and their shareholders through exposés in her paper
- that the women's strike was not a direct result of Besant's article nor her urgings
- that Besant became fully involved only *after* the strike had occurred
- that the strike had attracted public attention in its own right even before Besant gave it publicity

In summary, Mann reveals that the matchwomen were better strategists than any of the learned ladies and gentlemen of the Fabian Society, whose tactics were achieving little until the women decided to strike.

By the time Mann arrived at the docks on the afternoon of 14 August, the men had decided to widen their claim to include what would become the historic demand for 'the dockers' tanner' – an hourly increase of one penny. By 16 August 2,500 men were out at the East and West India and South London docks.[50] Under the guidance of Burns and Tillett, the strike had spread to neighbouring docks by the next day. Within a week 'half of East London was out'.[51] There would be more than 50 small strikes in a five-mile radius of East London over the summer of 1889, from Crosse and Blackwell's jam factory to Charrington's brewery. A strike by Jewish tailors, both men and women, involved 6,000 workers and continued until the end of September.[52]

On 17 August, striking dockers were 'parading some of the principal thoroughfares of the City, with a view to gaining sympathy'; they were 'groaning' loudly *en masse* as they passed Tilbury, where dockers had not yet come out, perhaps still wary after the previous October's unsuccessful strike.[53]

There were reports of the intimidation of strike-breakers, and worse: the *Daily News* on 20 August reported apparently revolutionary stirrings, typified by the words of a ship's painter who was preparing to join the strike: 'If the working-class hold together they can do just what they likes . . . they could cut the Queen's head off tomorrow.' Other men apparently disagreed: 'Better stow that sort of bosh, mate . . . we mean to hang together but we're going to keep quiet about it. Yes, sir: that's what Mr Tillett said . . . You keep orderly and respectable and you got the public with 'e.'[54]

This short exchange, if accurately reported, is interesting, and perhaps illustrates that there were sections of the strike force more radical than at least one of its leaders. Robert Blatchford would report that Tillett had, before the dock strike, been less than enthusiastic about 'social agitation', and after it was still no revolutionary, only moving his position so far as to speculate that 'if labouring men can show such power they ought to use it to get their own representatives in Parliament'.[55]

On 20 August the *Star* reported that 'trade after trade joins the labourers', making a rare reference to black workers on the docks and their solidarity in refusing to strike-break: 'the coolies' leaders decline: black men will not do the work white men won't do'.[56]

By now the dock company was feverishly putting up recruitment posters: 'Gentlemen Blacklegs' and other 'novice dockers' answered their call.[57] The East End was solidly behind the strike, and feeling in the area ran so high that a local baker sent a letter to the *Echo* begging to correct the 'malicious' rumour that he had sold bread to the dock company to feed strike-breakers.[58] On 21 August the *Standard* reported that a demonstration in Hyde Park was attended by around 100,000 supporters, with seven bands playing the 'Marseillaise', demonstrating the revolutionary feeling abroad.

On 22 August the *Irish Times* reported that 37,000 workers were now on strike. On 24 August the *Pictorial News* carried a double-page spread with illustrations of scenes from the strike, including John Burns addressing a mass meeting and telling the men that 'The matchgirls had formed a union and had got what they wanted, and so had the gas stokers at Beckton, and surely the Dock Labourers could do the same', to cries of 'Hear hear'.[59] It is notable here that Burns referred simply to 'the matchgirls' without any further explanation, and not, for example, to 'the matchgirls from Bryant and May's factory in Bow who went on strike last year'. He clearly expected his audience, comprising tens of thousands of men, to not only know exactly who the matchwomen were, but to be well aware of their strike and its outcome. Their response would seem to indicate that this was true, and to display enthusiasm for the matchworkers' example.

By the 25th there were an estimated 130,000 strikers in what the media were now calling the 'Great Dock Strike'. The *Observer* listed some of the professions who had joined the action: 'Stevedores, ship-painters, dockyard mechanics, carpenters, shipwrights, carmen, lightermen, workmen and biscuit and jam factories'.[60] The last two groups would have been largely female and, as has been previously shown, jam-making was an alternative often chosen by matchwomen during high summer when the match trade was slack.

By 27 August the docks were like 'a city of the dead',[61] completely deserted. On this day Burns made reference to the matchwomen at a rally following an enormous procession from the East End to the city, complete with brass bands, floats and banners of every kind: '... stand shoulder to shoulder. Remember the matchgirls, who won their fight and formed a union.'[62] Such processions were now becoming an almost daily occurrence. Tom Mann remembered the matchworkers being invoked by Burns on at least one other such occasion, when he told the assembly that 'resolution had won the match girls' strike as it would yet win the dockers'.[63]

Resolution was indeed sorely needed. Although donations were pouring in, they were not sufficient to feed even a tenth of those on strike. On their marches, dockers carried rotting fish-heads and vegetables on spikes to show the sort of food for which they and their families had to scavenge to survive. Their wives, some of whom would have been matchwomen, declared a rent strike: banners strung across the Commercial Road by wives read: 'Husbands on strike: landlords need not call here'; and rather more poetically:

> Our husbands are on strike; for the wives it is not honey
> And we all think it is not right to pay the landlord money.
> Everyone is on strike; so landlords do not be offended.
> The rent that's due we'll pay when the strike is ended.[64]

By the end of the month the men and their families were starving. Just at the point when the men might have been hungered back to work, over £30,000 arrived from Australian port workers. Fresh supportive strikes were still occurring, the

East London Observer reported on 31 August, including many female workers – with matchworkers among them: 'The present week might not inaptly be called a week of strikes – coal men, printers' labourers, match girls ... are all out.'[65] While Bryant and May's name is not specifically mentioned here, it must be considered extremely likely that this referred to their workforce: as we have seen from John Burns' speeches, 'matchgirls' and 'Bryant and May matchworkers' were synonymous in the East End. It also seems plausible that matchworkers who were wives and daughters of dockers would have carried on working through the first days of the strike in order to maintain some income for the household.

Female participation in the strike was again demonstrated when 150 tinplate workers, 'mostly girls', came out in solidarity, and 'when a procession of Dock Labourers passed [them] ... they followed in the rear, singing and dancing and playing mouth-organs'.[66]

The *Evening News and Post* was now referring to 'London on strike' and the *Daily News* remarked that it would be easier to list those who were not affected by the strike than those who were. There was 'panic among the shipowners' and the price of coal doubled, but still the dock company refused the men's terms. The *East London Observer* asked: 'Is the strike a Socialist rising?' *Justice* hoped it could be: 'Burns and Mann [are] very careful to keep any references to Socialism or the Red Flag out of their speeches but ... [are] pushing on the cause of a social revolution, whether they know it or not.'[67] (*Justice* would famously criticize the two men for refusing to allow the red flag to be flown at the dock gates, though Engels thought they were tactically correct in this: the presence of the flag 'would have ruined the whole movement and ... driven [the dockers] back into the arms of the Capitalists'.[68])

On 2 September the *Star* recorded a (presumably misspelled) Mr Frederick Engels as donating five shillings to the dockers' strike fund. There was a call for a general strike, and shipowners and merchants rushed to Lloyds to insure against riot.[69] The call was quickly withdrawn for fear of alienating public sympathy, but militancy continued. The *East London News* of 7 September was headlined STRIKE FEVER and noted that

> coal men, Matchgirls, parcels postmen, carmen, rag, bone and paper-porters and pickers and employees in jam, biscuit, rope, iron ... clothing and railway works have found some grievance ... and ... followed the infectious example of coming out on strike.[70]

The establishment was becoming increasingly concerned. Pressure was mounting on the dock company from all sides, including ship and wharf owners, but the company remained stubbornly resistant. In desperation, the owner of Butler's Wharf began separate negotiations with the strike committee, and the chairman of P & O shipping suggested that shipowners might take over the discharge of ships. On 5 September the Lord Mayor of London formed the Mansion House Committee to try to bring resolution. The committee included Cardinal Manning, the Catholic Archbishop of Westminster, who had demonstrated some sympathy for the dockers' cause, though some subsequent commentators have regretted his considerable and moderating influence on the strike at this stage.[71]

The Dock Company eventually acceded to almost all of the strikers' demands, and Manning met the dockers on 10 September to persuade them to accept the employers' terms, with new payments to begin on 4 November. The strike committee finally agreed, and the return to work was settled for 16 September. On Sunday 15 September a last huge procession was held, culminating with a vast rally in Hyde Park, and 'All along the Commercial Road, the women turned out in thousands to see their husbands and their sons pass in triumph.'[72]

This newly burgeoning political awareness would produce the 'tremendous harvest' of New Unionism.[73] Hundreds of new unions and trade councils were established over the next few years, and old unions were given fresh impetus as the gains of unskilled workers spread to the wider movement. Although the new movement was considerably driven back by a new employers' offensive after 1891, and the TUC's old guard, led by Henry Broadhurst, did their best to prevent change, 'history was against them'.[74] The new unionists, with Kier Hardy a prominent spokesman, had successfully dislodged them by 1890.

Engels declared: 'The people are now putting their shoulders to the wheel in quite a different way ... drawing into the struggle far greater masses, shaking up society far more profoundly, and bringing forward far more radical demands...'[75]

By 1890, the number of trade unionists in the country had more than doubled, from 860,000 in 1889 to nearly 2 million in 1890. Not all of the new unions would last the course, but there was also massive expansion in pre-existing unions. In 1885 Charles Booth estimated that there were only 3 unions in London that were more than 2,000 strong; by 1894, there were 26.[76]

The Gasworkers' Union remained strong despite an unsuccessful strike between December 1889 and February 1890, which cost the union £10,000. The union had 60 branches in 1891 including a women's branch in Silvertown, and by 1892 had some 16,000 members. The aforementioned tailors' strike of 1889 achieved much in uniting sweated workers in the East End with the comparatively affluent West End bespoke craftspeople.[77] Lewis Lyons and James Macdonald helped to forge unity by amalgamating proposals appealing to the craftsmen's desire for greater local autonomy with those for the opening of membership to women and factory workers: although initially rejected by the union's conference in 1891, it was later accepted.[78]

The socialist and militant Boot Operatives' Union brought 10,000 members out on strike in 1890, and attempted a return to old craft values in the face of increasing mechanization and division of labour in their work. The new national unions of Shop Assistants and Clerks would prove significant, the former founded by socialists. In the building industry three large new unions were established, the biggest of which was the Navvies, Bricklayers' Labourers and General Labourers' Union led by John Ward, himself a former 'navvy' and an SDF member, and later one of the founders of the ILP. After a series of strikes Ward founded the

National Federation of Labour Union alongside Jack Williams, also of the SDF.[79] The federation had 13 branches by the end of 1889.

London's first May Day demonstration was held in 1890 in Hyde Park. 'It seemed,' wrote a contemporary observer, 'as though the whole population of London poured parkwards.'[80] It has been estimated that 500,000 people marched, and a further indication of ties between matchworkers and dockers comes from the *Star*'s eyewitness report of 5 May 1890:

> There was the banner of the Postmen's Union ... a slight break and up came the dockers, an interminable array with multitudinous banners ... Then came a large contingent of women ... match-makers, among others. Looked at from above they advanced like a moving rainbow, for they all wore the huge feathers of many colours which the East End lass loves to sport when she is out for the day ...[81]

The Employer strikes back

Almost as soon as New Unionism had begun to take hold, the employers, initially wrong-footed by the scale and suddenness of events, began their inevitable retaliation. New unions of unskilled workers were the first targets. By the end of 1889 the South Metropolitan Gas Company had abolished the eight-hour day and decimated its workers' union.[82] The shipowners, the wealthiest of the capitalists, who had previously sought negotiation with the dockers and condemned the Dock Company, now formed the Shipping Federation with the sole purpose of crushing the seamen's and port workers' unions. Lockouts in Cardiff and Hull destroyed unions there, and employers nationwide united to follow suit. Membership in some unions plummeted: the National Union of Dockworkers had 50,000 members in 1890, but only 8,463 by 1892.[83]

The National Procedure Agreement heralded a new style of industrial relations: strike action had now to be 'applied' for to a joint committee of union and management representatives.[84] The new unions which did survive showed themselves in many cases to be willing to negotiate with management in preference to militancy.

The counteroffensive was cemented by two legal decisions, *Lyons v. Wilkins* in 1896, which outlawed picketing, and the notorious Taff Vale ruling of 1901, enabling employers to sue unions for losses resulting from strike action.[85] However, the advances of New Unionism would never be completely reversed: the changes it brought to concepts of trade unionism would remain, and the ground was prepared for general unionism. If the next few years would prove to be something of 'an anticlimax',[86] a new period of strong trade unionism would emerge after 1909.

WOMEN AND NEW UNIONISM

After the first upheaval of New Unionism, trade unions were no longer actively closed to women, but nor would they display particular enthusiasm for recruiting them. The Gasworkers' Union formed a women's branch in the aftermath of New

Unionism, as we have seen: but whether it actively or adequately campaigned to recruit women must remain open to question, since its entire female membership was only 800 by 1906.[87]

The WPPL became more involved with working women in the 1880s, being renamed the Women's Trade Union and Provident League in 1891 in the aftermath of New Unionism, and the league became more politically militant.[88] The Women's Trade Union Association was founded in 1889 and later merged with the WIC, but as has been shown both of these organizations would ultimately blame the supposedly 'inferior' quality of women's work for their position in the labour market.

At the end of 1890, a 19-week strike by a largely female workforce at Manningham Mills in Bradford began. The workers, like the matchwomen, had seen their wages reduce year on year. Now, confronted with a further proposed reduction, they felt they would be doing an injustice 'not only . . . to ourselves but to the whole textile industry in the West Riding of Yorkshire by accepting the proposition'. 5,000 workers would join the stoppage. Women workers went out to secure donations, and a number of trade unions supported the call for funds. In April 1891, disturbances broke out in Bradford when the authorities tried to prevent the strikers from holding mass meetings and rallies. The culmination was a riot in the city centre, with the Durham Light Infantry making bayonet charges on the crowd. The strike ultimately failed in its objectives and the strikers were forced back to work, but its legacy was a growth of radical politics in the city, leading to the formation of the Bradford Labour Union. The union was radical and socialist in its politics, and because of its work Bradford hosted the founding conference of the ILP in 1893.

There was also agitation among laundresses in London in 1891, and Tom Mann was called upon to address them too. By the efforts of such women more male trade unionists began, albeit slowly, to understand the need for organization among women workers, as a delegate of the Amalgamated Society of Tailors expressed it at the union's 1892 AGM: 'Women should be allowed to work out their own political and social questions for themselves, the same as men are doing now.'[89]

New Unionism was a beginning rather than an end for women trade unionists: they would face – and indeed continue to face – a long battle for true equality and representation within the movement. It was, however, their first significant advance since the 1840s, and membership among women grew steadily from 50,000 in 1888 to 432,000 in 1913.

The matchwomen had helped to change perceptions of the 'factory girl': by 1896, Frances Hicks saw them as ideal unionists. She praised their 'rough and ready intelligence', resourcefulness and 'adherence to their own code of honour' as far more relevant to the modern woman than the 'angel of the house' qualities of 'humility and sweet content'.[90] She admired their solidarity, noting that 'factory girls always have girl-mates' ready to make collections for them in times of trouble, standing at the factory gates at pay-time 'with her apron held out'. Noting that strikes among women workers were 'not as uncommon among girls' as generally believed, she allowed that the women had 'no lack of intelligence to see the necessity of it' when the occasion arose.[91] Hicks further argued that after 'a few more years of education and development', they could become powerful agents of social change: 'Unfettered by precedent, they will make their own freedom, and through them the freedom of a nation of workers . . . servants they have been, fellow-workers they are, and comrades they will be.'[92]

Looking back on the matchwomen's strike in later years, both Mann and Tillett would make it clear that the women's victory had been an important inspiration, and a highly significant event for New Unionism: to Tillett, indeed, it was 'the beginning of the social convulsion which produced New Unionism'.[93] Mann agreed: '. . . the girls won. This had a stimulating effect upon other sections of workers, some of whom were also showing signs of intelligent dissatisfaction . . .'[94] Engels, also a keen observer of the London political scene in the 1880s who knew Besant, called the matchwomen's strike simply 'the small push that was needed for the whole avalanche to move'.

In 1940 Ernest Bevin wrote privately to surviving dock strikers with his assessment of the overall gains of New Unionism:

> Fifty years ago . . . you were among those who were involved in . . . a great industrial upheaval – virtually a revolution against poverty, tyranny and intolerable conditions. You little thought during those weeks . . . that you were laying the foundation of a great Industrial Movement.[95]

CONCLUSIONS

We can now see that the matchwomen's groundbreaking victory was vital to New Unionism, and that this was actually never denied by the leaders of the dock strike: according to Ben Tillett, it quite simply began the movement. The dockers were among the workers who contacted Besant, as Matchworkers' Union secretary, for advice in the aftermath of the women's victory.

The matchwomen's ability to self-organize is now clear. Though the independence and significance of the women's action continues to be undervalued by historians, in the light of both new and re-examined evidence, it is hard to sustain the arguments of some as to the 'isolated' nature of the matchwomen's strike, and their supposed difference from New Unionists like the dockers as a group of workers.

Research on primary accounts of the dock strike has yielded clear evidence of the matchwomen's participation and support in the dock strike. It has also shown the months between the two strikes to be far from the fallow period suggested by Hunt's conclusion that the matchwomen's strike came 'too early' to be judged significant to New Unionism.[96]

As to the matchwomen's influence on the dockers' strike, union leaders like Tillett and Mann seem to have been fully aware of it. Not just in the heat of their own action, but also in later years, both acknowledged it in their memoirs, heralding it as a key event in the beginning of New Unionism.[97]

Despite the controversies among theorists over some aspects of New Unionism, the significance of the events of this period to the overall development of the British labour movement is generally accepted. In the light of the above evidence, and of the discovery that the matchworkers' action was genuinely self-organized, there is no sustainable reason to continue to deny the women their part in it. Furthermore, as the matchwomen's victory clearly influenced the dockers and began a wave of activity which connected the two strikes, there is no reason why we should not to conclude, as did Tillett and Mann, that the 1888 strike was the true beginning of New Unionism.

8

Matchwomen, Dockers and the London Irish Community

INTRODUCTION

In this chapter we will examine the evidence for connections between the matchwomen and dockworkers. We have seen that few historians have explored, and some have dismissed, the idea of any connections between the two groups. Using interview evidence, primary accounts, census records, and maps of the relevant area at this time, I will test the hypothesis that the matchwomen were 'too different' to have influenced other New Unionist strikes like the dockers.

I carried out this research by analysing the occupations of the residents in 'matchwomen's streets' – firstly, a sample of those which occurred with the greatest frequency on the 1888 strike fund register, and secondly, the home streets of the matchwomen who I discovered to have been members of the Strike Committee (later the Matchmakers' Union committee) and did this. The streets and neighbourhoods where the matchwomen lived have been analysed and I have located the relevant streets, where possible, on contemporary maps and in census records. Distance from the docks has been measured, and occupational mix of residents noted with particular reference to incidences of matchwomen and dockers living in close proximity.

We have already examined some evidence that ties between the dockers and the matchwomen predated their industrial struggles, reinforcing the idea that the dockers would have been aware of the women's strike and their victory. Shared Irish heritage may have been an important component of this connection, and this link will be explored through primary evidence including an analysis of strikers' surnames using an official index of Irish householders.

'DOCK LABOURERS AND THEIR FAMILIES'[1] AND THE LONDON IRISH

John Hollingshead, journalist and theatre manager, published *Ragged London*, a volume of social investigation, in 1861. Writing of the Whitechapel area, he noted of the Wentworth Street neighbourhood, the home of Mary Driscoll in 1881, that:

> [its] inhabitants are chiefly Dock Labourers, and their families a class who form one-half of the population of this district ... The female population in these courts and alleys, as usual, forms the greatest social difficulty to be dealt with. Their husbands may be Dock Labourers, earning, when employed, if on the 'permanent list', 3s. a day – if on

the 'casual list', only 2s. 6d. a day; their children, after an education in the streets or the ragged schools, may be drafted off into Lucifer-match or brush factories, where cheap and juvenile labour is in much demand . . .[2]

Beatrice Potter, in Charles Booth's survey of East London workers, noted that Bryant and May's matchwomen were 'often the daughters of Dock Labourers',[3] and would later become 'Dock Labourers' wives'.[4] Of the handful of matchwomen visited by Potter, three were dockers' daughters. Charles Dickens, in *Travels in the East*, recorded a visit to a matchwoman who was both widow and mother to dock labourers, and to her neighbour, a girl of 13 working for Bryant and May while her father worked on the docks.[5] The Queen's Counsel Montagu Williams, familiar with the matchwomen through his legal work, observed that 'many a match girl of sixteen marries a dock labourer . . . no older'.[6]

Although connections between the matchwomen and the Irish community are rarely made, Bryant and May director William Wilberforce Bryant said in an interview before the strike, rather surprisingly with the *Girls' Own Paper*, that 'all our hands, men and women, hail from the Emerald Isle by birth or lineage'.[7] At the time of the strike, the factory manager, Mr Rix, had also told the *East London Advertiser* '[m]ost of the females are of Irish extraction'.[8] The strike register confirms that many of the women lived in predominantly Irish neighbourhoods and streets, including Sophia Street: the vicinity of which we will later see Charles Booth describe disparagingly as an 'Irish den'.[9] Twenty-three lived in one area known as the 'Fenian Barracks'.[10] This places the women in one of the most politically active communities in East London at the time, along with many of the 1889 dock strikers. Booth patronizingly noted that 'Paddy enjoys more than his proportional share of dock work',[11] and one of the best-organized unions prior to New Unionism, the Stevedores' Union, was 'manned and officered by the London Irish', and in fact developed out of the Irish Land and League movement.[12] The majority of the dockers' strike committee were Irish and their meeting place, the Wade Arms, was an Irish pub.[13]

Irish birth or descent would have made the matchwomen part of a socially and geographically close-knit, and extensive, community: by the 1860s London was Britain's largest centre of Irish settlement.[14] This might reasonably be suggested to have increased their sense of solidarity and identity; James Connolly believed that the experiences of Irish workers in England, when combined with the oppression they had fled, also led to a heightened sense of class as well as national consciousness.[15]

Certainly there is good evidence that the working-class Irish community in the Victorian East End was a politicized one. The London Irish brought with them traditions of what Swift and Gilley have called 'passive mass defiance, street violence and armed rebellion'.[16] Their political aims were encouraged and supported by English socialists and radicals in London, the country's political centre; and, as we have seen, the focus of a vibrant socialist revival. Charlton posits that Irish solidarity and mistrust of the British state was an important component of New Unionism.[17] Terry McCarthy also recognises this, and notes the Irishness of the matchwomen, in his book on the Dublin General Strike of 1913–14.[18]

However, with these exceptions, this 'Irish Factor' and the possibility that the strong ties of shared community may have contributed to the matchwomen's famous solidarity is rarely considered and has not previously been examined in detail. Swift and Gilley have argued that it is the very outcast status of the London Irish community which had 'prevented historians from bothering much about them' until late into the twentieth century. But even more recent histories of the Irish in British cities – including their own – ironically tend to ignore the matchwomen, neither claiming the 1888 strikers as a notable group of Irish workers, nor including matchmaking among typical occupations of the Irish in London. The opposite is true of the '89 dock strikers and of dock workers in general, who are given much attention.

The Irish migrants who came to London at this time had to struggle to find a means of entering the city's economy. Having little or no capital, most were restricted to poorly paid casual work, which tended to be concentrated in already overcrowded areas. In the East End, many able-bodied Irishmen were forced to join the desperate 'call-ons' at the docks, and search for affordable lodgings for themselves and their families in the dockside slum communities.

There is evidence that English working men, already struggling hard themselves for a livelihood, were more likely to regard Irish incomers – as they often did women workers – with hostility, and as an economic threat, than as people to be emulated. Much has been written about the outsider status of the London Irish community, set apart by nationality, religion and sometimes language,[19] 'ostracized and locked in an urban ghetto ... relegated to the side streets and back alleys of their neighbourhoods'.[20]

However, if the Irish were met with indifference or hostility, they apparently displayed a marked lack of enthusiasm for the host population in return, which had its roots in their experiences in Ireland, '[their] sense of obligation or of gratitude ... nullified ... by their belief that it was Britain's misgovernment of Ireland which had caused them to be uprooted in the first place'.[21]

The Irish community in the East End was close-knit, and Irish neighbours would help each other out both financially and practically in difficult times.[22] Aided by its religious, political and social organizations, the community also managed to maintain itself and its sense of Irishness in the face of blatant prejudice and hostility. Charles Booth demonstrates the anti-Irish feeling, but also the community's solidarity, when writing about Gale Street in the East End:

> This block sends more police to hospital than any other in London. 'Men are not human', they are wild beasts. You take a man or a woman, a rescue is always organised. They fling bricks, iron, anything they can lay their hands on. All are Irish cockneys. Not an Englishman or Scotchman would live among them.[23]

Irish workers in London were often the worst paid, making them unwelcome economic competition for the established workforce, as Marx noted:

Every industrial and commercial centre in England possesses a working class divided
into two hostile camps, English proletarians and Irish proletarians. The ordinary English
worker hates the Irish worker as a competitor who lowers his standard of life. In relation
to the Irish worker he feels himself a member of the ruling nation and turns himself into
a tool of the aristocrats and capitalists of his country thus strengthening their domination
over himself.[24]

The matchwomen, then, could be seen as trebly disadvantaged, being Irish,
female and working-class. Though not all of their number who came from Irish
families would have been born in Ireland, the Irish migrant community of this
period was exceptional in maintaining a strong sense of original identity into
third and fourth generations and beyond.[25]

By the 1880s a new wave of nationalist activity in Ireland, the socialist revival,
and an influx of unskilled Irish workers, had brought matters in London to a
head. Michael Davitt, veteran of the Fenian struggles, worked in London to try
to unite English and Irish workers, addressing a rally in 1885 thus:

The industrial classes in these countries can, if they combine at the polls, hurl the party
of wars and waste, of land monopoly and labour . . . from the helm of the state . . .[26]

Socialists campaigned with the Irish community to build mass meetings, which
became a regular fixture of London life. In 1887, 150,000 men, women and children
marched to Hyde Park from dockland communities including Bermondsey,
Rotherhide and Poplar to demonstrate against the Crimes Bill, introduced in
response to a boycott of landlords by Irish tenants led by the National Land
League, the Bill proposed the removal of the right to trial by the tenants involved.
The authorities responded by banning mass meetings, but to no avail. On Sunday
13 November, a rally was dispersed so brutally by police that hundreds were injured
and one man killed. 'Bloody Sunday' sparked national outrage. The matchwomen
must have been aware of such demonstrations, and may well have participated
along with their communities. We know that when they first met Besant the
women already knew who she was, recognizing her from her appearance on the
speakers' platforms of East London's mass demonstrations.[27]

SURNAMES ON THE STRIKE REGISTER

In order to test Bryant's assertion about the workforce's heritage, I have used the
Irish Primary Evaluation Survey, known as the Griffith's Evaluation, to analyse
the surnames of strikers for possible Irish origin. Each of the names of strikers
from the Victoria factory, where it is believed that the strike may have begun,
has been compared against the names of Irish householders on the survey. The
surname etymology and history has been studied in each case.

The Griffiths evaluation was published between 1848 and 1864, and listed
every householder and landholder in Ireland. Because of the destruction of Irish

records from 1821 to 1851 in a fire at the Public Record Office, and the pulping, by government order, of the 1861 and 1871 censuses, the evaluation remains the only reliable record of the names of Irish householders for this period. It has been possible to use it to trace the surnames of many of the striking matchwomen to Ireland, and sometimes even to the counties in which they were most commonly found.

The individual results for each surname are shown at Appendix [p. 227]. As previously mentioned, the strike fund register was compiled at some speed at mass meetings, so understandably contains spelling errors. In obvious cases – for example, when both of the Driscoll sisters' surnames are spelled differently – the likely correct surname has also been recorded in the Appendix. The names of the four women from this factory who would later be on the union's committee, including that of Eliza Martin, who seems to have been a key figure in the strike, have been capitalized. While it is accepted that this is not a definitive analysis, the findings suggest that as many as 76 per cent of strikers from the Victoria factory, and three out of the four union committee members in the factory, could well have been of Irish descent.

MATCHWORKERS' NEIGHBOURHOODS: ANALYSIS OF ADDRESSES

'The streets,' recalled one child of Victorian East London, 'were all alive': children had their own world in the courts and rookeries of the East End.[28] Often turned out of the house by day to play outside with others from the street, children were used to those outside their family keeping an eye on them and looking after them, or not – they encountered distant as well as close neighbours as they roamed far afield, and quickly learned who would indulge them, and who they annoyed at their peril.[29] Neighbours might, of course, also be relatives of some kind: in many areas, familial connections could link almost everyone in a given street.[30] The East End's network of reciprocal favours, essential for surviving poverty, has already been remarked upon, and this increased the sense of community and interdependence.[31] All of these factors increase the likelihood that dockers living closely together with matchwomen in the East End would have known about their strike action and subsequent victory.

In order to establish neighbourhood connections between matchwomen and dockers beyond doubt, a variety of addresses from the strike fund register have been located in the 1891 Census. The occupations of all recorded residents on each street have been noted, and where these are matchmaking, dock labour or related work, this has been recorded.

In the first section, four streets which occur repeatedly on the strike fund register have been taken as 'typical' matchwomen's addresses and located on the 1891 Census, the closest one taken to the strike. Each street has been studied in its entirety and the entry for every occupant examined. Resident matchbox-makers have been recorded as well as match factory workers, my research among descendants having confirmed that women often alternated between factory work and outwork for Bryant and May as circumstances dictated, and that factory workers and outworkers associated together – and that matchbox-making may even have been undertaken in the factory itself. Therefore, connections between matchbox-makers and dockers are also of significance.

Difficulties over handwriting, spelling and map location were frequently encountered. As outlined in my introduction, for example, Bloomfield Street occurred multiply on the register, not always with the same spelling, but ultimately had to be rejected for analysis, as it could not be located on either the census or Bacon's 1888 street map. With these provisos, the streets chosen for the first analysis were: Sophia Street (which occurs the highest number of times in the register), Tidey Street, Box Street and Gill Street all of which have more than five matchwomen listed as residents on the register.

Selected Streets

Sophia Street is not listed in the index of G. W. Bacon's 1888 *Ordnance Atlas of London and Suburbs*: Charles Booth's original notebooks for his poverty survey had to be used to approximately locate it. Booth classified it as 'dark blue', indicating 'very poor, casual [workers], chronic want' according to his colour-coding system, and he headlines his entry 'Rook Street and Sophia Street: Irish'. Booth goes on to record that these two streets are 'a regular Irish den . . . all the vices of the Irish rampant, murder, rows, riot etc. . .'[32] From his notes it is clear that Sophia Street is just off Poplar High Street, therefore directly above the West India Docks, and probably the small street, illegibly labelled on Bacon's map, that runs between East India Dock Road and the High Street. This was a short distance from the homes of union committee members Julia Gamelton and Mary and Mog Driscoll in 1888.

Tidey Street is not listed in Bacon's index either, but actually does appear on the map itself: with the help of Charles Booth's 'poverty maps' in the Booth Archive (it was necessary to look at Booth's originals as these are clearer than facsimiles) it has been located less than a mile from the West India Docks – just below Whitethorn Street, where union committee member Eliza Martin was living in 1888.[33] It is accordingly close to the area Charles Booth recorded as being locally called the 'Fenian Barracks'. Booth's notebooks recorded neighbouring Blackthorn Street and Whitethorn Street as 'dark blue', and adding 'Inhabited by many Irish and workers in the Gas Works. A rough lot, given to drinking and racing and betting.'[34]

Gill Street is also unlisted in Bacon's map, and again had to be located via Booth's maps and notebooks. It is 200 yards west of Sophia Street, and about the same distance from the West India Docks. Booth has no more to say about it than that it was part of a 'nest of brothels' frequented by sailors.[35]

FINDINGS

Sophia Street

Sophia Street residents who were matchworkers and appeared on the strike fund register in 1888, listed by house numbers:

1 Mary Halford
2 Ellen Halford
   Nellie Lay
8 Kate Stanton
   Ellen Frazer
10 Kate Sheen
12 Annie Wenborn
19 Mary Cunningham
25 Mary Hash
26 Laura Stanton
31 Margaret Laura
35 Mary Marney
37 H. Ward
   Ellen Sheehan
39 Kate Crawley
40 B. Flack
43 Mog Pier

Sophia Street residents as shown in the 1891 Census:

1–4 uninhabited
  5 Three dock labourers
  6 One dock labourer, of Irish birth
     Bridget Lawler, matchmaker
     Margaret Lawler, matchmaker
  7 Margaret Peal [Mog Pier?]
     Mary Sullivan or McMahon
  9 Margaret Slatterly and Kate? [illegible], matchmakers
 11 Two dock stevedores, one Irish-born
 12 Annie Wenborn, matchmaker
     Margaret Wenborn, matchmaker
     Three Irish-born stevedores
 13 Dock labourer
 14 Two dock labourers
 15 Stevedore
 17 Mary Cunningham, matchmaker [was at no. 19 in strike fund register]
     Catherine Cunningham (sister of above), matchmaker
     Maggie Cunningham (sister of above), matchmaker

(*continued*)

One dock labourer

21 Irish-born stevedore

23 Four dock labourers, sons of Irish-born mother

24 One Irish-born dock labourer

Two dock labourers with Irish-born mother

Rebecca Duhig, matchmaker

One Irish-born shipyard labourer

27 One dock labourer

28 One dock labourer

Catherine Coughlan, matchmaker with Irish-born mother

29 Irish-born dock labourer

30 Irish-born dock labourer

32 Irish-born dock labourer

35 Mary Minehan, matchmaker [could this be Mary Marney as per strike fund register?]

Irish-born dock labourer

35 Irish-born dock labourer

Dock labourer

Shipyard labourer

37 Ellen Sheen, matchmaker [likely to be Ellen **Sheehan** as per strike fund register, who lived at this address]

Her father, an Irish-born dock labourer

Sarah Ward, matchmaker

39 Catherine Crawley, matchmaker [as per strike fund register]

Her father, an Irish-born dock labourer

Census analysis:

Dock labourers or related work – 23 men

Matchmakers – 16

Matchmakers on strike in 1888 and still present in 1891–4 or 5

Dock workers and matchworkers under the same roof at – 7 addresses

Gill Street

Gill Street residents as shown on matchworkers' strike fund register in 1888:

23 Rachel Leonard

39 Annie Waters

41 Sarah Branton

42	May Hickey
44	Ellen Elsey
44	Annie Elsey
51	Louie Buck

Gill Street residents as shown in the 1891 Census:

2	Warehouse porter
4	Stevedore
13	Dock labourer
14	Dock labourer
15	Dock labourer
16	Wharf foreman
17	Barge lighterman
18	Delivery wharf foreman
19	Barge lighterman
20	Two dock labourers
	Bargeman
29	Dock labourer
35	Dock stevedore
37	Dock labourer
40	Dock labourer
42	Dock labourer
49	Stevedore
	Dock labourer
	Louisa Buck, matchmaker [as per strike fund register]
	Rachel Leonard, matchmaker [was at no. 23 in strike fund register]
	Dock labourer
	Dock engine stoker
	Shipyard labourer
	Bargee
54	Dock labourer
57	Barge builder
80	Barge lighterman
95	Stevedore
103	Shipyard labourer
105	Dock labourer

(*continued*)

Census analysis:

Dock labourers or related work – 29 men

Matchmakers – 2

Matchmakers on strike in 1888 and still present in 1891–2

Tidey Street

Tidey Street residents as shown on matchworkers' strike fund register in 1888:

20 Liz Butler

20 Clara Peacock

31 Emma Walker

    Mary Harrington

    Emma Harrington

    Francis Sermon

Tidey Street residents as shown in the 1891 Census:

  2 Dock labourer

  3 Shipyard labourer

20 Clara Peacock '[Match?] Factory hand' [as per strike fund register]

28 Three dock labourers

31 Emma Walker; [no occupation listed] [as per strike fund register]

33 Dock labourer

34 Dock labourer

37 Two shipyard workers

43 Warehouseman

46 Gas fitter at docks

47 Barge lighterman

49 Dock labourer

Census analysis:

Dock labourers or related work – 13 men

Matchmakers – 2

Matchmakers on strike in 1888 and still present in 1891–2

MAPPING THE STRIKE COMMITTEE

In the next analysis, the addresses of the Matchmakers' Union committee have been located, where it is possible to do so, on Bacon's 1888 maps (see p. x). This was complicated by the fact that, as with the previous analysis, some of the streets appear on Charles Booth's maps but are not named on the Bacon map (though the street itself may be shown, unmarked). Some streets could not be found on either map, but their approximate location was later established through reading Booth's notes on his survey walks. For example, Jane Wakeling's 'Lomas Buildings' could not be found on the maps, but Booth's notebooks tell us that it was 'off Ben Johnson Road', which lies about 100 yards north of Eastfield Street (Eliza Martin's marital address, which is in turn less than 50 yards from the site of the shops Mary Driscoll went on to own).

Other previously encountered problems again presented themselves. The street spelled 'Gayesley' in the register, for example, is 'Gaselee' on both the 1888 map and in Booth's notebooks. Some smaller streets are not named on Bacon's map but are on Booth's 'poverty maps'. Booth's maps, and his survey notebooks, were also used to discover more about these streets and their inhabitants. Gaselee Street, Cottage Street, Love Lane and Cornwall Street are particularly close to the docks. All were within a mile of one of the East London docks except for Alice Francis' Jefferson Street, a small street less than a hundred yards long, and just over a mile from the East India Docks.

All of the women on the committee were found to have lived within a two-mile square area of East London. Eliza Price's and Eliza Martin's 1888 addresses were only one road apart, as were Martin's and Staines', all in an area directly between the West India Docks and Bryant and May's. Louisa Beck's address in Cornwall Street and Kate Slater and Ellen Johnson's home in Love Lane are also just a street apart, again in close proximity to the docks. Only Sarah Chapman's address, Swan Place, could not be found in the 1891 or 1881 censuses, though there was a proliferation of 'Swans' in the area, including Swan Court, Swan Yard and Swan Street. Presumably Swan Place was too small to be named individually and was instead classified as part of Mile End Road. Kelly's Directory shows that a pub, The Swan or The White Swan, was at 229 Mile End Road from at least 1851.

Mary Driscoll: Cottage Street and Gloucestershire Court

At the time of the strike, the Irish Driscoll sisters, Mary and 'Mog', were living with their family in Cottage Street. This runs between East India Dock Road and Poplar High Street, and is in the immediate vicinity of both the West India and East India docks. Cottage Street is not mentioned by name by Charles Booth, but appears on one of the maps in the Charles Booth Archive as 'Cottage Row' and on another as 'Cottage Street'. Bacon's 1888 map shows it as Cottage Street and it is still known by that name today. The 1891 Census shows a Cottage Street running into Cottage Row. It may be that this is the area described by Booth in 1896: 'Down along the Poplar High Street . . . then into a little village of small houses occupied by dock employees, each with a small garden, known as *W. India Dock Cottages* . . .'[36] If so, Patrick Driscoll must presumably have been a fairly senior or permanent dock employee at this time. He is only ever known to have worked on the docks, and in 1881, when the census confirms him as still in this role, he was 50 years old. This is a reasonable age for such demanding physical work, and the fact that he was still employed by the dock company might suggest some seniority.

It is not known at this stage whether the family had any connection to one of the key figures of the Great Dock Strike and signatory of the strike call, Dennis Driscoll.

Cottage Street had its fair share of dock-based employees in 1881, as well as several matchmakers:

Cottage Street

Cottage Street residents as shown in the 1881 Census:

1	Waterman
	Carman
5	Carman
7	Three matchmakers
	Two dock labourers [These five workers were brothers and sisters]
8	Matchmaker
13	Dock labourer
25	Port watchman
30	Shipping clerk, head of household, daughter a matchmaker
44	Stevedores' labourer
58	Port signalman
	'J. R. Boy' (Port signalman)
	Seaman
	Stevedore
60	Dock labourer
	Carman
61	Ship's rigger
	Ship's scraper

Gloucestershire Court

The Driscoll family's earlier home in Gloucestershire Court, a short distance from Commercial Road, was within the civil parish of Limehouse, traditionally a dockers' area, and less than three-quarters of a mile from both the St Katherine's and London docks. As shown in Chapter Nine, Mary and her sisters would marry dock labourers. Joan Harris, Mary's granddaughter, lived near Tilbury for most of her adult life, and confirmed that the docks had been a constant factor in her life and those of her relatives: 'My family lived and died by the docks.'[37]

While this address was a reasonable distance – more than two miles – from Bryant and May's, the census shows that several matchmakers as well as dockers lived in the court in 1881:

1 Four matchmakers

2 Two dock labourers

3 The Driscolls:

  Dock labourer

  Matchmaker [subsequently 3 more matchmakers]

6 Three matchmakers

  Dock labourer

7 Three stevedores

Louisa Beck, 1888: Cornwall Street, Shadwell

1891 Census Information: RG12/286 Folio 172

Louisa Beck was no longer at no. 8 in 1891. At that address was a William Butcher, 'coffeestall holder', and his family. As might be expected from its location so close to the London Docks, a large number of dock labourers and workers in allied trades are present:

3 Ship scraper

4 'Stevedore's Labourer – Dock'

13 Two dock labourers

16 Two dock labourers

17 Dock labourer

19 Stevedore

22 Dock labourer

33 Dock labourer

35 Dock labourer

40 Dock labourer

  Dock labourer

41 Barge lighterman

  Dock labourer

49 Dock labourer

51 Dock labourer

59 Dock labourer

61 Dock labourer

67 Dock labourer

Mrs Knowles, 1888: Giraud Street

1891 Census Information: RG12/330 Folio 1–11

Giraud Street still exists, less than half a mile away from the former West India Docks, classified by Charles Booth as 'Light Blue: Poor'. This was a street dominated by dockers in the 1890s – Mrs Knowles was not then at no. 96, but two dock labourers were.

  1 Dock labourer

10 Barge lighterman
      Barge lighterman
      Port messenger
      Barge lighterman
      Barge lighterman

13 Dock labourer

14 Dock labourer

21 Match factory hand

22 Dock labourer

24 Shipwright

25 Dock labourer

28 Shipwright
      Shipwright

40 Four dock labourers
      Stevedore

41 Dock labourer

45 Dock labourer

57 Dock labourer

65 Dock labourer
      Matchbox filler

69 Dock labourer

71 Dock labourer
      Matchbox filler (wife of above)

75 Dock labourer

85 Dock constable
      Dock labourer

87 Stevedore

96 Two dock labourers

97 Dock labourer

Kate Slater and Ellen Johnson, 1888: Love Lane, Shadwell

1891 Census Information: RG12/290 Folio 30

Again, neither woman was at the same address, no. 9 Love Lane, in 1891. This very short road is close to Cornwall Street, also running off Cable Street, and so equally close to the London Docks.

- 9 Barge lighterman
  Carman
- 15 Carman
- 25 Dock wharf labourer
- 31 Dock wharf labourer
  Stevedore
  Barge builder

Julia Gamelton, 1888: Gaselee Street

1891 Census Information: RG12/333 Folio 118

Julia Gamelton was not at Gaselee Street in 1891: her former home, no. 43, was uninhabited. The street ran between the West and East India Docks, and contained a high proportion of matchmakers as well as dockers.

- 5 Dock labourer
  Shipyard labourer
- 8 Matchmaker
- 16 Matchmaker
- 18 Two dock labourers
- 19 Shipyard labourer
- 20 Three matchmakers
- 26 Bargeman
- 31 Barge waterman
  Matchmaker
- 36 Dock labourer
- 38 Shipwright
- 40 Six dock labourers
- 41 Shipyard labourer
- 46 Barge lighterman
- 49 Barge lighterman
  Dock labourer
- 53 Two matchmakers

Alice Francis, 1888: Jefferson Street

1891 Census Information: RG12/319

Alice Francis was the only committee member to be found still at her 1888 address in 1891.

2 Dock labourer
4 Match factory hand
11 Matchbox packer
19 Alice Francis, age 28, 'Match Factory Girl'
32 Dock labourer
34 Two matchmakers
37 Warehouseman

Jane Wakeling, 1888: Lomas Buildings

1891 Census Information: RG12/308 Folio 136

Lomas Buildings was located off Ben Johnson Road, about half a mile from the Regent's Canal Docks. It was one street away from Eastfield Street, where Eliza Martin lived with her husband, and this in turn was next-but-one to Parnham Street, where Mary Driscoll would keep two shops.

2 Dock labourer
4 Dock labourer
5 Dock labourer
6 Two dock labourers
7 Dock labourer
12 Dock labourer
14 Dock labourer
17 Dock labourer
21 Dock labourer
23 Dock labourer
26 Dock labourer
    Matchmaker
29 Dock labourer
31 Dock labourer

Julia Staines, 1888: Streatfield Street

1891 Census Information: RG12/229

Streatfield Street was off Devon's Road, close to Fairfield Road and over a mile from any docks. Julia Staines could not be found in 1891, but there were a number of dock workers in the street.

 2 Shipwright (retired)
 3 Warehouseman
 9 Ships' joiner
10 Barge lighterman
11 Barge lighterman
14 Ships' clerk
18 Barge lighterman
19 Dock labourer (retired)
20 Barge lighterman
23 Barge lighterman
   Boatbuilder
24 Barge lighterman
31 Barge lighterman
34 Sailmaker
36 Shipwright
38 Dock landing clerk

Eliza Price, 1888: Thomas Street

1891 Census Information: RG12/298 Folio 79

Eliza Price was no longer at no. 15 Thomas Street in 1891. The street is about half a mile from both the Regent's Canal Docks and the West India Docks.

 3 Ship's engineer
 5 Barge lighterman
   Ship's rigger
12 Dock foreman
13 Dock labourer
14 Marine engineer
18 Barge lighterman
   Mastmaker
   Port shopboy
29 Dock labourer

(continued)

38 Lighterman (retired)
39 Customs' boatman
41 Shipwright
    Barge lighterman
63 Dock labourer
67 Dock labourer
73 Dock labourer
85 Dock labourer
87 Stevedore dock labourer
97 Dock labourer

Eliza Martin, Whitethorn Street

Eliza Martin's family testify that Eliza had a sister who married into a local family of dockers, the Farncourts. Her daughter, Rosie, also married a docker, and had three sons who went on to work on the docks. Eliza's daughter Polly also married a docker: Whitethorn Street was 'a dockers' area' according to Eliza's grandchildren. Her grandson Jim Best has said that in any case matchwomen and dockers were 'all the same people, from the same families'.[38]

1891 Census Information

 4 Dock labourer
 7 Two matchmakers
 9 Carman
15 Dock labourer
16 Matchbox filler
    Carman
    Match factory labourer
17 Dock labourer
    Matchmaker
19 Dock labourer
22 Matchmaker
26 Carman
28 Shipyard labourer
38 Carman
39 Shipping clerk

CONCLUSIONS

The evidence provided in this chapter confirms the impression given by numerous contemporary commentators, and the comments of dockers' leaders: the matchwomen and dockers were far from being members of two isolated groups, but in fact were well known to each other as friends, neighbours and relatives.

The 'Irish factor' may have been important to connections between the two groups of workers, and perhaps helped to foster a sense of kinship between the matchworkers themselves, as well as between matchwomen and dockers. Social connections between members of the Irish community may also have helped to bring about relationships that led to actual kinship, as must the proximity caused by the natural propensity of the Irish as immigrants to initially settle close to one another on arrival in London.

Census and map evidence, as well as information drawn from interviews (which is presented in full in the next chapter), all speak eloquently of ties between matchwomen and dockers, and primary accounts too suggest that these were two groups who were traditionally linked, living close together and intermarrying. The matchwomen's strike and victory seem likely to have been the talk of these East End communities, if these indeed were the wives, mothers and neighbours of dockers who would strike in 1889.

9

In Search of the Matchwomen: Case Study and Primary Evidence

INTRODUCTION

Having stripped away some of the layers of myth and misunderstanding, we are left with a very different matchwomen's strike from the traditional version. We can see that it was neither planned by Annie Besant and the Fabians nor welcomed by them; and that the matchwomen and the dockers were closely associated, both as private individuals and as strikers in '88 and '89.

However, there is still a void at the heart of the story. We now know who did *not* lead the strike, but not who did. The history books tell us nothing of the matchwomen's individual lives and experiences, and without this it is hard to draw accurate conclusions about their motivations, or what their actions and victory might have meant to them. All the evidence points, overwhelmingly, to a self-organized strike: but the strikers were not interviewed during their lifetimes, unlike the Melbourne tailoresses, so we lack confirmation from the women themselves. No biographical information about the matchwomen's lives has so far been published, in contrast with an immense amount of material about Besant and key figures in the Great Dock Strike.

Despite the obvious difficulties in correcting this historical imbalance after so many years, as I've previously explained, I became increasingly convinced that it was important to at least attempt it. Some sense of the matchworkers as individuals might help to test the new hypothesis of self-organization, and perhaps illuminate their famous solidarity, which enabled them to successfully challenge their employers from such an apparently vulnerable position, breaking the 'rules' of Victorian womanhood to boot.

The two known photographs taken during the strike, and the information which can be gleaned from them, will also be discussed in this chapter. Both photographs have helped me to establish the identities of those who were really at the forefront of the strike. The better-known photo is of a small group of striking women; the second, of the Matchworker's Union committee, with Annie Besant and Herbert Burrows also pictured. The Committee photograph appears in a number of books, but only Besant and sometimes Burrows are named.

We know why the Committee photograph was taken and what it shows us; however the circumstances of the first photograph are not known. Why would a photographer have pictured just a few women, and these particular women, out of over a thousand strikers? If the idea was simply to record the strike, it would have made more sense to pull the camera back, both to create the context by making the Fairfield match works, where I believe it was taken, more visible, and to show the extent of the strike by picturing more strikers. I felt that anything I could discover about this photograph might add a piece to the puzzle.

The whereabouts of the original photograph are currently unknown, despite extensive enquiries. However, an enlargement made directly from it is in the collection of the People's History Museum in Manchester. The enlargement was made at the National Museum of Labour History (NMLH) in Limehouse, it is thought in the 1980s. The Museum was run, between 1975 and 1986, in Limehouse Town Hall by the Trade Union, Labour and Co-operative History Society (TULC). It displayed the TULC's collection of labour history documents and ephemera. On its closure in 1986 the museum's collections were kept in storage until the opening of the People's History Museum in Manchester in 1990.[7]

In the course of my research I found that the notes on the photograph provide a fascinating link with the Great Dock Strike of 1889. They state: 'Enlargement from the original photo formerly belonging to John Burns (in the possession of S. Marks) Trade Union, Labour, Co-operative Democratic History Society'.[8] Therefore, the original photograph had been owned by John Burns, the dockers' leader.

As regards the second photograph, as we know that the strike committee was voted for by the strikers en masse, any information which could be gleaned about those who were chosen might shed light on the beginnings of the strike – and perhaps show us whether or not Bryant and May were right in suspecting certain matchwomen of being its true leaders. If so, the leaders were presumably respected by their workmates and so might well be among the committee members. That would in turn confirm that the committee was democratically elected by the women, without undue influence from Besant.

We've already seen that there is a dearth of autobiographical evidence; no diaries or unpublished autobiographies of matchwomen have as yet been discovered. In fact collectors of working-class autobiography from this period have noted a general 'silence'[1] of women: Vincent located only a small handful of female autobiographies; Rose too found that women made up only 15 per cent of autobiographers in the manuscripts he studied for the period 1870 to 1889. (Though this increased dramatically after 1890 – the reasons for which might repay research in themselves – they still represented only 30 per cent of accounts between 1890 and 1929.)[2] It would not be surprising that even women workers who could write and believed, against the weight of prevailing ideology, that their lives were worth recording, may not have found the time for autobiography between the demands of home and family. This makes the photographs, and whatever we can learn from them, all the more important.

TRACING DESCENDANTS

I used various approaches in an attempt to find information that would fill the gaps in the matchwomen's story.

As the lack of primary evidence from the matchwomen themselves became clearer, so the idea of tracing descendants became more important.

This search lasted several years. I wrote articles about my research for national and local newspapers and trade union journals, asking for descendants to come forward. I contacted local history societies and gave talks which included appeals for information. I made appeals on BBC Radio London and spoke at the Museum of London's Museum in Docklands and East London's Ragged School Museum, among others. These talks proved by far the most successful means of reaching descendants: I was fortunate to find the grandchildren of three matchwomen in this way.

The resulting testimony is inevitably two generations removed. The length of time since the strike and lack of other biographical information increases its rarity and value, but it is also important in its own right, giving a good sense of the real lives and individuals behind the generic tag of 'matchgirls'. Despite the time lapse, much of the testimony comes from people who knew matchwomen well – indeed were practically brought up by them in two cases. Another fortuitous aspect – beyond the finding of such sources at all against the odds – is that these were such good interviewees: enthusiastic about the project, lucid and illuminating in their testimony, and generous with their time, histories, and personal artefacts such as family photographs.

The grandchildren of matchworkers Eliza Martin, Mary Driscoll and Martha Robertson were ultimately interviewed. All three of the women were working for Bryant and May at the time of the strike. Crucially, Driscoll and Martin were among the five women suspected of being the prime movers in the strike. Both women feature in the strike fund register, as does Mary Driscoll's sister 'Mog' (Margaret), the great-aunt of Joan Harris.

The resulting information represents the first published details about the lives of the Bryant and May matchwomen. I hope that this, in conjunction with the other material presented, begins the process of restoring to them a sense of individual identity and agency. All four were powerful women within their own families and communities.

The first descendant I found, after a talk at the Museum of Docklands, was Joan Harris, granddaughter and great-niece respectively of Mary and Mog Driscoll. Mary Driscoll was one of the five names listed on Bryant and May's list of 'troublemakers': but Driscoll was a relatively common surname in the East End of the time; there were several Driscolls on the strike fund register alone. However, as will be shown, subsequent evidence strongly suggests that this Mary Driscoll was a key figure in the strike and a member of the union committee. It also transpired that, unbeknown initially to Joan Harris herself, her great-aunt had also been a committee member.

Located next, when I spoke at the Ragged School Museum in Tower Hamlets, were Jim Best and Ted Lewis. Jim Best is the grandson of Eliza Martin (later Best), also one of the five on the firm's list. His grandmother died before he was born, but family tradition had always held that she was central to the strike: she had told her son (Jim's father) that she and her friends had begun it. The third interviewee, Ted Lewis, is the grandson of Martha Robertson, a matchbox-maker and matchmaker for Bryant and May for many decades. Martha was extremely young at the time of the strike, just six years old, and therefore died more recently than the other two grandmothers, surviving until the 1960s. There are therefore more living witnesses who remember her, and their recollections are more recent. Martha knew the strikers well, and worked alongside them for many years: therefore, while she was too young to be a central figure in the strike herself, the testimony of Ted, his wife Bett and Ted's cousin Larraine has been extremely valuable in adding to our understanding of the women's lives.

Before considering the interview evidence in more detail, we'll look more closely at three 'artefacts' of the strike: the two photographs and the strike fund register.

THE FACTORY PHOTOGRAPH

The first photograph is of unknown date, of a group of seven young women. A very young-looking matchbox seller is wearing a tray of boxes around her neck. This girl would have been a street seller, the embodiment of Anderson's 'Little Matchgirl'. She may feature in the photograph just to give context – without her, there's nothing to indicate that we're looking at matchwomen – or because she supported the strike, as we know that homeworking matchbox makers did. Six other young women are also featured – five faces are clear, one blurred, as if the woman has moved at the last second.

The women in the photograph have always been identified simply as being striking matchwomen, and it has become iconic: it is the image which is most associated with the strike, and is invariably used to illustrate articles about it. It is displayed in the windows of the UNITE headquarters in Holborn. However, its provenance has been lost over time: we do not know the identities of the women featured; why they in particular were selected; or when and by whom it was taken. We know that Besant spoke to a 'handful' of women; that the firm identified five 'troublemakers'; and also that immediately after the first walkout, six matchwomen were chosen by colleagues to go and out their demands to management – the number shown could therefore be significant.

The group look younger and less confident than the women in the second photograph, who are also noticeably better dressed. Those in the first photograph appear to be in their teens, and more closely resemble the vulnerable waifs of the popular imagination. They look anxious and a little shell-shocked, dressed in what look like heavy coats and jackets, with white aprons and kerchiefs at their necks. All but one wear or carry hats: the matchbox seller wears a masculine-looking bowler, but the other women have what look like the fancier velvet numbers worn 'clapped on the head like a clam shell' which contemporaries tell us the matchwomen favoured.[3]

At first sight the clothing looks inappropriate for a July day, which might cast doubt on its credentials as a strike photograph: but in researching the weather I found that temperatures in July 1888 were in fact unseasonably low: snow fell in Kent on 11 July, ice disrupted the fishing fleets out at sea and the whole summer was notably chilly.[4] After looking closely at the outside walls of the Bryant and May factory in Bow, which fortunately remains intact, I'm also satisfied that the photograph was taken outside it.

So the location fits, as does the clothing, and the focus on a handful of women

The 'factory' photograph. With thanks to the People's History Museum, Manchester

may also point to the picture having been taken in the early days of the strike. Their sturdy, practical clothing and aprons, especially when contrasted with the clothes in the second photograph, suggest work clothes; which also suggests that the women had been working that day. If this is the case then this must be Day One of the strike. This would also explain their wary expressions: as well as probably being unused to being photographed, they had just taken a dramatic step and faced an uncertain future.

The whereabouts of the original photograph are currently unknown, despite extensive enquiries. However, an enlargement made directly from it is in the collection of the People's History Museum in Manchester. The enlargement was made at the National Museum of Labour History (NMLH) in Limehouse, it is thought in the 1980s. The museum was run, between 1975 and 1986, in Limehouse Town Hall by the Trade Union, Labour and Co-operative History Society (TULC). It displayed the TULC's collection of labour history documents and ephemera. On its closure in 1986 the museum's collections were kept in storage until the opening of the People's History Museum in Manchester in 1990.[5]

In the course of my research I found that the notes on the photograph provide a fascinating link with the Great Dock Strike of 1889. They state: 'Enlargement from the original photo formerly belonging to John Burns (in the possession of S. Marks) Trade Union, Labour, Co-operative Democratic History Society'.[6] Therefore, the original photograph had been owned by John Burns, the great

The matchwomen's strike committee, 1888. With thanks to the People's History Museum, Manchester

leader and orator of the '89 dock strike. I am grateful to Terry McCarthy, former director of the Limehouse museum, for confirming that S. Marks is Sid Marks, one of the museum's founders.

When I was speaking at the Museum in Docklands and first met Joan Harris, my visual of this photograph was still displayed on the wall behind me. Joan was convinced that Mary Driscoll was the tallest woman, right at the centre of the photograph, half-smiling and looking very directly at the camera. We noticed that another girl, hatless and with a heavy fringe, was behind her, apparently standing on something, and with her left hand on Mary's shoulder. Later research has shown that this is likely to be Mary's devoted younger sister Mog. The close sisterly pose is repeated down the years in family photos in Joan's possession (see Appendix p. 235).

THE COMMITTEE PHOTOGRAPH

Besant, Burrows and 12 matchworkers feature in this second photograph, of members of what was initially the strike committee, and then the Matchmaker's Union committee. The photograph seems likely to have been taken in Charrington's Hall on the Mile End Road before or after a distribution of funds, the main distributions of which took place on 14 and 21 July: an entry in George Bernard Shaw's diary for the 14th records that a Charlotte Roche took photographs at this meeting. (I am indebted to Paul Williams, then custodian of 'Shaw's Corner', the writer's former home in Hertfordshire, for identifying Roche as the niece of artist Felix Mosceles.[7])Shaw first mentions Roche in April 1888, where he records that she delivered an 'incoherent' lecture at an SDF meeting. She was evidently an active photographer, photographing Shaw himself – on 1 July, the day before the strike began – as well as 'innumerable socialists and musicians'.[8] She seems therefore a likely candidate for our photographer in this case, and 14 July for the date.

Although this group looks so different, at least some are the same individuals shown in the first photo. The Strike Committee look more mature, poised and elegant; but I think circumstances explain this. By the time of the second photograph things were very different on more than just the surface. The strike had been underway for some time, and garnered considerable publicity and support. The women had spoken at huge public meetings, met face-to-face with and impressed MPs, and may have been something close to heroines in their neighbourhood – all of which must have increased their confidence exponentially. The Committee members would also have had time to look their best for the photograph – style their hair, put on their best clothes, borrow outfits from friends or redeem their 'Sunday Best' from the pawnbrokers (it was common practice for poor working people to take their most valuable possessions in and out of pawn as they needed money, sometimes on a weekly basis. The song 'Pop Goes the Weasel' commemorates East End garment workers doing just this: 'Up and down the City Road, In and Out the Eagle (pub): That's the way the money goes, pop goes the weasel'- to 'pop' something was slang for pawning it, and a weasel was a small dressmaker's iron).

I've previously mentioned that Jim Best recalled his father pointing out his grandmother on a reproduction of the union committee photograph printed in a local paper at some time in the 1980s. He remembered that the names and addresses of all the members of the committee were printed underneath.

I spent some time trying to locate the article at Colindale Newspaper Library, but without an exact date or year this meant potentially searching through every copy of the newspaper (the East London Advertiser) for a decade. I began this attempt, looking at newspapers for a few possible dates, like those around the strike's anniversary, but found nothing and had to make the decision to abandon it for practical reasons. However, Jim spoke about this to his family, and a year later one of his brothers was able to find an original copy of the East London Advertiser containing the article.[9] The fact that it had been carefully preserved by Eliza's family for almost twenty years is further proof of their respect for the tradition of her participation. Crucially, I now had the names of all of the women on the strike committee. This was the first Joan Harris or I knew of Mary and Mog Driscoll's involvement with the Committee.

The article was written by historian Tom Ridge and custodian Lynne Fox, of East London's Ragged School Museum. The 12 committee members are as follows, with those whom Bryant and May believed to be 'ringleaders' are shown in italics, and those whose descendants have been located and interviewed are in bold type:[10]

From the Victoria factory:
Eliza Martin, 14 Whitethorn Street, Bow Common.
Louise Beck, 8 Cornwall Street, Shadwell.
Julia Gamelton, 43 Gayesley Street, Poplar.

Wax and Box Stores:
Jane Walking, 4 Lomas Buildings.
Jane Staines, Devons Road.
Eliza Price, 15 Thomas Street, Bromley.

Patent:
Sarah Chapman, 2 Swan Place, Mile End Road.
Alice Francis, 19a Jefferson Street.
Polly [sic] and Mary Driscoll, 24 Cottage Street, Poplar.

Seated on the right of the photograph:
Mrs Knowles, Giraud Street.

Behind her:
Kate Slater and Ellen Johnson, 9 Love Lane, Shadwell.

The last three women must be from the fourth section of the factory, the Centre and Top Centre, and Ellen Johnson's entry in the strike fund register indeed confirms that she worked there. This last piece of evidence confirms the credibility of the interviewees' evidence; and also Bryant and May's suspicions. The very existence of their list, together with family testimony, greatly supports the self-organized hypothesis of the strike.

I cross-checked the list of names against the strike fund register in the TUC archives. All except Mrs Knowles and Kate Slater were on it. (There is a 'K. Slater', no. 21 on the register, who appears as 'K. Flaser' in the first part of the register and later as 'Slater', but the address is 266 St Leonards Road. This striker does, however, work in the correct part of the factory, the Centre and Top Centre. Mrs Knowles presumably worked there too, but no trace of her having accepted money from the strike fund can be found. Perhaps, as the only married woman on the committee, she had a husband earning enough to temporarily support her, and she declined assistance.)

The following are the women's names, addresses, marital status, occupations, 'Wages Last Week', and home circumstances ('Dependent or Independent'), according to the register:

Extract from Strike Fund Register:
[Those whom Bryant and May believed to be 'ringleaders' are shown in italics, and those whose descendants have been located and interviewed are in bold type:]

Victoria:
Eliza Martin. 14 Whitethorn Street, Bow Common. Single. Cutting down, 6/5. Parents.
Louise Beck. 8 Cornwall Street, Shadwell. Cutting down. 7/7.5. Parents.
Julia Gamelton. 43 Gayesley Street, Poplar. Single. Cutting down. 6/4. Parents.

Wax and Box Stores:
Jane Walking, ['Wakeling' on register] 4 Lomas Buildings, Stepney. Single. Wax Filler. 4/8. Father.
Jane Staines, 3 Streatfield Road, Devons Road. Single. Wax Filler. 4/-. Father.
Eliza Price, 15 Thomas Street, Bromley. Single. Wax filler. 5/-. Father.

Patent:
Sarah Chapman, 2 Swan Place, Mile End Road: Patent, 14/-.
Alice Francis, 19a Jefferson Street. Single. Patent. 5/11. Mother.
Polly Driscoll, 24 Cottgae [sic] Poplar. Patent. 6/6. Father.
Mary Driscoll, 24 Cottage Street, Poplar. Patent. Single. 6/6. Father.

Centre and Top Centre:
Ellen Johnson, 9 Love Lane, Single, Packer, 5/3, Parents.

Apart from Mrs Knowles, Kate Slater and Ellen Johnson, we don't know who is whom in the photograph. However, after close comparison of photographs of the women in later life, I think it is very likely that Mary and Mog Driscoll may be the two women standing on the platform next to Annie Besant, Mary with her hand on Mog's shoulder. The differences in height and body-shape between the two women appear to correspond and Mary's upright bearing is again striking.

EAST END LADIES: MARY, MOG AND ELIZA

I first interviewed Joan Harris, Jim Best and Ted Lewis in their respective homes. Jim and Ted still lived in the East End, while Joan had moved out to Essex.

When I interviewed Jim, he mentioned that he had never seen inside walls of the match factory, which had become a private, gated housing development known as the Bow Quarter in the 1980s.

I organised a group visit to the factory so that the grandchildren could meet one another, after which we repaired to the Matchmaker pub on Roman Road for a rather more informal and convivial interview.

(1) Mary Driscoll

Mary Driscoll was the child of two Irish parents, and was born in London on 14 January 1874. Her father was Patrick Driscoll of County Kerry, and her mother Elizabeth Cunningham of Skibbereen, County Cork. 'Driscoll' is shown by the Griffith's Evaluation of Irish householders to have been a typical Cork surname: 1,017 of 1,276 Driscoll households in Ireland at this time were in Cork.[11]

Mary's mother Elizabeth Cunningham first came to England with her family to escape the famine in 1844, when she was 12, but their stay was brief. Family tradition has it that the Driscolls were sheltering in a barn overnight; all were asleep except, fortunately, Patrick, who overheard a gang of robbers planning to attack them. He roused the others and they managed to escape, but Patrick was so appalled at this first experience of England that he evidently decided it would be better to take their chances back in Ireland, and they returned home.

When Elizabeth was older she returned to England alone to make her living. Like her daughters, she regularly worked for Bryant and May. She later met and married Patrick Driscoll, who worked all his adult life as a dock labourer.[12]

The Driscoll family

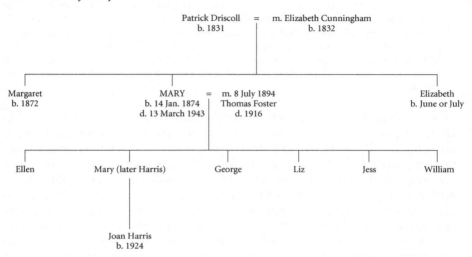

The 1881 Census shows the Driscoll family living in the East End at 3 Gloucestershire Court:

The Driscoll's 1881 Census Entry

3 Gloucestershire Court		
Patrick Driscoll, Head	aged 50	Dock Labourer, born Ireland, Co. Kerry
Elizabeth Driscoll, Wife	aged 49	Lead worker, born Ireland, Cork
Katherine	aged 17	Match maker
Margaret	aged 9	Scholar
Mary	**aged 7**	**Scholar**
Elizabeth	aged 10 months	

Gloucestershire Court is not named on Bacon's 1888 *Ordnance Atlas of London and Suburbs*, nor is it marked on Charles Booth's maps of the area. However, the folio pages in the 1881 Census show that it was near to Ann's Court, one of several small courts Booth recorded around Wentworth Street, between Whitechapel High Street and Bishopsgate Street. The archivist of the Booth collection has confirmed that this is the most likely location.[13] Built around a communal courtyard, 'courts', belying the pleasant name, were often the worst kinds of housing in the East End. The Reverend Samuel Barnett (vicar of a church in Commercial Road and later the first warden of Toynbee Hall) described the scene in 1873:

... the whole parish is covered with a web of courts and alleys. None of the courts have roads ... [in some] the sanitary accommodation was pits in cellars; in other courts the houses were lower, wooden and dilapidated, a stand pipe at the end providing the only water. Each chamber was the home of a family who sometimes owned their indescribable furniture, but in most cases the rooms were let unfurnished for 8 pence a night. In many instances broken windows had been repaired with rags, the banisters had been used for firewood, and the paper hung from the walls which were the residence of countless vermin.[14]

Mary's mother Elizabeth, sometime matchmaker, is shown as a lead worker in 1881, but given the changeable nature of women's 'casual' employment at the time this is not surprising. Daughter Katherine is shown as a matchmaker, but it is her presence which is the one unexpected factor. Neither Joan Harris nor any other surviving family members who knew Mary Driscoll was aware of Katherine's existence. It was not unknown for families at this time to stop talking about family members who became estranged for some reason, but the circumstances of Katherine's life remain a mystery at this point and she disappears from later census entries. However, cross-referencing with the names index for the census shows that of several Patrick Driscolls, this is the only one in the right area and with children of the right age in 1881. The names, ages and places of birth of the other five family members are all correct, as is Patrick Driscoll's occupation, so it must be assumed that this is the right family.

Joan Harris knew her grandmother for eighteen years, and had a close relationship with her. The health of Joan's mother, Mary Harris, was precarious: she had pneumonia on five separate occasions, so severely that each time she was given the Last Rites. Because of this Joan's grandmother effectively brought Joan up for much of her childhood. Joan adored her, to the extent that her exasperated mother would exclaim, 'She *has* got her faults you know!'[15]

Joan's great-aunt, Mary's sister Margaret Driscoll, always known as Mog, also worked at the factory and joined the strikers in 1888. The strike fund register shows Mary and Mog working in separate factories but living at the same address: it is interesting to note that Mary's name is recorded only one line above that of Sarah Chapman, who would later attend the Trades Union Congress on behalf of the union; the two women clearly worked at the same job and in the same part of the factory.

Register Entries

Wax & Box stores & patent

		Single/ Married	Occupation	Wage	
195	Mary Driscoll 24 Cottage St	S	Patent	6/6	Lives with Father

| 198 | Sarah Chapman 2 Swan Place | S | – | 14/- | Helps to keep Father |

Victoria Factory

| 51 | Mog Driscol 24 Cottgae [sic], Poplar | S | Cutting Down | 7/1 | Lives with Parents |

The matchworkers' strike register records that Mary was working in the 'Wax & Box stores & patent'. 'Wax vestas' were friction matches which used a wax or wax-braided stem, appearing around 1833. They are still made in some countries today, including China and India, though wooden matches have long since superseded them in Britain.[16] Mary Driscoll's occupation is listed as 'Patent'. Bryant and May seem to have referred to their safety matches as 'Patent Safety Matches' (having bought the patent for them from Lundstrom), and as simply 'Patents' in advertisements of the period.[17] Other jobs in the same part of the factory are associated with boxes and box-making: 'box sewer, box inverter, box carrier', etc. Mog Driscoll describes herself as living at Cottage Street with 'parents', so although Mary only mentioned her father (probably as the head of the household), both Patrick and Elizabeth are likely to still have been alive at this point.

Cottage Street would have been an improvement on Gloucestershire Court, where they were living in 1881– there is a full analysis of both addresses and the surrounding areas in Chapter Eight. By 1891 the family had left Cottage Street, and Mary married three years later.

Joan Harris makes the point that, like most young people, she was not especially interested in the past when she knew her grandmother. Although she became fascinated by East End history in later years, to her subsequent regret she did not ask her grandmother much about her younger years. However, she remembers her grandmother, and also her mother, talking about pay and conditions in the match factory, treatment by foremen, and health and safety as the issues that most concerned the women, and she does not recall any mention of Annie Besant or her involvement.

Mary Driscoll does not in any case seem to have been a woman necessarily impressed by social status. Far from being in awe of middle-class philanthropists, Joan remembers that Mary was 'canny' about manipulating them when necessary to help her family. The Salvation Army used to distribute free cocoa to those in the neighbourhood they considered to be 'deserving poor', and amenable to their message. Mary would tell her – Catholic – children to go along and pretend to be part of the 'Church Army', singing the appropriate hymns in order to secure their share of cocoa.[18] Later in her life, Mary was on good terms with an aristocratic woman who did 'good works' in the area, and occasionally advised her on these activities. Mary continued to visit this woman for many years, but considered that the relationship was one of equals rather than 'charity

case' and 'philanthropist'. There is no doubt, however, that the family survived
on very little: Joan remembers her aunts talking about going out to pick up
'specks' (left-over bruised bits of fruit and vegetables) from street markets to feed
themselves.[19]

Mary's notably upright bearing was individual and distinctive enough to help
her granddaughter to identify her in the 'factory' photograph of the striking
women nearly a hundred and twenty years later. She had deliberately adopted
this way of carrying herself, evidently as a very young woman, and perhaps as a
mark of self-respect in the face of early poverty. Clearly it meant something to
her, as she was insistent that her children and grandchildren did the same: Joan
remembers her frequently telling them, 'Always hold your head up. Remember
you're as good as anyone.'

Mary married Thomas Foster, a dock worker, on 8 July 1894.[20] Their marriage
certificate shows that the couple had been next-door neighbours in St Dunstan's
Road, which is presumably how they met. Joan recalled that Foster 'had to go on
the cobbles' – he had to join the call-ons for casual dock work, never making it
to a secure position.[21] Two of her sisters, Mog and youngest sister Lizzie Driscoll,
would also marry dockers who worked on the 'Royal' group – the Albert, Victoria
and George docks.

Mary gave birth to eleven children, only five of whom survived. Foster was a
heavy drinker and could be violent: he once pushed Mary down a flight of stairs
when she was pregnant. His wife, 'a very hard-working and independent lady',[22]
took in washing both before and after Foster's death and effectively supported
herself after her marriage: she had little choice as 'if he [Foster] earned a penny
he'd spend it on drink'.[23] In order to afford new shoes for the family each year,
Mary took the children hop-picking each summer, the traditional summer
holiday, or the closest thing to it, for many matchwomen and dockers. Even the
strike could not interrupt the tradition: as Annie Besant remarked in July 1888,
many of the fourteen hundred Bryant and May strikers had taken themselves off
to the hop-fields so were not drawing strike pay, accounting for the fact that only
just over half of them appear on the strike fund register.

Much has been written about hop-picking, but not always from the perspective
of those who did it. It is often described as a kind of rural idyll, at least when
compared to the everyday lives of East End workers. Joan, however, remembered
the hard work and discomfort too, and intensely disliked the annual trip, though
others in her family enjoyed it enough to go hopping even when they didn't need
the money. Joan recalled long days in the fields and, at night, the itchy straw
mattresses in the huts provided for the pickers, as well as the seemingly endless
rain drumming on corrugated iron roofs. She vividly remembers her relief one
summer when her father, coming to visit and finding Joan in the middle of the
field in the pouring rain trying to shelter underneath the vines, picked her up
and took her straight home.

Thomas Foster died in 1916 when Mary was in her final pregnancy. Her son
William would himself die three years after his father, on Armistice Day 1918.

'Billie' was a victim of 'Spanish flu', a highly virulent strain of influenza which is thought to have killed between 20 and 40 million people worldwide, more than World War One itself. Mary never entirely recovered from the loss of her last child.

It is thought that Foster may have died on the docks: though accounts are vague, Joan remembers hearing his death attributed to a head injury sustained during a fall at work. After her husband's death Mary flourished, and somehow managed to set herself up as a shopkeeper. Her two shops, a cats' meat shop and a corn chandler's, were next door to one another in Parnham Street, now demolished, off Salmon Lane near Limehouse Cut. Her first profession perturbed at least one middle-class investigator:

> ... the catsmeat interest is liberally represented, no less than five establishments of that character flourishing in the market. How is this? Do the squalid court and alley dwellers, with their proverbial extravagance, each keep a cat? or – No; the supposition is too dreadful.[24]

Had the above author read his Mayhew, he would have been reassured to learn that it was a well-established and profitable trade: Mayhew recorded some 300 cats' meat sellers in London's markets in his surveys earlier in the century, most operating from stalls or barrows:[25]

> The supply of food for cats and dogs is far greater than may be generally thought ... There are upwards of twenty of such yards in London; three or four are in Whitechapel, one in Wandsworth, two in Cow-cross – one of the two last mentioned is the largest establishment in London – and there are two about Bermondsey.[26]

By Mary Driscoll's time the selling was taking place in shops as well as from the barrows most of Mayhew's subjects used. A photograph of her shop from the 1920s (p. 204) shows that an array of general groceries was also being sold. Where Mary got the funds to establish her shop remains a mystery. If Foster's death was an accident on the docks, Mary might have got compensation for her widowhood; certainly, her granddaughter Joan believes, she would have made sure she obtained any payment she was entitled to, as she was extremely financially astute: 'You couldn't do her out of a penny.'[27] Joan also remembered that she had 'an admirer' in her insurance agent. She was unlikely to have had help from her parents-in-law: Mary detested her mother-in-law, a hospital matron; she had taken out insurance on her mother-in-law's life, and she threw a party with the dividend when she died in 1930.

They were quite small, local shops, one of which was in Mary's own front parlour, so would not have been excessively expensive to establish or to run, though still beyond the means of many poor East Enders. Booth describes Parnham Street as 'respectable', and Joan remembers the street itself in the 1920s as clean and quite pleasant, although Mary's own living quarters, like so many in the East End, were infested with black beetles.

Mary was a competent businesswoman, who worked extremely hard and expected her children to do likewise: 'Even if [one of her daughters] was rushing off to a date she'd say, hang on, go and serve that customer next door first, and they'd complain at being made late.'[28] Mary was known for her financial acumen and, despite not being able to read or write, she kept a constant mental check on takings: 'She could always tell you down to the last penny what was in the tills in either shop, at any time.'[29] Local shopkeepers were figures of some standing in their neighbourhoods, particularly as they could give or withhold 'tick', the vital credit on which many poor households ran. As Hobsbawm noted:

> When workers lost their employment – which they might do at the end of the job, of the week, of the day or even of the hour – they had nothing to fall back upon except their savings, their friendly society or trade union, their credit with local shopkeepers . . .[30]

Mary would leave £13 in her will, a reasonable sum for someone born into poverty.

Mary's Irish heritage was a source of pride to her, and she remained a staunch Republican all her life. Joan remembers large pictures of Robert Emmett, executed for fighting for Irish Independence, and Michael Collins, prominent Sinn Fein member and participant in the 1916 Easter Rising, having pride of place in Mary's rooms throughout her life. We saw in Chapter Three that Emmett and his passionate final speech remained a radicalizing influence on Irish migrants to London like Communist Party member John Gibbons, more than a century after his death.[31] 'The Bold Robert Emmett' was among the extensive repertoire of Irish 'rebel' songs which Mary used to sing. ('My crime is the love of the land I was born in, A hero I lived and a hero I'll die.') Arthur Morrison also recalled of his mother, who made matchboxes for Bryant and May, that 'When she was well boozed she used to sing Irish songs: "Bold Robert Emmett who died with a smile". It was a famous song with her.'[32]

Joan was 'brought up on those songs'.[33] Joan's mother also felt herself to be Irish, and shared her mother's Republican politics. Joan inherited this sense of identity, though all of the women came to dislike the course the Republican movement would later take.

Though usually a quiet woman, Mary Driscoll was a strong character who would 'fight her corner', with what her daughter Mary called an 'Irish temper'. Joan says she could accept the idea of her grandmother leading a strike if she felt she and her colleagues were being badly treated, but found it harder to imagine her being 'told what to do' by Annie Besant or any other 'outsider': 'She was too sensible to have done herself out of her wages just because someone told her to. But she would have done it if it was something she believed in.'[34]

It was only discovered during the course of this research that Mary had been a strike committee member, along with Mog. Both Mary and Mog are named as present in the committee photograph: from comparisons with later photographs of the two women, it is believed that they may be the two women immediately

Mary Driscoll's shop in Parnham Street, 1920s. Joan Harris and her mother in doorway. With thanks to Joan Harris

to Annie Besant's left on the platform (see p. 192). They are identified as 'Mary and Polly' Driscoll of 24 Cottage Street, Poplar; however, it was in fact Mary not Margaret who was nicknamed 'Polly', so this is evidently a mistake.

Mary Driscoll survived the intensive bombings of the 1940–41 Blitz un-harmed, although her house in Parnham Street had no air-raid shelter. During one air raid she ran through the streets with her newborn grandchild in her arms, desperate to find a church in which to baptize him – and didn't return home until she'd succeeded. She retained her sense of independence all her life, and was unhappy when the war finally caused her to be evacuated to Taunton in Somerset: 'She could never,' Joan said, 'be comfortable living in anyone else's home', preferring to be under her own roof in Parnham Street, for all that Joan remembers it as a 'dreadful place' with no inside toilet or more than a tin bath to wash in, and infested with black beetles. This must have been hard for a woman as fastidious as Mary evidently was, but she never complained about the conditions, though she was overwhelmed on first seeing the Harris family's new home in Essex – exclaiming to her daughter: 'Oh, Mary, it's a palace! An indoor toilet and bathroom!'[35]

Joan Harris was a flight mechanic during the war, and so had to request home leave during Mary's last illness in 1943. She had to fight to get it, from a superior officer who said, 'But she's only your grandmother.' 'Yes,' Joan replied, 'but she means the world to me.' Because of this delay, by the time she arrived home it was too late – Mary had died of 'dropsy' (oedema), aged 69, on 13 March 1943.

(2) Eliza Martin

Eliza Martin's grandson Jim Best has worked for most of his adult life as a London taxi driver. He and his wife Mary lived on the Isle of Dogs when I first interviewed them, but have since moved to Romford (still in East London).

Jim Best's grandmother Eliza Martin lived at 14 Whitethorn Street, Bow during the strike. Her grandson knew the house well as it remained in the family for some time. He did not know his grandmother – she died before he was born, the first of the four matchwomen researched to die, and probably not from natural causes. Only one photograph of Eliza survives. However, Jim was close to her surviving children, his uncles and aunts, and learned about Eliza from them and from his father.

Family tradition had always asserted that Eliza was one of the strike leaders. As Jim recalls:

> I remember my Dad showing me the article in the *East London Advertiser* and saying, 'That's your Nan, son.' Eliza told Dad that she and her friends started the strike and we were proud of that. There was never any doubt in our minds it was their strike, the girls' strike, not anyone else's.[36]

Contemporary evidence from the *Star* newspaper, which had a reporter at the scene of the strike from its earliest hours, wrote about the key role of an 'Eliza':

> One of the leaders of the strike – who, with her companions on the Committee, stood behind the table and checked entries – was Eliza, a girl with a Titian-like bloom on her handsome face, the figure of an Amazon, and the softest violet eyes.[37]

There were two 'Elizas' on the committee, Eliza Price and Eliza Martin. Of the two, Eliza Martin seems the more likely candidate for the woman described above, having been one of the five mentioned by Bryant and May as leaders of the strike. No photographs of her as a young woman exist, but she evidently had eyes of a striking and unusual blue – which could perhaps have been rendered violet with a little poetic licence. Eliza's sister married into a local family of dockers, the Farncourts, and had a daughter, Rosie, who also married a docker and had three sons with him, who also worked on the docks in their turn.

Eliza herself married George Best, a fishmonger, in December 1892 in Mile End, and went to live with him in Eastfield Street. Charles Booth noted that this street was the residence of several fish curers, and also dock labourers. Jim Best says that it had a reputation as a 'tough' street in his grandmother's time. The Bests had done comparatively well for themselves through their family business, and George was considered a good catch – in financial terms at least. The family owned their own 'smokehole', a large shed in the back garden where fresh fish were smoked over wood chippings. The fish were picked up in the early hours of every morning from the Billingsgate market, then smoked and sold – sometimes back to Billingsgate. The Bests also had a fish stall outside a local pub. The family owned their own double house in front of the 'smokehole'.

Eliza and George had nine surviving children: Eliza, Larly, George, Bet, Polly (née Mary), Joe, Nelly, Jim and Tom (the father of my interviewee). Eliza and her children worked in the family business: like Mary Driscoll's and Martha Robertson's families, their only break was a summer's hop-picking in Kent.

Eliza had a close relationship with all of her children. However, George Best turned out to be a violent and 'very cruel'[38] man. He beat his children, so severely that they bore the marks for the rest of their lives. Jim remembers that when he knew them decades later, scars were clearly visible on their wrists and forearms where they had raised their arms in front of their faces to try to protect themselves from their father's whip. From what Jim knows of Eliza, he believes that she would have done what she could to protect her children: she 'could look after herself' physically, and if George had hit her 'she would probably have hit him back'.[39] Certainly Eliza is known to have fought physically when necessary to protect her daughters from unwelcome sexual advances and harassment from local men. However, George Best was an intimidating man whose family feared him. This, and Eliza's devotion to her children, is believed to have led to her premature death.

Eliza had charge of the family's money, but was supposed to account to her husband for everything that she spent, and never knew when he would ask to see how much was left. She had secretly been spending more than was allowed on her children, and over time this built up to a larger deficit in funds than she could make up. She knew that her husband would eventually discover this, and that if he found out where the money had gone, he would be more than capable of taking out his anger on the children. Eliza's daughter Polly told Jim's wife Mary what was believed to have happened next:

> Eliza's daughter Polly . . . said that [Jim's father] Tom found their mother dead in bed when he was 11 years old. This would have been in 1921. It was kept from Tom because he was only young, but his Nan used to look after the family money, as they were quite well off. And there was not as much money there as there should have been. As . . . [George Best] was a very wicked spiteful man, Eliza was so afraid of her husband [finding out] that she took her own life.[40]

When George Best died his son Jim took control of the family business. His brother Tom, the father of my interviewee, later left to work on building sites – he felt his brothers were leaving him to do far more than his fair share of the hard work, including getting up at 2 a.m. every morning to fetch the fresh fish from Billingsgate. Jim committed suicide around 1960. George (junior) was 'gassed' in France during World War Two and never married.

Their sisters had a reputation in the neighbourhood for being strong women who could look after themselves. When Jim Best was young, he witnessed an occasion when the locals used this for their own amusement:

> One day Nell was queuing up in the local betting shop when this toff came in and lined up behind her. I saw one of the local lads reach past him to pinch Nell's bottom, knowing what she'd do. She wheeled round and punched the bloke behind her, the toff, knocking him out with one punch.[41]

Polly Best also used to 'chase men away from the family women'.[42] She married a docker: Whitethorn Street was 'a dockers' area', and Jim Best said that to him matchwomen and dockers were very closely allied: 'all the same people, from the same families'.[43]

(3) Martha Robertson

Martha Robertson was born in 1882, but was working at the Bryant and May factory at the time of the strike, making matchboxes. She later became a matchmaker working inside the factory

Her grandson, Ted Lewis, is an expert on community history and helped to establish the Ragged School Museum in Copperfield Road, Tower Hamlets, on the site of the largest ragged school in London, his knowledge of the East End past and present has been tremendously helpful. He and his wife Bett both grew up in the East End and still live in Bow, a few minutes walk from Fairfield Road.

Ted had a very close relationship to his grandmother, who died when he was an adult. Martha's mother Jane was also a matchbox-maker, and her father George a dock labourer. Martha's future husband James Lakin was the son of a docker, William Lakin, and a matchbox-maker, Mary Lakin. The Lakin family were of Irish descent. Martha and her family 'always mixed with lots of dockers and dockers' families'.[44] Information about Martha's life has been compiled through interviews with Ted Lewis and his wife Bett, who also knew her, and with the use of an unpublished family history written by Ted's cousin Larraine Gardner. The latter includes Martha's own reminiscences recorded by Larraine.

Martha Robertson. With thanks to Ted Lewis

The Robertson family in the 1891 Census: 19 Harold Street (RG12/267)

The census shows the family of nine living at Harold Street, Bethnal Green, in two rooms. Also resident at the same address were ten other people from two different families, including another matchbox-maker. The street no longer exists, and nor do the streets immediately bordering it, but with the help of the Booth archive I have located it running off Green Street, close to Victoria Park and less than a mile from the Fairfield Works. Charles Booth's notebooks from 1898 to 1899 comment on it only in passing, along with four neighbouring streets: 'Harold Street, Type Street, Norton St., Sydney St ... Harold St and Type St. dark blue as map'.[45] Booth's notes for dark blue streets read 'Very poor, casual. Chronic want'.[46]

Census Entry

George Robertson (father) aged 33, born 1858, 'labourer', born Bethnal Green	
Jane Robertson (mother) aged 32, born 1859, 'box maker', born Bethnal Green	
Children	
Jane	aged 13 (born 1878)
George	aged 12 (born 1879)
Emily	aged 10 (born 1881)
Martha	**aged 8 (born 1882)**
Sarah	aged 6 (born 1886)
James	aged 3 (born 1888)
Harry	aged 1 (born 1890)
Born after the census	
Fred	born 1891
Mari and Eliza (twins)	born 1892
Also resident at the same address:	
Albert [?] Staerck – Slipper maker	
Wife Hannah	
Son William	
Ann Cousins – Matchbox Maker + six children, including	
Jane Cousins (daughter) Matchbox Maker	

The Lakin family in the 1891 Census: 42 Walter St (RG12/272)

Martha's future husband James lived at Walter Street in 1891, not far from the Mile End Road, with his family of seven; thirteen other people also lived in separate lodging rooms in the same house.

Walter Street does not feature on Bacon's map, but I have located it from Charles Booth's maps, just over a mile from both the Bryant and May factory in Fairfield Road and the London Docks. Booth classified the street as dark blue, though somewhat condescendingly noted 'one or two houses at the West End rather better – one with books on the table – mostly novels'.[47] Walter Street is also close to the Robertsons' rooms in Harold Street, which were a short walk away, through Victoria Park cemetery.

Census Entry

Father: William, aged 37, born 1854, dock labourer
Mother Mary, aged 31, born 1859, box-maker

Children	
William	aged 13, born 1878
James	**aged 11, born 1880**
Henry	aged 9, born 1882
Richard	aged 8, born 1883
George	aged 3, born 1888
Born after the census	
Florence	
Elizabeth	

Martha was one of six children in 1888, a further three being born after her. Even when she was a very young child her earnings from matchbox-making were important to the family economy. Her recollections, written down by her granddaughter Larraine, provide insight into a young matchbox-maker's day, which for Martha began at 5 a.m:

> Scrambling out of the large bed she shared with her siblings, she would get dressed and begin her chores . . . her clothes were hand me downs and her shoes were whatever she could find in the cupboard under the stairs. Often not a matching pair, those were saved for the older children. She would begin by clearing the grate and laying a new fire, then walk to the Bryant and May factory and join the queue with many other children. Martha would sit and make her quota of matchboxes for the princely sum of 2½d per gross. She was happy to do it to help her family, and always recalled her own mother with love and not resentment, saying how hard her life had been . . . On her way back home she would buy some bread and milk – in order for the family to have some breakfast before they started their day. Sometimes she would sit with her mother and make the matchboxes as 'homework', sometimes by herself in the factory, but it was always Martha's responsibility to walk to the factory to collect and deliver them.[48]

This is the first account of matchbox-making being performed *in* the factory rather than at home, but it seems that Martha was clear about this. If it was the case, perhaps lack of space at home was a factor: it must have been hard for Martha and her mother to find the room to work and to lay out all the materials necessary for their work when the whole family lived in two rooms with seven other family members.

As Arthur Harding's recollections of his mother and sister's matchbox-making show, this was space-consuming work: 'The floor being the drying ground for the matchboxes, there was no room to move about. The matchboxes had to be spread out to dry and you couldn't afford to tread on them.'[49] Harding's mother was disabled, and unable to walk to the factory; in any case, older women worked at home out of necessity, to try to accommodate the demands of family, but it may be that Bryant and May allowed children, or perhaps anyone with insufficient space indoors, to work on the premises. This would certainly have been an advantage to the employer in giving them immediate access to the finished product, which could then be filled straightaway; and as Fairfield Road was an enormous, sprawling complex, allocating space would probably not have been a problem.

The particular significance of this new information is that it means there would have been less of a division between at least some box-makers and factory workers, explaining the support they later offered to the strike, and meaning that ties between matchbox-makers and dockers, like those in the Lakin family, are more important in supporting the hypothesis of connected strikes than have previously been supposed. The WPPL would note in 1890 that many matchbox-makers' husbands were unionized dockers.[50]

Martha had only basic schooling, and left school at 13 to work full time at the Bryant and May factory, again demonstrating the interchangeable nature of the two types of work.

Marriage and later life

Martha Robertson's marriage certificate records her marriage on 15 August 1901 to 22-year-old James Lakin, then a tea porter (possibly working at a dock), of 42 Walter Street, Green Street. Martha was married from her childhood home, 22 Cambridge Road.

Cambridge Road (now Cambridge Heath Road) and Walter Street lie close together in Bethnal Green. Reflecting on the area in general in the late nineteenth century, Booth noted that it showed 'a general tendency . . . to become poorer', and in an analysis which could have applied to the whole of the East End and beyond, concluded that 'The first people to be affected by cheaper locomotion are the richer classes. Life of the poor more sociable and more bound up with neighbours than life of richer. Therefore rich go, poor remain.'[51] This again emphasizes the importance of community, and the almost communal element of life in the neighbourhoods that were home to matchwomen.

Booth recorded that in the late 1880s, the streets around Cambridge Road and Green Street had a high proportion of poor and very poor residents:

'mostly casual labourers and people under-employed in the furniture and dress trades. Only 4.2 per cent were classed as middleclass, small manufacturers and shopkeepers.'[52]

Booth categorized Cambridge Road itself as 'mixed' to 'fairly comfortable', though on the east side of it were 'two very bad roads'.[53] The 1891 Census seems to bear this out, showing a number of Cambridge Road residents in trades which were considered more 'respectable' and were probably better paid and less unpleasant than those typically found in poorer East End roads. Several residents reported that they were 'living on their own means', although this could presumably have covered a multitude of possibilities apart from some kind of private wealth or income. However, Cambridge Road also boasted one lawyer, a teacher and several shopkeepers (including a grocer, fishmonger and newsagent), elevating it towards respectability by the standards of the time. The Robertson family were not there at this time – a family called Levy, who were cake-bakers, were at number 22. There were several dock and associated workers, including a dock foreman, a warehouseman, two carmen, and a family of dockers – interestingly enough called Tillett. There were several more dock workers in Walter Street.

Martha and James Lakin had five children by the time James enlisted as a rifleman in the First World War. Jenny, Jim, Harry, Clara and Bett survived: a fourth daughter, also named Martha, died in infancy in 1903, as did son George in 1904. When James got leave from France in 1915, their daughter Jenny was conceived. Some time after his return, Martha received official notification that rifleman Lakin was 'lost in action – missing presumed dead'.[54]

The Lakin family home was at 50 Libra Road, off the lively market street, Roman Road. It is also near 'Annie Besant Close', though this was not built until the 1970s, just outside Martha's lifetime.[55] Libra Road was categorized by Charles Booth in his poverty map for 1898–9 as 'Poor. 18s. to 21s. a week for a moderate family'. The Lakins were certainly not well off. The house, now demolished, was a Victorian terraced 'airy' house (the 'airy' being the local name for the large basement area) divided into three storeys; but far from luxurious inside, with 'a leaky roof, "wonky" stairs, lead pipes which froze in the winter, ill-fitting windows' and an outside toilet.[56] The top floor consisted of two rooms and a landing; the kitchen was two floors below with 'a copper in one corner, an old meat safe and a stone floor, and a flight of stairs down to the lower passage and "airy"'.[57] Chickens and rabbits were kept in the 'yard', where Martha also grew dahlias.

The Lakins originally rented two rooms in the basement. The landlord had stipulated a maximum of two children, but when he called round unannounced on one occasion he counted five; however, he 'took pity' on Martha, whom he assumed to be widowed. Ted surmises that the landlord may have been one of Martha's 'admirers', of whom there would be several: 'she got about a bit'.[58] In any event, he allowed her and her family to stay, and she remained there all her life, eventually moving upstairs where she had three rooms and a scullery. This was not luxurious: 'There were no carpets, just rice sacks on the floor: it was pretty grotty really but no one knew any different – they didn't often leave the area so there was nothing to compare it to.'[59]

Martha was 'very well respected' in the community – 'she was the one all the others in the street would go to in a crisis'. She also acted as the unofficial neighbourhood midwife and undertaker, so she both delivered babies and laid out the dead.[60] Because of her standing, Martha was approached by the army in 1916 to help identify badly wounded local soldiers. These were men whose injuries had left them not only disfigured but unable to communicate. Walking the wards with her sons, Martha said later that she felt 'drawn' to a man bandaged from head to foot who was unable to communicate except with unintelligible groans. 'Then she suddenly looked into his eyes and said – "Jim . . . is it you?" He fell back on the bed with tears streaming down his bandaged face. Martha fainted, her two sons holding her up.'[61]

Her badly wounded husband was immediately discharged into her care. Martha was expected to nurse him on her own without any medical or financial assistance, as well as looking after her family and working full time. James was finally discharged as 'no longer fit for war service' in June 1917.[62] Permanently and severely facially disfigured, as photographs in his later life make clear, he was a different man, and 'never the same again after his pain and suffering. Those that . . . remember him try hard to find good things to say about him.'[63] People who knew him described him as having 'half his face blown away', and family photographs confirm the extent of his injuries; it was difficult, as his granddaughter acknowledges, 'to be cheerful under those circumstances'.[64] However, he and Martha remained together and had three more children. After his death Martha married an Irishman, William Leary, a 'dear old man' who had been a childhood sweetheart, and had remained a drinking buddy who accompanied her on many a 'beano'.[65] They married in 1956 and had five years together before his death.

Martha's 'happiest time of year' was always the family's annual excursion to the hop-fields in Pluckley, Kent. Martha would go on ahead of the rest of the family to ensure everything was in order for their stay, freshly wallpapering and preparing the huts they would sleep in, and making sure she got the best quality straw to stuff their mattresses. The rest of the family would load all of their baggage onto a lorry and drive down, 'singing all the way'.[66] Martha, unsurprisingly after so many years of hard physical labour, suffered from a bad back and could only sleep well in her own bed, so that came to Pluckley too.

It was during one year's hop-picking, however, that Martha suffered a tragedy. Her infant son Dickie, who was just crawling, found his way under a tree and ate some poisonous berries. The local doctor was on holiday, and the locum refused to come out on a Sunday. Having no other option, Martha carried her baby for two hours to the nearest hospital, but he died in her arms before she could reach it. He was buried in Pluckley churchyard. To the end of their lives Dickie's siblings never forgot the injustice surrounding his death, recalling it with 'anger and bitterness'.[67]

Martha's life was a constant fight against poverty, but she was an excellent manager who somehow kept her large family fed on virtually nothing. Ted Lewis remembers a large stewpot permanently simmering over the fire in Libra Road, for which he would often be sent to the butcher's for 'two pen'orth of bones and leave the meat on'. When he was very young Martha would always tell him they were having 'duck' if he asked what was for supper – she kept ducks in the garden. It wasn't until he was older that he realized she had been teasing him: the duck population had remained constant, and they'd actually been eating something rather less fancy – probably faggot stew.[68]

Ted remembered her with 'her hands always busy' at one kind of homework or another, never stopping even when visitors called – in fact, guests were likely to be 'roped in' to help her. Martha continued to make matchboxes for Bryant and May, as well as pickling onions for the local pickle factory. Matchbox-making 'was done as-and-when – women at home would pick it up and put it down when they could fit it in', often needing to work 16-hour days to make any kind of money.[69]

Despite hardship and tragedy Martha had enormous strength of character and remained 'a fairly happy person' who was popular and sociable:

> She liked a drink and socializing: her favourite pubs used to be the 'Cornwallis', at the bottom of Libra Road in Old Ford Road, the 'Lady Franklin', and the 'Milton Arms'. She'd usually bring a crowd of friends back from the pub with her to the house in Libra Road, and they'd all sing and play the piano until late.[70]

Martha had great 'pride in herself and her children'. The family was extremely close, and talked about the 'funny Lakin ways' which seemed to have given them an almost supernatural connection with one another. Martha would sometimes wake in the morning saying that she was worried about one of the children, and he or she would often appear wanting to speak to her before the day was out, 'unannounced but not unexpected'.[71] Of necessity Martha was always extremely shrewd with her money – as Ted put it, 'artful': 'If we were in the pub and I offered to buy her a drink she'd always say, "Oh no, no Ted, you keep your money . . ." but it didn't take that much persuasion, she'd always take it in the end'.[72]

Ted met a number of Bryant and May matchwomen who were his grandmother's friends to the end of her life. They used to take trips to the seaside together, what they called their 'beanos', which often involved a fair amount of drinking:

> [The Bryant and May workers] were all like part of a family. They were very strong characters, all of them, very efficient and strong. They might not have been what people outside would have called ladies, but to us they were. They were East End ladies.[73]

Ted also remembered the matchworkers as well able to look after themselves if in any trouble. He recalled that even when she was an old woman with a fractured hip and a walking stick, if he and Martha were in a pub where trouble was brewing, 'she'd say, if it kicks off, just prop me up in a corner and I'll take 'em on with my stick'.[74] Martha was bedridden at the end of her life, but never lost her sense of humour or gave up her social life. She would receive her visitors in her bedroom, where she

> lay in bed singing pub songs. In the morning she'd listen out for the pot and pan man pushing his barrow down Libra Road. There was a loose manhole cover which almost always tripped him up, making half the pots fall off his barrow. It always made her laugh. She said it was better than an alarm clock, and used to chuckle and say, 'That poor sod won't have anything left to sell.'[75]

Martha died in 1962, just over a year after her second husband.

Although Martha was extremely young at the time of the strike she still had some memory of it, and also heard about it from the strikers themselves, whom she came to know well – they were her friends and workmates for many years when she worked in the factory. Ted confirms that she never talked about the strike as being led from outside, and he could not remember her ever mentioning Annie Besant. His belief, from knowing the Bryant and May women, is that the strikers

> did it for themselves, and for their families and communities too, from a sense of right and wrong. Because they knew the way they were being treated in the factory, the low wages and so on, was wrong, and that their employers were doing very well out of them. They knew it was wrong, morally wrong, and they didn't need anyone from outside to come along and tell them that. They weren't the sort of women to be told what to do by anyone anyway.[76]

Martha also remembered Bryant and May's chagrin at being forced to improve conditions after the strike; the employers evidently tried to compensate for their financial loss by attempting not to apply the improved terms to new or younger workers.

Ted Lewis was inspired by what his grandmother and parents had been through in their lives to become a trade union activist himself, as a member of the TGWU (Transport and General Workers Union, now merged with Amicus to form UNITE). He worked on the docks after the war, as both a docker and a crane driver, though he didn't much enjoy dock work, and preferred his later job at Billingsgate fish market. Ted saw his trade union activism as 'a class struggle', motivated by the hardship his grandparents and parents had endured all their lives.[77] Ted's sisters were also trade unionists, and took an active part in a long strike at a bakery where they worked.

Ted's wife Bett, who also became close to Martha – and was the only one of his girlfriends of whom she approved – worked at Bryant and May at Fairfield Road in the 1950s. It was, she says, then considered 'one of the best' for employment practices, as a result of continuing improvements made since the strike but also, she believes, because of continuing sensitivity to the 'bad name' the strike had given the firm: even after so many years the memory of it was very much present.[78] (This is borne out by papers in the company archive, mentioned earlier, which show that the firm were still extremely reactive, verging on the litigious, to reminders of 1888. They continued to attempt to get their name expunged from film and musical scripts about the strike into the 1960s, until their solicitor finally had to advise them that they had to accept the association as a 'fact of history'.)

Martha's reminiscences also provide an interesting new interpretation of an enduring East End legend. As discussed in Chapter Six, the statue of Gladstone which Bryant and May caused to be built using forced contributions from the workforce still stands on the Bow Road, and continues to have red paint thrown at it for reasons, and by persons, unknown. It has been said that this was revived as a protest about the converting of the building into 'yuppie flats' in the 1980s. Ted reported that according to the matchworkers' tradition they themselves threw the first paint, after dark, to represent their 'blood', which had paid for it.[79] We do know that the matchwomen voiced this same objection at the unveiling ceremony, from their reports of it to Besant when interviewed for 'White slavery in London'.

It has not as yet been possible either to confirm this. I can see that the 'culprits' may be unwilling to admit to what probably constitutes criminal damage, but it would be fascinating to know who continues the tradition, and whether they have any connection to the matchworkers.

CONCLUSIONS

The Bryant and May strikers have previously been nameless faces in photographs, frozen in time in one moment in 1888. While the historical account of Besant's life moves forward from that year, history has, until now, had nothing to tell us about the matchwomen's individual lives after the strike.

As we have seen, the rich and valuable testimony of these three matchwomen's grandchildren allows us to see the women growing up and becoming mothers, wives and grandmothers. Far from being downtrodden, all were figures of some standing in their communities, and well respected despite not conforming to popular notions of female 'respectability'. That they drank, sometimes fought physically, and in some cases took lovers, made no difference to their status.

All three were matriarchal figures within their large families. Mary Driscoll moved on from the match factory and a difficult marriage to an alcoholic to become a successful shopkeeper, while Martha Robertson was an unofficial community leader and midwife. All of the women showed competence and strength of character in their lives, and each is recalled as a strong personality with a strong sense of self. As Carl Chinn notes in 'They Worked All Their Lives', his study of urban working-class women, there is an important and sometimes overlooked dichotomy between the class status accorded to women like Driscoll, Martin and Robertson by outsiders and their personal standing at home:

> [their matriarchal role] enabled the mothers of this section to exercise a power within their own ... communities, which contrasts with the general lack of authority exercised by women of more prosperous classes during the period.[80]

Mary Driscoll is remembered for her pride in herself and her insistence that she and her family were anybody's equals, regardless of class. Martha Robertson and Eliza Martin had the courage and confidence to defend themselves and their loved ones, physically if necessary. All were financially astute, and balanced family and sometimes business budgets.

On the basis of the interview and life-history evidence, these women do not seem likely to have agreed to take strike action, with no financial or job security, simply because outsiders told them to. Certainly none of the interviewees could imagine the women they knew doing so.

Thanks to Eliza Martin's family, it has been possible to identify the women who were on the union's committee, and to show that the women on Bryant and May's list of troublemakers were all also on that committee. This strengthens the idea that these were the true leaders of a self-organized strike; among them may have been one or more of the women who first spoke to Besant.

The matchwomen whose lives have emerged from this research were certainly, according to their grandchildren's accounts, capable, popular and charismatic enough to have earned the respect of colleagues, and sufficiently indomitable to have stood up to their employers in the cause of what they believed was right.

Matchwomen's grandchildren Ted Lewis, Joan Harris and Jim Best, outside the former Bryant and May factory in Fairfield Road, 2005 (photograph Louise Raw)

All survived hardships and tragedies in their lives, a common factor being the deaths of children and marriages to difficult men. Mary Driscoll, celebrating the Irish rebel tradition and unconcerned by the Blitz, and Martha Robertson, uncomplainingly nursing a disfigured and unhappy, possibly shell-shocked, husband, are far removed from the helpless, easily led waifs of popular 'matchgirl' history.

Less is known of Eliza Martin, but she raised nine children and worked in the family business in spite of her own suffering as the wife of an extremely abusive husband. In her youth she may well have been one of the actual leaders of the strike, and confident enough to address public mass meetings as a very young woman, winning the obvious admiration of the *Star*'s reporter.

Two out of the three grandchildren were virtually or partly brought up by their grandmothers, and all regard themselves as staunch East Enders. Though Joan Harris had left the area she regularly makes the journey back to the East End, sometimes weekly. All have a high level of knowledge about the area and its history, and have therefore been valuable interview subjects who have provided, as well as recollections of their grandmothers, a sense of the community to which the women belonged, and of the legacy of the strike in the memory of that community.

The descendants' testimonies have shed new light on the strike, and on the two photographs of the women which, despite being well known, had previously revealed so little. If, as her granddaughter suspects, Mary Driscoll features in the 'factory' photograph of the striking women, the picture was possibly taken of this group rather than any other because of their role in what took place, and it might be a photograph of the strike's leaders.

Connections to the dockers run through the women's lives: Mary Driscoll was a docker's daughter and married a docker, Martha Robertson married a docker's son, and Eliza Martin's brother-in-law and nephews were dockers. As Jim Best put it, the idea that the matchworkers were too dissimilar as a group of workers from the dockers to have influenced the latter's strike does not stand up to the evidence: they were each other's friends, relatives and neighbours: to all intents 'the same people'.[81]

10

Final Conclusions

The starting point for this book was an unanswered, and seemingly unanswerable, question about the mechanics behind a legendary strike.

The traditional story of the 1888 Bryant and May dispute had become such a cliché of labour history that, if fame was the only measure of importance, it seemed an unpromising prospect for further research. As Askwith's comments at the time of the Black Country Strike showed, its example was remembered and invoked at times of industrial unrest decades later; and it probably has more resonance with a non-academic audience even today than other recognized 'New Unionist' strikes.

However, the orthodox account was a curious conundrum: it had made the strike well known while keeping the women at its heart completely unknown, and virtually anonymous. While Annie Besant appears in glorious Technicolor, a storybook heroine rushing to the aid of the oppressed, the matchwomen are little more than a shadowy mass huddled around her. They were, we are told, fourteen hundred desperately poor women, yet were willing to lay down their livelihoods for one middle-class journalist, who almost instantly became their leader. My initial question, which none of the secondary sources I consulted would answer was, simply: How? How had a virtual stranger from a very different background, at a time when class was an inflexible divide, persuaded the matchwomen *en masse* to adopt this course? I could find nothing which even began to consider how this astonishing feat had been achieved.

The revelation that Annie Besant had not, and could not have, been the prime mover of the strike came relatively early in my research. A thorough and chronological reconstruction of events showed that she was not present when the strike began. More surprisingly, she was also clearly unaware that it had begun until a visit from a delegation of strikers.

Besant's own accounts, her political views at the time, and the policies of the Fabian Society, added a further question to my research: Why would she have wanted to lead a strike of a group of workers that she, her political allies and most of the established labour movement believed to be inherently unorganizable? Many of Besant's ideas were radical for her time, but among them can be found no trace of revolutionary socialism or early syndicalism. She saw trade unionism for such women as having the benefits of an improving social club; it might 'teach [women] comradeship and stir up social feeling, and improve their business faculty, and brighten their lives in many ways'; but it would do them no material good – 'raise their wages – no'.[1] Leaving aside the fact that anyone with good knowledge of the Bryant and May women would have known that they had little to learn about 'comradeship', Besant explicitly stated at the same time that unionization would be counterproductive:

> Suppose a union was formed [at Bryant and May's], and the girls went on strike: the foreman would simply announce that so many hands were required at so much an hour, and their doors would be besieged within hours.[2]

If Besant *had* led the strike, therefore, this would have entailed an extremely rapid change of heart, even for a woman known for her ideological about-turns. Even then, as Besant explicitly stated that she expected mass dismissals to result from a strike, it is logical to assume that someone of her political experience would have made advance attempts to raise funds: even if the women were not sacked by Bryant and May, they would draw no wages while on strike. However, it is clear that no money had been set aside, that the strikers suffered several days of hardship on account of it, and that they took matters into their own hands: as the *East London Advertiser* tuttingly noted, they 'marched up and down the streets soliciting coppers, and were quite willing to pour their tale of hardships into every sympathetic ear'.[3] Several hundred also took themselves off to the hop-fields to support themselves.

It was becoming obvious, then, that a lack of attention to historical detail, as well as to the technicalities of industrial disputes, had allowed a myth to be created.

However, I wanted to do more than provide a corrective to the orthodox version of events. A book which showed only that Besant did *not* lead the strike would still have conformed to the 'Besant-centric' mode of telling the story – placing her at the centre, albeit from a new angle. My research has been concerned with looking beyond conventional accounts for what has been ignored, overlooked, or hidden by history and by ideology.

Removing Annie Besant from the leadership role initially left a vacuum, resulting from an historical vicious circle: the failure to re-evaluate the strike had meant that its importance was not understood, and the episode did not seem to warrant the more detailed examination that would have revealed its significance. Unlike the participants in other 'female' strikes, such as the Melbourne tailoresses' dispute discussed in Chapter Two, the matchwomen were not interviewed in their lifetime. An explanation in their own words of what happened, and why, was therefore completely lacking. The tracing of descendants therefore seemed an important part of the attempt to obtain missing information and details: though an unusual approach in an historical study, it was one way, and perhaps the only way, in which the matchwomen's voices might now be heard.

This attempt was time-consuming, taking several years, and traditional research methods such as tracing census records were not fruitful. These had to be put aside in favour of more unconventional means of gaining possible informants' attention, through media articles and especially public talks. Thanks also to Bryant and May's scrupulous preservation of information, I was able to find the names of the five suspected 'ringleaders' of the strike, and to eventually confirm that my interviewees were the descendants of two of the five.

Meeting and talking with the relatives of those who, I believe I can now say with confidence, were among the true leaders of this legendary strike has been a privilege, and I owe them a great deal. It has also confirmed the truth of primary accounts which presented the matchwomen in a very different aspect from the helpless waifs of popular imagination. At least one of the five women named by Bryant and May told her family that she and her friends had begun the strike. Her grandson's assistance made it possible to confirm the names of all of the 12 women who were elected to the initial strike committee, later the union committee, by their colleagues. Another interviewee had known two of the committee members, her grandmother and her great-aunt, well, despite the length of time since the strike. The naming of committee members has also shown that Bryant and May's estimation of the workers' leaders – from their perspective, the troublemakers – among its workforce was probably accurate: all of the five women they named were on the committee.

I was then able to work on 'mapping' committee members' addresses to show familial and geographic closeness to East London dock workers. The connections proved ubiquitous. The family case studies also demonstrated individual connections to the dockers in two out of three cases, and strong Irish roots in one, again concurring with much of the generally overlooked primary evidence. The politicization of the London Irish community, to which many of the matchwomen may have belonged, has been posited as a significant factor in the dock strike, and New Unionism generally;[4] it has been argued here that there is no reason why this should not have been equally true of the matchwomen's strike.

The significance of these findings is not the revelation that Annie Besant did not lead the strike, but that the matchwomen did. This means that an extremely disadvantaged and exploited group of workers defied class and gender stereotypes to take their own action against a powerful employer. The matchwomen's action and victory offered a huge challenge to Victorian beliefs about women, the working classes, unskilled workers, and the Irish, beliefs held not just by the establishment but by the labour movement too. Even the syndicalists believed that only workers in 'key industries' could influence others by striking – and match manufacture would hardly have counted as 'key'. The match strike, the dock strike and other disputes of 'New Unionism' share many similarities: the same people were often involved – Thorne, Burns, Tillett, Champion, Mann, Besant and Eleanor Marx. Most of the strikes took place within the same small area of London. All challenged accepted notions of working-class solidarity. One has been undervalued for more than a hundred years, because of the status and gender of those involved. The myth that Besant and her socialist colleagues planned and orchestrated the strike has persisted for many years, despite changes in historical thinking, and although it has been shown that Besant's own published accounts clearly contradict it.

Importantly, in terms of the matchwomen's overall place within British labour history, it has been possible to show that in striking successfully they provided clear and acknowledged inspiration for the workers who went on to be New Unionists – in direct contravention of the conclusions of some eminent labour historians.

A thorough re-examination of primary sources on the Great Dock Strike has yielded considerable supporting evidence of the matchwomen's influence. Dockers' leaders Tom Mann and Ben Tillett were both unequivocal, indeed generous to an almost surprising degree, in attributing to the matchwomen's action the very beginnings of New Unionism.[5] Tillett described the matchwomen's victory as quite simply 'the beginning of the social convulsion' which produced the movement.[6] As a key New Unionist himself he was surely in a position to know; and he might have been expected to want to claim this accolade for 'his' strike, had he any cause to believe otherwise. Mann also invoked the matchwomen's example in the course of the dock strike, and revealed both the independence and effectiveness of their action: despite the socialists' efforts, he stated that only the women's action brought 'any change for the better'.[7] A further previously unknown new link between the two strikes came with the discovery that the better known photograph of the striking matchwomen had originally been in the possession of John Burns.

Despite this, the matchwomen's strike has continued to be regarded as too isolated from the rest of New Unionism, and the strikers too different from other New Unionists, to have influenced the movement. The familial and geographical evidence provided here, both from official records and from interview testimony, dramatically challenges the latter assumption. The matchwomen and the dockers in fact came from the same communities, streets and even families in East London: to those who knew them, they were essentially 'the same people'.[8]

We have also found that the two strikes were not separated by a year-long vacuum of industrial action, but connected by a steadily increasing number of strikes, including an attempted dock strike in October 1888, just three months after the matchworkers' victory.

There is, then, considerable evidence to support the idea that the matchwomen's strike was both self-organized and influential. Once I had compared the myth against the reality suggested by primary evidence, I faced a second conundrum – why misunderstandings about the strike had persisted for so long, with evidence being overlooked or hidden *by* history, in the successive 120 years.

The matchwomen's strike took place against a background of what Honeyman and Goodman have identified as particularly intense gender conflict in the workplace,[9] and it has been a contention of this book that this is highly significant: the dominant gender ideology of the period contributed not only to the strike itself, but also to the way in which the women and their action was perceived; and, ultimately, to the fallacious belief that it was necessary for middle-class activists to 'lead' the action in the first place.

The matchwomen's gender has in fact both contributed to and detracted from the strike's fame. The fact that these were 'factory girls', about whom there was much contemporary concern and some prurient interest, undoubtedly added to the picturesque nature of the strike, and drew public attention to it. On the other hand, their gender also contributed to the idea that the strikers could not have organized themselves, at a time when the possibility of female militancy was considered not just implausible but threatening to the *status quo*.[10]

We have seen that as industrial workers, the matchwomen fell short of the contemporary domestic ideal of womanhood, presenting a potential problem for their supporters, who may accordingly have chosen consciously to portray them as helpless waifs rather than militant 'factory girls'. Equally, the effects of the dominant class and gender ideologies of the day may have affected the way in which even their middle-class champions saw them.

The mythical 'matchgirl' image, while colourful and enduringly popular, has obscured the reality. The failure to theoretically encapsulate both class and gender in orthodox British labour history must also be held partly to account.

That the matchwomen should have been neither helpless 'little matchgirls' nor slatternly 'factory girls', but industrial workers pursuing a genuine grievance on their own account, has seemingly been a stretch too far not only for many Victorian imaginations, but for some since. It has proved easier to accept that the women were somehow 'made' to go on strike by outsiders. The idea that the women were acting for themselves and may even have been influenced to a degree by the politically charged atmosphere of the East End of the time remains controversial, and I have encountered some hostility to it during my research. However, a critical examination of the politics of London's working class, using such accounts as are available, shows that these were often far from as self-serving and unsophisticated as had sometimes been suggested. The matchwomen said that they recognized Besant from socialist meetings, and in a note to her expressed a desire to attend more meetings if she would give them details. A large component of the workforce was of Irish heritage, and we know that the sense of Irish identity and an admiration for Irish rebels was strong in the Driscoll/ Harris family, and in the London Irish community in general. The example of the Melbourne tailoresses proves that female workers in the 1880s were quite capable of looking at their situation politically. As Martha Robertson's grandson Ted has said, why should the lessons of socialism be lost on the very workers who knew only too well how it felt to be exploited by ruthless industrial capitalism?

We know too that the matchwomen had well-established traditions of militancy on which to draw in 1888, belying their employers' contention that they were a docile and contented workforce prior to this point. There is considerable evidence for this, and the degree to which it has been overlooked is surprising.

Bernard Shaw, a key figure in devising Fabian policy, would later argue that 'The Fabian Society succeeded because it addressed itself to its own class.'[11] That, I believe, is exactly what Besant intended to do here: to initiate a middle-class war of words and consumer boycotts between the Fabians and the employers, in which the matchwomen themselves were intended to have little part. Besant provided an extremely effective exposé of their working conditions, and possibly hoped to provoke Bryant and May into ill-considered libel action. She may have wanted to keep the workers out of the affair for the best of motives: they were vulnerable to instant dismissal and potential financial disaster. However, she certainly did not plan or orchestrate the strike, and was candid about her dismay when she realized that fourteen hundred strikers were on the streets of the East End. That Besant herself tells us that this realization only came some days after the strike began, should long since have put an end to the idea of external leadership. Even without that vital chronological detail, Besant made several denials of direct involvement. Though a remarkable woman in many ways, she was not and did not claim to have been a strike leader.

Once the distractions of the popular myth are cleared from view, the match-women themselves emerge at the forefront of events. The wonderful testimony of their grandchildren allows us to discover the strike's leaders as real women, all of whom survived hardship to become matriarchs and respected figures in their communities. They were far from the 'angels of the house' stereotype: fortunately for them, as it is unlikely that such delicate creatures of the Victorian imagination would have fared well in the streets of the East End, or withstood the matchwomen's lot of relentless work and childbearing, poverty and loss. Hans Christian Andersen's angelic 'Little Match Girl' was possessed of the requisite feminine helplessness, and in turn was an archetypal victim: she did not survive to womanhood. The three matchwomen researched in this account went on to raise twenty surviving children between them, and are still remembered with affection by their families 120 years after their strike.

It is hoped that this study will go some way towards rescuing these women and their workmates from what has indeed been, in E. P. Thompson's words, the 'enormous condescension of posterity'. In arguing for their acceptance as the mothers of the modern trade union movement, and exposing the 'gender blindness' which has kept them from their rightful place, I hope also to contribute to the re-opening of discussion on the necessity of a 'double vision' which can encompass both class and gender in labour history. We cannot be sure that there will be no further attempts to sideline women's experiences in the future, especially when influential historians like David Starkey actually advocate it. This makes it yet more imperative that the matchwomen's true contribution to the British labour movement becomes known. This goes beyond the righting of an historical inaccuracy. As Spender has convincingly argued, the exclusion of women from history has been incorporated into the education system.[12] This is not an abstract issue, but has directly affected the way generations of women feel about themselves and their abilities, and the value society places on them. We have recent proof of this: in 2006, in a study by clinical psychologist Penelope Lockwood demonstrated the importance of same-sex role models to young women's self-esteem. In the study male and female students were given articles to read about either a man or a women who had succeeded in their field. Afterwards, female students who had read about a successful woman rated themselves more highly than those who had read about a man; there was no such division among male students[13]. The true story of the matchwomen should be known to every schoolgirl and boy – and I have considerable correspondance from both teachers and pupils to confirm that it does interest them.

It's a shame that the modern labour movement didn't previously reassess the strike. It has had its own problems, of course: the movement only began comparatively recently to address the 'democratic deficit' within its ranks, and particularly within its leadership. The under-representation of women in the decision-making processes and structures of unions became a matter of widespread concern only when political and economic changes in the 1980s saw traditional male membership decimated. Women, not male manufacturing workers, were becoming the paradigmatic trade unionists[14] – but only when trade union membership dropped by almost 50 per cent did the movement begin to actively pursue the recruitment of marginalized workers. Nearly a hundred years after the matchwomen's strike, Cockburn could still conclude that 'men have continued to monopolise positions of influence within trade unions despite greater female participation in the labour force'.[15]

In 1994 the TUC launched a 'New Unionism' campaign in recognition of this. Had the movement learned from the matchwomen's strike about the capability and solidarity of women workers, it is possible that this would never have become necessary.

To dismiss the importance of the matchwomen's strike is to dismiss the importance of the dock strike, and of new unionism itself, which, although short lived, ultimately transformed the image of poor unskilled workers, and their view of themselves. No longer seen as a 'feckless rabble'[16] but as a group who could gain real collective power, they had proved themselves as more than capable trade unionists. The movement laid the basis for the general trade unionism to come, and extended trade unionism beyond the skilled elite to the most vulnerable in the labour market: the men, women and children who could be thrown out of work at any time, and who were at the mercy of employers and trade cycles. Even if women themselves had to do most of the work to recruit and organize their sisters, they now had the example of the matchwomen before them.

In conclusion, new evidence has shown that the matchwomen's strike has for more than a century been a victim of what Sarah Boston has called 'the myths about women workers and organisation which . . . do not stand up to historical scrutiny'.[17] In March 1940, surviving dock strikers received a medal from the Transport and General Workers' Union, with an accompanying letter from then general secretary Ernest Bevin, to commemorate the 'jubilee' year of the strike. In the letter he hailed their involvement in laying the foundation on which the entire modern trade union movement had been built:[18]

> It must be some compensation to you to have lived and witnessed how, as a result of your banding together, this great movement has grown; how it has spread world-wide; how literally millions of your fellow-men have benefited as a result of that great effort; and

how you helped to raise the status of the so-called unskilled workers of the country and make them as proud of themselves today as they were despised then.[19]

If this was true of the dock strikers then, we must now, finally, grant an equal tribute to the Bryant and May matchwomen.

Appendix

GRIFFITHS' EVALUATION APPLIED TO SURNAMES ON STRIKE FUND REGISTER

Victoria Factory, Page One, Numbers 1–30 on Strike Register.

Surname	Nos. of Same Name on Irish Primary Valuation, 1848–1862
LOUISE BECK	92
Webb	224
Bouquet	0
ELIZA MARTIN	3,335
Ince	7
Lary	3
Miller	967
Llewelyn	0
Cary	33
Thirsty	0
Murphy	13,359
Hayes	2,625
Conners	15
JULIA GAMELTON	0
Dean	55
Waters	634
Hall	1,027
Branton	2
Leonard	999
Collins	3,090
Bridman	0
Sheen	0 (but if Sheehan, 1,870)
Prouse	0

Surname	Nos. of Same Name on Irish Primary Valuation, 1848–1862
O'Brien	3,654
Carthy	534
Raffe	0
Collins	3,090
Perry	261
Page	68

Victoria Factory, Page Two, Numbers 30–58 on Strike Register.

Surname	Nos. of Same Name on Irish Primary Valuation, 1848–1862
Cunningham	92
Luck	0
Collingin	0
Carthy	534
Sheen	0 (but if Sheehan, 1,870)
Donovan	2,367
Bligh	54
Belquim	0
Belquim	0
Daniels	2
Morgan	1,236
Turner	350
Hoxton	0
Donovan	2,367
Collingin	0
Crawley	210
Peacock	76
Lee	1,086
Goddard	7
Gutridge	0
Alender	1– or if Allender, 12
MOG DRISCOL	Known to be DRISCOLL– 1276
Wade	350
Donovan	2,367

Surname	Nos. of Same Name on Irish Primary Valuation, 1848–1862
Smithers	0
Smith	5,982
Begley	259
Herbert	233
Chipp	0

Victoria Factory, Page Three, Numbers 59–87 on Strike Register.

Surname	Nos. of Same Name on Irish Primary Valuation, 1848–1862
Driscol	Likely to be DRISCOLL– 1276
Sheen	0 (but if Sheehan, 1,870)
Butler	1870
Stanton	67
Ince	7
Marney	2
Laura	0
Alender	1– or if Allender, 12
Feeney	208
Murphy	13,359
Samuels	3
Sullivan	7,859
Dean	55
Connoly	8
Buck	51
Stone	104
Pier	0
Smith	5,982
Sullivan	7,859
Foley	2,407
Wood	131
Garrett	148
Helster	0
Cole	180
Marney	2

Surname	Nos. of Same Name on Irish Primary Valuation, 1848–1862
Smith	5,982
Cunningham	92
Sweeney	640
Harris	459

Victoria Factory, Page Four, Numbers 88–115 on Strike Register.

Surname	Nos. of Same Name on Irish Primary Valuation, 1848–1862
Roffe	0
Thorn	0
Connoley	0
Connoley	0
Howard	515
Donovan	2,367
Haley	28
Sheen	0 (but if Sheehan, 1,870)
Ripsher	0
Hestall	0
Mills	420
Stanton	67
Donovan	2,367
Day	284
Walker	1,241
Carr	1,241
Chambers	546
Soundy	0
Dabs	0
Hering	0
Harrington	0
Heeney	978
Sermon	49
Lloyd	277
Drake	76
Cary	33

Surname	Nos. of Same Name on Irish Primary Valuation, 1848–1862
Harrington	0
Nellen	0

Victoria Factory, Page Five, Numbers 116–45 on Strike Register.

Surname	Nos. of Same Name on Irish Primary Valuation, 1848–1862
Fay	251
Stevenson	321
Taylor	1,359
Roley	0
Shedwick	0
Peacock	76
Russell	1,303
Potts	104
Emerton	0
Elsworth	0
Goss	49
Goss	49
Morr	0
Cannon	604
Ellis	355
Roley	0
Belsham	0
Tant	0
Dow	2
Sawle	0
Prior	182
Cox	607
Hogwood	0
Sandell	0
Townsend	134
Prior	182
Berles	0
Long	1,050

Surname	Nos. of Same Name on Irish Primary Valuation, 1848–1862
Maccalow	0
Daley	13

Victoria Factory, Page Six, Numbers 146–73 on Strike Register.

Surname	Nos. of Same Name on Irish Primary Valuation, 1848–1862
Dabbs	0
Baker	352
Matthews	242
Plummer	25
Pearson	96
Wenner	0
Aplin	0
Wenner	0
Webb	224
Hitchin	0
Daniels	0
Quick	6
Quick	6
Hunt	631
Bowkett	0
Astall	0
Heaford	0
Bentley	53
Bentley	53
Hives	2
Hosier	3
Woolhead	0
Strickland	13
Cronin	1,122
Maloney	95
O'Brien	3,654
Cura	0
Riley	15

Victoria Factory, Page Seven, Numbers 174–86 on Strike Register.

Surname	Nos. of Same Name on Irish Primary Valuation, 1848–1862
Sermon	0
May	227
Mahoney	62
Harris	459
Macarty	0– if McCarty 77
Haines	31
Westwood	2
Macarty	0– if McCarty 77
Downing	126
Nevitt	0
Mills	420
Yeoman	0
Marsh	44

Mary Driscoll, seated, far right; Mog Driscoll (behind, with hand on Mary's shoulder)

Notes

Notes to Introduction

1 In addition, the smaller streets and courts where many casual workers lived were often the poorest addresses and vulnerable to demolition, for either 'slum clearance' or new road-building.
2 According to the research of Clara Collet, in C. Booth, 'The trades of East London connected with poverty', Charles Booth Archive, ref. A2, and cited in C. Chinn (1988), *They Worked All their Lives*, p. 217.
3 S. Rowbotham (1975), *Hidden from History*.
4 S. Boston (1987), *Women Workers and the Trade Unions*, Introduction, p. 1.
5 D. Thornton: 'Factory girls: gender, empire and the making of a female working class', PhD thesis, University of Melbourne, 2007. Interview, Danielle Thornton/Louise Raw, 24 August 2008.
6 E. H. Carr (1990), *What is History?*, pp. 7–30.
7 E. H. Hunt (1981), *British Labour History 1815–1914*, p. 305.
8 *Ibid.*
9 A. Portelli (1991), *The Death of Luigi Trastelli and Other Stories*, p. 31.
10 A. L. Morton and G. Tate (1956), *The British Labour Movement*, p. 185.
11 C. Willis (1998), 'Victim or virago? Popular images of the Victorian factory girl', paper for Birkbeck College, p. 6.
12 *The Times*, 14 July 1888, Bryant and May archives, Hackney Archives Department.
13 Records of Bryant and May's AGM, 1888, company archives bundle D/B/BRY/1/2/540.
14 The *Link*, 23 June 1888.
15 C1023/30 C1, Roy Palmer Collection, item 28: 'Talk about the matchgirls' strike'.
16 The *Link*, 30 June 1888.
17 *The Times*, 14 July 1888; the *East London Advertiser*, 7 July 1888; the *Link*, 7 July 1888.
18 H. Pelling (1963), *A History of British Trade Unionism*, p. 97.
19 N. Soldon, (1978), *Women in British Trade Unions*, p. 30.
20 *Ibid.*
21 *Ibid.*, p. 87. Black was also the first female factory inspector, and had given a speech on female labour to the Fabian Society meeting at which Besant first heard about conditions at Bryant and May.
22 A. L. Morton, and G. Tate (1956), *op. cit.*
23 *Ibid.*, p. 189.

24 P. Thompson (1967), *Socialists, Liberals and Labour*, p. 45.

25 J. F. C. Harrison (1990), *Late Victorian Britain 1875–1901*, p. 142.

26 *Ibid.*

27 E. J. Hobsbawm (1987), *The Age of Empire 1875–1914*, p. 212.

28 E. J. Hobsbawm (1974), *Labour's Turning Point 1880–1900*, p. 78.

29 *Ibid.*

30 *Ibid.*, p. 79.

31 P. Thompson (1967), *Socialists, Liberals and Labour: the Struggle for London 1885–1914*, p. 45.

32 B. Harrison, 'The politics of ill-health in late-nineteenth-century Britain: the case of the match-making industry', *Sociology of Health and Illness*, vol. 7, no. 1, 1995, 20–1.

33 A. J. Reid (2004), *United We Stand*, p. 234.

34 *Ibid.*, p. 235.

35 A. Besant (1893), *op. cit.*, p. 211.

36 Trade Union Histories card file, TUC Library Collections, London Metropolitan University.

37 Labour MP John Scurr quoted in the *Morning Star* on the centenary of the strike, Saturday 10 July 1988. In TUC archives MISC HD 53699.

38 S. Boston (1987), *op. cit.*; M. Davis (1993), *Comrade or Brother?*, p. 94.

39 J. Scott (1988), 'Women in The Making of the English Working Class', in *Gender and the Politics of History* (1988).

40 E. J. Hobsbawm, *Man and Woman in Socialist Iconography*, History Workshop 6, 1978.

41 E.g. B. Taylor (1983), *Eve and the New Jerusalem*; L. Tilly and J. Scott (1978), *Women, Work, and Family*.

42 M. Doolittle, 'Close relations? Bringing together gender and family in English history', *Gender and History*, vol. 11, no. 3, November 1999, 542.

43 A detailed discussion of this is contained in Selma Leydesdorff's article 'Gender and the categories of experienced history', *Gender and History*, vol. 2, no. 3, November 1999, 597–611.

44 R. Shoemaker and M. Vincent (1998), 'Gender history: the evolution of a concept', 'Introduction' in R. Shoemaker and M. Vincent, (eds) (1998), *Gender and History in Western Europe*, p. 2; and G. Block, 'Women's history and gender history: aspects of an international debate', pp. 25–42 in *ibid.*, p. 28.

45 J. Tosh, 'What should historians do with masculinity?' in Shoemaker and Vincent (1998), *op. cit.*, pp. 66–84.

46 R. Shoemaker and M. Vincent, (eds) (1998), *op. cit.*, p. 11.

47 K. Honeyman and J. Goodman, 'Women's work, gender conflict, and the labour market in Europe, 1500–1900', pp. 353–76, in *ibid.*, p. 353.

48 Tosh (1998), *op. cit.*, pp. 65–72.

49 J. Kelly (1984), *Women, History, and Theory*, p. 2.

50 J. Lewis, 'The working-class mother and state intervention 1870–1918', Chapter 4 in J. Lewis (1986), *Labour and Love*, p. 102.

51 E. Roberts, 'Women's Strategies, 1890–1940', Chapter 9 in J. Lewis, (1986), *op. cit.*, p. 230.

52 Labour MP John Scurr quoted in the *Morning Star*, Saturday 10 July 1988, in TUC archives MISC HD 53699.

53 Lily Harrap, matchwoman's great-granddaughter, in the *East London Advertiser*, 25 July 2002.
54 J. Rose (2002), *The Intellectual Life of the British Working Classes*, p. 2.
55 Interview, Anna Davin/Louise Raw, 4 June 2003.
56 *Ibid.*
57 Interview, Anna Davin/Louise Raw, *ibid.*
58 A detailed discussion of this is contained in Selma Leydesdorff (1999), *op. cit.*
59 E. H. Hunt (1985) *op. cit.*, p. 305.
60 C. Dickens (1884, 1987), *One Dinner a Week and Travels in the East*, p. 92.
61 T. Mann (1923), *Memoirs*, cited in A. Briggs (1988), *Victorian Things*, p. 102.
62 J. Charlton (1999), *It Just Went Like Tinder*.
63 S. Fagence Cooper (2001), *The Victorian Woman*, pp. 87–8.
64 From publisher's website, www.vam.ac.uk.
65 Simon Schama's (2002) *History of Britain 1776–2000*, p. 189.
66 A. Davin (1997), *Growing Up Poor*.
67 M. Cohen and H. Fagan (eds) (1984), *Childhood Memories Recorded by some Socialist Men and Women in their Later Years*.
68 M. Brodie, 'Politics stirs them very little: Conservatism and apathy in the East End of London 1885–1914', PhD thesis, Oxford University, 1999.
69 G. Stedman Jones (1971), *Outcast London*.
70 A. John (ed.) (1986), *Unequal Opportunities*.
71 T. R. Gourvish and A. O'Day (eds) (1988), *Late Victorian Britain 1867–1900*.
72 S. Rowbotham, 'Approaches to home working in the nineteenth and twentieth century'; G. Holloway, 'Origins of the women's trade union movement'; M. Davis, 'Women's work and trade unions in the 19th and 20th centuries', papers for 'Women: Fighting for Rights at Work' conference, Black Country Living Museum, 17 October 2005.
73 T. Mann (1923), *op. cit.*; H. H. Champion (1890), *The Great Dock Strike in London, August 1889*; W. Kent (1950), *John Burns*; J. Schneer (1982), *Ben Tillett*, (1910) *A Brief History of the Dock Strike;* and (1931) *Memories and Reflections;* T. McCarthy (1988), *The Great Dock Strike*.
74 R. Gray (1981), *The Aristocracy of Labour in Nineteenth Century Britain c.1850–1914*.
75 R. Penn (1985), *Skilled Workers in the Class Structure*.
76 Paul Thompson is the author of *The Voice of the Past* (1978) and *The Myths We Live By* (1990), among other works.
77 Interview, Anna Davin/Louise Raw, 4 June 2003.
78 British Library Sound Archive Transcription Service, copies of The Roy Palmer Collection tapes C1023/29 and C1023/30: Samuel Webber.
79 Bryant and May archives, Hackney Archives Department: bundles P/B/BRY/1/2/538–564.
80 The *Star*, 23 July 1888, p. 3.
81 E.g. A. Perkyns, 'Age checkability and accuracy in the censuses of six Kentish parishes, 1851–1881', and 'Birthplace accuracy in the censuses of six Kentish parishes, 1851–1881', Chapters 12 and 19 respectively in D. Mills and K. Schurer (1996), *Local Communities in the Victorian Census Enumerators' Books*.
82 As evinced by E. A. M. Roberts, 'Women's strategies 1890–1940', Chapter 9 in J. Lewis (1986), *op. cit.*

83 See A. Davin (1997), *op. cit.*

84 D. R. Mills and K. Schurer, 'Migration and population turnover', Chapter 4 in D. Mills and K. Schurer (1996), *op. cit.*, pp. 218–28.

85 M. Tebutt, 'Telling family histories: everyday landscapes and the meanings of place', public history seminar paper, Ruskin College, May 2002.

86 D. R. Mills and K. Schurer, 'Migration and population turnover', Chapter 4 in D. Mills and K. Schurer (1996), *op. cit.*, pp. 218–28.

87 I arrived at this decision after advice from Professors Jerry White and Mary Davis, and staff at the British Library.

88 As will be discussed later, Mary and Mog Driscoll's surnames are spelled 'Driscoll' and 'Driscol', and their address '14 *Cottage Street*' and '14 *Cottgae*'.

89 Letter from Housman to Alfred Pollard, 28 October 1889, cited in T. Stoppard (2006), *A.E.H.–A.W.P.: A Classical Friendship.*

90 The *Irish Times*, 27 July 2002; The *Irish Post* 10 October 2002; *Connect*, Communication Workers Union, December 2003; The *Whitechapel Journal*, July 2005.

91 The Museum in Docklands, 3 June 2004 and 8 March 2005; The Ragged School Museum in East London, 11 November 2004; St Albans Museum, 1 March 2005; Barnet Historical Society, 11 May 2005.

92 The *Star*, 23 July 1888, p. 3.

93 *Ibid.*

94 R. Grele (1991), *Envelopes of Sound*, p. 8.

95 R. Grele, 'Movement without aim: methodological and theoretical problems in oral history', in R. Grele (1991), *ibid.*, pp. 126–55.

96 A. Portelli, 'Oral history as genre' in M. Chamberlain and P. Thompson (1998), *Narrative and Genre*, p. 31.

97 A. Portelli (1998), *op. cit.*, p. 31.

98 P. Clough *et al.* (2004), *Researching Life Stories*, p. 457.

99 S. Benison, panel discussion on oral history, Radio WFMT Chicago, IL, 13 April 1973, in R. Grele (1991), *op. cit.*, p. 64.

100 Interview Joan Harris/Louise Raw, 8 June 2004.

101 R. Grele, panel discussion on oral history, Radio WFMT Chicago, IL, 13 April 1973, in R. Grele (1991), *op. cit.*, p. 87.

102 A. Portelli (1991), *op. cit.*, Introduction, p. ix; and *ibid.*, quoting Nathaniel Hawthorne in the introduction to *The House of the Seven Gables.*

103 G. Etter-Lewis, in R. Perks and A. Thomson (2006), *The Oral History Reader*, p. 89.

104 A. Portelli (1991), *op. cit.*, Introduction, p. ix.

105 E. Gordon (1991), *Women and the Labour Movement in Scotland 1850–1914*, p. 102.

106 R. Grele, 'Movement without aim: methodological and theoretical problems in oral history', in R. Grele (1991), *op. cit.*, p. 132.

107 R. Perks and A. Thomson (2006), *op. cit.*, p. 96.

108 Testimony of Rigoberta Menchu, in C. Salazer, 'A Third World women's text: between the politics of criticism and cultural politics', Chapter 6 in S. B. Gluck and D. Patai (eds) (1991), *Women's Words*, p. 94.

Notes to Chapter 1: Angels in the House and Factory Girls

1   The *Daily News*, 8 October 1888. The full report is as follows:
    'The following may be taken as samples of the many letters concerning which rumours were current on Saturday. Intimation was given to the City police on Saturday morning that Messrs. Bryant and May had received a letter from a person signing himself J. Ripper, couched in the following terms: "I hereby notify that I am going to pay your girls a visit. I hear that they are beginning to say what they will do with me. I am going to see what a few of them have in their stomachs, and I will take it out of them, so they can have no more to do on the quiet. (Signed) John Ripper. P.S. I am in Poplar today."'
2   *Ibid.*
3   A. Besant, 'White slavery in London', the *Link*, 23 June 1888.
4   H. C. Andersen (1845, 1981), *The Little Match Girl.*
5   E. P. Thompson (1963), *The Making of the English Working Class.*
6   W. Fishman (1988), *East End 1888*, p. 1.
7   R. Bridenthal *et al.* (eds) (1987), *Becoming Visible*, p. 309.
8   R. Shoemaker and M. Vincent (eds) (1998), *Gender and History in Western Europe*, p. 11.
9   'A present to a servant maid', cited by D. George (1930), *London Life in the Eighteenth Century*, p. 169.
10 J. S. Mill, cited in *ibid.*, p. 251.
11 *Ibid.*, pp. 180, 181.
12 M. Sweet (2001), *Inventing the Victorians*, Introduction, p. xvi.
13 T. Hunt (2004), *Building Jerusalem.*
14 D. Newsome (1997), *The Victorian World Picture*, p. 74.
15 M. Davis (1990), *Comrade or Brother?*, p. 112.
16 'Women and coverture', Harvard Business School summary at www.hbs.edu.
17 M. Davis (1990), *op. cit.*, p. 112.
18 S. Boston (1987), *Women Workers and Trade Unions*, p. 18.
19 *Ibid.*, p. 4; A. John (ed.) (1986), *Unequal Opportunities*, Introduction, p. 2.
20 M. Vincinus (1985), *Independent Women*, p. 209.
21 C. Patmore (1891), *The Angel in the House*, Introduction, p. 1, e-text version published online by Project Gutenberg (2003) at http//www.Gutenberg.org.
22 S. Eron, *Poet or Ventriloquist?: Reinterpreting Gender and Voice in Coventry Patmore's 'The Angel in the House' and 'Victories of Love'*, published online at www.victoriaweb.org.
23 Professor L. Melani (2001), *Landmarks of Literature*, CUNY School of Literary Criticism website, at http://academic.brooklyn.cuny.edu.english.
24 Woolf, V., (1942) Professions for Women, in 'The Death of the Moth and Other Essays', published posthumously)
25 C. Patmore (1891), *op. cit.*, *The Cathedral Close*, p. 1.
26 J. S. Moore (1998), *Bulwer-Lytton.*
27 *Ibid.*
28 *Ibid.*
29 E. E. Walford and J. Gillies (eds) (1908), *The Politics and Economics of Aristotle.*
30 Cited in M. Vincinus (1985), *op. cit.*, p. 4.
31 *Ibid.*

32   J. E. Butler (1868), *The Education and Employment of Women*, p. 26. Transcribed by
     Kathryn Benedict for the Victorian Women Writer's Project, University of Indiana,
     www.indiana.edu.
33   J. Harris (1993), *Private Lives, Public Spirit*, p. 25.
34   *Ibid.*
35   J. E. Butler (1868), *op. cit.*, p. 26.
36   *Ibid.*
37   M. Vincinus (1985), *op. cit.*, p. 2.
38   E. P. Thompson (1991), *The Making of the British Working Class*, p. 60.
39   A. Davin (1997), *Growing Up Poor*, p. 143.
40   M. Vincinus (1985), *op. cit.*, p. 215.
41   *Ibid.*
42   H. Bosanquet (1896), *Rich and Poor*, p. 60, cited in *ibid.*, p. 99.
43   M. Vincinus (1985), *op. cit.*, p. 215.
44   Interview, Louise Raw and Joan Harris, granddaughter of matchworker Mary
     Driscoll, 3 June 2004; interview, Louise Raw and Ted Lewis, grandson of Martha
     Robertson, 23 February 2005.
45   The title of an epic poem published in 1874 by James Thomson, describing a
     symbolic night-time journey through desolate London streets.
46   M. Harkness writing as John Law (1893), *Captain Lobe*.
47   G. Stedman Jones (1971), *Outcast London*, p. 14.
48   A. Besant (1887), *Is Socialism Sound? Verbatim report of a four nights' debate between
     Annie Besant and G. W. Foole*, p. 16.
49   W. Fishman (1988), *East End 1888*, p. 1.
50   *The Nineteenth Century XXIV* (1888), p. 262, cited in W. Fishman (1988), *op. cit.*,
     p. 1.
51   T. H. Huxley, cited in R. Beer (1979), *Matchgirls' Strike 1888*, p. 1.
52   A. Besant (1887), *op. cit.*, p. 16.
53   *Ibid.*, p. 260.
54   A. Palmer (1989), *The East End*, p. 44.
55   J. H. Mackay (1891), 'The anarchists', in T. McCarthy (1988), *The Great Dock Strike*,
     p. 21.
56   Cited in W. F. Aitken (1902), *Canon Barnett, Warden of Toynbee Hall*, 1902, p. 77.
57   C. Dickens (1996), *Dickens' Journalism, Volume 2*, (ed. M Slater), p. 225.
58   C. Dickens (1996), *op. cit.*, p. 226.
59   G. B. Shaw, in S. Weintraub (ed.) (1969), *George Bernard Shaw*, p. 114.
60   A. Mearns (1883), *The Bitter Cry of Outcast London*, p. 87.
61   The *Pall Mall Gazette* (1986), p. 7.
62   H. Hyndman (1912), 'Further reminiscences', p. 4, cited in A. Taylor (1992), *Annie
     Besant*, p. 167.
63   J. Lewis, 'The working-class wife and mother and state intervention 1870–1918', in
     J. Lewis (ed.) (1986), *Labour and Love*, p. 101.
64   M. Vincinus (1985), *op. cit.*, p. 39.
65   R. Shoemaker and M. Vincent (1998), *Gender and History in Western Europe*, p. 11.
66   M. Vincinus (1985), *op. cit.*, p. 5.
67   P. E. Johnson (2001) *Hidden Hands*, p. 5.
68   *Ibid.*
69   J. Morris (1986), *Women Workers and the Sweated Trades*, p. 85.

70 R. A. S. Hennessey (1969), *Factories*, p. 10.
71 M. Perrot (1992), *Writing Women's History*, p. 54.
72 I. Pinchbeck (1981), *Women Workers and the Industrial Revolution*, p. 111.
73 E. J. Hobsbawm (1995), *The Age of Empire*, p. 199.
74 J. Rendall, *The Origins of Modern Feminism*, p. 185, cited in A. John (1986), *op. cit.*, p. 200.
75 *Ibid.*
76 Commissioner Symonds, 'Mining Report', 1842, cited in P. E. Johnson (2001), *Hidden Hands*, p. 19.
77 R. A. S. Hennessey (1969), *op. cit.*, p. 61; I. Pinchbeck (1981), *op. cit.*, 1981, p. 4.
78 K. Marx (1976), *Capital, Volume One*, pp. 620–1.
79 P. E. Johnson (2001), *op. cit.*, p. 4.
80 Labour MP John Scurr quoted in the *Morning Star*, Saturday 10 July 1988, in TUC archives MISC HD 53699.
81 *Ibid.*, p. 80.
82 A. Mearns (1883), *op. cit.*
83 T. Oliver (ed.) (1902), *Dangerous Trades*, cited in R. Beer (1979), *op. cit.*, p. 11.
84 G. Sims (1882), *How the Poor Live*, cited in C. Willis (1998), 'Victim or Virago?', p. 12.
85 A. Davin (1997), *op. cit.*, p. 75.
86 F. Hicks, 'Factory girls', in A. Reid (ed.) *The New Party*, (1896), p. 315.
87 M. Williams QC (1894), *Round London*.
88 Charles Booth Archive, B346/75–77.
89 Interview with Poplar resident from Anna Davin's personal archives.
90 Interview Jim Best/Louise Raw, 7 February 2005.
91 M. Cohen and H. Fagan (eds) (1986), *Childhood Memories Recorded by some Socialist Men and Women in their Later Years*, p. 65.
92 E.g. A. Davin (1997), *op. cit.*, p. 173.
93 R. Bridenthal *et al.* (eds) (1987), *op. cit.*, p. 316.
94 S. Rowbotham (1973), *Hidden from History*, Chapter 10: 'Feminism and rescue work'.
95 F. Engels (1888), *The Condition of the Working Class in England in 1844*.
96 K. Marx (1976), *op. cit.*
97 F. Engels (1888), *op. cit.*
98 S. Mitchell (1988), *Victorian Britain*, p. 142.
99 'Bishop Frazer on the social evil', the *Northern Echo*, 27 October 1871.
100 J. Butler, 'The double standard of morality', *The Philosopher*, October 1886.
101 *Ibid.*
102 B. Hemyng, a pseudonym for Heming, 'Prostitution in London', from H. Mayhew (1851, 1961), *London Labour and the London Poor, Volume Four*.
103 *Ibid.*
104 A. Marshall, 'The housing of the London poor: (1) Where to house them', *Contemporary Review*, February 1884, 228, cited in G. Stedman Jones (1971), *op. cit.*, p. 128.
105 Sir J. Cantlie, President of the Royal Society of Tropical Medicine and Hygiene, 'Degeneration amongst Londoners', lecture delivered at Parkes Museum, London, 27 January 1885, published transcript.
106 Charles Booth Archive, *op. cit.*
107 *Ibid.*
108 *Ibid.*

109   Anon, probably M. Harkness (1889), British Weekly Commissioners, *Toilers in London; or Inquiries concerning Female Labour in the Metropolis* cited in J. Charlton (1999), *It Just Went Like Tinder*, p. 21.
110   M. Williams QC (1894), *op. cit.*, p. 16.
111   *Ibid.*
112   *Ibid.*
113   *Ibid.*, p. 17.
114   *Ibid.*
115   *Ibid.*
116   *Ibid.*
117   A. John (ed.) (1986), *op. cit.*, p. 5.
118   A. Davin (1997), *op. cit.*; J. Lewis, 'The working-class mother and state intervention 1870–1918', Chapter 4 in J. Lewis (1986), *op. cit.*
119   C. Booth (1889), *Life and Labour of the People, Volume 1*, p. 63.
120   A. Davin (1997), *op. cit.*, p. 75.
121   Interview, Louise Raw and Joan Harris, June 2004.
122   *Ibid.*
123   A. Davin (1997), *op. cit.*, p. 75.
124   Anon, probably M. Harkness (1889), *Toilers in London; or Inquiries concerning Female Labour in the Metropolis* cited in J. Charlton (1999), *It Just Went Like Tinder*, p. 35.
125   Interview, Louise Raw/Ted Lewis, 23 February 2005.
126   A. Davin (1997), *op. cit.*
127   *Ibid.*
128   *Ibid.*
129   *Ibid.*
130   R. Gray (1981), *The Aristocracy of Labour in Nineteenth Century Britain c.1850–1914*, p. 38.
131   Interview Louise Raw/Ted Lewis, 23 February 2005.
132   *Marx and Engels: Selected Correspondence*, p. 479; in R. Beer (1979), *op. cit.*, p. 1.
133   P. Thompson (1967), *Socialists, Liberals and Labour: the Struggle for London 1885–1914*, p.45.

Notes to Chapter 2: Haunted by the Woman Question: The Victorian Labour Movement and Women Workers

1   K. Hunt (1996), *Equivocal Feminists*, p. 1.
2   *The Times*, 7 July 1888.
3   N. Soldon (1978), *Women in British Trade Unions*, p. 2.
4   A. Clark (1995), *The Struggle for the Breeches*, p. 135.
5   H. Pelling (1963), *A History of British Trade Unionism*.
6   J. Wade on a strike by 1,500 women mill workers in 1835, from *History of the Middle and Working Classes* (1835), pp. 570–1, in C. Willis (1998), *Victim or Virago?*, p. 1.
7   N. Soldon (1978), *op. cit.*, p. 2.
8   M. Davis (1993), *Comrade or Brother?*, p. 38.
9   K. Offen, *op. cit.* p. 344, in R. Bridenthal *et al.* (1987), *Becoming Visible*, p. 336.
10   S. Rowbotham (1977), *Hidden from History*, p. 44.
11   *Ibid.*, p. 39.

12   H. Pelling (1963), *A History of British Trade Unionism.*
13   J. Scott, 'Gender: a useful category of historical analysis', in R. Shoemaker and M. Vincent (eds) (1998), *Gender and History in Western Europe*, p. 44.
14   *Ibid.*
15   *Ibid.*, p. 56.
16   J. Hannam and K. Hunt (2002), *Socialist Women*, p. 57.
17   E. H. Hunt (1981), *British Labour History 1815–1914*, p. 25, cited in A. John (1986), *Unequal Opportunities*, p. 8.
18   G. Holloway (2005), *Women and Work in Britain Since 1840*, p. 76.
19   *Ibid.*
20   S. Boston (1987), *Women Workers and the Trade Unions*, p. 17.
21   *Ibid.*
22   M. Davis (1993), *op. cit.*, p. 79.
23   S. Alexander (1994), *Becoming a Woman and Other Essays in Nineteenth and Twentieth Century Feminist History*, pp. 28–9.
24   *Ibid.*
25   *Ibid.*
26   A. Clark (1995), *The Struggle for the Breeches*, p. 119.
27   *Ibid.*, p. 115.
28   *Ibid.*, p. 135.
29   E. Mappen, 'Social feminist approaches to the problem of women's work', Chapter 8 in A. John (1986), *op. cit.*, p. 244.
30   *Ibid.*
31   *Ibid.*
32   E. Roberts (1986), 'Women's strategies 1890–1940', Chapter 9 in J. Lewis (ed.) (1986), *Labour and Love*, p. 237.
33   The *Link*, 23 June 1888, and the strike fund register, TUC archives.
34   *Ibid.*
35   A. Clark (1995), *op. cit.*, p. 40.
36   B. Taylor (1983), *Eve and the New Jerusalem*, cited in A. Clark (1995), *op. cit.*, p. 82.
37   A. Clark (1995), *op. cit.*, p. 2.
38   Charles Darwin was among those who cited the inspiration of Malthus' (1798) *Essay on the Principle of Population*: University of California, Berkeley (2005): Evolution Website; Evolutionary Thought; Thomas Malthus. Available from http://www.ucmp.berkely/edu/history/malthus.
39   Place was prominent in the London Corresponding Society. A. Clark (1995), *op. cit.*, p. 2.
40   G. Holloway (1998), *op. cit.*, p. 178.
41   Quoted in *Women's Trade Union Review*, July 1897, p. 17, and cited in E. Gordon (1991), *Women and the Labour Movement in Scotand 1850–1914*, p. 106.
42   M. Barrett and M. McIntosh (1980), *The Family Wage: Some Problems for Socialists and Feminists, Capital and Class 2*, pp. 51–72, cited in G. Holloway (1998), *op. cit.*, p. 178.
43   M. Davis (1993), *op. cit.*, p. 100.
44   S. Boston (1987), *op. cit.*, p. 73.
45   D. Thom, 'The bundle of sticks: women, trade unionists and collective organisation before 1918', Chapter 9 in A. John (ed.) (1986), *op. cit.*, p. 277.

46 M. Llewelyn Davies (1984), *Life as We Have Known It: By Co-operative Working Women*, p. 40, cited in G. Holloway (1998), *op. cit.*, p. 175.

47 Fawcett's letter to the *Standard*, 23 July 1898, cited in D. Rubinstein (1991), *A Different World for Women*, p. 104.

48 *Ibid.*

49 B. Harrison (1996), *Not Only the Dangerous Trades*, p. 68.

50 G. Holloway (1998), *op. cit.*, p. 185.

51 G. Holloway, 'Origins of the women's trade union movement', paper for 'Women: Fighting for Rights at Work' conference, Black Country Living Museum, 17 October 2005.

52 S. Rowbotham(1977), *Hidden from History*, p. 60.

53 G. Holloway, 'Origins of the women's trade union movement', paper for 'Women: Fighting for Rights at Work' conference, Black Country Living Museum, 17 October 2005.

54 S. Alexander (1994), *op. cit.*, p. 63.

55 G. Holloway (2005), *op. cit.*

56 I. Ford (1906), *Women and Socialism*, cited in J. Liddington and J. Norris (2000), *One Hand Tied Behind Us*.

57 *Ibid.*

58 T. Olcott, 'Dead centre: the women's trade union movement in London 1874–1914', the *London Journal*, vol. 2, no. 1, May 1976, 40.

59 *Ibid.*

60 From 'Women's Protective and Provident League annual report for 1889', Gertrude Tuckwell Collection, TUC Library, London Metropolitan University. For full discussion see Chapter 7.

61 From 'Women's Protective and Provident League annual report for 1890', Gertrude Tuckwell Collection, TUC Library, London Metropolitan University.

62 D. Thom (1986), *op. cit.*, p. 279.

63 H. Pelling (1963), *A History of British Trade Unionism*, p. 86.

64 J. Harris (1993), *Private Lives, Public Spirit*, p. 26.

65 D. Thom (1986), *op. cit.*, p. 262: it should be noted, however, that, as Isabella Ford pointed out, many early socialists of the period, like William Morris, were equally middle class; she could of course have included the names of Marx, Engels, and many more. It may be therefore that some of the apparent resentment over class concealed hostility over gender.

66 *Ibid.*, p. 262.

67 J. Kelly, 'The doubled vision of feminist theory', in *Women, History, and Theory* (1984), pp. 51–64.

68 M. Davis, 'The making of the English working class revisited: history theory and practice', professorial inaugural lecture, London Metropolitan University, 4 June 2003.

69 *Ibid.*

70 S. Boston (1987), *op. cit.*, Introduction, p. 1.

71 E.g. F. Engels (1888), *The Condition of the Working Class in England in 1844*, and K. Marx, *Capital, Volume 1*, cited in M. Davis (2003), *op. cit.*

72 M. Davis (2003), *op. cit.*

73 C. and W. Staples, '"A Strike of Girls": gender and production politics at the Kenrick factory during the Black Country Strike of 1913', paper for the American Sociological Association, New York, 1996, online at learn.aero.und.edu., p. 9.

74 The *Birmingham Gazette*, 8 April 1913, cited in *ibid.*, p. 29.
75 C. and W. Staples (1996), *op. cit.*, p. 29.
76 *Ibid.*
77 S. Lewenhak (1977), *Women and Trade Unions: An Outline History of Women in British Trade Unions*, cited in *ibid.*, p. 6.
78 C. and W. Staples (1996), *op. cit.*
79 *Ibid.*, p. 4.
80 D. Thom (1986), *op. cit.*, cited in *ibid.*, p. 5.
81 H. Clegg, *A History of Trade Unions Since 1889, Volume 2, 1911–1933*, cited in *ibid.*, p. 4.
82 C. and W. Staples (1996), *op. cit.*, p. 4.
83 C. and W. Staples (1996), *op. cit.*, p. 5.
84 *Ibid.*
85 The *Age*, 30 December 1882, and the *Argus*, 18 January 1883, cited in D. Thornton (2005), *op. cit.*, p. 2.
86 *Ibid.*, p. 2.
87 D. Thornton, 'Gender, class and activism in the Melbourne Tailoresses' strike, 1882–3', paper presented at 'The Past Is Before Us: The Ninth National Labour History Conference', University of Sydney, 30 June–2 July 2005.
88 *Ibid.*
89 *Ibid.*, p. 1.
90 The *Argus*, 14 July 1874, cited in *ibid.*, p. 2.
91 *Ibid.*, p. 3.
92 *Ibid.*, p. 6.
93 E. Creswell, Royal Commission into the Factory Act, 1882, cited in D. Thornton (2005), *op. cit.*, p. 6.
94 H. Robertson, 'A pioneer interviewed', *Clothing Trades Gazette*, no. 15, May 1922, in D. Thornton (2005), *op. cit.*, p. 10.
95 *Ibid.*, p. 10.
96 *Ibid.*, p. 16.
97 *Ibid.*
98 M. Davis (1999), *Sylvia Pankhurst*, p. 1.
99 J. Kelly, 'The doubled vision of feminist theory', in *Women, History, and Theory* (1984), pp. 51–64.
100 C. and W. Staples (1996), *op. cit.*
101 N. Ferguson (2004), *Empire*.
102 N. Ferguson, 'Welcome to the new imperialism: the US must make the transition from informal to formal empire', The *Guardian*, Wednesday 31 October 2001.
103 *Ibid.*
104 *Ibid.*
105 A. Vickery, 'Golden Age to seperate spheres? A review of the categories and chronolgy of English women's history.' *Historical Journal 36* (1993), 383–414.
106 J. Puris, 'David Starkey's History Boys', 2nd April 2009, The *Guardian*, retrieved from guardian.co.uk
107 M. McMillan (1927), *The Life of Rachel McMillan*, p. 137, cited in S. Rowbotham (1977), *Hidden from History*, p. 63.

Notes to Chapter 3: Life, Work and Politics in the Victorian East End

1   Sylvia Pankhurst (1977), *The Suffragette Movement*, p. 416.
2   A. Mearns (1883), *The Bitter Cry of Outcast London*; W. T. Stead – journalism including 'Outcast London – where to begin?', the *Pall Mall Gazette*, 23 October 1883; 'The maiden tribute to modern Babylon', Parts I–IV, the *Pall Mall Gazette*, 6, 7, 8 and 10 July 1885.
3   A. Wells (2001), *Political Culture and Communication in Britain*, p. 2.
4   S. Koss (1986), *The Rise and Fall of the Political Press in Britain, Volume 1*.
5   *The Times*, 7 July 1888.
6   B. Harrison, 'Women's work and health in the East End 1880–1914', in *Rising East*, vol. 2, no. 3, 20–45.
7   'Fifth Report of the House of Lords Select Committee on the Sweating System', 1980, pp. xvii (Cd 169) pxlii, cited in J. Morris (1986), *Women Workers and the Sweated Trades*, p. 8.
8   J. Morris (1986), *op. cit.*, pp. 1–2.
9   S. Rowbotham, 'Approaches to home working in the nineteenth and twentieth century', paper for 'Women: Fighting for Rights at Work' conference, Black Country Living Museum, 17 October 2005.
10 *Punch*, 16 December 1843. Published online in E. C. Stedman (ed.) (1895), *A Victorian Anthology, 1837–1895: Selections Illustrating the Editor's Critical Review of British Poetry in the Reign of Victoria*.
11 *The Times*, 'White slaves of London', 27 October 1843, p. 4.
12 J. Morris (1986), *op. cit.*, p. 5.
13 The *Pall Mall Gazette, op. cit.*, 1986, p. 7.
14 *The Times*, 11 October 1884, in J. Morris (1986), *op. cit.*, p. 7.
15 J. Morris (1986), *op. cit.*, p. 7.
16 *The Times*, 10 February 1888, cited in *ibid.*, p. 292.
17 1884, cited in J. Morris (1986), *op. cit.*, p. 7.
18 PP. 1984 LXXXI cd.7564, cited in *ibid.*, p. 12.
19 G. Bosio (1981), *Il Tratore ad Acquanegra*, cited in A. Portelli (1995), *Italian Oral History*, p. 1.
20 J. R. Shanley, 'Outlines of working people in history', FTAT Record November 1978, TUC archives.
21 Rosa Luxembourg, speech to Foundation Congress of the German Communist Party, 1918, cited in R. Hyman (1971), *Marxism and the Sociology of Trade Unionism*.
22 M. Brodie, 'Politics stirs them very little: Conservatism and apathy in the East End of London 1885–1914', Oxford University PhD thesis, 1999; G. Stedman Jones (1971) suggests that the limited consciousness of the 'casual poor' was a great hindrance to groups like the SDF and to the dockers' leaders: *Outcast London*, pp. 344–8.
23 G. Stedman Jones (1971), *op. cit.*
24 A. Besant (1890), *The Trade Union Movement*, p. 28.
25 G. Stedman Jones (1971), *op. cit.*, p. 341.
26 *Ibid.*, p. 343.
27 *Ibid.*
28 *The Times*, 9 February 1886, p. 5, and *Daily News* of the same date, p. 6, quoted in M. Brodie (1999), *op. cit.*, p. 27.

29 B. Gidley (2000), *The Proletarian Other*, p. 6 and M. Brodie (1999), *op. cit.*, p. 29.
30 M. Brodie (1999), *op. cit.*, p. 23.
31 Brodie quotes figures of 50% in the East End and 59.9% nationally from J. Garrard (1970), *The English and Immigration 1880–1910*, p. 73.
32 M. Brodie (1999), *op. cit.*, pp. 12–13.
33 M. Cohen and H. Fagan (eds) (1984), *Childhood Memories Recorded by some Socialist Men and Women in their Later Years*.
34 A collection of journalist and later Independent Labour Party (ILP) member Blatchford's articles from the *Clarion*, published in 1893. It sold over 2 million copies.
35 M. Cohen and H. Fagan (1984), *op. cit.*, p. 6.
36 *Ibid.*, p. 7.
37 *Ibid.*
38 *Ibid.*, p. 10.
39 *Ibid.*, p. 50.
40 *Ibid.*, p. 30.
41 G. Stedman Jones, *op. cit.*, p. 341.
42 J. Rose (2002), *The Intellectual Life of the British Working Classes*, pp. 45–6.
43 *Ibid.*, pp. 40–1.
44 *Ibid.*, 2002, p. 45.
45 E. H. Hunt (1985), *British Labour History 1815–1914*, p. 305.
46 A. Harding (1981), *East End Underworld*, (ed. R. Samuel).
47 A. Davin (1997), *Growing Up Poor*, p. 63.
48 *Ibid.*
49 *Ibid.*, p. 66.
50 *Ibid.*, p. 67.
51 C. Booth 1890, cited in A. Davin (1997), *op. cit.*, p. 51.
52 A. Davin (1997), *op. cit.*, p. 50.
53 T. Wright (1967), *Some Customs and Habits of the Working Classes, by a journeyman engineer*. New York: A.M. Kelly.
54 B. Jones, cited in Cohen, M. and Fagan, H. (eds) (1984), *Childhood Memories recorded by some Socialist Men and Women in their later years*. Self-published manuscript.
55 Interview, Joan Harris/Louise Raw, 8 June 2004.
56 A. Davin (1997), *op. cit.*, p. 54.
57 *Ibid.*
58 E. Baillie, *The Shabby Paradise*, p. 14, cited in A. Davin (1997), *op. cit.*
59 A. Davin (1997), *op. cit.*, p. 56.
60 R. A. Bray, *The Town Child*, pp. 123–4, cited in *ibid.*
61 A. Davin (1997), *op. cit.*, p. 54.
62 *Ibid.*, p. 66.
63 *Ibid.*
64 *Ibid.*, p. 15.
65 *Ibid.*, p. 66.
66 Phyllis H., eldest of eight, Anna Davin's personal notes from SE1 People's History Group, 13 May 1980.
67 M. E. Loane (1909), *An Englishman's Castle*, p. 116.
68 A. Davin (1997), *op. cit.*, p. 88.

69   *Ibid.*
70   *Ibid.*, p. 90.
71   Report of the Commissioners, Factory and Workshop Acts, Session 8 February–15 August 1876, vol. xxix, pp. 961–3.
72   Special Committee *Administration Byelaws* report, 1890, p. 68, cited in A. Davin (1997), *op. cit.*, p. 105.
73   *Ibid.*, p. 91, cited in A. Davin (1997), *op. cit.*, p. 108.
74   R. Church, cited in A. Davin (1997), *op. cit.*, p. 72.
75   A. Davin (1997), *op. cit.*, p. 116.
76   R. L. Stevenson (1881), *Virginibus Puerisque*, pp. 28–9, cited in A. Davin (1997), *op. cit.*, p. 119.
77   A. Davin (1997), *op. cit.*, p. 120.
78   F. Willis (1948), *101 Jubilee Road, a Book of London Yesterdays*, p. 5, cited in A. Davin (1997), *op. cit.*, p. 120.
79   *Ibid.*
80   R. Church, *op. cit.*, p. 142, cited in A. Davin (1997), *op. cit.*, p. 121.
81   G. Sims (1882), *How the Poor Live*, cited in C. Willis (1998), 'Victim or Virago?', p. 32.
82   A. Davin (1997), *op. cit.*, p. 147.
83   Interview, Ted Lewis/Louise Raw, 23 February 2005.
84   Employment of Schoolchildren, PP 1902, evidence of Miss Ella Holme, Appendix 19 and q. 2, 268.
85   Interview, Joan Harris/Louise Raw, 8 June 2004: see Chapter 9.
86   Ragged School Union Reports, 20 September 1868, pp. 200–1, in A. Davin (1997), *op. cit.*
87   A. Davin (1997), *op. cit.*, p. 147.
88   *Ibid.*, p. 161.
89   *Ibid.*, p. 170.
90   *Ibid.*, p. 173.
91   Charles Booth Archive, 'Eliza B Poplar 1900', transcript B13.
92   Booth Poverty Map 1, p. 158.
93   W. Fishman, *East End 1888*, p. 51.
94   E. Roberts (1996), *A Woman's Place*.
95   *Ibid.*
96   *Ibid.*
97   *Ibid.*
98   Bill Jones' recollections in M. Cohen and H. Fagan (eds) (1986), *op. cit.*, p. 65.
99   A. Davin (1997), *op. cit.*, p. 37.
100 *Ibid.*
101 M. Cohen and H. Fagan (eds) (1986), *op. cit.*, p. 65.
102 J. Foster (1974), *Class Struggle and the Industrial Revolution*, cited in S. Moore (1986), *op. cit.*, p. 208.
103 N. Hewitt, 'Beyond the search for sisterhood: American women's history in the 1980s', *Social History*, vol. 10, no. 3, 1985, cited by S. Moore (1986), *op. cit.*, p. 14.
104 *Ibid.*
105 S. Moore (1986), *op. cit.*, p. 5.
106 *Ibid.*, p. 12.
107 E.g. A. Davin (1997), *op. cit.*; J. Lewis (1986), *Labour and Love*.

108 E.g. P. Long, 'The women of the Colorado fuel and iron strike, 1913–1914', in R. Milkman (ed.) (1984),*Women, Work and Protest*; H. Penn Lasky, 'When I was a person: the ladies' auxiliary in the 1934 teamsters', in R. Milkman (ed.) (1984), *op. cit.* All cited in S. Moore (1986), *op. cit.*, p. 13.

109 T. Kaplan, *Female Consciousness and Collective Action in Barcelona 1910–1918*, cited in S. Moore (1986), *op. cit.*, p. 16.

110 Cited in S. Moore (1986), *op. cit.*, p. 14.

111 *Ibid.*, p. 209.

Notes to Chapter 4: Liberals and Lucifers: Bryant and May and Matchmaking

1 Hackney Archives, D/B/BRY/4/8/1.

2 Rev. A. O. Jay (1986), *A Story of Shoreditch*, p. 80, cited in M. Brodie, 'Politics stirs them very little: Conservatism and apathy in the East End of London 1885–1914', PhD thesis, p. 127, Oxford University, 1999.

3 Labour MP John Scurr on the matchwomen and their community, the *Morning Star*, Saturday 10 July 1988, in TUC archives MISC HD 53699.

4 J. Harris, 'Final flicker of a British flame', *New Scientist*, issue 1919, 2 April 1994, 40.

5 K. McGrath (ed.) (1999), *World of Invention*.

6 H. Spencer, cited in A. Briggs (1988), *Victorian Things*, p. 181.

7 W. Smith (1886), *Morley*, p. 17.

8 Calculation made using John J. McCusker, 'Comparing the purchasing power of money in Great Britain from 1264 to any other year including the present', Economic History Services, 2001. http://www.eh.net/hmit/ppowerbp/.

9 As will be shown, statistics of toxicity and morbidity are unreliable, due in large measure to under-reporting and deliberate concealment by companies like Bryant and May.

10 *Westminster Gazette*, 3 June 1898, cited in B. Harrison, 'The politics of ill-health in the late nineteenth century Britain: the case of the match making industry', *Sociology of Health and Illness*, 17,1,1995.

11 G. Augustus Sala (1859), *Gaslight and Daylight: with some London scenes they shine upon.* Place unknown. Chapman and Hall, p. 286.

12 Recalled by James Wright as a reminiscence of his grandmother who lived in Bow, at public lecture 'A match to fire the docks', given by Louise Raw at Museum of London, Docklands, 3 June 2004.

13 Factory Department Annual Returns cited in B. Harrison, 'The politics of ill-health in late-nineteenth century Britain: the case of the match-making industry', *Sociology of Health and Illness*, vol. 17, no. 1, 1995.

14 1863 Children's Employment Commission, First Report (v. 18): *Mr. White's Report on the Lucifer Match Manufacturer.*

15 Letter from W. J. Brown, solicitors, referring to Bill Owen and Tony Russell's musical *The Matchgirls*, first produced at the Globe Theatre in 1966. Bryant and May archives bundles P/B/BRY/1/2/538–564.

16 B. Harrison, *op. cit.*, p. 23.

17 Kings College Archives, Kings College, London: Biographical and Administrative Details, John Syer Bristowe, reference GB 0100 TH/PP BRISTOWE.

18 'The match girls' strike', *Freedom*, vol. 2, no. 23, August 1888, 1–2.

19 1863 Children's Employment Commission, *op. cit.*

20 *Ibid.*

21 A. Miles (1972), 'Phosphorus necrosis of the jaw: phossy jaw', *British Dental Journal* vol. 133, 203–6, and National Safety Council briefing, 'Phosphorus', www.nsc.org. library/chemical/phshor.

22 Recalled by James Wright as a reminiscence of his grandmother who lived in Bow, at public lecture 'A match to fire the docks', given by Louise Raw at Museum of London, Docklands, 3 June 2004.

23 B. Harrison (1995), *op. cit.*, p. 23.

24 Various reports, the *Star* and *Daily Chronicle*, 2 June 1888, describing death of Bryant and May worker Cornelius Lean.

25 *Ibid.*

26 Chief Inspector of Factories Report 1899, cited in B. Harrison (1995), *op. cit.*, p. 24.

27 H. G. Hubbard, 'Evolution of the match', *The Rushlight*, vol. 1, no. 1, November 1934, at www.rushlight.org/research.

28 B. Harrison (1995), *op. cit.*, p. 23.

29 *Ibid.*

30 R. Squire (1927), *Women in the Public Service, an Industrial Retrospect*, p. 54, cited in B. Harrison, *op. cit.*, pp. 22–3.

31 A. Davin (1997), *Growing Up Poor*, p. 191.

32 *Munby Diaries Volume 9*, p. 74, 30 July 1861, cited in *Ibid.*, p. 191.

33 Report of the Commissioners, Factory and Workshop Acts, Session 8 February–15 August 1876, vol. xxix, p. 963.

34 Cited in B. Harrison (1995), *op. cit.*, p. 23.

35 *Ibid.*

36 B. Harrison, (1996) *Not Only the 'Dangerous Trades'*.

37 W. Booth (1890), *In Darkest England and the Way Out*, Introduction, p. 3.

38 Interview with CNN, 'Your business', CNN archive, 2000.

39 R. Howell, 'Quaker theologies', paper for the Northern Monthly Extension Committee Meeting of the Religious Society of Friends in Aotearoa/New Zealand, January 1998.

40 W. Glenny Crory (1876), *East London Industries*, Chapter 6, 'The manufacture of matches', p. 43.

41 Mr White's Report on the Lucifer Match Manufacturer; Children's Employment Commission, First Report (v. 18), 1863.

42 Bryant and May with P. Beaver (1985), *The Matchmakers* (company history), p. 38.

43 R. Howell (1998), *op. cit.*

44 Considerable email correspondence took place with the following Society of Friends historians/archivists: Dr Robert Howell (see below), 4 October 2005, 10 October 2005; Chris Lawson, 11 October 2005; Jennifer Barraclough of the Woodbrook Quaker Study Centre, 25 October 2005.

45 Records of Bryant and May partnership, Bryant and May archives, ref. D/B/ BRY/1/1.

46 W. Glenny Crory (1876), *op. cit.*, p. 48.

47 The *Link*, 14 July 1888.

48 *Ibid.*

49 John J. McCusker, 'Comparing the purchasing power of money in Great Britain from 1600 to any other year including the present', Economic History Services.

50 The *Link*, 23 June 1888.
51 The *Commonweal*, vol. 4, no. 132, 21 July 1888, p. 225.
52 D. C. Mitchell and S. Gwyn Smith (1896), *The Matchbox Collectors' Scrapbook*, Bryant and May catalogue no. 2.
53 L. Rigby (2000), *Stoke Poges*.
54 See *East London Advertiser* reports and editorials for July 1888, Chapter 6.
55 W. Glenny Crory (1876), *op. cit.*, p. 44.
56 *Ibid.*, p. 45.
57 Report of the Commissioners, Factory and Workshop Acts (1876), *op. cit.*, pp. 961–3.
58 *Ibid.*
59 *Ibid.*, p. 962.
60 *Ibid.*
61 *Ibid.*, ciii 94.
62 *Ibid.*, ciii 94.
63 *National Reformer* 1885, cutting in Bryant and May archives D/B/BRY/1/1; T. Mann (1986), *What a Compulsory Eight Hour Working Day Means to the Workers*, pp. 25–6.
64 'How it is done – at Bryant and May's match factory', *Cassell's Saturday Journal*, 10 December 1887, 249–50.
65 *Ibid.*
66 *Ibid.*
67 *Ibid.*
68 The *Daily Chronicle*, 2 June 1898.
69 *Ibid.*
70 The *Commonweal*, vol 4, no. 132, 21 July 1888, p. 225.
71 *Ibid.*
72 Cited in *ibid.*
73 As discussed in the *Echo*, 20 July 1888: see Chapter 6.
74 *Ibid.*
75 B. Harrison, 'Women's work and health in the East End 1880–1914', *Rising East*, vol. 2, no. 3, 20–45.

Notes to Chapter 5: The 'Notorious' Annie Besant: The Strike Leaders Reconsidered

1 A. Wood Besant (1893), *An Autobiography*, p. 295.
2 E. Pease (1925), *The History of the Fabian Society*, p. 40.
3 A. Wood Besant (1893), *op. cit.*, p. 24.
4 *Ibid.*
5 *Ibid.*, p. 42.
6 *Ibid.*
7 *Ibid.*, p. 6.
8 *Ibid.*, p. 40.
9 *Ibid.*, p. 47.
10 Besant was pro-suffrage, though never a suffragette – she affronted Emmeline Pankhurst with her modern 'short skirts and short hair', which the latter thought 'hideous'. R. Manvell (1976), *Trial of Annie Besant*, p. 94.
11 *Ibid.*

12 Bradlaugh would cause a furore on his election to parliament in 1880 by refusing to take the required oath 'on the faith of a Christian'. The conflict over this continued for several years and became a national issue, with the working classes broadly supporting Bradlaugh.

13 A. Taylor (1992), *Annie Besant*, p. 70.

14 *Ibid.*

15 A. Wood Besant (1893), *op. cit.*, p. 127.

16 *Ibid.*, p. 129.

17 *Ibid.*, p. 130.

18 *Ibid.*

19 *Ibid.*, p. 188.

20 *Ibid.*

21 *Ibid.*, p. 189.

22 *Ibid.*, p. 295.

23 *Ibid.*

24 The *Link*, 23 June 1888.

25 A. H. Nethercot (1961), *The First Five Lives of Annie Besant*. Two years later Nethercot also published *The Last Four Lives of Annie Besant*.

26 None appears, for example, in 'Annie Besant's quest for truth', *Journal of Ecclesiastical History*, vol. 50, 1999, 215–39.

27 *The Times*, 7 July 1888.

28 *Justice*, 21 June 1884, in A. Taylor (1992), *op. cit.*, p. 172.

29 J. Hannam and K. Hunt (2002), *Socialist Women*, p. 7.

30 'History of the names and years of officers of the members of the Executive Committee 1884–1924', Appendix III in E. Pearse (1925), *op. cit.*, p. 285.

31 E.g. J. Martin (1999), *Women and the Politics of Schooling in Victorian and Edwardian England*, p. 68; J. Hannam and K. Hunt (2002), *op. cit.*, p. 2.

32 Morton and Tate (1956), *The British Labour Movement*.

33 *Ibid.*, p. 173.

34 J. Hannam and K. Hunt (2002), *op. cit.*, p. 3.

35 *Ibid.*

36 G. B. Shaw (1928), *The Intelligent Woman's Guide to Socialism, Capitalism, Sovietism and Fascism, Volume 1*, p. 185.

37 *Ibid.*, p. 201.

38 *Ibid.*, p. 205.

39 H. M. Hyndman (1883), *The Historical Basis of Socialism*, pp. 287–91, cited in E. J. Hobsbawm (1974), *Labour's Turning Point 1880–1900*, p. 74.

40 *Justice*, 7 September 1889, cited in M. Crick (1994), *The History of the Social-Democratic Federation*, p. 60.

41 *Justice*, 21 September 1889, cited in Crick (1994), *op. cit.*

42 M. Crick (1994), *op. cit.*, p. 60.

43 S. Weintraub (ed.) (1986), *Bernard Shaw, The Diaries 1885–1897*, p. 392.

44 *Ibid.*, p. 393.

45 Roche will be mentioned further in discussion of the Matchwomen's Union committee photograph in Chapter 9.

46 S. Weintraub (ed.) (1986), *op. cit.*, p. 393.

47 *Ibid.*, p. 395.

48 A. Besant, 'Industry under socialism', in G. B. Shaw (ed.) (1891), *Fabian Essays in Socialism*, p. 94.
49 *Ibid.*, p. 111.
50 S. Webb, 'English progress towards democracy', Fabian Tract 15 (1892), cited in E. J. Hobsbawm (1974), *op. cit.*, p. 74.
51 Fabian Society leaflet (1897), cited in E. J. Hobsbawm (1974), *op. cit.*, pp. 64–5.
52 N. and J. McKenzie (eds) (1982), *Diary of Beatrice Webb*, p. 222.
53 B. Anderson and J. Zinsser (1988), *A History of their Own*, p. 383.
54 M. Davis (1999), *Sylvia Pankhurst*, p. 9.
55 *Ibid.*
56 J. Hannam and K. Hunt (2002), *op. cit.*, p. 5.
57 E.g. J. Liddington and J. Norris (2000), *One Hand Tied Behind Us*, p. 44.
58 K. Hunt (1996), *Equivocal Feminists*; J. Hannam and K. Hunt (2002), *op. cit.*
59 S. Pankhurst (1977), *The Suffragette Movement*, p. 111.
60 E. Crawford (1999), *The Women's Suffrage Movement*, p. 333.
61 *Ibid.*, p. 57.
62 *Ibid.*, p. 60.
63 *Ibid.*, p. 91.
64 *Ibid.*
65 G. Holloway, '"Let the women be alive!"', Chapter 7 in E. J. Yeo (ed.) (1998), *Radical Femininity*, p. 172.
66 *Ibid.*, p. 177.
67 A. Nield Chew (1982), *The Life and Writings of Ada Nield Chew remembered and collected by Doris Nield Chew*, p. 234.
68 *Ibid.*, p. 57.
69 *Ibid.*, p. 168.
70 Source: *Time* magazine, 29 June 1962; *Time* magazine online archive, http: www. time.com.
71 *The Duchess of Duke Street*, BBC Drama, 1976–7.
72 G. Holloway (1998), *op. cit.*, p. 177.
73 The *Link*, 23 June 1888.
74 *Ibid.*
75 A. Besant (1890), *The Trade Union Movement*, p. 28.
76 Cited in A.Taylor (1992), *op. cit.*, p. 317.
77 Source: the Theosophical Society, Britain.
78 Besant in *The Ancient Wisdom: An Outline of Theosophical Teachings* (1897), cited in A. Taylor (1992), *op. cit.*, p. 242.
79 *Ibid.*
80 Besant, *op. cit.*, p. 204.
81 *Marx and Engels Collected Works Vol. 38*, p. 88. Letter to Karl Kautsky (Stuttgart), 30 April 1891 (pp. 86–8), cited in H. A. O. de Tollenaere, 'Marx and Engels on spiritualism and Theosophy', online article at http://www.stelling.nl/simpos/simpoeng.htm.
82 *Marx and Engels Collected Works Vol. 38*, p. 191. Letter to Karl Kautsky (Stuttgart), 25 October 1891 (pp. 190–1), cited in *ibid.*
83 H. A. O. de Tollenaere (1996), *The Politics of Divine Wisdom*.
84 G. B. Shaw (1979), cited in N. and J. Mackenzie, *The First Fabians*, p. 46.
85 E.g. N. and J. Mackenzie (1979), *op. cit.* p. 45, who state that 'conversion was personified in an attachment to a new make of idol'.

86 A. Wood Besant (1893), *op. cit.*, p. 197.
87 H. Burrows' journal, Spring 1889, from the archives of the American Theosophical Society, www.theosophical.org.
88 *Ibid.*
89 'Report from the Committee on the Bill to regulate the labour of children in the mills and factories', 1832: Parliamentary Papers, 1831–1832, xv, pp. 454–5.
90 M. Sweet (2001), *Inventing the Victorians*, p. 62.
91 *The Times*, 27 October 1843, p. 4.
92 *Ibid.*
93 'The needlewomen of London', the *Manchester Guardian*, 4 November 1843.
94 M. Sweet (2001), *op. cit.*, pp. 62–9.
95 *Ibid.*
96 Four shillings in 1888 would equate to around £15 a week in 2004, according to John J. McCusker, 'Comparing the purchasing power of money in Great Britain from 1600 to any other year including the present', Economic History Services, 2001, http://www.eh.net/hmit/ppowerbp/.
97 A. Besant, 'White slavery in London', the *Link*, 23 June 1888.
98 The Paragon is mentioned as a particular favourite of the women in *Round London*, by Montagu Williams QC (1894), p. 16.
99 A. Besant, 'White slavery in London', *op. cit.*
100 *Ibid.*
101 *Ibid.*
102 *Ibid.*
103 *Ibid.*
104 The *Link*, 23 June 1888.
105 *Ibid.*
106 The *Star*, 6 July 1888, p. 3.
107 A. Besant, 'White slavery in London', *op. cit.*
108 *Ibid.*
109 'Report of the Truck Committee, Vol. 1: report and appendices', vol. lix, no. Cd.4442, 1908.
110 'Royal Commission of Children's Employment, Report', 1863, Sessional Papers xviii, Paper 3170 1862, Reports.
111 'The Sweating System: first report from the Select Committee of the House of Lords', vol. xx, paper 361, 1888.
112 A. C. Bryant, cited in A. Taylor (1992), *op. cit.*, p. 206.
113 A. Wood Besant (1893), *op. cit.*
114 The Women's Industrial Council, 'Married women's work. Being the report of an enquiry undertaken by the Women's Industrial Council', 1909.
115 A. Wood Besant (1893), *op. cit.*, p. 210.
116 *Ibid.*, p. 209.
117 *Ibid.*, p. 211.
118 The *Link*, 23 June 1888.
119 Printed in each case on 3 July 1888.
120 Besant and Burrows' Theosophy will be further discussed in Chapter 7.
121 Annie Besant confirms this in her autobiography (1893, *op. cit.*) and in the *Link*, 23 June to 7 July 1888.
122 Records of Bryant and May's AGM, 1888, company archives, bundle D/B/BRY/1/2/540.

123 Bryant and May's response to Annie Besant, quoted in the *Link*, 7 July 1888.
124 The *Link*, Saturday 7 July 1888, p. 3.
125 'The Sweating System: first report from the Select Committee of the House of Lords', *op. cit.*
126 The *East London Advertiser*, 30 June 1888, p. 3.
127 The *Link*, 14 July 1888.
128 A. Wood Besant (1893), *op. cit.*, p. 334.
129 The *Link*, 30 June 1888.
130 Annie Besant in the *Link*, 7 July 1888.
131 *Ibid.*
132 *Ibid.*
133 J. R. Shanley, 'Outlines of working people in history', FTAT Record, November 1978, TUC archives.
134 The *Link*, 7 July 1888.
135 M. Cole, in preface to B. Potter, (1987), *The Co-operative Movement in Great Britain*, p. xxxv.
136 A. Besant, *op. cit.*, p. 13.

Notes to Chapter 6: 'One Girl Began': The Strike and the Matchwomen

1 The letter commenting on the dismissal, from Burrows and Besant, was published on 3 July and must have been written at least one day before publication.
2 The *Star*, 3 July 1888.
3 The *East London Advertiser*, 'Bryant and May's match girls on strike: who fans the flames?', 7 July 1888.
4 The *Star*, 4 July 1888, p. 4.
5 *Ibid.*
6 *Ibid.*
7 Besant's journal, cited in A. Taylor (1992), *Annie Besant*, p. 55.
8 Correspondence preserved in the strike fund register, which was originally Burrows' cuttings book, shows him living at Aberdeen Road in Highbury, North London: TUC archives.
9 The *Link*, 7 July 1888.
10 *Ibid.*
11 *Ibid.*
12 The *Link*, 14 July 1888.
13 Bryant and May archives, Hackney Archive Department, bundle D/B/ BRY1/2/538.
14 The *Star*, 6 July 1888.
15 The *East London Advertiser*, *op. cit.*, 7 July 1888.
16 The *Star*, 4 July 1888, p. 4.
17 *Ibid.*
18 The *Star*, 6 July 1888.
19 *Ibid.*
20 The *East London Advertiser*, *op. cit.*, 7 July 1888.
21 The *East London Observer*, Saturday 14 July 1888, 'The match girls on strike. Bryant and May interviewed', p. 5.
22 *Ibid.*

23 *Ibid.*
24 *Ibid.*
25 The *Star*, 6 July 1888.
26 *Ibid.*
27 *Ibid.*
28 *Ibid.*
29 *Ibid.*, p. 3.
30 The *East London Advertiser, op. cit.*, 7 July 1888.
31 *Ibid.*
32 The *East London Advertiser*, 7 July 1888, p. 5.
33 The *Star*, 6 July 1888, p. 3.
34 *Ibid.*
35 E.g. John Charlton (1999), *It Just Went Like Tinder*, p. 15.
36 The *Link*, 7 July 1888.
37 *Ibid.*
38 Besant in the *Link*, 7 July 1888.
39 *Ibid.*
40 *Ibid.*
41 *Ibid.*
42 A. Wood Besant (1893), *Annie Besant.*
43 The *Link*, 7 July 1888.
44 *Ibid.*
45 *Ibid.*
46 The *Star*, 7 July 1888, p. 2.
47 *Ibid.*, p. 2.
48 *Ibid.*, p. 2.
49 *Ibid.*
50 *Ibid.*
51 *Ibid.*
52 The *Star*, 9 July, p. 3.
53 *Ibid.*
54 A. Wood Besant (1893), *op. cit.*, p. 175.
55 *Justice*, 9 July 1888.
56 A. Wood Besant (1893), *op. cit.*, p. 175.
57 *Ibid.*
58 *Ibid.*
59 The *Star*, 11 July 1888, p. 3.
60 J. Poynter, 'The London Trades Council and the New Unionism', dissertation for University of North London, 2001, p. 45.
61 *Ibid.*
62 The *East London Advertiser*, Saturday 21 July 1888, p. 6.
63 The *Star*, 13 July 1888, p. 3.
64 *Ibid.*
65 The *Pall Mall Gazette*, 9 July 1888, cited in R. Beer (1979), *Matchgirls' Strike 1888*, p. 41.
66 The *Link*, 14 July 1888.
67 The *Star*, 14 July 1888.
68 The *East London Advertiser*, 14 July 1888, p. 6.

69 The *Eastern Post*, Saturday 21 July 1888, p. 9.
70 Anon, probably M. Harkness (1889), British Weekly Commissioners, *Toilers in London*, cited in J. Charlton (1999), *op. cit.*, p. 21.
71 *Ibid.*
72 The *Star*, 14 July 1888.
73 The *Star*, 17 July 1888, in R. Beer (1979), *op. cit.*, p. 43.
74 *Ibid.*, p. 43
75 The *Echo*, 20 July 1888, in R. Beer (1979), *op. cit.*, p. 42.
76 The *East London Observer*, 'The match girls' strike', Saturday 21 July 1888, p. 6.
77 The *Eastern Post*, 21 July 1888, p. 9.
78 *Ibid.*
79 The *East London Advertiser*, 21 July 1888, p. 6.
80 Clara Collet in C. Booth, 'The trades of East London connected with poverty', Charles Booth Archive, ref. A2, and cited in C. Chinn (1988), *They Worked All their Lives*, p. 217.
81 The *Commonweal*, 21 July 1888.
82 The *Eastern Post*, 21 July 1888, p. 9.
83 The *East London Advertiser*, 14 July 1888.
84 The *East London Advertiser*, editorial, 21 July 1888.
85 The *Star*, 18 July 1888.
86 Mile End MP John Scurr·in 1923, quoted in the *Morning Star* on the centenary of the strike, Saturday 10 July 1988. In TUC archives, MISC HD 53699.
87 J. Kelly (1984), *Women, History, and Theory*, p. 2.
88 N. and J. McKenzie (eds) (1982), *Diary of Beatrice Webb*, p. 222.
89 R. Shannon (1999), *Gladstone, Heroic Minister 1865–98*, p. 77.
90 A. Briggs (1988), *Victorian Things*, p. 193.
91 R. Beer (1979), *op. cit.*, p. 35.
92 *Ibid.*
93 *Ibid.*
94 *Ibid.*
95 *The Times*, 25 April 1871, p. 10, quoted in R. Beer (1979), *op. cit.*, p. 35.
96 The *Standard*, 2 May 1871, Bryant and May archives.
97 *The Times*, 25 April 1871, *op. cit.*, p. 35.
98 Copy of the British Library Sound Archive/Roy Palmer Collection tape C1023/30: Samuel Webber.
99 My transcript of *ibid.*, item 28, 'Talk about the matchgirls' strike'.
100 C. A. Brown (1960), *The Story of our National Ballads*, p. 206.
101 *Ibid.*
102 *Ibid.*, p. 210.
103 *Ibid.*
104 Digital Tradition Folk Music database at www.mudcat.org.
105 *Ibid.*
106 F. Holcroft (1992), *A Terrible Nightmare*, p. 163.
107 *Ibid.*, p. 163.
108 J. Lloyd, Llanteg Historical Society, 'The wooden horse', online article at www.BBC. co.uk/wales/southwest.
109 E. P. Thompson (1991), 'Rough music: le charivari anglais', Chapter 8 in *Customs in Common.*

110 Papers of the Mathias family, cited by J. Lloyd, Llanteg Historical Society, *op. cit.*
111 Original manuscript in National Library of Wales, viewable online at www.llgc.org. uk. See also J. Powell (2000), 'Early references to tree fruit in Welsh literature', for Rhwydwaith Afalau'r Gororau at www.marcherapple.net.
112 *Ibid.*
113 *Ibid.*
114 *Ibid.*
115 R. Jones, 'Women, community and collective action: the "Ceffyl Pren" tradition', Chapter 1 in A. John (ed.) (1991) *Our Mother's Land*, p. 9.
116 J. Davies (1993), *A History of Wales*, p. 380.
117 Cited in *ibid.*
118 A. Marvell (1667), *Last Instructions to a Painter*. Collected in A. Marvell (1689), *A Collection of Poems on Affairs of State*.
119 E. P. Thompson (1991), 'Rough music: le charivari anglais', Chapter 8 in *Customs in Common*.
120 R. Jones (1991), *op. cit.*, p. 9.
121 *Ibid.*, p. 11.
122 *Ibid.*, p. 12.
123 *Ibid.*
124 *Ibid.*
125 *Ibid.*, p. 15.
126 *Ibid.*, p. 15.
127 *Ibid.*, p. 16.
128 From 'White slavery in London', The *Link*, 23 June 1888, p. 2, Bryant and May archives.
129 Mark Hutton, Development and Renewal officer, Tower Hamlets Council: telephone conversation with the author, 29 March 2006.
130 Interview L. Raw/T. Lewis, 23 February 2005.
131 *National Reformer* 1885, cutting in Bryant and May archives; T. Mann (1986), *What a Compulsory Eight Hour Working Day Means to the Workers*, pp. 25–6.
132 Charles Booth, *op. cit.*
133 Records of Bryant and May's AGM, 1888, company archives bundle D/B/ BRY/1/2/540.
134 Appended to Charles Booth's notebook, Charles Booth Archive, LSE B178, p. 62.
135 Interview with Miss Nash in *ibid.*
136 *Ibid.*
137 T. Mann (1923), *Memoirs*, p. 58.

Notes to Chapter 7: The Matchwomen, the Great Dock Strike and New Unionism

1 G. D. H. Cole (1948), *A Short History of the British Working Class Movement.*
2 J. F. C. Harrison (1990), *Late Victorian Britain 1875–1901*, pp. 142–3.
3 P. Thompson (1967), *Socialists, Liberals and Labour*, p. 531.
4 J. F. C. Harrison (1990), *op. cit.*, p. 142.
5 E. J. Hobsbawm (1964), *Labouring Men*, cited in J. Lovell (1977), *British Trade Unions 1875–1933*, p. 20.
6 E.g. J. Lovell (1977), *op. cit.*, p. 23.
7 J. F. C. Harrison (1990), *op. cit.*, p. 143.

8   E. H. Hunt (1982), *British Labour History 1815–1914*, p. 135.
9   A. L. Morton and G. Tate (1956),*The British Labour Movement*, p. 106.
10 J. Strauss, 'Engels and the theory of the labour aristocracy', in the *Link* no. 25, January to June 2004, online journal at http://www.dsp.au.links/back/issues.
11 T. Ramsay, Durham miners' leader, cited in *ibid.*
12 B. and S. Webb (1920), *The History of Trade Unions*, p. 235.
13 A. L. Morton and G. Tate (1956), *op. cit.*, p. 145.
14 See: A. Clark (1995), *The Struggle for the Breeches*, p. 119; K. Honeymen and J. Goodman, 'Women's work, gender conflict and the labour market in Europe, 1500–1900', Chapter 15 in R. Shoemaker and M. Vincent (1998), *Gender and History in Western Europe*. A fuller discussion of masculinity and skill occurs in Chapter 3.
15 M. Davis (1993), *Comrade or Brother?*, p. 79.
16 George Potter, trade unionist and journalist, in the *Reformer*, 5 November 1870, cited in R. Gray (1981), *The Aristocracy of Labour in Nineteenth Century Britain c.1850–1914*, p. 8.
17 R. J. Morris, 'The labour aristocracy in the class struggle', *Recent Findings of Research in Economic and Social History*, no. 7, Autumn 1988, 2.
18 J. Field, 'British Historians and the Concept of the Labor Aristocracy', p. 61 in *Radical History Review* Winter 1978–1979, pp. 61–85).
19 A. L. Morton and G. Tate (1956), *op. cit.*, pp. 145, 149.
20 A. Wood Besant (1893), *Annie Besant*, p. 117.
21 From: 'Women's Protective and Provident League Annual Report for 1889', Gertrude Tuckwell Collection, TUC Library, London Metropolitan University.
22 From: 'Women's Protective and Provident League Annual Report for 1890', Gertrude Tuckwell Collection, TUC Library, London Metropolitan University.
23 J. Schneer (1982), *Ben Tillett*, p. 27.
24 B. Tillett (1910), *Dock, Wharf, Riverside and General Workers' Union*, p. 14.
25 A. L. Morton and G. Tate (1956), *op. cit.*, p. 185.
26 Quoted in the *Daily News*, 19 August 1889. In A. Stafford (1961), *A Match to Fire the Thames*, p. 107.
27 The *Daily News*, 19 August 1889, in A. Stafford (1961), *op. cit.*, pp. 110–11.
28 Interview with Paddy Logue of the Derry Trades Council, 11 August 2002.
29 *Ibid.*
30 Palmer's *Index to The Times*, 1888–1889.
31 Both strikes are cited by Sheila Rowbotham in *Hidden From History* (1977), p. 61.
32 As recorded in Palmer's *Index to The Times*, 1888–1889.
33 W. Thorne, from *My Life's Battles*, pp. 69ff., cited in E. J. Hobsbawm (1974), *Labour's Turning Point*, p. 79.
34 *Ibid.*
35 *Ibid.*
36 W. Thorne (1989), *My Life's Battles.*
37 *Ibid.*
38 *Ibid.*
39 *Ibid.*
40 T. Mann (1923), *Memoirs*, p. 59.
41 G. D. H. Cole and R. Postgate (1938), *The Common People*, cited in W. Kent (1950), *John Burns.*

42	E. J. Hobsbawm (1964), *Labouring Men*, p. 158.
43	*Ibid.*, pp. 163–5.
44	J. Charlton (1999), *It Just Went Like Tinder*, p. 32.
45	*Ibid.*
46	H. Mayhew (1861), *London Labour and the London Poor*, p. 65.
47	T. Mann (1923), *op. cit.*, p. 31.
48	*Ibid.*, p. 38.
49	*Ibid.*, p. 58.
50	The *Morning Advertiser*, 16 August 1889.
51	*Ibid.*
52	J. Charlton (1999), *op. cit.*
53	*Ibid.*
54	The *Daily News*, 20 August 1889.
55	A.M. Thompson (1937), *Here I Lie*, p. 60.
56	The *Star*, 20 August 1889.
57	The *Echo*, 21 August 1889.
58	M. S. Carter, grocer, of 24 High Street, Poplar: letter in the *Echo*, 21 August 1889.
59	The *Pictorial News*, August 24 1889.
60	The *Observer*, 25 August 1889.
61	The *Star*, 27 August 1889.
62	T. Mann (1923), *op. cit.*
63	The *Star*, 27 August 1889.
64	J. Charlton (1999), *op. cit.*, p. 98.
65	The *East London Observer*, 31 August 1889.
66	The *Evening Standard*, 27 August 1889.
67	*Justice*, 31 August 1889.
68	The *Daily Chronicle*, 1 July 183, cited in M. Crick (1994), *The History of the Social-Democratic Federation*, p. 30.
69	J. Charlton (1999), *op. cit.*, p. 119.
70	*Ibid.*, p. 99.
71	*Ibid.*
72	The *Evening Standard*, 16 September 1889.
73	A. L. Morton and G. Tate (1956), *op. cit.*, p. 185.
74	*Ibid.*, p. 196.
75	Engels to Sorge, 7 December 1889, cited in *ibid.*, p. 195.
76	Cited in P. Thompson (1967), *op. cit.*, p. 53.
77	*Ibid.*, p. 54.
78	*Ibid.*
79	*Ibid.*, pp. 55–7.
80	A. L. Morton and G. Tate (1956), *op. cit.*, p. 195.
81	The *Star*, 5 May 1889.
82	A. L. Morton and G. Tate, *op. cit.*, 1956, p. 206.
83	H. A. Clegg *et al.* (1977), *A History of Trade Unions Since 1889*, p. 17.
84	*Ibid.*, p. 97.
85	*Ibid.*
86	*Ibid.*, p. 58.
87	P. Thompson (1967), *op. cit.*, p. 45.
88	M. Davis (1993), *op. cit.*, p. 100.

89 Mr Flynn, in 'Women's trade union quarterly report', 18 January 1892, cited in S. Rowbotham (1990), *A Century of Women*, p. 62.
90 F. Hicks, 'Factory girls', in A. Reid (ed.) (1896), *The New Party*, p. 315.
91 *Ibid.*, p. 320.
92 *Ibid.*, pp. 325–6.
93 B. Tillett (1931), *Memories and Reflections*, p. 122.
94 T. Mann (1923), *op. cit.*, p. 55.
95 Letter from Ernest Bevin to John Ravey and survivors of the 1889 'Great Dock Strike', property of Ravey's grandson John Rooney, interviewed 29 July 2002.
96 E. H. Hunt (1982), *op. cit.*, p. 135.
97 B. Tillett (1931), *op. cit.*, p. 122.

Notes to Chapter 8: Matchwomen, Dockers and the London Irish Community

1 J. Hollingshead (1861), *Ragged London*, p. 46
2 *Ibid.*, pp. 46, 49.
3 B. Potter, in C. Booth (1889), *Life and Labour of the people, Volume 1*, p. 473.
4 *Ibid.*, p. 476.
5 C. Dickens (1884, 1987), *One Dinner a Week and Travels in the East*, p. 92.
6 M. Williams (1894), *Round London*.
7 G. Rose (1982), 'The strike at Bryant and May's Match factory, East London, July 1888', extract from *An Atlas of Industrial Protest 1850–1900*, pp. 100–4, in TUC archives, HD5367.
8 The *East London Advertiser*, 'Bryant and May's match girls on strike: who fans the flames?', 7 July 1888.
9 *Ibid.*
10 Charles Booth, B346, p. 79)
11 C. Booth (1889), *op. cit.*, p. 194.
12 E. J. Hobsbawm (1974), *Labour's Turning Point*, p. 30.
13 J. Charlton (1999), *It Just Went Like Tinder*, p. 89.
14 L. Hollen Lees (1979), *Exiles of Erin*, p. 19.
15 J. Connolly (1910), *Labour In Irish History*, Chapter 16.
16 R. Swift and S. Gilley (1985), *The Irish in the Victorian City*, p. 3.
17 *Ibid.*, pp. 82–92.
18 T. McCarthy (2008), *Labour v. Sinn Fein – The Dublin General Strike 1913/14: The Lost Revolution*. Labour History Movement.
19 R. Swift and S. Gilley (1985), *op. cit.*, p. 8.
20 L. Hollen Lees (1979), *op. cit.*, p. 63.
21 R. Swift and S. Gilley (1985), *op. cit.*, p. 20.
22 A. Davin (1997), *Growing Up Poor*, p. 54.
23 C. Booth (1889), *op. cit.*
24 J. Charlton (1999), *op. cit.*, pp. 82–3.
25 L. Hollen Lees (1979), *op. cit.*, p. 63.
26 M. Davitt, in T. W. Moody (1953), *Michael Davitt and the British Labour Movement*, cited in J. Charlton (1999), *op. cit.*, p. 86.
27 J. R. Shanley, 'Outlines of working people in history', *FTAT Record*, November 1978, TUC archives.
28 A. Davin (1997), *op. cit.*, p. 53.

29 *Ibid.*
30 *Ibid.*, p. 54.
31 *Ibid.*, p. 55.
32 Charles Booth Archive, B346, p. 99.
33 Charles Booth Archive.
34 Charles Booth Archive, B23, p. 18.
35 Charles Booth Archive, B346, p. 85.
36 *Ibid.*, p. 17.
37 Interview, Joan Harris/Louise Raw, 8 June 2004.
38 Interview, Jim Best/Louise Raw, 7 February 2005.

Notes to Chapter 9: In Search of the Matchwomen: Case Study and Primary Evidence

1   D. Vincent (1981), *Bread, Knowledge and Freedom*, p. 7.
2   J. Rose (2001), *The Intellectual Life of the British Working Classes*, Preface, p. 2.
3   *Justice*, 14 July 1888, in A. Taylor (1992), *Annie Besant*, p. 211.
4   Sources: BBC Kent weather record for July 1888 at http://www.bbc.co.uk/kent/weather/history/weeklyfacts, and the Central England Temperature Series, which has records of English temperature fluctuations from 1659 to date, cited in 'Historical weather events' at http://homepage.ntlworld.com/booty.weather/climate/1850_1899.htm
5   A. R. Bell, J. Martin and S. McCausland, 'Labour's memory: a comparison of labour history archives in Australia, England, Wales and Scotland', *Labour History*, no. 88, May 2005, electronic article, 25–44.
6   Provided by the People's History Museum, Manchester, 16 August 2008. It is assumed that the S. Marks is Sid Marks, one of the founders of the NMLH.
7   Correspondence from Paul Williamson, National Trust custodian of 'Shaw's Corner', Ayot St Lawrence, Herts, 29 April 2006.
8   S. Weintraub (ed.) (1986), *Bernard Shaw, The Diaries 1885–1897*.
9   Article from the *East London Advertiser*, 15 December 1989, p. 18.
10 The *East London Advertiser*, 'Make a match', 15 December 1989, p. 18.
11 Griffith's Evaluation records, published by the *Irish Times*, and online at scripts. Ireland.com.
12 Interview, Joan Harris/Louise Raw, 8 June 2004.
13 Sue Donnelly, archivist at LSE/Charles Booth Archives, personal communication 29 March 2006.
14 Cited in W. F. Aitken (1902), *Canon Barnett, Warden of Toynbee Hall*, p. 77.
15 Interview, Joan Harris/Louise Raw, 8 June 2004.
16 *Tradekey International Trade Directory 2006*, Watch Match Manufacturers, www. tradekey.com.
17 E.g. two adverts placed in the *Surrey Advertiser*, 3 February and 10 February 1872, for 'Bryant and May patent safety matches', at www.newspaperdetective.co.uk.
18 Interview, Joan Harris/Louise Raw, 9 September 2004.
19 *Ibid.*
20 Marriage certificate provided by Joan Harris, 8 June 2004.
21 Interview, Joan Harris/Louise Raw, 9 September 2004.
22 *Ibid.*

23 *Ibid.*
24 J. Greenwood (1867), *Unsentimental Journeys; or Byways of the Modern Babylon.*
25 H. Mayhew (1851, 1861–2), *London Labour and the London Poor.*
26 *Ibid.*
27 Interview, Joan Harris/Louise Raw, 9 September 2004.
28 *Ibid.*
29 Interview, Joan Harris/Louise Raw, 8 June 2004.
30 E. J. Hobsbawm (1999), *Industry and Empire*, rev. edn.
31 M. Cohen and H. Fagan (eds) (1984), *Childhood Memories Recorded by some Socialist Men and Women in their Later Years*, p. 50.
32 A. Harding (1986), *East End Underworld*, (ed. R Samuel).
33 Interview, Joan Harris/Louise Raw, 8 June 2004.
34 *Ibid.*
35 *Ibid.*
36 Interview, Jim Best/Louise Raw, 7 February 2005.
37 The *Star*, 23 July 1888, p. 3.
38 Interview, Jim Best/Louise Raw, 7 February 2005.
39 *Ibid.*
40 Interview, Mary Best/Louise Raw, 7 February 2005.
41 Interview, Jim Best/Louise Raw, 7 February 2005.
42 *Ibid.*
43 *Ibid.*
44 Interview, Ted Lewis/Louise Raw, 23 February 2005.
45 Charles Booth Archive, B349, pp. 210–11.
46 Charles Booth Archive.
47 Charles Booth Archive, B350, 1898–99, p. 23.
48 As told by Martha Robertson to Laraine Gardner, daughter of Martha's daughter Frances ('Hett'), and recorded by her in 'Falling leaves', an unpublished family history/scrapbook kindly lent by Ted Lewis.
49 A. Harding(1986), *op. cit.*
50 From 'Women's Protective and Provident League Annual Report for 1890', Gertrude Tuckwell Collection, TUC Library, London Metropolitan University.
51 Charles Booth Archive, B350, p. 79.
52 From 'Bethnal Green: building and social conditions from 1876 to 1914, a history of the county of Middlesex: Volume 11: Stepney, Bethnal Green' (1998), pp. 126–32, http://www.british-history.ac.uk/report.
53 Charles Booth Archive, B350, p. 31.
54 Copy of official notification in L. Gardner's 'Falling leaves', p. 11.
55 Source: Mark Hutton, Development and Renewal officer, Tower Hamlets Council, telephone conversation, 29 March 2006.
56 Interview, Ted Lewis/Louise Raw, 23 February 2005.
57 *Ibid.*
58 *Ibid.*
59 *Ibid.*
60 *Ibid.*
61 L. Gardner, *op. cit.*, p. 11.
62 *Ibid.*, p. 13.
63 *Ibid.*, p. 11.

64 *Ibid.*
65 *Ibid.*, p. 155.
66 Interview, Ted Lewis/Louise Raw, 23 February 2005.
67 L. Gardner, *op. cit.*, p. 32.
68 Interview, Ted Lewis/Louise Raw, 23 February 2005.
69 *Ibid.*
70 *Ibid.*
71 L. Gardner, *op. cit.*, p. 33.
72 Interview, Ted Lewis/Louise Raw, 23 February 2005.
73 *Ibid.*
74 *Ibid.*
75 *Ibid.*
76 *Ibid.*
77 *Ibid.*
78 Interview, Bett Lewis/Louise Raw, 23 February 2005.
79 Interview, Ted Lewis/Louise Raw, 23 February 2005.
80 C. Chinn (1988), *They Worked All Their Lives*, p. 11.
81 Interview, Jim Best/Louise Raw, 7 February 2005.

Notes to Chapter 10: Conclusions

1   The *Link*, 23 June 1888.
2   *Ibid.*
3   The *East London Advertiser*, 14 July 1888, p. 6.
4   J. Charlton (1999), *It Just Went Like Tinder*, p. 89.
5   T. Mann (1923), *Memoirs*, p. 203; B. Tillett (1931), *Memories and Reflections*, p. 122.
6   B. Tillett (1931), *op. cit.*, p. 122.
7   T. Mann (1923), *op. cit.*, p. 58.
8   Interview, Jim Best/Louise Raw, 7 February 2005
9   K. Honeyman and J. Goodman, 'Women's work, gender conflict and the labour market in Europe, 1500–1900', Chapter 15 in R. Shoemaker and M. Vincent (1998), *Gender and History in Western Europe*, p. 353.
10 J. Wade, on a strike by 1,500 women mill workers in 1835, from *History of the Middle and Working Classes* (1835), pp. 570–1, in C. Willis (1998), *Victim or Virago?*, p. 1.
11 M. Holroyd (1997), *Bernard Shaw*, p. 46.
12 D. Spender, *Women of Ideas and What Men Have Done to Them*, cited in G. Holloway (1998), *ibid.*, p. 178.
13 Cited in 'Someone to look up to', Kira Cochrane, the *Guardian*, Monday 1st November 2010, pp. 10–11).
14 C. Howell (1996), 'Women as the paradigmatic trade unionists? New work, new workers and new trade union strategies in Conservative Britain', *Economic and Industrial Democracy*, vol. 17, no. 4, 511–43.
15 C. Cockburn (1985), *Machinery of Dominance*, p. 86.
16 J. Charlton (1999), *op. cit.*, p. 53.
17 S. Boston (1987), *Women Workers and the Trade Unions*, p. 1.
18 Letter to surviving dock striker John Ravey (1861–1947), provided by his son John Rooney, 29 July 2002.
19 *Ibid.*

Bibliography

PRIMARY SOURCES

Copy of letter from Ernest Bevin to John Ravey, provided by John Rooney (see 'interviews' below), 29 July 2002.

'Degeneration amongst Londoners' (27 January 1885), lecture by James Cantlie. London: The Leadenhall Press.

W. Glenny Crory (1876), *East London Industries*. London: Longmans, Green and Co.

F. Engels (1888), *The Condition of the Working Class in England in 1844*. William Reeves: London.

William Morris's Correspondence and Papers: British Library, GB 0058 ADD, MS 45338–45353.

British Library Sound Archive Transcription Service, copies of The Roy Palmer Collection tapes C1023/29 and C1023/30: Samuel Webber.

Report of the Commissioners, Factory and Workshop Acts, Session 8 February–15 August 1876, vol. xxix, pp. 961–3.

NEWSPAPERS

The *Commonweal*
The *East London Advertiser*
The *East London Observer*
The *Echo*
Justice
The *Link*
The *Pall Mall Budget*
The *Pall Mall Gazette*
Palmer's Index to *The Times*, 1790–1905 and 1888–1889
The *Star*
The *Times*

ARCHIVES

Bryant and May archives, Hackney Archives Department: bundles P/B/BRY/1/2/538–564, including company correspondence, records of company meetings, extensive press cuttings and correspondence relating to the 1888 strike, and scripts, playbills and media reviews 1960–72.

Charles Booth Archive, London School of Economics: notebooks and notes A2, B23, B346, B349.

Museum in Docklands archives, including transcript of talk given by Bob Aspinall at the

DHG meeting, 6 September 1989: 'Reflections on the 1889 Dock Strike'; dock strike newspaper cuttings Books 1 and 2; Record Book 116/3743.
The Trades Union Congress archives, University of North London, including original matchworkers' strike register, 1888 and matchworkers' files HD5367.

PAMPHLETS AND MEMOIRS

Beer, R. (1979), *Matchgirls' Strike 1888: The Struggle Against Sweated Labour in London's East End*, National Museum of Labour History Pamphlet.
Besant, A. (1887), *Is Socialism Sound? Verbatim report of a four nights' debate between Annie Besant and G.W Foote*. London: Progressive Publishing Co.
Besant, A. (1887), *The Socialist Movement*, self-published pamphlet.
Besant, A. (1890), *The Trade Union Movement*, self-published pamphlet.
Besant, A.(1912), *The Masters*. Madras, India: The Theosophical Publishing House.
Wood Besant, A. (1893), *Annie Besant: An Autobiography*. London: Fisher Unwin.
Besant, W. (1908), *Shoreditch and the East End*. London: A. & C. Black.
Cohen, M. and Fagan, H. (eds) (1984), *Childhood Memories Recorded by some Socialist Men and Women in their Later Years*, self-published manuscript.
Hyde Champion, H. (1890), 'The Great Dock Strike', Swan Sonnerschein and Son: London, in British Library collection 'Tracts on Socialism 1875–91'.
'The Eight Hours' Movement: Verbatim Report of a Debate between Mr H. M. Hyndman and Mr C. Bradlaugh' (1890). London: Freethought, collected in *Ibid*.
Mann, T. (1986), *What a Compulsory Eight Hour Working Day Means to the Workers*: Reprints in Labour History. London: Pluto Press.
Mearns, A. (1883), *The Bitter Cry of Outcast London*. London: James Clarke and Co.
Stead, W. T.: journalism including 'Outcast London – where to begin?' in the *Pall Mall Gazette*, 23 October 1883; 'The maiden tribute to modern Babylon', Parts I–IV in the *Pall Mall Gazette*, 6, 7, 8 and 10 July 1885.
Thompson, D. (1989), *British Women in the Nineteenth Century*, Historical Association pamphlet.
Webb, S. (1908), *The Basis and Policy of Socialism* (reprinted from Fabian Society tracts). London: A. C. Fifield.
Williams, M. (1894), *Round London: Down East and Up West*. London: Macmillan.

INTERVIEWS

Interviews were conducted with the following individuals:
Joan Harris, granddaughter of matchworker Mary Driscoll, 3 June 2004, 8 June 2004, 9 September 2004, 27 October 2005.
Ted Lewis, grandson of Martha Robertson, 23 February 2005, 27 October 2005.
James Best and Anne Chapman, grandchildren of Eliza Martin, 7 February 2005.
James and Mary Best, 27 October 2005.
Anna Davin, historian, 4 June 2003.
John Rooney, grandson of surviving dock striker John Ravey (1861–1947), 29 July 2002.
Paddy Logue, historian and writer, formerly of the Derry Trades Council, 11 August 2002.
Jim Corcoran, Irish trade unionist, 29 July 2002.
Mark Hutton, Development and Renewal officer, Tower Hamlets Council, by telephone, March 2006.

LECTURES AND CONFERENCE PAPERS

Davis, M., 'The making of the English working class revisited: history theory and practice', professorial inaugural lecture, London Metropolitan University, 4 June 2003.

Holloway, G., 'Origins of the women's trade union movement', paper for 'Women: Fighting for Rights at Work' conference, Black Country Living Museum, 17 October 2005.

Rowbotham, S., 'Approaches to home working in the nineteenth and twentieth century', paper for 'Women: Fighting for Rights at Work' conference, Black Country Living Museum, 17 October 2005.

Thornton, D., 'Gender, class and activism in the Melbourne Tailoresses strike 1882–3', paper presented at 'The Past Is Before Us': The ninth National Labour History Conference, University of Sydney, 30 June–2 July 2005.

DIARIES AND AUTOBIOGRAPHIES

Besant, A. (1893), *Annie Besant: An Autobiography*. London: T. Fisher Unwin.

Harding, A. (1981), *East End Underworld: Chapters in the Life of Arthur Harding* (ed. R. Samuel). London: Routledge.

McKenzie, N. and J. (eds) (1982), *Diary of Beatrice Webb*. London: Virago.

Mann, T. (1923), *Memoirs*. The Labour Publishing Company.

Weintraub, S. (ed.) (1986), *Bernard Shaw, the Diaries 1885–1897 with Early Autobiographical Notebooks and Diaries, and an Abortive 1917 Diary*. University Park, PA: Pennsylvania State University Press.

THESES AND DISSERTATIONS

Brodie, M. (1999), 'Politics Stirs Them Very Little: Conservatism and Apathy in the East End of London 1885 –1914'. PhD thesis for Oxford University.

Livesey, R. (1999), 'Women, Class and Social Action in Late Victorian and Edwardian London'. PhD thesis for Warwick University.

S. Moore (1986), 'Women, Industrialisation and Protest in Bradford, 1780- 1845'. PhD thesis for University of Essex.

Julia Poynter (2001), 'The London Trades Council and the New Unionism', Dissertation for University of North London MA in Labour and Trade Union Studies.

SECONDARY SOURCES

Aitken, W. F. (1902), *Canon Barnett, Warden of Toynbee Hall: His Mission and its Relation to Social Movements*. London: S. W. Partridge and Co.

Alexander, S. (1994), *Becoming a Woman and Other Essays in Nineteenth and Twentieth Century Feminist History*. London: Virago.

Anderson, B.S. and Zinsser, J.P. (1988), *A History of their own: women in Europe from prehistory to the present*. New York: Harper and Row.

Andersen, H. C. (1981), *The Little Match Girl*. Kingswood: Kaye & Ward.

Arch, J. (1986), *From Ploughtail to Parliament: An Autobiography*. London: The Cresset Library.

Ashplant, T. G., 'Anecdote as narrative resource in working-class life stories', in M. Beddoe (1998), *Discovering Women's History*. London: Longman.

Behagg, C. (1991), *Labour and Reform: Working-Class Movements 1815–1914*. London: Hodder and Stoughton.

Bennett, O. (1988), *Annie Besant*. London: Hamish Hamilton.

Benson, J. (1989), *The Working Class in Britain 1850–1939*. London: Longman.

Blaxter, L. (ed.) (1996), *How to Research*. Open University Press.

Blewett, M., 'Diversities of class and gender experience and the shaping of Labor politics: Yorkshire's Manningham Mills strike, 1890–91 and the Independent Labour Party', *Labor History*, no. 4, November 2006, 511–35.

Booth, C. (1889), *Life and Labour of the People, Volume 1: East London*. N.p.: Williams and Norgate.

Booth, C. (1891), *Life and Labour of the People, Volume II: London Continued*. [S.I.]: Williams and Norgate.

Booth, W. (1890), *In Darkest England and the Way Out*. London: Wiliam Burgess.

Bornat, J. and Diamond, H., 'Women's history and oral history: developments and debates', *Women's History Review*, vol. 10, no. 1, February 2007, 19–39.

Boston, S. (1987), *Women Workers and the Trade Unions*. London: Lawrence and Wishart.

Bridenthal, R., Koonz, C. and Stuard, S. (eds) (1987), *Becoming Visible: Women in European History*. Boston, MA: Houghton Mifflin Company.

Briggs, A. (1968), *Victorian Cities*. London: Penguin.

Briggs, A. (1990), *Victorian Things*. London: Pelican.

Brown, C. A. (1960), *The Story of our National Ballads*. New York: T. Y. Crowell.

Bryant, E. and Patton, L. (eds) (2005), *The Indo-Aryan Controversy: Evidence and Inference in Indian History*. London: Routledge.

Bryant and May (1961), 'Making matches'. London: Press and PR Ltd.

Bryant and May with P. Beaver (1985), *The Matchmakers*. London: Bryant and May.

Burnett, J. (1966), *Plenty and Want*. Harmondsworth: Pelican.

Burnett, J. (1994), *Destiny Obscure: Autobiographies of Childhood, Education and Family from the 1820s to the 1920s*. London: Routledge.

Cain, P. and Hopkins, A. (1993), *British Imperialism: Innovation and Expansion 1688–1914*. London: Longman.

Carr, E. H. (1990), *What Is History?* London: Penguin.

Chamberlain, M. and Thompson, P. L. (eds) (1998), *Narrative and Genre: Contexts and Types of Communication Transaction*. London: Transaction Publishers.

Champion, H. H. (1890), *The Great Dock Strike in London, August 1889*. London.

Chanfrault-Duchet, M., 'Narrative structures, social models, and symbolic representations in the life story', in S. B. Gluck and D. Patai (eds) (1991), *Women's Words: The Feminist Practice of Oral History*. London: Routledge, pp. 77–92.

Charlton, J. (1999), *It Just Went Like Tinder: The Mass Movement and New Unionism in Britain 1889, a Socialist History*. London: Redwords.

Chinn, C. (1988), *They Worked All their Lives: Women of the Urban Poor in Britain 1880–1939*. Manchester: Manchester University Press.

Clark, A. (1995), *The Struggle for the Breeches: Gender and the Making of the British Working Class*. London: Rivers Oram Press.

Clegg, H. A., Fox, A. and Thompson, A. F. (1977), *A History of Trade Unions Since 1889, Volume 1 1889–1910*. Oxford: Clarendon Press.

Coates, K. and Topham, T. (1974), *The New Unionism*. London: Pelican.

Cohen, G. A. (2000), *Karl Marx's Theory of History: A Defence*. Oxford: Clarendon Press.

Cohen, M. and Fagan, H. (eds)(1984) *Childhood memories recorded by some Socialsit men and women in their later years*. Self-published manuscript.

Cockburn, C. (1985), *Machinery of Dominance: women, men and technical know-how*. London: Pluto.

Cole, G. D. H. and Filson, A. W. (1967), *British Working Class Movements: Selected Documents 1789–1875*. London: Macmillan.

Connolly, J. (1910), *Labour in Irish History*. Dublin: Maunsel & Co.

Cooper, S. (2001), *The Victorian Women*, London: V&A Publications.

Crawford, E. (1999), *The Women's Suffrage Movement: A Reference Guide*. London: Routledge.

Crick, M. (1994), *The History of the Social-Democratic Federation*. Edinburgh University Press.

Crossick, G. (1978), *An Artisan Elite in Victorian Society: Kentish London 1840–1880*. London: Croom Helm.

Cullen, M. and Luddy, M. (eds) (1995), *Women, Power and Consciousness in Nineteenth-Century Ireland*. Dublin: Attic Press.

Davies, J. (1993), *A History of Wales*. London: Penguin.

Davin, A. (1997), *Growing Up Poor: Home, School and Street in London 1870–1914*. London: Rivers Oram Press.

Davis, M. (1993), *Comrade or Brother?: The History of the British Labour Movement 1789–1951*. London: Pluto Press.

Davis, M. (1999), *Sylvia Pankhurst: A Life in Radical Politics*. London: Pluto Press.

De Beauvoir, S. (1988), *The Second Sex*. London: Pan Books.

De Tollenaere, H. A. O. (1996), *The Politics of Divine Wisdom: Theosophy and Labour, National and Women's Movements in Indonesia and South Asia 1875–1947*. Nijmegen: Katholieke Universiteit Nijmegen.

Dickens, C. (1884, 1987), *One Dinner a Week and Travels in the East*. High Wycombe: Peter Marcan.

Dickens, C. (1996), *Dickens' Journalism, Volume 2: The Amusements of the People and Other Papers: Reports, Essays and Reviews 1834–1851* (ed. M. Slater). London: Dent.

Dinnage, R. (1986), *Annie Besant*. Harmondsworth: Penguin.

Eron, S. (2004) 'Coventry Patmore's marriage to Emily Augusta Andrews 1847–1860', published online at www.victorianweb.org.

Evans, L. (1970), *British Trade Unionism 1850–1914*. London: Edward Arnold.

Farson, D. (1991), *Limehouse Days*. London: Michael Joseph.

Ferguson, N. (2004), *Empire: how Britain made the modern world*. London: Penguin.

Fishman, W.J. (1988) *East End 1888: a year in a London borough among the labouring poor*. London: Duckworth.

Fried, A. and Elman R. (eds) (1971), *Charles Booth's London*. London: Pelican.

Ganzl, K. (1986), *The British Musical Theatre, Volume 2 1915–1984*. Oxford University Press.

George, M.D. (1930), *London Life in the Eighteenth Century*. Place and publisher not known.

Gidley, B. (2000), 'The Proletarian Other: Charles Booth and the politics of Representation'. Occasional paper for Goldsmith's College, Centre for Urban and Community Research.

Gluck, S. B. and Patai, D. (eds) (1991), *Women's Words: The Feminist Practice of Oral History*. London: Routledge.

Goodley, D., Lawthorm, R. and Clough, P. (2004), *Researching Life Stories: Method, Theory and Analyses in a Biographical Age*. London: RoutledgeFalmer.

Gordon, E. (1991), *Women and the Labour Movement in Scotland 1850–1914*. Oxford: Clarendon Press.

Gormersall, M. (1997), *Working-Class Girls in Nineteenth-Century England: Life, Work and Schooling*. London: Macmillan.

Gourvish, T. R. and O'Day, A. (eds) (1988), *Later Victorian Britain 1867–1900*. Basingstoke: Macmillan Education.

Gray, R. (1981), *The Aristocracy of Labour in Nineteenth Century Britain c.1850–1914*. London: Macmillan.

Greenwood, J. (1867), *Unsentimental Journeys; or Byways of the Modern Babylon*.

Grele, R. (1985), *Envelopes of Sound: The Art of Oral History*. Chicago: Precedent.

Hannam, J. (1989), *Isabella Ford*. Oxford: Basil Blackwell.

Hannam, J. and Hunt, K. (2002), *Socialist Women: Britain, 1880s to 1920s*. London: Routledge.

Harris, J. (1993), *Private Lives, Public Spirit: Britain 1870–1914*. London: Penguin.

Harrison, B. (1996), *Not Only the Dangerous Trades: Women's Work and Health in Britain, 1880–1914*. London: Taylor & Francis.

Harrison, J. F. C. (1990), *Late Victorian Britain 1875–1901*. London: Fontana Press.

Hennessey, R. (1969), *Factories*. London: Batsford.

Hobsbawm, E. J. (1964), *Labouring Men: Studies in the History of Labour*. London: Weidenfeld and Nicolson.

Hobsbawm, E. J., 'Trade union history', *Economic History Review*, vol. XX, no. 2, August 1967.

Hobsbawm, E. J. (1977), *The Age of Revolution*. London: Abacus.

Hobsbawm, E. J. (1977), *Labour's Turning Point, 1880–1900*. London: Harvester Press.

Hobsbawm, E. J. (1987, 1995), *The Age of Empire*. London: Weidenfeld and Nicolson.

Hobsbawm, E.J. (1999), *Industry and Empire from 1750 to the present day*. London: Penguin.

Holcroft, F. (1992), *'A Terrible Nightmare': The Cotton Famine Around Wigan*. Wigan: Wigan Heritage Service.

Hollingshead, J. (1985), *Ragged London in 1861*. London: Garland.

Holloway, G., '"Let the women be alive!": the construction of the married working woman in the industrial women's movement, 1890–1914', in E. J. Yeo (ed.) (1998), *Radical Femininity: Women's Self-Representation in the Public Sphere*. Manchester: Manchester University Press.

Holloway, G., 'Writing women in: the development of feminist approaches to women's history', in W. Lamont (ed.) (1998), *Historical Controversies and Historians*. London: UCL Press, pp. 177–87.

Holloway, G. (2005), *Women and Work in Britain since 1840*. London: Routledge.

Holroyd, M. (1997), *Bernard Shaw*. London: Chatto and Windus.

Honeyman, K. (2000), *Women, Gender and Industrialisation in England 1700–1870*. London: Macmillan.

Hopkins, E. (1979), *Social History of the Working Classes 1815–1945*. London: Arnold.

Hunt, E. H. (1985), *British Labour History 1815–1914*. London: Weidenfeld and Nicolson.

Hunt, K. (1996), *Equivocal Feminists: The Social Democratic Federation and the Woman Question, 1884–1911*. Cambridge University Press.

Hunt, T. (2004), *Building Jerusalem: the rise and fall of the Victorian City*. London: Weidenfeld and Nicolson.

Hyman, R. (1971), *Marxism and the Sociology of Trade Unionism*. London: Pluto Press.

Hyman, R. (1972), *Strikes*. London: Fontana.

Hyman, R. (1975), *Industrial Relations: A Marxist Introduction*. London: Macmillan.

John, A. (ed.) (1986), *Unequal Opportunities: Women's Employment in England 1800–1918*. Oxford: Blackwell.

John, A. (ed.) (1991), *Our Mother's Land: Chapters in Welsh Women's History 1830–1939*. UWP: Cardiff.

Johnson, P. E. (2001), *Hidden Hands: Working-Class Women and Victorian Social-Problem Fiction*. Ohio University Press.

Judd, D. (1970), *The Victorian Empire 1837–1901: A Pictorial History*. London: Weidenfeld & Nicolson.

Kelly, Joan (1984), *Women, History, and Theory*. University of Chicago Press.

Kent, W. (1950), *John Burns: Labour's Lost Leader*. London: Williams and Norgate.

Knox, J. (1558), *The First Blast of the Trumpet Against the Monstrous Regiment of Women*. J. Crespin: Geneva.

Koss, D. (1986), *The Rise and Fall of the Political Press in Britain, Volume 1*. London: Hamish Hamilton.

Labossiere, M. (2008), *Philosophical Provocations: What Don't You Know?* London: Continuum.

Lane, T. (1974), *The Union Makes Us Strong*. London: Arrow.

Law, J. (pseudonym of Margaret Harkness) (1888), *Captain Lobe: Or In Darkest London*. London: Apollo Press.

Law, J. (pseudonym of Margaret Harkness) (1888), *Out Of Work*. London: Sonnenschein & Co.

Lawrence, E. (1994), *Gender and Trade Unions*. London: Taylor and Francis.

Lees, L.H. (1979) *Exiles of Erin: Irish migrants in Victorian London*. Manchester: Manchester University Press.

Lenin, V. (1982), *Imperialism, the Highest Stage of Capitalism*. Moscow: Progress.

Levene, P. (2002), *Unholy Alliance: A History of Nazi Involvement with the Occult*. London: Continuum.

Lewis, J. (ed.) (1986), *Labour and Love: Women's Experience of Home and Family 1850–1940*. Oxford: Blackwell.

Liddington, J. and Norris, J. (2000), *One Hand Tied Behind Us: The Rise of the Women's Suffrage Movement*. London: Virago.

Loane, M.E. (1909), *An Englishman's Castle*. London: Edward Arnold.

Lovell, J. (1969), *The Stevedores and the Dockers: A Study of Trade Unionism in the Port of London, 1870–1914*. London: Macmillan.

Lovell, J. (1977), *British Trade Unions 1875–1933*. London: Macmillan.

Macintyre, S. (1986), *A Proletarian Science: Marxism in Britain 1917–1933*. London: Lawrence and Wishart.

Mackenzie, N. and J. (1979), *The First Fabians*. London: Quartet.

Manvell, R. (1976), *The Trial of Annie Besant*. London: Elek/Pemberton.

Martin, J. (1999), *Women and the Politics of Schooling in Victorian and Edwardian England*. London: Continuum.

Marvell, A. (1689), *A Collection of Poems on Affairs of State*. London: Publisher not known.

Marx, K. (1973), *Grundrisse*. London: Penguin.

Marx, K. (1976), *Capital, Volume One*. Harmondsworth: Pelican.

Marx, K. and Engels, F. (1996), *The Communist Manifesto*. London: Phoenix.

Mauch, J. and Birch, J. (1989), *Guide to the Successful Thesis and Dissertation: Conception to Publication*, 2nd edn. New York: Dekker.

Mayfield, S. (1988), *Women and Power*. London: Dryad.

Mayhew, H. (1985), *London Labour and the London Poor*. Harmondsworth: Penguin.

McCarthy, T. (1988), *The Great Dock Strike*. London: Weidenfeld and Nicolson.

McCarthy, T. (2008) *Labour v. Sinn Fein – The Dublin General Strike 1913/14: The Lost Revolution*. Labour History Movement.

McFeely, M. D. (1991), *Lady Inspectors: The Campaign for a Better Workplace 1893–1921*. Athens, GA: Georgia University Press.

McGrath, K. (1999), *World of Invention*. Detroit: Gale.

Midgley, C. (1998), *Gender and Imperialism*. Manchester: Manchester University Press.

Miller, R. L. (2000), *Researching Life Stories and Family Histories*. London: Sage.

Mills, D. and Schurer, K. (1996), *Local Communities in the Victorian Census Enumerators' Books*. Oxford: Leopard's Head Press.

Mitchell, D. C. and Gwyn Smith, S. (1896), *The Matchbox Collectors' Scrapbook*. Bryant and

May catalogue no. 2. London: Vesta Publications.

Mitchell, S. (1988), *Victorian Britain: An Encyclopedia*. Westport, CN: Greenwood.

Moore, J. S. (1998), *Bulwer-Lytton*. SRP Publications at www.mith.demon.co.uk/Bulwer. htm.

Morris, J. (1986). *Women Workers and the Sweated Trades: the origins of minimum wages legislation*. Aldershot: Gower.

Morris, R. J. (1979), *Class and Class Consciousness in the Industrial Revolution, 1780–1850*. London: Macmillan.

Morton, A. L. and Tate, G. (1956), *The British Labour Movement*. London: Lawrence and Wishart.

Musson, A. E. (1972), *British Trade Unions 1800–1875*. London: Macmillan.

Nethercot, A. H. (1961), *The First Five Lives of Annie Besant*. London: Rupert Hart Davis.

Newsome, D. (1998), *The Victorian World Picture*. London: Fontana.

Nield Chew, D. (ed.) (1982), *The Life and Writings of Ada Nield Chew Remembered and Collected by Doris Nield Chew*. London: Virago.

Offen, K. (1987), 'Liberty, equality & justice for women: the theory & practice of feminism in 19th Century' in Bridenthal *et al.* (eds) *Becoming Visible: Women in European History*.

Olcott, T., 'Dead centre: the women's trade union movement in London 1874–1914', *The London Journal*, vol. 2, no. 1, May 1976.

Palmer, A. W. (1989), *The East End: Four Centuries of London Life*. London: Murray.

Pankhurst, S. (1977), *The Suffragette Movement*. London: Virago.

Patmore, C. (1891), *The Angel in the House*. [S.I.]: Cassell & Company.

Pearse, E. (1925), *History of the Fabian Society*. London: Fabian Society.

Pelling, H. (1963), *A History of British Trade Unionism*. Harmondsworth: Penguin.

Pelling, H. (1963), *Popular Politics and Society in Late Victorian Britain: Essays*. London: Macmillan.

Penn, R. (1985), *Skilled Workers in the Class Structure*. Cambridge University Press.

Perks, R. and Thomson, A. (eds) (2006), *The Oral History Reader*. London: Routledge.

Perrot, M. (1984), *Writing Women's History*. Oxford: Blackwell.

Pinchbeck, I. (1981), *Women Workers and the Industrial Revolution*. London: Virago.

Plekhanov, G. V. (1976), *The Role of the Individual in History*. London: Lawrence and Wishart.

Plummer, K. (2001), *Documents of Life 2: An Invitation to a Critical Humanism*. London: Sage.

Poovey, M. (1989), *Uneven Developments: The Ideological Work of Gender in Mid-Victorian England*. University of Chicago Press.

Portelli, A. 'Italian Oral History: Roots of a Paradox'. Essay published online, University of Hing Kong, www.hku.hk/sociodep/oralhistory.

Portelli, A. (1991), *The Death of Luigi Trastelli and Other Stories: Form and Meaning in Oral History*. Albany, NY: State University of New York Press.

Potter, B. (1987), *The Co-operative Movement in Great Britain*. Aldershot: Gower, in association with the London School of Economics.

Porter, R. (1994), *London: A Social History*. London: Penguin.

Reid, A. (1895), *The New Party, described by some of its members*. London: Hodder Bros.

Reid, A. J. (2004), *United We Stand: A History of Britain's Trade Unions*. London: Penguin/ Allen Lane.

Rendall, J. (1990), *Women in an Industrialising Society: England 1750–1880*. Oxford: Blackwell.

Reynolds, S. (ed.) (1986), *Women, State and Revolution: Essays on Power and Gender in Europe since 1789*. Brighton: Wheatsheaf.

Rigby, L. (2000), *Stoke Poges: A Buckinghamshire Village Through 1,000 Years*. Chichester: Phillimore.

Roberts, E. (1996), *A Woman's Place: An Oral History of Working Class Women, 1890–1940*. Oxford: Blackwell.

Rose, J. (2001), *The Intellectual Life of the British Working Classes*. Yale University Press.

Rose, S. O. (1992), *Limited Livelihoods: Gender and Class in Nineteenth Century England*. London: Routledge.

Ross, E. (1993), *Love and Toil: Motherhood in Outcast London, 1870–1918*. Oxford University Press.

Rousseau, J. J. (1902), *Emile: Or Concerning Education: Extracts Containing the Principal Elements of Pedagogy Found in the First Three Books* (ed. Jules Steeg, trans. Eleanor Worthington). Boston, MA: Heath.

Rowbotham, S. (1977), *Hidden from History: Three Hundred Years of Women's Oppression and the Fight Against It*. London: Pluto Press.

Rowbotham, S. (1990), *A Century of Women*. New York: Viking.

Royle, E. (1980), *Chartism*. London: Longman.

Rubinstein, D. (1986), *Before the Suffragettes: Women's Emancipation in the 1890s*. Brighton: Harvester Press.

Rubinstein, D. (1991), *A Different World For Women: The Life of Millicent Garrett Fawcett*. London: Harvester/New York: Wheatsheaf.

Rudestam, K. E. (2001), *Surviving Your Dissertation*, 2nd edn. Thousand Oaks, CA: Sage.

Sala, G.A. (1859), *Gaslight and Daylight: with some London scenes they shine upon*. Place unknown: Chapman and Hall.

Samuel, R. and Thompson, P. (eds) (1990), *The Myths We Live By*. London: Routledge.

Saul, S. B. (1985), *The Myth of the Great Depression 1873–1896*, 2nd edn. London: Macmillan.

Savage, M. and Miles, A. (1994), *The Remaking of the British Working Class*. London: Routledge.

Schama, S. (2002), *History of Britain 1776–2000*. London: BBC.

Schmiechen, J. (1984), *Sweated Industries and Sweated Labor: A history of the London Clothing Trades, 1860–1914*. London: Croom Helm.

Schneer, J. (1982), *Ben Tillett*. London: Croom Helm.

Schwarzkopf, J. (2004), *Unpicking Gender: The Social Construction of Gender in the Lancashire Weaving Industry, 1880–1914*. Aldershot: Ashgate.

Scott, J.W. (1988), *Gender and the Politics of History*. New York: Columbia University Press.

Selley, E. (1920), *Village Trade Unions in Two Centuries*. London: George Allen and Unwin.

Sewell, R. (2003), *In the Cause of Labour*. London: Wellread Publications.

Shannon, R. (1999), *Gladstone, Heroic Minister 1865–1898*. London: Penguin.

Sharpe, P. (ed.) (1998), *Women's Work: The English Experience, 1650–1914*. London: Macmillan.

Shaw, G. B. (ed.) (1891), *Fabian Essays in Socialism*, New York: Humboldt.

Shaw, G. B. (1928), *The Intelligent Woman's Guide to Socialism, Capitalism, Sovietism and Fascism, Volumes 1 and 2*. London: Penguin.

Shepherd, J. (2004), *George Lansbury: At the Heart of Old Labour*. Oxford University Press.

Shipley, S. (1983), *Club Life and Socialism in Mid-Victorian London*. London: Journeyman.

Shoemaker, R. (2004), *The London Mob: Violence and Disorder in Eighteenth-Century England*. London: Hambledon.

Shoemaker, R. and Vincent, M. (1998), *Gender and History in Western Europe*. London: Arnold.

Smith, W. (1886), *Morley: ancient and modern*. London: Longmans & Co.

Soldon, N. (1978), *Women in British Trade Unions*. London: Pelican.

Spender, D (1982) Women of Ideas and what men have done to them: from Aphra Ben to Adrienne Riche. London: Routledge and Kegan Paul.

Stafford, A. (1961), *A Match to Fire the Thames*. London: Hodder and Stoughton.

Stanley, L. and Wise, S. (1993), *Breaking Out Again: Feminist Ontology and Epistemology*. London: Routledge.

Steadman, L. (1973), *Life in Victorian London*. London: Batsford.

Stedman, E. C. (ed.) (1895), *A Victorian Anthology, 1837–1895: Selections Illustrating the Editor's Critical Review of British Poetry in the Reign of Victoria*. New York: Bartleby Press.

Stedman Jones, G. (1984), *Outcast London*. London: Penguin.

Sweet, M. (2001), *Inventing the Victorians*. London: Faber and Faber.

Swift, R. and Gilley, S. (1985), *The Irish in the Victorian City*. London: Croom Helm.

Taylor, A. (1992), *Annie Besant*. Oxford University Press.

Thompson, A. M. (1937), *Here I Lie: The Memorial of an Old Journalist*. London: Routledge and Sons.

Thompson, D. (1993), *Class, Gender and Nation*. London: Verso.

Thompson, D. (1993), 'Queen Victoria: the monarchy and gender' Occasional Paper no. 5, Institute for Advanced Research in the Humanities, University of Birmingham.

Thompson, E. P. (1991), *Customs in Common*. London: Merlin Press.

Thompson, E. P. (1991), *The Making of the English Working Class*. Harmondsworth: Penguin.

Thompson, P. (1967), *Socialists, Liberals and Labour: The Struggle for London 1885–1914*. London: Routledge and Kegan Paul.

Thompson, P. (2000), *The Voice of the Past: Oral History*, 3rd edn. Oxford University Press.

Thorne, W. (1989), *My Life's Battles*. London: Lawrence and Wishart.

Tillett, B. (1910), *Dock, Wharf, Riverside and General Workers' Union. A Brief History of the Dockers' Union. Commemorating the 1889 Dockers' Strike*. London: Twentieth Century Press.

Tillett, B. (1931), *Memories and Reflections*. London: J. Long.

TUC (1968), *The History of the TUC 1868–1968*. London: TUC Publications.

Tyler, P. (2007), *Labour's Lost Leader: The Life and Politics of Will Crooks*. London: I. B. Tauris.

Valenze, D. (1995), *The First Industrial Woman*. Oxford University Press.

Vicinus, M. (1985), *Independant Women: work and community for single women 1850–1920*. London: Virago.

Vickery, A., 'Golden age to separate spheres: a review of the categories and chronology of English women's history'. *Historical Journal* 36 (1993): 383–414.

Vincent, D. (1981), *Bread, Knowledge and Freedom: a study of working class nineteenth century autobiography*. London: Europa.

Walby, S. (1986), *Patriarchy at Work: Patriarchal and Capitalist Relations in Employment*. Cambridge: Polity Press.

Walford, E. E. and Gillies, J. (eds) (1908), *The Politics and Economics of Aristotle*. London: G. Bell and Sons.

Webb, B. and S. (1920), *The History of Trade Unions*. Self-published manuscript.

Weintraub, S., *George Bernard Shaw: An Autobiography, 1856–1898; Selected from his writings*. London: Max Reinhardt.

Welshman, J. (2006), *Underclass: A History of the Excluded, 1880–2000*. London: Continuum.

Williams, B. (1980), *Quakers in Reigate 1655–1955*. Self-published manuscript.

Winslow, B. (1996), *Sylvia Pankhurst: Sexual Politics and Political Activism*. London: UCL Press.

Woolf, V., (1942) Professions for Women, in 'The Death of the Moth and Other Essays':
    London: Hogarth Press].
Wollstonecraft, M. (1992), *A Vindication of the Rights of Woman*. London: Penguin.
Wright, T. (1967), *Some habits and customs of the working classes, by a journeyman engineer*.
    New York: A.M. Kelly.
Yow, V. (2005), *Recording Oral History*. Oxford: Altamira.

Index